£16.50

a

Feminist Companion

——— to ———

The Latter Prophets

edited by Athalya Brenner

The Feminist Companion to the Bible

8

Editor
Athalya Brenner

Sheffield Academic Press

224.6

Published by Sheffield Academic Press Ltd
Mansion House
19 Kingfield Road
Sheffield, S11 9AS
England

Printed on acid-free paper in Great Britain
by The Cromwell Press
Melksham, Wiltshire

British Library Cataloguing in Publication Data

A catalogue record for this book is available
from the British Library

ISBN 1-85075-515-9

To the memory of

Fokkelien van Dijk-Hemmes

ת·נ·צ·ב·ה·

CONTENTS

Abbreviations   11

ATHALYA BRENNER
    Preface   13

ATHALYA BRENNER
    Introduction   21

Part I
THE CASE OF 'HOSEA'

CAROLE R. FONTAINE
    Hosea   40

CAROLE R. FONTAINE
    A Response to 'Hosea'   60

ALICE A. KEEFE
    The Female Body, the Body Politic and the Land:
    A Sociopolitical Reading of Hosea 1–2   70

YVONNE SHERWOOD
    Boxing Gomer: Controlling the Deviant Woman
    in Hosea 1–3   101

NAOMI GRAETZ
    God is to Israel as Husband is to Wife: The
    Metaphoric Battering of Hosea's Wife   126

FRANCIS LANDY
Fantasy and the Displacement of Pleasure:
Hosea 2.4-17   146

JOHN GOLDINGAY
Hosea 1–3, Genesis 1–4 and Masculist Interpretation   161

MAYER I. GRUBER
Marital Fidelity and Intimacy: A View from Hosea 4   169

MARGARET S. ODELL
I Will Destroy Your Mother: The Obliteration of
A Cultic Role in Hosea 4.4-6   180

HELEN SCHÜNGEL-STRAUMANN
God as Mother in Hosea 11   194

MARIE-THERES WACKER
Traces of the Goddess in the Book of Hosea   219

Part II
ON THE PORNOPROPHETICS OF SEXUAL VIOLENCE

FOKKELIEN VAN DIJK-HEMMES
The Metaphorization of Woman in Prophetic Speech:
An Analysis of Ezekiel 23   244

ATHALYA BRENNER
On Prophetic Propaganda and the Politics of 'Love':
The Case of Jeremiah   256

ROBERT P. CARROLL
Desire under the Terebinths: On Pornographic
Representation in the Prophets—A Response   275

PAMELA GORDON AND HAROLD C. WASHINGTON
Rape as a Military Metaphor in the Hebrew Bible   308

F. RACHEL MAGDALENE
Ancient Near Eastern Treaty-Curses and the
Ultimate Texts of Terror: A Study of the Language
of Divine Sexual Abuse in the Prophetic Corpus 326

Part III
SHOULD WE TRUST THE GOD OF THE PROPHETS?

NANCY R. BOWEN
Can God be Trusted? Confronting the Deceptive God 354

Bibliography 366

ABBREVIATIONS

AB	Anchor Bible
ABD	D.N. Freedman (ed.), *Anchor Bible Dictionary*
AJSL	*American Journal of Semitic Languages and Literatures*
AnBib	Analecta biblica
ANET	J.B. Pritchard (ed.), *Ancient Near Eastern Texts*
AOAT	Alter Orient und Altes Testament
ATD	Das Alte Testament Deutsch
BA	*Biblical Archaeologist*
BARev	*Biblical Archaeology Review*
BASOR	*Bulletin of the American Schools of Oriental Research*
BBB	Bonner Biblische Beiträge
BDB	F. Brown, S.R. Driver and C.A. Briggs, *Hebrew and English Lexicon of the Old Testament*
BHS	*Biblia hebraica stuttgartensia*
Bib	*Biblica*
BibB	*Biblische Beiträge*
BibOr	Biblica et orientalia
BJRL	*Bulletin of the John Rylands University Library of Manchester*
BJS	Brown Judaic Studies
BKAT	Biblischer Kommentar: Altes Testament
BR	*Biblical Research*
BSac	*Bibliotheca Sacra*
BTB	*Biblical Theology Bulletin*
BZ	*Biblische Zeitschrift*
BZAW	Beihefte zur *ZAW*
CBQ	*Catholic Biblical Quarterly*
EncJud	*Encyclopaedia Judaica*
EvT	*Evangelische Theologie*
GKC	*Gesenius' Hebrew Grammar*, ed. E. Kautzsch, trans. A.E. Cowley
HALAT	W. Baumgartner *et al.*, *Hebräisches und aramäisches Lexikon zum Alten Testament*
HAR	*Hebrew Annual Review*
HAT	Handbuch zum Alten Testament
HBT	*Horizons in Biblical Theology*
HSM	Harvard Semitic Monographs

HTR	*Harvard Theological Review*
HUCA	*Hebrew Union College Annual*
IDB	G.A. Buttrick (ed.), *Interpreter's Dictionary of the Bible*
IDBSup	*IDB*, Supplementary Volume
IEJ	*Israel Exploration Journal*
Int	*Interpretation*
JAOS	*Journal of the American Oriental Society*
JBL	*Journal of Biblical Literature*
JewEnc	*The Jewish Encyclopedia*
JCS	*Journal of Cuneiform Studies*
JFSR	*Journal of Feminist Studies in Religion*
JQR	*Jewish Quarterly Review*
JR	*Journal of Religion*
JSOT	*Journal for the Study of the Old Testament*
JSOTSup	*JSOT* Supplement Series
JSPSup	*Journal for the Study of the Pseudepigrapha*, Supplement Series
JSS	*Journal of Semitic Studies*
JTS	*Journal of Theological Studies*
KAT	Kommentar zum Alten Testament
KB	L. Koehler and W. Baumgartner (eds.), *Lexicon in Veteris Testamenti libros*
NCB	New Century Bible
NRT	*La nouvelle revue théologique*
OBO	Orbis biblicus et orientalis
OTG	Old Testament Guides
OTL	Old Testament Library
OTWSA	*Oud Testamentiese Werkgemeenschap in Suid-Africa*
QD	Quaestiones Disputatae
RB	*Revue biblique*
RevExp	*Review and Expositor*
SBLDS	Society of Biblical Literature Dissertation Series
SBLMS	Society of Biblical Literature Mongraph Series
SJOT	*Scandinavian Journal of the Old Testament*
ST	*Studia theologica*
THAT	*Theologisches Handwörterbuch zum Alten Testament*
TQ	*Theologische Quartalschrift*
TS	*Theological Studies*
TZ	*Theologische Zeitschrift*
UF	*Ugarit-Forschungen*
VT	*Vetus Testamentum*
VTSup	*Vetus Testamentum*, Supplements
WMANT	Wissenschaftliche Monographien zum Alten und Neuen Testament
ZAW	*Zeitschrift für die alttestamentliche Wissenschaft*

PREFACE

Athalya Brenner

This volume of the Feminist Companion contains discussions of passages from the Latter Prophets (Hebrew: 'Last Prophets'): biblical books attributed to named persons designated as 'prophets' by the text and its interpreters. These books supposedly contain selections of sayings and teachings which were committed to writing and transmission, earlier or eventually as the case might be. Hence also the labels 'prophets of the written word' or 'classical prophets' which are sometimes used in Bible criticism.

Next to the Torah, so-called prophetic literature has been the most influential biblical text. Ideologies and concepts are diagnosed by exegetes and interpreters as 'prophetic', merely because of their recording and preservation within the books designated as such. The mystique attached to words like 'prophet' or 'prophecy' is not easy to resist: the sheer number of quotations from or references to 'prophetic' texts in the New Testament provides excellent testimony to this mystique and to its utilization in religious, hence also sociopolitical, ideology. But what does the Bible mean, what do *we* mean, when the term 'prophecy' and the phenomenology it designates are referred to?

The Hebrew root נבא and its derivatives, conveniently—and with ostensible ease—translated into various forms of 'prophesy', is actually quite problematic. Its etymological provenance is far from clear. Hence, biblical lexicology is quite vague on this point. The KB, for instance, suggests an Akkadian cognate with the sense of 'call, speak' and derives the Hebrew verb from the

noun-form נביא, 'caller, speaker': 'prophet'.[1] This is hardly
satisfactory. I am tempted to speculate that נבא is close in
meaning to נבע, 'come out of (a source)', used once in the *qal*
stem of water coming forth (Prov. 18.4) and three times in a
noun, 'water source' (Qoh. 12.8; Isa. 38.7; 49.10). The biblical
dictionaries view 'bubble (of water)' as the base of נבע, which is
corroborated by some Semitic cognates. But, statistically, the
root נבע in the *hiphil* stem, הביע, appears *ten* times, and means 'to
speak, bring forth (words), utter', sometimes expressly with the
'mouth' or 'lips' (Prov. 15.2; Pss. 49.8; 119.171). Significantly,
both the distribution of נבע *hiphil*, 'talk, utter', and the formation
itself are differentiated from those of נבא, 'be a prophet' or
'prophesy'. The former is specifically a *hiphil* stem, and appears
mostly in the Psalms[2] or wisdom literature (Proverbs and
Qoheleth). The latter root has no specific distribution, although
it is more prevalent in the books named 'prophetic books'. On
the other hand, it has nominal forms, and *niphal* and *hithpael*
verb formations.

Therefore, the sense 'talk, call' is quite suitable for both: a
'prophecy' is conceived of as the verbally pronounced outcome
emanating from some contact with the divine. Phonologically, of
course, a mutation of ע into א is irregular for classical (pre-exilic)
biblical Hebrew. I am not suggesting a mutation of consonants,
but a recognition that the common base sense of the two roots
is distinguishable by differentiated semantic usage more than by
etymological provenance. The common base derives from the
first two consonants, a principle acknowledged by scholars who
trace the original bi-consonantal structure of the more regular
tri-consonantal Semitic pattern. The third consonant, then,
carries a variation of the primary sense common to both.[3] It is
conceivable that a specialized sense of 'come forth' ('of speech,
especially 'divine speech') was attached to נבא quite early on,
while its twin נבע continued to be used for the coming forth of

1.   KB (1983), p. 588, for the presumably denominative verbal formations; pp. 625-26 for the presumable base noun, with a shorthand
bibliography for the derivation of the נבא words discussed.
2.   Where a verbal נבא does not feature at all; and נביא is rare (but see
Ps. 105.15).
3.   Thus already in GKC, §30, f-m.

water *and* speech, albeit in another stem and other textual contexts. A metaphor of words issuing from or coming forth out of the mouth 'like water' might have served as a contiguous link for both roots. On the other hand, both might have originally signified 'speech', and only secondarily 'bubble forth'. However, and for whatever it is worth, I can produce no cognates for supporting this theory. Neither can biblical scholarship ascertain, after many years of heated debate, what is the primary status of words containing the root-sequence נבא and the phenomenologies it represents.

The root's semantic range is quite broad: it encompasses 'augur', 'forecast', 'portend', 'foretell', 'predict', 'soothsay' and the like.[1] Therefore, to distinguish between these various activities and functions, and to apply the distinctions to occurrences of the root in divergent biblical contexts, requires exegetical dexterity. One way of coping with this multitude of significations, denotations and connotations is to order them into a developmental, chronologically linear sequence; that is, to point to trends of evolution from earlier, more primitive or naive 'prophecy' to later, 'classical' or 'written' prophecy. The earlier phenomena are defined as more technical and, simultaneously, more extroverted, intuitive and ecstatic. The later 'prophetic' phenomena are defined as relatively free of future-telling elements, while being more preoccupied with social and moral issues.

But even a cursory glance at prophetic personages and activities in biblical books will verify that apparent confusion reigns. The only certainty is that a 'prophet' is an intermediary or intercessor, sometimes self-styled (cf. Deut. 18.9-22), who delivers messages and nurtures a relationship between *his* god and *his*

---

1. Scholars sometimes rely on passages such as 1 Sam. 9.9, 'In the past in Israel a man said thus on going to seek God, let us go to the seer, for a prophet now was previously called "the seer" (Heb. ראה)', to distinguish between the functions of pre-classical prophecy (future-telling, often privately transacted) and classical prophecy (mainly concern with political, social, moral and religious agendas). The change of terminology, however, does not necessarily indicate a change in substance: moreover, terms like ראה and חזה ('seer') appear in the Latter Prophets too although, admittedly, in smaller numbers than נבא terms. Also, the activities attributed to Samuel in this passage and elsewhere in 1 Samuel problematize that distinction.

reluctant human audience by various means. However, in biblical literature such functions of intermediation or intercession are performed also by priests, monarchs and other leaders; the boundaries between various intermediary methods are not always easy to define. In addition, YHWH may occasionally reveal himself to his community and to individuals within it *without* any kind of mediation.

Other criteria for claiming prophetic status for narrated persons, or phenomena, or narratives, or poetic compositions—or the evolutionary line thereof—may lead us into trouble too. In what way are symbolical acts reportedly performed by an Isaiah or a Jeremiah singularly 'prophetic'? Is Ezekiel less ecstatic, say, than the naked Soul (1 Sam. 10.10-13; 19.20-24), or Elisha (2 Kgs 3.12-15)? Is Daniel less of a prophet than Jonah, although the book so named is late, thus incorporated into the Writings? The problematics of recognizing 'prophecy' are expressed in the Bible itself, in the Torah. In Num. 11.25-30 Moses reportedly affirms the legitimacy of popular prophecy. And in Numbers 12 Moses' prophetic prowess is juxtaposed with Miriam's and · Aaron's, especially the former; the crux is YHWH's admission with regards to the direct relationship between him and his 'prophet'. The uncertainty of recognizing the legitimacy or illegitimacy of a prophetic claim is dealt with in Deuteronomy 15. In Jer. 23.25-40 we have only the textual speaker's subjective word for his true affinity with God, against those he calls 'prophets who use my [God's] name falsely' (cf. also Jer. 28–29). The book of Ezekiel contains an extended section of ranting and raving against 'prophets' and 'prophesying' claims, of males and females, who the speaker-in-the-text considers false (Ezek. 12.21–14.23, esp. ch. 13). The same question of establishing prophetic authority informs the the story of the prophets and the two kings (1 Kgs 22.5-28). The claim for authority involves a claim for *truth*, that is, eventual materialization of the divine message professed; this is so not only in the Torah and in Kings, but also in Ezekiel and Jeremiah. Clearly, then, Scripture itself sees prophetic claims as far from settled; and so should we, in spite of centuries of pondering and an enormous mass of fervent scholarly debate.

And what about the claim made for the uniqueness of

Hebrew prophecy? The Bible itself belies this notion. It affirms the status of 'prophets' for worshippers of Baal and Asherah (1 Kgs 18; 19.1); if they are not 'true prophets', this is because the authority they claim (pagan gods) is rejected. Although Deut. 18.15, 18 restricts legitimate prophetic claims to Hebrew origins ('a נביא from within you, from your brethren', v. 15; 'I shall raise for them a נביא from among their brethren', v. 18), YHWH and his 'spirit' can come even to a foreigner, like Bileam (Num. 22–24). Modern scholarship has shown us that similar phenomena, again featuring forecast of the future by dreams, vision and direct contacts with the divine, were reported in other ancient cultures, notably Mari.

What נביא or נבואה signified for the *persons* named נביא in the Latter Prophets remains unclear as well. The historicity of 'prophets', not to mention the texts attributed to them in the MT or in other textual traditions (such as the LXX), is still hotly disputed. Assuming that Hosea, Jeremiah, Isaiah and so on are names that designate historical *persons*, can we ascertain that *they* saw themselves as 'prophets'? The editors of the biblical books so named obviously believed that they were 'prophets', and true ones, as evidenced by the superscriptions to those books. But 'Amos', for instance, rejects this notion roundly (Amos 7.14-16): the text draws a distinction between *being a prophet* and *uttering a prophecy*. Recognition of 'false prophesying', as in Jeremiah and Ezekiel, does not automatically imply a justified self-claim to 'prophecy'. Would-be prophetic messengers tend to reject their divinely-ordained role (Moses, Elijah, Jeremiah, Jonah—if a prophet he is; but cf. Isa. 6, and Ezekiel). Nonetheless we, the readers, are called upon by the voices-in-the-text as well as by compilers, editors and many generations of interpreters to accept the claim for a *truth* that is typical in those texts.

Scholarly interpretations of the 'prophetic books' are not immune from this claim. A recent dialogue in writing between Holt, Auld and Carroll[1] shows that escaping from the hold

1. Cf. *JSOT* 48 (1990). T.W. Holt ('Prophecy in History: The Social Reality of Intermediation', pp. 2-29 and 'It is Difficult to Read', pp. 51-54) presents a variation on the traditional approach to the prophetic books. G.A. Auld ('Prophecy in Books: A Rejoinder', pp. 31-32), and R.P. Carroll

written 'prophecy' exercises is a matter of courage—and personal convictions (or their lack). Auld and Carroll suggest that, because of the unresolved difficulties listed above and many others, the interpretive community would do well to regard the 'prophetic' texts as *poetry* rather than the elusive *prophecy*; or historiographical *prose*, as in some chapters of Isaiah and Jeremiah.

To summarize. It would seem that the primary meanings and functions of 'prophecy' or 'prophetic' or 'prophet', inasmuch as we can uncover them, are 'speech', 'speaking, calling', 'to speak out' and the like. A 'prophet', therefore, is primarily a public speaker (to come back to the meaning assigned in the KB and discussed above). Public speakers resort to propaganda in order to advance their ideas and ideologies. They appeal to addressees in order to gain influence over them. Their rhetoric may therefore include verbal exaggeration, symbolic acts and dramatization (to the point of performing street theatre, as some scholars maintain). The approach championed by, for instance, Auld and Carroll might seem too radical to some readers. But these scholars' premises enable us to go beyond the courteous mystique attached to the so-called prophetic texts, and to confront the teachings they embody. Recent scholarship emphasizes the political and social contents of those teachings, which are very much in evidence alongside the religious, cultic and moral concerns. Whether the concepts of gender obtainable therein are acceptable to feminist and womanly readers is a matter of taste and for debate. Such a debate is founded on rejection of 'prophetic' *authority* inasmuch as it contributes toward undermining that same authority. It is also informed by the notion that the so-called prophetic books, which exhibit an avid interest in everything political and social, continue to exert their influence in today's communities—be they academic or otherwise. The images of femaleness and woman that these books contain are significant for feminist criticism. However, if we comply as required with prophetic mystique, if we do not regard it with a degree of inquisitive scepticism, feminist critique

('Whose Prophet? Whose History? Whose Social Reality? Troubling the Interpretive Community Again: Notes towards a Response to T.W. Overholt's Critique', pp. 33-49) advance the opposite view.

of the prophetic books has no room for manoeuvre. Ultimately, it is perhaps more useful to regard the books of the Latter Prophets as a collection of related literary genres than as depictions of historical phenomena; and this is the approach that has been adopted in this volume.

Athalya Brenner

Female Images in Prophetic Books

Analyses of female images have been a priority of feminist Bible criticism and, to a very large extent, they still are. Proceeding from this perspective (which, to many conventionally trained scholars, is not the most urgent perspective for dealing with the prophecy genre), what images of femininity and femaleness are to be found in the texts attributed to the 'classical prophets'? Here are some of them.

1. *Women are Neither Acknowledged Public Leaders nor Prophets*
In other parts of the Bible women—Miriam, Deborah, Huldah, Noadiah—are named as 'prophetesses'. In the present collection, the Latter Prophets, no written reference to female 'prophecy' is to be found.[1] Although women prophets and other female leaders are known, for instance from Mesopotamia,[2] a 'prophetess' here, inasmuch as she is mentioned, seems to be a prophet's companion or wife, as in Isa. 8.3, 'and I came unto the

---

1.   There is a single reference to Miriam, together with Moses and Aaron, in Mic. 6.4. The reference reads: 'I [YHWH] brought you out from the land of Egypt, and delivered you from the house of slavery, and sent *Moses and Aaron and Miriam* in front of you'. There is no doubt that *leadership* is attributed to Miriam here. However, it seems to me that to claim *prophetic* status for her in this reference is to stretch the matter too far.
2.   Cf. B. Batto, *Studies on Women at Mari* (Baltimore: Johns Hopkins University Press, 1974); R. Harris, 'Biographical Notes on the Naditu Women of Sippar', *JCS* 16 (1962), pp. 1-12; *idem*, 'Independent Women in Ancient Mesopotamia', in B.S. Lesko (ed.), *Women's Earliest Records: From Ancient Egypt and Mesopotamia* (BJS, 166; Atlanta: Scholars Press, 1989), pp. 145-56.

prophetess and she conceived and gave birth to a son, and YHWH said to me, name him…and before the boy calls "my father", "my mother"'. Unlike the Torah and the Former Prophets, the Latter Prophets collection does not recognize 'prophetess' as an independent vocation. Here she is wife and mother, whose prerogative to name her child (much in evidence in the other texts) is taken over by the child's father, who gives the son a symbolic name.[1]

In Ezekiel, the possibility of female prophecy is dealt with in another manner. Here female prophecy is defined as 'prophesying' (in the Hebrew *hithpael* stem, 'pretend to be a prophet'?), which certainly means a demotion of practitioner and practice (cf. Ezek. 13 for both female and male 'prophesizers'). In short, women are not and should not be either public leaders or public speakers.

2. *Women Exert Bad Influence even when their Involvement in Public Affairs is Informal and Confined to the Domestic Sphere*

They are likened to cows, insatiable in their demands from their masters (!), hence perpetrators of moral and social corruption. Thus in Amos,

> Listen to this message, cows of the Bashan in the hill of Samaria,
> who pillage the destitute, crush the poor,
> who say to their[2] masters, bring and we shall drink.

---

1.   But cf. the celebrated passage of Isa. 7.14: 'Therefore, God will give a signal to *you*' (masc. plural). Here, the young woman (Hebrew עלמה) is pregnant, and will have a son; and '*you will call* (fem. singular, וקראת) his name Immanuel' (*she* will name him). The Hebrew gives the naming right to the mother. However, the switch in addressee is problematic. An emendation to 'and [he] will call (וקרא) his name'—presumably attributing the name-giving to YHWH, the only masculine singular subject in this passage—is suggested by *BHS*, on the basis of IQIsa and some LXX texts. While the emendation does little for the syntax of the passage, it manages to do away with one of the significant rights of women, that is, their right to name their sons. See Gen. 29.30-31, Ruth 4.17, and elsewhere.

2.   The Hebrew text has 'their masters', אדניהם, with the masc. genitive suffix, here and in the next verse ('to you'). In *BHS* an emendation to the fem. genitive suffix is suggested, as dictated by the context. However, since the apparently masc. plural suffix is used in classical biblical Hebrew to denote the fem. suffix too, together with the fem. plural suffix within the

YHWH god swears by his holiness that [such] days are coming to
you,
[that] you will be carried...
And brought out naked, and thrown into the harem[1] (Amos 4.1-3).

Urban women are expressly singled out for attack. Isa. 3.12-15a
is motivated by a specific complaint: the people are ruled by
women who repress them, especially the poor and disadvan-
taged among them. Apparently, when women allegedly have
political and social influence, injustice reigns. Let us remember
that the audience appealed to is an urban audience, especially
elite classes. Even when the prophet-speaker is presumably of
country stock (Amos, Jeremiah) he operates in the city, be it
Samaria or Jerusalem; his concerns are concerns of society and
state, and 'he' claims to come into contact with leaders and
people of substance. In that sense, the critique of urban, elite
women is the critique of *everywoman* within the textual microcosm. So it is in Amos (above) and also in Isaiah:

And YHWH said, Because the daughters of Zion exalt [themselves]
and walk about with tilted necks and painted eyes,
and they joust, walk and careen, and their legs tinkle—
God will stroke their heads with a skin disorder,
and expose their vulvas.[2]
And on that day, God will undo the splendour of their... (Isa.
3.16-18a).

Subsequent verses contain a catalogue of 21 (!) items of female
apparel and jewellery, some unparalleled in other biblical passages and quite obscure (3.18-23); whoever compiled that catalogue must have been familiar with such female finery. But,
according to some commentators, the list is an addition. Thus
for instance A.S. Herbert: 'the detailed list of feminine adorn-
ments was probably added to the oracle, perhaps by a disciple

same verses and context (cf. Ruth 1.8 [twice], 9, 11, 13), the emendation
seems unnecessary. And see also GKC, §135o.
   1.   The translation of this last verse (Amos 4.3) is approximate, for the
Hebrew is corrupt. Cf. *BHS* and the LXX for the passage.
   2.   Translating the Hebrew פתהן literally; but see other, mitigating versions in *BHS*. Most of the translations are, to a greater or lesser degree,
euphemistic.

of the prophet'.[1] No reason is given for this diagnosis. One might surmise that the catalogue belongs to another genre. However, does an admixture of genre necessarily imply another author? Or, alternatively, does the mystique attached to 'prophet' and 'prophecy' exclude the textual narrators' involvement in or intimate knowledge of such mundane feminine items? Knowledge of female finery seems to have informed the lament on Tyre in Ezekiel 27 too,[2] where the city is described in terms of a woman (and see below). At any rate, the Isaian text continues to relate the morbid fate envisaged for the daughters of Zion:

> And instead of perfume there will be decay,
> and rope instead of a belt
> and baldness instead of coiled hair
> and sackcloth for a sash.
> For instead of beauty...
> Your people will fall by the sword, and your heroes in war...
> And on that day, seven women will clutch at one man,
> saying, 'We shall eat our own bread, and wear our own garments;
> Only give us your name, do away with our shame!'[3] (3.24–4.1).

The designation of 'women' as daughters, in fact daughters of a daughter (for 'Zion' is a daughter herself), is interesting. This

---

1. A.S. Herbert, *The Book of the Prophet Isaiah: Chapters 1–39* (Cambridge: Cambridge University Press, 1973), p. 45.

2. Notably vv. 7, 16-18, 22, 24.

3. It seems that the 'shame' referred to is the shame of being unmarried or, at the very least, without male protection. The assumption, as so often in patriarchal ideology, is that a woman not properly attached to a household headed by a male remains outside the boundaries of the social order. Let us note that Jephthah's mother, whose status is unclear, is called זונה by the narrator (Judg. 11.1-2); that when the Levite's wife leaves him, her action is depicted as prostitution even though she returns to her father's house (ותזנה עליו פילגשו, Judg. 17.2); and that the unattached women who come to Solomon for judgment are 'prostitutes' (1 Kgs 3.16-27). Marriage is the norm: unattached females are shamed by the presentation of their sexuality as suspect. Interestingly Rahab (Josh. 2 and 6.22-25), who belongs to this same category of female, acquires respectability and a husband in both Jewish and Christian traditions.

title establishes their social status as dependent minors, their personal circumstances notwithstanding.[1]

3. Cities and Countries are Metaphorized into Women, Preferably 'Virgins' or 'Daughters'

These women's sexuality is impaired by war and their fate is to be physically exposed, raped and prostituted:

> Virgin Israel has fallen, she will not rise again
> she has been abandoned on her land [with] no one to lift her
> (Amos 5.2. Cf. 7.17; Nah. 3.5; Zech. 14.2; Isa. 4.4, 32.9-14; and more).

Babylon, Egypt, Israel, Judah and others are thus depicted and addressed. This literary phenomenon has long been noticed by commentators,[2] and given a slim grammatical justification: 'cities', 'nations' and 'countries' in Hebrew are grammatically of the feminine gender. The metaphor often contains an ingredient of sexual violence committed against women in war.[3] This constitutes a politicization of sexual abuse (often labelled by commentators 'female sexual fate at wartime'), rather than a commentary on the social and political ills that determine that abuse. When the metaphor is read on a continuum leading from 1 above through 2 to 3, its damaging potential for women and images of femininity is evident. Nevertheless, in a few passages in second Isaiah and elsewhere we also find the somewhat more comforting figure of Zion as mother (and see below, 5).[4]

1. The parallel designation 'daughters of Jerusalem' (Song 1.5; 2.7; 3.5 [of 'Zion', 3.10]; 5.8, 16; 8.4) might be construed as referring to *young, unmarried* women, hence legally 'daughters', because of the subject matter. However, even here the designation may be understood as another instance of patriarchal attitudes toward women.

2. Cf., for instance, recently and for additional literature J.F.A. Sawyer, 'Daughter of Zion and the Servant of the Lord in Isaiah: A Comparison', *JSOT* 44 (1989), pp. 89-107.

3. Cf. P. Gordon and H.C. Washington, 'Rape as a Military Metaphor', in this volume; and the articles in C.V. Camp and C.R. Fontaine (eds.), *Women, War and Metaphor* (*Semeia* 61 [1993]).

4. On Zion as mother and the relevance of the image for today see the recent article by H. Schüngel-Straumann, 'Mutter Zion im Alten Testament', in T. Schneider and H. Schüngel-Straumann (eds.), *Theologie zwischen Zeiten und Kontinenten: Für Elizabeth Gossmann* (Freiburg: Herder, 1993), pp. 19-43.

4. *The Divine Husband/Unfaithful Human Wife Metaphor*

This metaphor is probably affiliated to the foregoing images. In this metaphor (Hos. 1–3; Jer. 2–5 and elsewhere; Ezek. 16, 23; numerous passages in second Isaiah), YHWH is always the faithful, loving husband; the people, Judah/Israel or Jerusalem/Samaria, are always an adulterous, wayward wife. The marriage contract, broken unilaterally by the metaphorical wife, signifies the alleged unilateral breaking of the covenant with YHWH by the metaphorized people. The metaphor constitutes an act of religious propaganda anchored in preconceptions of gender relations and the nature of female sexuality which reinforces a vision of negative female sexuality as against positive or neutral male sexuality (and see below).

5. *The Figure of a Woman Giving Birth is a Symbol for Fear, Physical Infirmity and Suffering in Political Affairs and War*

If cities, countries or communities are imaged, like women, as unfit for public prominence, their presumably deserved fate may be metaphorized into the female pain par excellence. This image appears in Jeremiah (6.24; 22.23; 50.43) and Micah (4.9).[1] Here too an exclusive aspect of female (sexual/reproductive) experience is politicized. Similar use is made of images of bereaved mothers, or widows, whose image is at times combined with that of the city, nation or territory as woman (see, for example, Jer. 30.14; 31.3-4; Isa. 47.1-5, 9). In this latter combination, a reconstitution into 'virginity' or restored motherhood signifies a reversal in the fortunes of the woman/city.

6. *Professional Women, Women of Vocation, Do Not Feature Largely*

In Jeremiah mourning women are mentioned in passing (Jer. 9.16-20). For women as practitioners of magic skills, see 7.

7. *In Zechariah 5.5-11, Evil Itself Assumes the Guise of a Woman, Carried by Women*

This 'vision' seems to function as a not-so-distant relative of the 'prophesying' women in Ezekiel, and of the attribution of

---

1.   Also once in the Psalms (48.7). The parallel image of trembling in fear in Exod. 15.14 has the same Hebrew word, חיל, but lacks the comparison to 'woman in labour'.

witchcraft and necromancy specifically to women in other parts of the Bible. Why is evil depicted as a 'woman'? Possibly because:

8. *Women are Described as Active in the Cult, Albeit Not in* YHWH's *Cult*

In Jeremiah 7 and 44 they are accused of establishing and perpetuating an all-family cult of the Queen of Heaven in Jerusalem and elsewhere. In Ezek. 8.14 women are accused of mourning the Mesopotamian fertility god Tammuz at the Jerusalem temple. The 'whoredom' attributed to daughters and daughters-in-law in Hosea (for example, Hos. 4.13-14) seems, once again, like an angry exclamation against the involvement of women in non-Yahwistic cults. In the light of recent archaeological findings (as in Kuntillet 'Ajrud and Hirbet el-Qom) and scholarly research,[1] there can hardly be any doubt that Judahite and Israelite women, barred from the official cult of YHWH, found other venues for their religious impulses.

Such descriptions may be problematic for womanly readers. If we cooperate with the all-male (inclusive of the divine) voice of this literature, as dictated by the acceptance of the prophetic mystique, we have no choice but to condemn those women. But if, along the lines suggested by Cheryl Exum, we step out of the text's ideology,[2] then our evaluation of these textual women's religiosity and morality changes along with our understanding of ancient Israelite religion.

1. Cf. S. Ackerman, 'And the Women Knead Dough: The Worship of the Queen of Heaven in Sixth-Century Judah', in P.L. Day (ed.), *Gender and Difference in Ancient Israel* (Philadelphia: Fortress Press, 1989), pp. 109-22; D. Edelman, 'Huldah the Prophet—of Yahweh or Asherah?', in A. Brenner (ed.), *A Feminist Companion to Samuel and Kings* (The Feminist Companion to the Bible, 5; Sheffield: Sheffield Academic Press, 1994), pp. 231-50. M. Douglas, *In the Wilderness: The Doctrine of Defilement in the Book of Numbers* (JSOTSup, 158; Sheffield: JSOT Press, 1993), pp. 200-212, links women's worship to the story of Miriam on the one hand, and the husband-wife metaphor of covenantal relationship between YHWH and Israel on the other hand. See also S. Olyan, *Asherah and the Cult of Yahweh in Israel* (SBLMS, 34; Atlanta: Scholars Press, 1988).

2. J.C. Exum, *Fragmented Women: Feminist (Sub)Versions of Biblical Narrative* (JSOTSup, 163; Sheffield: JSOT Press, 1993).

It would seem, therefore, that women and womanhood are confined to specific functions in this kind of literature, not unlike the situation in other types of biblical literature. They are seldom imaged as independent, self-supporting figures. The images of wife/mother/widow and daughter are extended to denote other entities. Women are accused of other cults. Their membership in the 'prophetic', Yahwistic world is largely denied, unless they are positioned in traditional female roles. And even in those, their social situation is undermined by accusations levelled at urban women, and by the divine husband/unfaithful human wife metaphor.

Part 1: The Case of 'Hosea'

The book of Hosea has prompted much feminist comment in recent years, and understandably so. Of the images mentioned above, the book has an extensive (perhaps the historically primal) presentation of the marriage metaphor (4 above), and great emphasis upon the participation of women in presumably pagan cults (8), hence their corrupting influence (2). Clearly, the book exhibits a (male?) preoccupation, perhaps obsession, with things feminine and gender relations which are transformed into political and religious propaganda. The sociocultural impact of the androcentric views it contains cannot be underestimated.

The book begins with a story about the allegedly disastrous, albeit preordained, marriage of 'Hosea' himself (chs. 1–3). 'His' domestic affairs and wayward, 'prostitute' wife serve as symbolic representation of YHWH's covenantal relationship with his people. The metaphorized analogy between the human covenant of marriage and the divine/human covenant of exclusive monotheism attributes rigid roles to the partners and their respective sexualities. The male partner, human or divine, is assessed positively; the female partner, individual or community/territory, is evaluated as inherently negative. Whether this is a true story, a transformation of life experience into a mission, is largely a moot point. By the time we move on to read the rest of the book and its highly developed comprehension of other social issues and the political scene, our attitude has already been coloured by the opening hyperbole. And whereas male readers have tended to play down the hyperbole, womanly readers may find the confrontation with such a text painful.

Carole R. Fontaine's introductory survey of Hosea is the first essay on the book. Fontaine scans the sociopolitical and historical contexts of the book, the theological heritage it contains, and its literary features. For the purpose of the survey, the marriage metaphor is described rather neutrally as a symbolic representation in which Hosea's family life mirrors YHWH's relationship with Israel. Various aspects of the text are discussed briefly— the affinity between chs. 1 and 3, the ethics of the situation described, connections with fertility cults, women's status, the message signified by the metaphor, and so on. Fontaine then moves to a short description of chs. 4–14 and the poetic style. Throughout her analysis, first published in 1989, Fontaine retains an objective descriptive mode. In that sense, she can be seen to comply with the text and its messages.

However, Fontaine has also written a 'Response to (her) "Hosea"' for this volume. Here she declares openly that her introductory survey does not challenge traditional scholarly readings of Hosea concerning women and female sexuality, and explains why. Feminist concerns were not high on the agenda of biblical scholarship a few years ago and, although to a lesser extent, this is still the case now. M (Masculine/Male)[1] complicity with the suffering 'husband', be he 'Hosea' or YHWH, was sought and considered normative readerly practice. The wife's negativity was taken for granted. But what if we turn the tables? If we identify with the metaphorical, fictive or 'real' wife—a pleasure and task denied to F (Feminine/Female) readers in the past—then the ensuing reading will be greatly changed. In turn, a new F reading may promote a new F voice. Fontaine concludes with a personal midrash which assumes the perspective of Gomer, the much maligned 'wife' whose views are not heard in/by the text.

The question of fertility cults and their presence in or absence

1. For the terms M (Masculine/Male) and F (Feminine/Female) see A. Brenner and F. van Dijk-Hemmes, *On Gendering Texts: Female and Male Voices in the Hebrew Bible* (Leiden: Brill, 1993), esp. Brenner, 'Introduction', pp. 1-11.

from ancient Israel has been crucial for the understanding and eventual acceptance of the marriage metaphor, or for its rejection. In 'The Female Body, the Body Politic and the Land: A Sociopolitical Reading of Hosea 1–2', Alice A. Keefe proposes that Hosean imagery of female sexual transgression does not refer to fertility cults but to place- and time-bound sociopolitical conditions in Israel of the late eighth century BCE. Like Gruber and Odell,[1] Keefe rejects the notion, entertained by many commentators, that the reality of fertility cults motivates the sexual imagery. Instead, she links the female images with the land and agrarian developments instituted by royal activity. In this socioeconomic and political context, religious principles of the sacred link with the 'body' of the land are lost and, instead, everything becomes material and corporeal. In Keefe's analysis the female imagery employed in Hosea does not represent a rejected female otherness but a lost world, in which harmony between the sacred and the divine was possible. The central trope, then, is neither adultery nor fertility cult nor an inherent negativity of female sexuality but, rather, the lost land and everything the land stands for.

The boxing or battering of Gomer—the fictitious, real or symbolic wife—is the theme of Sherwood's and Graetz's articles. In 'Boxing Gomer: Controlling the Deviant Woman in Hosea 1–3', Yvonne Sherwood explores aspects of the solidarity implicitly sought between readers and text. The textual Gomer is an unacceptable woman: a wife but also promiscuous. Therefore, androcentric traditions—modern as well as ancient—seek to tame her. Ironically, both readerly modes resist the text in order to further their own views. Feminist critics, Sherwood warns, push their own agenda, as do mainstream critics. The feminist challenge is to avoid a romanticization of the female character(s) while deconstructing patriarchal attitudes and entities which are foisted onto women and female sexuality. Precisely because women occupy the cultural position of Other, as readers they can unlock biblical women's stories like Gomer's story. However, the unlocking should be carried out with caution.

---

1.   Gruber, 'Marital Fidelity and Intimacy', and Odell, 'I Will Destroy Your Mother', in this volume.

In 'God is to Israel as Husband to Wife: The Metaphoric Battering of Hosea's Wife', Naomi Graetz reads ch. 2. She surveys the standard mode for reading Hosea and Gomer's 'story' in Jewish midrashic texts: complicity with and sympathy for the textual husband and what he represents, condemnation of the wife and what she symbolizes. In the source text and the extra-biblical Jewish texts, Graetz finds traces of battering and abuse, verbal and otherwise, which are inflicted upon the 'wife' (Gomer/Israel) in the name of male and divine love. The 'marriage' is in trouble. The male spouse threatens the woman with violence. To attribute desperation and extreme emotion to the 'husband', thus to understand his words and threatening actions, is to agree that violence against women, especially married women, may be justifiable and necessary in the biblical source text as well as in ancient and modern Jewish interpretations. Graetz concludes by offering some ways for promoting change within the Jewish ritual tradition, so that women become a less convenient target for verbal and other kinds of abuse that are similar to those described in Hosea 2.

Feminist critiques, whatever their particular hue, are anchored in the recognition that conventional attitudes are male while claiming universal ('human', transgender) validity; that gender asymmetry operates in social as well as academic matters. And feminists often lament the fact that, by and large, they are in the business of converting the already converted, that is, engaging in a fruitful discourse with persons—mostly women—of similar convictions. While some feminists have despaired of breaking these boundaries, others are interested in the questions: how are male readers affected by feminist views? How does the feminist revolution, so-called, influence the attitudes and approaches of the other gender, if at all? The next three articles constitute different answers to these questions.

In his 'Fantasy and the Displacement of Pleasure: Hosea 2.4-17', Francis Landy attempts to bridge the obsessive battering of the metaphorical woman at the beginning of the passage with its promise of blissful reunion, and to establish its place within the pericope of chs. 1–3 and as a microcosm for the whole book. Landy builds on the results of previous feminist discussions of Hosea 2. In his analysis, the (male) fantasy shames and objectifies the metaphorical woman—land, people, children. The metaphor's boundaries are blurred, as are its specific referents. This is self-defeating and self-destructive. The threatened exposure of woman and children is analysed as sexual abuse and infanticide which emanate from divine jealousy and a projected sense of isolation. If a better end is envisaged after the obsessive bitterness of the accusations, this is possible because violence, finally, exhausts itself and other emotions must set in.

In his 'Hosea 1–3, Genesis 1–4 and a Masculist Interpretation', John Goldingay attempts a male reading of Hosea 1–3—with a difference. While he identifies with the Hosean figure-in-the-text (a traditional male choice), he does so from a fresh angle: that of an overtly masculine albeit relativized perspective which incorporates feminist concerns. Part of Goldingay's conclusion is that 'it is only when we have men and women together that we have the divine image represented'. And that is not much different from the theological viewpoint of avowed feminists.

Moving beyond the first three chapters of Hosea, in 'Marital Fidelity and Intimacy: A View from Hosea 4', Mayer Gruber reinterprets Hos. 4.10-19. He rejects most of the interpretations of the passage. With L.H. Ginsberg in his recent translation (JPS, 1985), Gruber reads in the passage an agricultural festival of eating and drinking, which leads to fornication (vv. 10-12). In party spirit, sexual promiscuity is practised by women and men alike. The men's behaviour is seen by the textual speaker ('Hosea'?) as ungodliness that drives the women related to them, daughters and brides, to the same kinds of sexual license (vv. 13-14).[1] According to Gruber, no cultic prostitution existed here or elsewhere in the Hebrew Bible. Rather, he sees in these and the following verses an egalitarian message for both genders to honour the covenant of marriage as a mature bond and adult religious commitment, and to practise sex only within its intimacy. The message of sexual commitment as condition for membership in the religious ('temple', v. 15) community is diametrically opposed to the occasional, teenage-like sexual patterns implied by non-monotheistic systems in the ancient

---

1. For a similar view see also Landy, 'Fantasy and Displacement'.

Near East. Thus, Gruber's interpretation has relevance for Hosean as well as contemporary theology of sexuality.

Still about ch. 4, in ' "I Will Destroy Your Mother": The Obliteration of a Cultic Role in Hosea 4.4-6' Margaret S. Odell discusses a difficult passage along lines similar to Gruber's. Who is the figure referred to by the appellation 'your mother', invoked in the passage? Odell considers the possibility that the 'mother' is the cultic superior of the addressed priest, and that this superior carries an honorific, official, maternal title. Odell reminds us that 'mother' is applied to Gomer too, again with fertility and cult associations. She suggests that the 'mother' functioned as leader within a Baalized Yahwistic context. As an example of female cult leadership which was suppressed and obliterated in/by the biblical text, the case of Miriam is cited.[1] Coming back to the sexual threat in Hosea, Odell shows by her reconstruction how the 'mother' figure was indeed destroyed, as promised in ch. 2.

The articles in this collection illustrate some of the ways in which the marriage metaphor is problematic for feminists. The metaphor disturbs not only because of the female imagery it contains, but also because of the figure of the husband/YHWH implied by readings which focus on the female figure. What kind of god will allegedly allow such brutal handling of a female figuration? This question is directly addressed by Francis Landy. It is indirectly addressed in Helen Schüngel-Straumann's article, 'God as Mother in Hosea 11'. Schüngel-Straumann admits that god-talk in Hosea is a difficult issue but, she argues, the portrait of YHWH drawn in/by the metaphor can be offset somewhat by reference to Hosea 11. There, in her opinion, YHWH is represented as a loving mother to his children (people). The alternative metaphor of YHWH-as-mother, she goes on, was repressed effectively by Christian theology which, traditionally, has focused on superior male positions of the

1. Cf. the section of articles on Miriam (some of which are cited by Odell) in A. Brenner (ed.), *A Feminist Companion to Exodus to Deuteronomy* (The Feminist Companion to the Bible, 6; Sheffield: Sheffield Academic Press, 1994), pp. 166-254. For a view of Miriam similar to Odell's, if from another perspective, see recently Douglas, *In the Wilderness*, pp. 196-216. Douglas also discusses the marriage metaphor (pp. 160-71).

biblical text rather than on positive representations of female positions. She concludes that although the Bible is undeniably patriarchal, there are passages in it that should and can be reinterpreted from a feminist theological perspective, so that they may appear beneficial for womanly interests.

The concern about god-talk bears different results in Marie-Theres Wacker's contribution. Wacker examines 'Traces of the Goddess in the Book of Hosea'. Looking for a/the goddess has been a favourite pursuit of some feminist critics; Wacker recommends that the search be conducted with caution and, indeed, demonstrates that this can be done. She looks for 'traces', not for fuller portraits. This means that she searches beneath and between lines for a goddess subtext. Like Schüngel-Straumann, Wacker's perspective is first and foremost theological. Her method is transdisciplinary. She moves from textual criticism of specific Hosean passages to extrabiblical literary, historical, archaeological and representational analogies. The article contains a discussion of the goddess-related status of women, and analyses of goddess icons and images (cow, tree) which were appropriated by the YHWH cult and its imagery.

Part II: On the Pornoprophetics of Sexual Violence

The essays of Part I show that feminist interpretations of Hosea, particularly of chs. 1–3, often focus on the violence expressed in and by the marriage metaphor about femaleness and female sexuality. One can perhaps mitigate the damage for women by pointing to the presumed motivations underlying the text, as do the authors of some essays. However, the textual anger and verbal violence are undeniable. It is difficult for any reader, even a resisting or suspicious reader, not to be affected by the recurrent, negative images of woman which are coded into the religio-political propaganda. The verbal violence of the marriage and other metaphors contains many references to females 'prostituting' themselves, which is also the regular practice of pornography. This recurrent accusation is socially devastating. It therefore remains to be asked if, and how, this type of religious propaganda makes use of pornographic representations of woman in Hosea and other books of the genre.

Four articles and one response are addressed to this issue. The first two, 'The Metaphorization of Woman in Prophetic Speech: An Analysis of Ezekiel 23' by the late Fokkelien van Dijk-Hemmes, and my 'On Prophetic Propaganda and the Politics of "Love"', extend the debate beyond Hosea. We both argue for viewing the marriage metaphor as not only abusive, but pornographic. Both of us begin by defining pornography and the characteristic features of realizing women and female sexuality in pornographic representations. Then, we apply these considerations to the different passages discussed. Van Dijk-Hemmes analyses Ezekiel 23 which, together with ch. 16 and Hosea 1–3, belongs to the set of fully-fledged articulations of the marriage metaphor. She shows how features like shaming the (metaphorical) female victim while attributing positive or neutral value to male sexuality operate within the metaphorization of Judah/Jerusalem and Israel/Samaria into women. These features, she points out, are potentially destructive for women's social standing and self-esteem. In my article, I try to trace the utilization of pornographic imagination in the representations of femaleness in Jeremiah 2–5. In order to affirm my conclusions I co-read a modern pornographic intertext, *Story of O*, together with the Jeremian texts. The comparison between the two disparate texts yields interesting if discomfiting results on the F and M images of each gender's fantasy and desire which they contain.

Van Dijk-Hemmes' and my conclusions are probably acceptable to many feminist and womanly readers but problematic for some, and certainly for many male readers. The issue of pornoprophetics is emotional, and hotly debated among feminists and between them and non-feminists. Robert P. Carroll's 'Desire under the Terebinths: Pornographic Representation in the Prophets—A Response' is a critique of the two articles and what Carroll, and many other non-feminist critics of the Bible, regard as the dangers inherent in our and similar feminist approaches of gendered sexual violence and desire in biblical literature. I asked Carroll to respond because his own position is criticized in van Dijk-Hemmes' and my articles; and also because his critique should serve as a mirror for feminist views and viewers, thus should not—in my opinion—be dismissed or suppressed as an expression of the Other. Carroll's remarks about the polyvalence of contemporary feminisms and *Ideologiekritik* is useful, especially if one wishes to engage in open dialogue with non-feminist thinkers.

In 'Rape as a Military Metaphor in the Hebrew Bible', Pamela Gordon and Harold C. Washington discuss prophetic verbal violence which contains anti-woman abuse from another angle, that of the examination of rape metaphors for war and military conquest. They analyse the sexual metaphor in which a conquered city is signified by a raped woman or raped women in prophetic literature and Lamentations, analogues for which abound in other ancient classical (Greek and Roman) literature. This metaphor, like the marriage metaphor, is a composite of images of woman and femininity. This kind of imagery can and should be resisted. To quote the authors, 'We reject the equation of bad women with bad cities, and we reject the idea that male violence (sexual and military, respectively) delivers just punishment'.

In 'Ancient Near Eastern Curses and the Ultimate Texts of Terror: A Study of the Language of Divine Sexual Abuse in the Prophetic Corpus', F. Rachel Magdalene discusses the two types of 'prophetic' texts: those defined as abusive and pornographic (van Dijk-Hemmes, Brenner) and those defined as abusive and rapist (Gordon and Washington). Although Magdalene concedes from the outset that such texts are, to use Phyllis Trible's idiom, 'texts of terror', she claims that cultural differences between ancient texts and modern readers should not be overlooked. Ancient Israel's concept of rape was different from our understanding of rape as the violation of a woman's body against *her* will. Self-controlled female sexuality of any kind was considered an offence. Granting that, the source of the violent rhetoric should be looked for elsewhere. Magdalene argues that the source of the violent assault metaphors is to be found in ancient Near Eastern treaty-curses. Patriarchal reception must have made the curses embodying women's fate in rape and war very real for Israelite male members of the community, hence the religious significance and effect of the metaphors. Magdalene concludes that understanding the source of YHWH's representation as rapist and abuser of female figures is not enough: one must mourn for all the victims of these biblical texts.

Part III: Should We Trust the God of the 'Prophets'?

In conclusion, we return to a question already broached by some articles, directly or otherwise (Landy, Schüngel-Straumann, Wacker, Magdalene). Can we trust this god who is imaged as a patriarchal male: husband, father, king, warrior, rapist? Or should one opt for feminist/female images of the deity: goddess (Wacker), mother (Schüngel-Straumann), cult official (Odell), Wisdom? In 'Can God Be Trusted? Confronting the Deceptive God', Nancy R. Bowen explores another unsavoury image of the divine: YHWH as deceiver, mainly in Ezek. 14.1-11. Bowen suggests that recognition of YHWH's occasional deceit may be liberating for womanly readers. The divine deceptions discussed facilitate transition from an existing situation toward an alternative reality, not necessarily of liberation but of hope. Although the idea of divine deception is painful, this divine trickster-style behaviour can be read as functional. Feminists may note that, in spite of the disturbing dimensions of prophetic (and other biblical) texts and images of gender relations and female sexuality, a deconstructive element is operational in them. And this may afford a measure of hope.

Or, it may not.

Part I
THE CASE OF 'HOSEA'

HOSEA*

Carole R. Fontaine

The prophet Hosea, the only native Israelite among the great 'writing' prophets of the eighth century BCE (Amos, First Isaiah, Micah), has often been characterized as the 'prophet of love' over against Amos, the 'prophet of doom'. As with most stereotypes, there is both truth and falsehood lodged within this conception of the prophet, whose name in Hebrew means '[God] has saved'. As he foresees the turbulent end of the northern kingdom (Israel), Hosea's message is as violent as any delivered by Amos, and his use of familial imagery is by no means always positive or evocative of tender feelings. Indeed, because of the overall tone of the book, many scholars have come to doubt that such hopeful passages as 14.1-9 (MT 14.2-10) and so on could have originated with the author of the bulk of the work.

The book comes from a time period falling approximately between the death of Jeroboam II in 746 and the fall of Israel (the northern kingdom, also referred to as 'Ephraim' by Hosea, in order to distinguish it from the southern kingdom of Judah) to Assyria in 722–721 BCE. The prophet's oracles were probably collected and preserved by disciples who fled to safety in Judah when the Assyrians destroyed the capital city, Samaria, and deported the upper-class Israelite population. As with the lives of most of the great prophets, we do not know what became of Hosea at that time. His work may have undergone one or more reorganizations and supplementations in the hands of Judean editors both in the early seventh century and during the Babylonian captivity, when the message of Hosea was particularly relevant for those seeking to understand the meaning of

*   This article originally appeared in B.W. Anderson (ed.), *The Books of the Bible* (New York: Charles Scribner's Sons, 1989), I, pp. 349-58.

Judah's sufferings.[1] In its final form, the book may be divided into two unequal complexes, the first comprising chs. 1–3 (Hosea's family mirrors God's relationship with Israel), and the second comprising chs. 4–14 (prophetic utterances). One noted scholar[2] further subdivides the second part into 4.1–11.11 and 11.12–14.9 (MT 12.1–14.10).

Sociopolitical Context

As with any prophetic book, it is impossible to grasp the major concepts of Hosea without some understanding of the social and political realities to which his prophecies were directed. Even though there is considerable debate about the proper chronological order of the oracles found in the work, the broad outlines of the period from which the book comes are clear, and these give some insight into the time frame and meaning of the individual passages.

The politics and social practices of the northern kingdom of Israel were always conditioned by the peculiar geographical position of that nation. Israel was a land of rich, productive valleys and upwarped hill country. Along with Judah, its less geographically favored sibling to the south, it lay nestled like a choice nut in the politically volatile nutcracker formed by the great river valley civilizations to the south (Egypt) and east (Assyria and Babylon). Pressures exerted by the great imperialistic powers inevitably crushed those small states occupying the Palestinian land bridge that had the misfortune to lie directly in the path of Egyptian and Mesopotamian ambitions, and the two often appear together as a word pair in Hosea's doom-filled prophecies (7.11, 9.6, 11.5, 11.11, 12.1 [MT, 12.21]). Periods of ascendancy in the political fortunes of Judah and Israel always came during times when the great empires of the river valleys

1. F.I. Andersen and D.N. Freedman, *Hosea: A New Translation with Introduction and Commentary* (AB, 24; Garden City, NY: Doubleday, 1980).

2. H.W. Wolff, *Hosea: A Commentary on the Book of Hosea* (Hermeneia; Philadelphia: Fortress Press, 1974). This standard commentary on Hosea makes use of frequent emendations of biblical texts and takes a form-critical approach in the explication of the units. For a very different treatment of the text of Hosea, see Andersen and Freedman, *Hosea*.

were weakened at home or overextended abroad, thus allowing 'breathing space' to the petty kingdoms of the Levantine.

The survival of Judah for almost two centuries following the
fall of Israel owed more to its geographical inaccessibility and
undesirability when compared with the privileged position of
the northern kingdom than to any moral or theological superiority on Judah's part. Geographically, Israel occupied a territory
where the great north–south and east–west trade routes
crossed. Although this location gave the kingdom access to
greater trade possibilities and foreign interchange, it also made
the land a primary target for Egyptian or Mesopotamian kings
who wished to march their armies through it to meet their great
rival in the quickest, most efficient way available. (The only
other possibilities for crossing the land bridge lay far to the
north in the Palmyrene Corridor or in the south through the
waterless Negev.) Like Belgium in the era of modern world
wars, Israel simply happened to be in the way of the power
struggles and expansionist policies of two great adversaries.
Hosea, of course, envisions Israel's coming destruction as the
result of the country's apostasy from Yahweh, the delivering
God of Moses and the ancestors. However, the geographical
and political realities undergirding the situation of the eighth-
century kingdoms of Israel and Judah make one wonder
whether any degree of faithfulness, however strong, could
have averted the catastrophes that lay ahead.

In the tenth century BCE, the recently divided kingdoms of
Judah and Israel had been devastated by an Egyptian invasion
led by the pharaoh Sheshonk I. By the mid-ninth century, Egypt
lay dormant and the Assyrian menace from the northeast had
forced the kings of Israel into an alliance with Aram-Damascus
and other local kingdoms against the Assyrian Shalmaneser III.
They were briefly successful, apparently defeating the 'Great
King' at the battle of Qarqar on the Orontes River in 853.
However, this allied victory was short-lived, for in 841 the
Israelite usurper-king Jehu was forced to pay heavy fines to
keep his kingdom (he is shown kissing Shalmaneser's feet in
submission on that king's 'Black Obelisk'). For about a century
afterward, Assyria was occupied with reorganization and
problems in its own territory, allowing Judah and Israel a period

of recovery that issued in the prosperous reigns of Uzziah of Judah and Jeroboam II of Israel. It was during this time of false security and blind optimism that Amos of Judah took his message of coming disaster to the northern kingdom and was met with a predictably negative response. Chapters 1–3 of Hosea may reflect the fortunes of the nation at the very end of Jeroboam II's reign.

Following Jeroboam's forty-one-year reign, his son, Zechariah, was assassinated within a year of his father's death in 746, thus bringing Jehu's dynasty, begun in violence in the Jezreel Valley, to a fittingly violent end. More palace coups followed, with King Menahem (c. 745–c. 738) emerging as the victor. Like Jehu before him, this king's policy for keeping his throne included pacification of the Assyrians by payment of huge amounts of tribute, for which he had to levy cruel taxes on Israelite landholders. This naturally alienated him from his local power base, and with Menahem's death the series of assassinations returned as pro-Assyrian factions struggled with Israelite nationalists. His son Pekahiah was assassinated after two years by Pekah, who was in turn assassinated by Hoshea, Israel's last king. In part, the anarchy in Israel was prompted by the all-too-evident resumption of Assyrian aggression with the accession of Tiglath-pileser III in 745.

The rule of the new king, an able administrator and warrior, spelled the beginning of the end for Israel and the neighboring petty states. Subduing his Babylonian enemies to the south, Tiglath-pileser defeated the kingdom of Urartu in the north and waged war as far away as the Caspian Sea. This accomplished, he turned his attention to the west and implemented previous policies with new zeal. Rather than simply punishing rebellions with massive displays of military might, this king annexed as Assyrian provinces any vassal states who refused tribute. Wholesale deportations of the ruling social classes of conquered states now held as provinces eroded local resistance by those peasants left on the land. Given that submission to Assyria was the only sure way for a ruler to retain some remnants of autonomy for himself and his country, Menahem's payment of tribute to Tiglath-pileser suddenly becomes understandable in the light of the unpleasant alternatives. It is clear from subsequent events, however, that the heavy tax burdens imposed by Menahem fueled the assassination of his son Pekahiah by anti-Assyrian factions.

Pekah, the usurper, made common cause against Assyria with Rezin, the king of Damascus, and certain Philistine allies along the coast. They tried to press Judah into joining their doomed alliance, and, finding first Jotham of Judah and then his son Ahaz unwilling to join their coalition, invaded Judah from the north (2 Kgs 15.37). In desperation, young King Ahaz sent to Tiglath-pileser for help (against the advice of the prophet Isaiah) and voluntarily made Judah an Assyrian vassal (2 Kgs 16.7-19, Isa. 7.1-17). This episode is known as the Syro-Ephraimite War; Hosea's oracles in 5.1-4, 5.8–6.6, 7.8-12, 8.7-10, 9.11-14, 11.1-7, and 12.1 (MT 12.2) probably come from the period immediately preceding the war and during the war itself.

With the Syro-Ephraimite coalition of Pekah and Rezin at the gates of Jerusalem intending to depose Ahaz, Tiglath-pileser was swift to respond. Attacking the coalition from the north, Judah was spared as Israel and its anti-Assyrian allies were driven into fighting the Great King long before planned and with a hostile Judah at their back. First destroying Philistia in 734 (and thereby rendering potential aid to the coalition from Egypt impossible), Tiglath-pileser then devastated Israel, annexing Israelite holdings in the Galilee and Transjordan and deporting their ruling populations. At this point, Pekah was assassinated by Hoshea, who then wisely surrendered to Assyria. In 732 the Assyrians conquered Damascus, executing Rezin and proceeding with annexation and deportation of the Syrian kingdom.

When Shalmaneser V succeeded his father, Tiglath-pileser, in 727, Hoshea tried to take advantage of the unrest that inevitably attended the death of a powerful king. Making overtures to Egypt for support, Hosea refused tribute to Shalmaneser. Israel's fate was thus sealed: Shalmaneser attacked in 724 and took Hoshea prisoner. The capital Samaria held out for two years as the Assyrians occupied the territory remaining to Israel after the earlier annexations of 733, but finally fell in 722–721 to Shalmaneser's successor, Sargon II. As thousands more were deported to Mesopotamia and Media, some fled to the relative safety to be found in Judah, carrying the sacred traditions of the now-defunct northern kingdom. Israel had come to an end, but the literary and theological heritage of its people endured.

The book of Hosea accurately reflects the social and political turmoil that attended the last days of Israel. The heavy burdens of vassalage to Assyria were various and demoralizing, since the price of survival was greater than the simple payment of tribute. The draining away of resources from the vassal country worsened its economic situation automatically, since surpluses could not be amassed for normal trade, nor could profits be plowed back into the land. Large, wealthy landholders routinely passed their tax burdens to the crown along to the peasant tenants who worked their land. General indebtedness rose, small landholdings—the 'heritage' of the poor—were swallowed up by greedy land speculators, and the ranks of the poor swelled. Similarly, the constant struggle to unite against Assyria, the Syro-Ephraimite war against Judah, and the court rivalries between pro- and anti-Assyrian factions also exacerbated the economic situation, since money siphoned away for militaristic reasons could not be used to improve the lot of the common folk.

Part of the price tag of vassalage usually included the adoption of the religious practices of the conquering suzerain. Although there is no direct evidence that Assyria interfered in Israel's cult before the fall of Samaria,[1] from the time of Jehu's submission to Shalmaneser III, Israel's exclusive worship of Yahweh had been threatened by the demands of political expediency. Actually, outside influences on its religious practices had always been a problem for the northern kingdom, at least in part because of its geographical position. Not only did Israel have greater contact with outsiders than did Judah, on account of its position on the international trade routes, but from the

---

1. M. Cogan, *Imperialism and Religion: Assyria, Judah, and Israel in the Eighth and Seventh Centuries BCE* (Missoula, MT: Scholars Press, 1974). This revised doctoral dissertation catalogues the effects of Assyrian imperialism on the states of the Palestinian land-bridge, concluding that Assyria did not interfere in internal religious affairs until Israel's annexation as an Assyrian province.

beginnings of statehood, its territories contained a fairly large, unassimilated population of Canaanite city-states. These people naturally tended to retain their own religious traditions of Baal worship. Marriage alliances with the Phoenician city of Tyre in the ninth century brought official toleration of Baal worship to Israel in the person of Queen Jezebel, since foreign princesses were permitted to retain their religions of origin as a matter of course in imperial marriages. Jehu's purging of Tyrian Baal worship as he founded his own ruling house did not deal with the popular fusion of Yahweh with local b^e'$al\hat{i}m$ and left unaddressed the problems of two coexisting populations with differing and purportedly inimical religious traditions. Further, the various alliances with Aram-Damascus against Assyria brought Israel into close contact with Syrian religious practices, at least some of which may have included human sacrifice, though only as a last resort during times of public or national emergencies.

In a modern age that values ecumenical dialogue (or at least religious tolerance), it is often difficult to understand the bitter hatred of the 'conservative' Israelite Yahwists for the fertility religions that surrounded them. It is important to remember that the rivalry between Yahwism and Baalism was based on far more than Israelite sensibilities about the inappropriateness of sexuality as a legitimate from of worship. One modern reconstruction of this conflict focuses on the social and political differences between Israel and surrounding neighbors.[1] Israel had covenanted with Yahweh, the redeemer god of the slaves in Egypt, to worship that god exclusively. Such fidelity was to be manifested not simply in the purity of Israel's cult (much of which was, in fact, adapted from Canaanite neighbors) but in a new social order that overturned the ruling ideologies of the surrounding city-states. There, the local king stood as a representative of the god Baal (whose name means simply 'owner' or 'master'), and by his celebration of the sexual act with a priestess representing a goddess who was Baal's consort, fertility for the land was assured. Like Baal, the king owned the land and

---

1. N.K. Gottwald, *The Hebrew Bible: A Socio-Literary Introduction* (Philadelphia: Westminster Press, 1985). Gottwald emphasizes social, scientific and literary approaches in his reconstruction of Israelite and Judean tradition and history.

all the people on it; power was concentrated in the hands of the few members of a military aristocracy who exploited all those beneath them. Cults that worshiped the royal dead effectively took grain surpluses out of the bellies of the poor and put them into the control of the priesthood that served the royal houses. This practice reduced possibilities for trade and growth and kept the lower-class population trapped in the struggle for simple daily survival. The manipulative sexuality that sought to stimulate divine fertility provided a convenient focal point for all the abuses of a religion that served and cemented an unjust social organization. To adopt parts of this worship for Yahweh's cult or to publicly profess the religion of the overlord was equivalent to a rejection of Yahweh's call for justice and equality among Israelite and Judean men. (Unfortunately, the patriarchal biases of the ancient world had a negative impact on Yahwism's ability to proclaim equality for women and certain others considered 'outsiders'.)

Thus, for the great prophets, both foreign alliances and foreign worship, however expedient politically, were sinful lapses from true fidelity to Israel's god. From Hosea's perspective—one he shares with all the eighth-century prophets—reliance on Egyptian, Assyrian or Aramaean allies instead of a reassertion of dependence on God through covenantal relationships and the social justice they entailed only witnessed to Israel's fundamental moral and theological bankruptcy. This, more than any particular sexual perversity, represents the core of the nation's 'harlotry', though the prophets certainly took the strongest exception to the presence of cultic sexual practices that had infiltrated the worship of Yahweh.

Theological Heritage

Quite naturally, the book of Hosea reflects the particular perspective of its native Israelite author, and this difference is felt in both diction and content. While frequent mention of Judah is made (perhaps the additions of a zealous Judean editor of later times), Hosea is primarily interested in the theological history and future of his own land, as the prophet's continued use of the northern term 'Ephraim' suggests. Hosea's emphasis on

Israel's past history is more than a mere rehearsal: Israel's present and future realities can be intuited from an understanding of the nation's past relationship to God, for the notion of 'corporate identity' infuses all the prophetic writings of the Hebrew Bible. The entire people living at any time was felt to bear the characteristics, and hence the potentialities and liabilities, of its forebears. Thus the Jacob traditions mentioned in 12.2-4, 12.12-13 (MT 12.3-5, 12.13-14) indicate the contentious nature of the Israelite people in the eighth century; the deliverance experienced in the exodus of the Late Bronze Age (11.1-4) foreshadows Yahweh's present anguish and future compassion (11.8-11); and so on. Hosea's use of national traditions makes it clear that, from the outset, faithlessness had marked Israel's response to Yahweh's redemptive labors on the people's behalf. The defection to Baal at Baal-Peor recorded in Numbers 25 is recalled in 9.10; the bloody beginnings of Jehu's dynasty find their way into a symbolic name for one of Hosea's children in 1.4. In 9.15 and 13.10-15, the beginnings of kingship at Gilgal, where Saul was chosen as the United Kingdom's first monarch, marks another wrong turning point in the people's history.

Hosea's particular attention to the beginning and end of ruling dynasties (8.4, 13.10-11) is naturally related to the violence that marked the political fortunes of the royal houses in the eighth century, when assassination became the rule rather than the exception. However, more ancient northern traditions are reflected here as well. First, Israel and Judah each had their own covenant traditions, and prophets tended to articulate their messages from the perspective of the covenant that had been most important in their national history. In Judah the covenant with David and his house was viewed as 'unconditional': God swore to preserve David and his descendants on the throne as reward for their past fidelity, and while such rulers might be chastised for wrongdoing, the covenant was viewed as inviolable and unbreakable (2 Sam. 7). In the North, the Mosaic or 'conditional' covenant model prevailed: the people swore to fulfill certain obligations in gratitude for Yahweh's delivering acts in the exodus. If the people did not uphold their side of the agreement, the Mosaic covenant could be broken and God would no longer be Israel's protective deity

(Exod. 19–20). When Hosea names his second son 'Not-my-people', he is giving symbolic form to his belief that Israel's apostasy had resulted in God's rejection of the now-broken Mosaic covenant.

Because of the importance of the differing views of the two covenant traditions, it is no surprise that both Judah and Israel viewed the legitimacy of political power in ways compatible with their individual covenants. From the division of the united kingdom upon the death of Solomon in the tenth century, rulership in Israel tended to find its legitimation through prophetic circles. Since there was no stable ruling house (comparable to the one in Judah) that was authorized by the Davidic covenant, charismatic leadership confirmed by prophetic approval became the method whereby Israelite rulers gained and held power. Likewise, prophetic challenge to a royal house could bring it down (cf. 1 Kgs 19). It is easy to see, then, why Amos's prophetic challenge to Jeroboam II resulted in his expulsion from the land (Amos 7.10-15). Hosea's oracles and the symbolic actions revolving around his family life no doubt earned him the same public dislike and humiliation that attended the careers of the other great prophets of Israel. His positive view of the true prophet's vocation (12.10, 13 [MT 12.11, 14]) and scathing attacks on the rulers of Israel show that he stands firmly in the heritage of the northern prophetic traditions.

Given the strong theological affinities found between Hosea's thinking and that expressed in the book of Deuteronomy, it is not unlikely that both were influenced by the traditions kept alive among the circles of the Levites, Israel's teaching priesthood, and that the survival of both works is owed at least in part to Levites who fled to Judah after 722–721. Certainly, those who edited the book of Hosea shared many theological attitudes with those who produced Deuteronomy and the Deuteronomistic History in Joshua–Kings. Such contact points included a belief of the unity of Israel and Judah (hence the prophetic message to one could be applied to the other, as in 5.10, 12-14 and so on), the future reuniting of Israel and Judah under the House of David (3.5), and a fervent hope that the events of 722–721 were not God's last word on Israel's future

(14.4-8 [MT 14.5-9]).[1] The effects of this theological outlook may
be felt throughout the book, where originally negative prophecies are toned down and 'updated' in the process of editing:
though some scholars believe that at least a few of the hopeful
passages, such as 11.8-9, may contain the authentic wording of
the prophet. Such a reversal from doom to hope is not unique in
the prophetic writings: Isaiah, Jeremiah and Ezekiel all shift to
the articulation of more hopeful messages concerning long-term
survival as they see their predictions of doom fulfilled.

Literary Features

Prophetic works usually contain three types of materials:
(1) autobiographical passages in prose or poetry, including 'call
passages' (where a prophet is commissioned as such by God),
reports of visions, and explanations of symbolic actions; (2) narrative passages in the third person, usually assumed to be from
the hand of disciples, which relate significant events in the
prophet's career and the nation's history; and (3) prophetic
utterances, generally in poetic form, which may include prophecies of doom, oracles of salvation, 'woe' oracles, threats,
reproaches, and covenant lawsuits. Many speakers may be
heard in the poetic oracles: sometimes the voice speaking is conceived of as that of God (2.1-5 [MT 2.3-17], 7.11-16, 11.1-9 and
so on); sometimes it is that of the prophet, either speaking as
himself (7.8-10, 9.7-9 and so on) or satirizing the people's responses to the prophetic message (6.1-3). In Hosea, chs. 1–3 contain third-person (1.1-9) and first-person (3.1-5) prose accounts
that explain the meaning for Israel of the symbolic actions taking
place in Hosea's family. A poetic lawsuit between Yahweh and
Israel in ch. 2 is sandwiched between the two accounts of
Hosea's domestic troubles, giving the lawsuit context and
meaning. Prophetic utterances form the rest of the work in
chs. 4–14, with the book ending on a decidedly didactic note in
14.9 (MT 14.10) which, borrowed from the wisdom tradition,
exhorts the audience to take the prophet's message seriously.

---

1.   R.E. Clements, 'Understanding the Book of Hosea', *RevExp* 72 (1975),
pp. 405-23. Clements argues for a Judean editing of the text of Hosea, and
looks at the complex in chs. 1–3 from this perspective.

The reader without knowledge of Hebrew will probably wonder at the great range of modern translations given for a single passage in Hosea. This is due to the poor condition of the original text, which is second in difficulty only to the book of Job. Some speculate that the corrupt state of the text is a result of the adverse effects of political and social turmoil during the period in which it was written and smuggled to safety in Judah.

Hosea's Family Mirrors God's Relationship with Israel (Chapters 1–3)
One of the most interesting features of the prophetic ministry is the performance of 'symbolic' actions. When commanded by God (as in 1.2, 4, 6, 9; 3.1), prophets would carry out unusual or unexpected acts that became 'visual aids' illustrating their messages. In all likelihood, such behavior was influenced by both the concepts underlying 'sympathetic magic' and the belief that words, like actions, had magical power to create the very thing to which they referred. It is not clear whether the prophets themselves believed that they were merely 'illustrating' the present and future circumstances of the people, or if they thought they were actively forging the fates of doom or restoration to which they pointed symbolically through their actions. It is clear from the political and priestly authorities' reactions to prophetic symbolic actions that the latter, more 'magical', view held sway in the minds of those in power, who felt threatened by the prophet's ministry. Hence, we see typical responses of repression, attempted censorship, and physical coercion used to attempt to restrain such prophetic behaviors, lest they create the doom-filled outcome by their peculiar acts. Symbolic actions are often dramatic and outrageous by the standards of their communities; often they may seem simply inexplicable or silly (for example, in Jer. 32 that prophet purchases a plot of land in Anathoth when Judah is about to fall to the Babylonians). By the very drama that surrounds them, symbolic actions are designed to get the attention of a hostile or panic-stricken audience. They baffle and excite the imagination. Perhaps the best-known and most intriguing of all symbolic actions performed by the Hebrew prophets is Hosea's marriage to a woman named Gomer.

Symbolic actions that are rooted in the normal (and not so

normal) events of family life are not unique to Hosea, though it is there that they make their first appearance among the 'Writing Prophets'. Like Hosea, Isaiah also gave his children symbolic names that heralded events in the nation's future (Isa. 7.14, 8.4). Jeremiah is commanded not to take a wife in order to dramatize the coming rupture in Judah's daily life (Jer. 16.2), and Ezekiel is told not to mourn the death of his wife, the 'delight of his eyes', as a sign of the grief to come (Ezek. 24.15-24). However, no other prophet was commanded to make quite so long-term and distressing a commitment as was Hosea when told to wed a 'woman of harlotry'. Such scandalous behavior on the part of a Hebrew prophet seems so inconceivable to some that a few scholars have attempted to give the events recounted in Hosea 1–3 an entirely allegorical meaning. However, since we see the family as an acceptable arena for symbolic actions in the other prophets, there is little reason to allegorize Hosea's reports.

Hosea's marriage was, no doubt, as interesting a topic for gossip in eighth-century Israel as it is for scholarly reconstructions in the present. Unfortunately, the text is by no means clear as to what actually transpired: does chs. 3 recapitulate the same events as ch. 1, now viewed from a later perspective, or does it refer to a subsequent reconciliation with Gomer, Hosea's encounter with yet another woman, or something else altogether? Not only is it difficult to sort out the identity of the woman (women?) in chs. 1–3, but the actual status of Gomer is unclear, since the text does not call her a prostitute per se. It has been suggested that 'wife/woman of harlotries' in 1.2 might mean someone who shares the general ethos of her surroundings, that is, a member of a 'harlotrous' people (see Isa. 6.5 for a similar situation), rather than referring to Gomer's alleged profession or adulterous behavior.[1]

To further complicate matters, we cannot say whether Gomer, if she was a prostitute, was merely a secular prostitute

---

1. R. Gordis, 'Hosea's Marriage and Message', in *idem* (ed.), *Poets, Prophets, and Sages: Essays in Biblical Interpretation* (Bloomington: Indiana University Press, 1971), pp. 230-54. Gordis reviews the various options for understanding the actions described in Hos. 1–3. He concludes that we have two accounts, from different time periods, of the same incident.

or was attached in some way to cultic activities, which would have scored considerably higher on the scale of sinfulness in prophetic thinking. One scholar has suggested that Gomer was not a prostitute, but rather took part in the supposedly common practice of dedicating her virginity to Baal by servicing a stranger within the precincts of the temple, in return for the blessings of fertility from the god.[1] However, sources used to reconstruct a 'sex cult' in eighth-century Israel are late and speculative at best. Even in Mesopotamia, where better documentation for the existence of a cult of sacred sexuality exists, the relationship between 'secular' and 'sacred' practises is unclear.[2]

It is Hosea's particular literary and theological achievement that he is able to use the very form of the practices he hates (sacred sexuality) as a vehicle for his message about Yahweh. While vehemently denying the appropriateness of conceiving of Yahweh in ways influenced by Baal worship (2.12-13, 16 [MT 2.14-15, 18), Hosea then images Yaweh in a marital relationship with Israel, and attributes to Israel's God all the bounties and acts usually associated with Baal, the fertility deity (2.8, 21-22; 14.5-8 [MT 2.10, 23-24; 14.6-9]). One wonders whether the 'mixed messages' sent by this technique were confusing to those hearing his oracles. It may be that the fusion of Yahweh with Baal was so complete that such an approach was the only one that could have made the psychic connection between the people's espoused theology and Hosea's insights about God.

The marriage metaphor used to describe God's relationship to Israel, though laden with dangerous overtones of the fertility religions, provides an excellent illustration of the prophet's conception of Yahweh's suffering over Israel's faithlessness. Marriage in the patriarchal societies of the ancient world served varied social purposes and was the foundational unit of society.

1.   Wolff, *Hosea*, on ch. 1.
2.   G. Lerner, 'The Origin of Prostitution in Ancient Mesopotamia', *Signs* 11 (1986), pp. 236-54. Lerner reviews the cuneiform evidence from Mesopotamia on prostitution, with special attention to the way the sexual control of women cemented the power and class relations in ancient society.

By the acquisition of wives and the production of sons, young men were acknowledged as adults and gained social standing. In this respect, wife and children were living extensions of the husband's ego boundaries, enhancing his social position and personal power. Since women and children were absolute dependents (though later legal traditions restrict somewhat the father's right to dispose of wife and children in wholly arbitrary ways), the thought that they might turn against the one who supported and owned them was probably a dreadful one to men, who profited from this social system (cf. Est. 1.13-22). Women's sexuality was closely guarded because through it male inheritance passed from father to son; women who had more than one partner struck at the very heart of patriarchal society's transmission of power, standing and the means of production. For this reason an adulterous wife did more than betray the man who owned and supported her; the living symbol of disorder, she lessened him in his own eyes and the eyes of society. Hence the husband's confusion, hurt and anger in such a situation would have been extreme and would have been experienced as humiliating and shameful.

Hosea's experience of these emotions brings him to a point where he sees them as a human mirror of God's response to the people's apostasy. What Hosea does not see is that a covenant built on a master–slave relationship like that embodied in patriarchal marriage or the conditional covenant (which was developed from models of vassal treaties between a great king and those just defeated by him) can never satisfy the deep emotional needs of the one in the position of the slave. Hosea's use of the parental metaphor to describe Yahweh's love for Israel actually predominates outside of chs. 1–3 and represents a more hopeful model in his theology than does the husband–wife relationship. Male children—and Israel is always conceived of as male—outgrow their position of dependence in ways not allowed to women in the ancient world, becoming mature, responsible and productive companions for their parents. Thus the parent–child relationship better embodies the kind of developmental growth that God envisions for Israel.

It has been argued that the meaning of Hosea's marriage is to be found not in the passages that look to a hopeful restoration of the marital relationship (that is, 2.14–3.5 [MT 2.16–3.5]) but in the symbolic names given to Hosea's children (1.4-8). In ancient society the name held a power that harks back to the magical power contained in all words. The name explained the essence of a person or thing, conferring the power of that knowledge on all those who knew it. It was definitely not the custom to give children negative names, since this would certainly shape their destinies. The names given Hosea's children would have been vivid, daily reminders of the unpleasant fate in store for the nation. In this reconstruction, the positive interpretations later given these names, the hope for marital restoration, and the insights about the enduring nature of love are seen as additions by disciples or Judean editors after the prophecies of doom had come to pass.[1]

Prophetic Utterances (Chapters 4–14)
At first glance, one is struck by the loose, 'collection'-like character of the second complex comprising the book of Hosea. Abrupt shifts in speaker and topic occur throughout, openings and closings of units are not clearly marked, and prose and poetic styles intermingle in a way that has been suggested as characteristic of eighth-century prophecy. Not all of these features need be attributed to the hands of later well-meaning editors. As we come to understand pre-exilic prophecy better, some commentators are beginning to find a greater unity in style and content in Hosea than was previously thought.

Viewed in terms of literary form, the second complex is composed mainly of divine speeches (4.4-9; 5.1-3; 5.8–7.16; 8.1-12; 9.10-13, 15-16; 10.9-15; 11.1-9, 11; 12.10-11 [MT 12.11-12]; 13.4-14; 14.4-8 [MT 14.5-9]), with a smaller number of prophetic speeches where God is spoken of in the third person. This varied structure accounts for the shifts in speaker, often occurring within a single unit (cf. 4.10-15; 8.11-13; 11.12–12.14 [MT 12.1-15]). The language of legal disputes is prominent in 2.2 (MT 2.4); 4.1, 4; 12.2 (MT 12.3) and laments, complaints, exhortations, threats and diatribes also make an appearance. The presence of wisdom forms in 8.7 and the affinity of parts of

---

1. Clements, 'Understanding the Book of Hosea'.

Hosea with wisdom thinking on the natural order has led some to suggest that Hosea was trained as a sage. However, this may be too great a conclusion to draw from the evidence, since wisdom forms occurred among the folk as well as among the educational elite in ancient Israel. Generally, the book of Hosea is difficult for form criticism, that branch of biblical literary criticism which attempts to pinpoint original 'generic' form, social context and use. Little precise historical information is present in the second complex, and this effectively limits the critic's ability to assign a given oracle to a particular time and place.

Hosea's style is particularly notable for its use of varied similes and extended metaphors, drawn mostly from the natural world and the life of the family. Both Yahweh and Israel are imaged in innovative and striking ways. Yahweh is pictured as a devouring lion (5.14; 13.7-8), a she-bear robbed of her cubs (13.8), a leopard (13.7), a moth and dry rot (5.12), an evergreen tree (14.8 [MT 14.9]) and dew (14.5 [MT 6]), as well as by the more typical images of parent (11.1-4), husband (2.2-21 [MT 2.4-23]), fowler (7.12), owner of stock animals (10.11; 11.4) and doctor (7.1; 11.3; 14.4; [MT 14.5]). Israel/Ephraim appears as a child (11.1-4), an adulterous wife (2.2-21 [MT 2.4-23]), an invalid (5.13; 7.1, 9; 14.4 [MT 14.5]), an unborn child and mother in labor (13.13). Similes from the natural world are also used to characterize Israel, including various birds (7.11-12; 9.11), cattle (4.16; 10.11), grapes and a grapevine (9.10; 10.1; 14.6 [MT 14.8]), figs and lilies (9.10; 14.5 [MT 14.6]), chaff, smoke, dew and mist (13.3), the olive tree and the forests of Lebanon (14.6-7 [MT 14.7-8]). More colorfully, the people are like a smoldering oven and a half-baked cake (7.4-7), with leaders who are like snares and nets (5.1). The sheer variety of imagery used in this one small book is an index of the poetic creativity of its author; it must have had a powerful effect on hearers, who were left unable to imagine God absent from even the most mundane spheres of action.[1]

The second complex in the book is difficult to characterize in terms of structure of poetic units, in part because opening and closing formulas are usually absent. Hosea prefers the use of

---

1. Wolff, *Hosea.*

synomomous parallelism (where the second half-line restates the thought of the first) in the creation of his poetic lines, with bicola (two half-lines to a verse) and tricola (three lines to a verse) predominating as his favorite forms. A typical example of his use of synonomous bicola is found in 6.6: 'For I desire steadfast love and not sacrifice, the knowledge of God rather than burnt offerings'.

Hosea's use of tricola may be observed in 9.4; 9.6, and often at the beginning and end of oracles, as in 8.9, 13 and 9.3, 6.[1] Hosea's poetry plays with typical Hebrew word order, and this characteristic contributes to a feeling of 'distance' in the prophet's message, almost as though the grammar of the oracles reflects the movement of God away from the people. One scholar has suggested that such 'delaying' tactics may also have served the purpose of holding the attention of an angry or indifferent audience for the duration of the oracle.[2] The routine use of poetic parallelisms creates an air of expectation in the hearers, who are naturally primed to wait for the second half of the verse to complete the poetic thought. By postponing this fulfillment, Hosea puts his audience on edge and gains more time to hammer home his point.

Hosea's creative use of language, tradition and theology lends a power to his message that transcends the events of the eighth century. His masterful depiction of the pathos of a betrayed God and a faithless people is given special force by the parallel events taking place in his own family. As the celebrated Jewish theologian Abraham Heschel puts it in his penetrating study *The Prophets* (1962), Hosea—perhaps because of his own experiences—has intuited the 'dramatic tension' existing between God's burning anger and intense compassion for the people.[3] Such passages as 1.34-8 and 11.1-9 resound with a

1. Cf. Wolff, *Hosea*; and also J.R. Lundbom, 'Poetic Structure and Prophetic Rhetoric in Hosea', *VT* 29 (1979), pp. 300-308. Lundbom looks at Hosea's use of broken bicola to convey a message of divine distance.

2. Lundbom, 'Poetic Structure'.

3. A.J. Heschel, *The Prophets* (New York: Schocken Books, 1962), I–II. Heschel provides excellent, extremely readable discussions of the phenomenon of prophecy in ancient Israel and Judah. Especially notable is Heschel's treatment of divine pathos in Hosea.

divine fury at betrayal, which is, nevertheless, held in check by
an unquenchable love:

> When Israel was a child, I loved him,
>   and out of Egypt I called my son.
> The more I called them,
>   the more they went from me;
> they kept sacrificing to the Baals,
>   and burning incense to idols.
> Yet it was I who taught Ephraim to walk,
>   I took them up in my arms;
>   but they did not know that I healed them.
> I led them with cords of compassion,
>   with bands of love,
> and I became to them as one who eases the
>   yoke on their jaws,
>   and I bent down to them and fed them.
> They shall return to the land of Egypt,
>   and Assyria shall be their king,
>   because they have refused to return to me.
> The sword shall rage against their cities,
>   consume the bars of their gates,
>   and devour them in their fortresses.
> My people ar bent on turning away from me;
>   so they are appointed to the yoke,
>   and none shall remove it,
> How can I give you up, O Ephraim!
>   How can I hand you over, O Israel!
> How can I make you like Admah!
>   How can I treat you like Zeboyim!
> My heart recoils within me,
>   my compassion grows warm and tender.
> I will not execute my fierce anger,
>   I will not again destroy Ephraim;
> for I am God, and not man,
>   The Holy One in your midst,
>   and I will not come to destroy (11.1-9).

Hosea's marriage taught him more than the meaning of
betrayal and humiliation. If a human parent could feel a sustaining love for the living fruit—legitimate or not—of his unhappy
union, how much more abiding must be the love of a divine
parent for wayward Ephraim! Though he could not avert the
terrible fate that overtook the northern kingdom, Hosea left a

literary and theological legacy whose influence is still felt. By delving into the deepest darkness of human emotions, Hosea came into contact with the heart of his god. It is this luminous moment of understanding between creator and creature, captured so powerfully in Hosea's writing, that has continued to move and enlighten readers of the book over the centuries.[1]

---

1. Additional material on Hosea can be found in G.I. Emmerson, *Hosea: An Israelite Prophet in Judean Perspective* (JSOTSup, 28; Sheffield: JSOT Press, 1984); J.J. Schmitt, 'The Gender of Ancient Israel', *JSOT* 26 (1983), pp. 115-25. Emmerson looks at the various levels of editing of Hosea and comes to conclusions that are strikingly different from those of Andersen and Freedman (*Hosea*). Schmitt surveys the use of masculine and feminine imagery to designate Israel. He concludes that the harlot metaphor in the prophetic writings originates in city language (cities are feminine in Hebrew), while the gender of Israel remains overwhelmingly masculine in the Hebrew Bible.

A RESPONSE TO 'HOSEA'

Carole R. Fontaine

It is by now a commonplace in feminist interpretation of the Bible to challenge the traditional readings assigned to any given book or tradition, and to raise questions about the legitimacy of the portraits of women and female imagery found there.[1] My short introduction to the prophetic book of Hosea to which I respond here originally appeared as part of a standard format, two-volume commentary on the Bible. It is fair to say that, while not rejected outright, feminist readings of Hosea were by no means part of the agenda of the editors or publishers. Because of limits on space assigned to the book and the historical-critical focus for the introductions written, the article did not adequately reflect the research or findings of the author at the time, and certainly no longer represents the approach I would now take if asked to write on Hosea. In many ways, the research that went into this article left me furious and outraged by what critical scholarship *cannot* or *will not* address, and sealed my fate as a scholar who chooses to stand with the Loyal Opposition. By the time I had finished writing on the so-called 'Prophet of Love', the only things I disliked more than the prophet and his god were the writings of modern commentators about Hosea.

Hosea left me with a bad taste in my mouth and a deep suspicion about my own motives for writing as a historical critic. In this instance, I had departed from my usual studies in wisdom traditions and goddess religions because the assignment paid

---

1. See, for example, T.D. Setel, 'Prophets and Pornography: Female Sexual Imagery in Hosea', in L.M. Russell (ed.), *Feminist Interpretations of the Bible* (Philadelphia: Westminster Press, 1985), pp. 86-65, as well as other essays in this volume.

well, and my health insurance for a chronic condition (one affecting mainly women, as it turns out) had just been discontinued. Hence, I was in a Gomer-esque frame of mind, and I drastically underestimated what it would do to my psyche to return to the rigid and reified constraints of historical-critical work. I had just completed a folkloristic study of a Late Bronze Age Hittite text by a queen, and had discovered, to my own surprise—I had been classically trained, after all—that there was a world of difference between the way a woman approaches her goddess in prayer and the way she speaks to a god in the very same position.[1] Since much of the analysis of this remarkable woman's prayer required a foray into socio-historical research, I am by no means suggesting that interpretation of biblical or other ancient texts should proceed in a literary vacuum that pays no attention to history or culture. Rather, what I found infuriating about the Hosea project as assigned to me was the way the typical procedures of biblical historical criticism *leave out* the very questions that any sensible person would put to the text. The ideological biases of the classical commentators, so in harmony with the patriarchal agendas of Hosea and the god he represented, functioned to obscure rather than reveal the text, as far as I was concerned.

Many of the commentators (not all of whom appear in the final bibliography, due to space constraints) displayed an almost prurient interest in Hosea's marital partner, and their outrage at her alleged behavior echoed Hosea's. To be sure, the text is unclear about the real meaning of Gomer's 'harlotry' as well as the identity of the woman in ch. 3,[2] but that did not stop comments on her actions which ranged from erotic fantasy to moralistic condemnation. Scholars eagerly debated the chronology of

1. 'Queenly Proverb Performance: The Prayer of Puduḥepa (KUB XXI, 27)', in K.G. Hogland, E.F. Huwiler, J.T. Glass and R.W. Lee (eds.), *The Listening Heart: Essays in Wisdom and the Psalms in honor of Roland E. Murphy, O. Carm.* (JSOTSup, 58; Sheffield: JSOT Press, 1987), pp. 95-126.

2. See the work of Robert Gordis, cited in my 'Hosea' article. More recently, Phyllis Bird has discussed the meaning of harlotry in ' "To Play the Harlot" ': An Inquiry into an Old Testament Metaphor', in P.L. Day (ed.), *Gender and Difference in Ancient Israel* (Minneapolis: Augsburg Fortress, 1989), pp. 75-94.

events and identity of the players in Hosea 1–3, but never stepped outside the text's construction of the *meaning* of those events and characters. All the sympathy was, naturally enough, on the side of the reportedly deserted husband and the affronted deity. The voice of Gomer or her children played no role in the scholarly speculations—and the intense discussions of the actual evidence for fertility cults and the practice of sacred marriage in Israel and surrounding cultures revealed that the scholarly consensus on such customs was based on no more than speculation. Yet, for many of the male interpreters of Hosea, Gomer's harlotry was 'a done deal', despite the poor quality of the 'evidence'; no 'hermeneutics of suspicion' troubled the outlook of the traditional commentaries. Exposition of the methodological fallacies of the arguments could not be accommodated within the space allotted to me; within the standard methodology, it was more important to rehearse the histories of the kings of Israel, histories important to the content and context of Hosea's 'message', than to question how extremely late texts from many centuries *after* Hosea could legitimately be used to reconstruct cultic sexual activities purported to have been practiced hundreds of years earlier.

I came away from my studies wondering if Gomer had been 'framed' by the requirements of the marital metaphor, because at that time I saw no hard and fast, external proof of her participation in a sex cult, or even her supposed activity as a secular prostitute. The text *needed* to stigmatize Gomer as a 'woman of harlotry' so that the symbolic action of Hosea's disastrous marriage would function properly. Unlike modern commentators who have often preferred to think of this marriage as an intensely personal 'object lesson' which caused Hosea to understand God's message to Israel in a certain way, the text explicitly states that the prophet married Gomer *on purpose,* that is, because of her harlotry and not in spite of it. Unlike the clerical commentators who wished to dismiss the text's report of Gomer's audacious behavior because it was morally unsuited to the wife of an honored prophet, I found myself working with a nascent feminist hermeneutic which preferred to see the reports of Gomer as the exaggerated and hysterical response of a patriarchal male/text which must, at all costs, paint Gomer as negatively as possible due to her associations with the land and the people, the real targets of Hosea's/God's polemic. Both approaches fail to hear the text because of the present-day interpreters' discomfort with the sexual activity reported there. If writing now, I would start with the bare notices in the text, and ask not, 'What *really* happened?', but rather, 'What does this *mean* within the text's ideological construction of reality, and what might it mean about the realities of women's lives, then and now?'

So what if she *did* have more than one partner, I asked myself. Did that signal the end of the world as the patriarchal male, human or divine, knew it? (Yes.) 'Stop whining!', I wanted to shout, 'You knew what she was like when you married her!' There was a basic injustice in castigating the woman for the very behavior that caused her to be chosen in the first place. Clearly, the text placed Gomer in a 'no-win' situation. Was this simply another case of male fear of female independence, the ingrained horror that patriarchal society feels when faced with a female sexuality which is judged to be 'out of control'? And where did the character of God fit into all this? I found that I could not separate the voice of the shamed prophet from the voice of the deity he claimed to represent. The historical-critical methods limiting me offered no effective means to clarify the situation, for in such settings questions of inspiration, authority or even point-of-view are considered 'theological' and 'subjective'; as such they are out of bounds for the objective, cool-headed historian.

But I knew that the kind of 'love' represented by Hosea and his god did not seem very much like my idea of love. The silenced and humiliated Gomer, abused into submission during her supposedly 'honeymoon'-like reunion with her master, became less of an 'object lesson' about inappropriate female behavior and more like an icon of what women may expect from the biblical god and his male representatives. From beginning to end Gomer and her children figured within the text merely as plot devices in the much bigger (and more important?) male story of domination and abusive relationship. From their point of view, Hosea's 'God of Love' ultimately was disclosed to be a patriarch of very human dimensions: obsessed with control, he could not brook the natural and normal individuation attempted by partner and offspring. Beloved only in their dependence on the patriarch (11.1, 3), any bid for autonomy or the ability to exercise choice (8.4) is construed as a shaming insult to their forgotten 'maker' (8.14). Whether spoken of as errant wife or fractious son, only when Israel is willing to live under the 'shadow' of God's patriarchal power is favor and fruitfulness to be restored (14.7). Further, this angry father or spouse is willing to use any violent means necessary to control his household in order to restore his delicate honor.[1] That these violent means so easily pass for 'love' in the eyes of the ancient author, audience and modern interpreter is a telling commentary on societies in which domestic violence against women and children is so customary that it has attained the status of unexamined norm. In the reality of patriarchal marriage and the theologies drawn from it, it makes precious little difference in status or treatment whether Gomer says 'my husband' or 'my Baal'—with the possible exception that 'my Baal' at least represents her own choice.

The traditional methods of biblical studies fail dismally when the interpreter is seeking not some positivistic answer to the question 'what happened?', but rather to give a hearing to the silenced and betrayed voices within the text. The inherent limitations of the methods themselves restrict the interpreter by failing to acknowledge the ideologies that dominate texts and force them to tell their story as they do. Hence, the voice of the narrator is fused with the voice of God and his prophet, and the allurements of that voice seduce the unwary, ancient *or* modern, into its violence. This seduction can take place even when interpreters are looking for 'relevance' to women's questions, as long as readers do not permit themselves to step outside of the text's ideology.[2] A truly feminist 'introduction' or commentary on the Bible must eschew the traditional structures

1.   See Renita Weems's discussion of sexual violence in Hosea, 'Gomer: Victim of Violence or Victim of Metaphor', *Semeia* 47 (1989), pp. 87-104.

2.   See, for example, C. Newsom and S. Ringe (eds.), *The Women's Bible Commentary* (Philadelphia: Westminster Press, 1992), where the premise appears to be that feminist interpretation can function as an 'add-on' to historical-critical enterprises, without the recognition that at least *some* versions of feminist criticism call that very enterprise into question.

of such works as defined by the guild of biblical scholarship, and learn to embrace new formats if it wishes to unleash the ravaged and battered female voice. The gaps and silences of the text must be viewed not as inconvenient difficulties of text transmission to be explained away by the commentator, but as fertile nests where the interpreter is invited to brood, participate and imagine, ultimately giving birth to new texts and new readings.

When viewed in this way, the ambiguities in our understanding of Gomer and her 'harlotry' scream their message across the centuries. Suppose there *was* a ritual cult where female sexuality was coded with divine meaning and carried cosmic consequences (Hos. 2.8). Suppose, further, that its appeal was so strong and compelling to the women of ancient Israel that they continued to bake cakes to the Queen of Heaven, with or without their husbands' consent (Jer. 44.19), and that such worship was in fact a family affair (Jer. 7.18). Suppose, in addition, that the women's interpretation of the fates of Israel and Judah might be correct—that it was the abandonment of their goddess's cult in favor of a exclusive, male-dominated religion that estranged the people from their land and led to their eventual downfall (Jer. 44.17-18). Suppose our ancient biblical mothers *did* lay themselves down eagerly on every high hill and under every green tree, welcoming lovers and their own satisfaction as though it were the most natural, divine and important thing in the world, regardless of the teachings of Deuteronomy. I am not necessarily suggesting that all these suppositions are true, but only that there are a variety of ways of reading this text, and that modern difficulties with sexuality are as blinding as ancient paradigms of male honor and shame. Perhaps these women mean what they say, and that fact ought to be taken seriously, along with the validity of the text's negative reports on their activities.

Compare the vitality of this exotic, erotic re-visioning of Israel's 'apostasy' (non-elite, popular worship) to the pallid and limp male-exclusive rituals with which it competed. At the very least, the presence of such popular religion in ancient Israel and Judah suggests that the cult of YHWH left unmet some of the emotional and spiritual needs of many, especially women.

Perhaps there are profound and deeply spiritual reasons why the goddess of ancient Israel, Asherah, was worshipped in YHWH's temple far more often than she was absent from those sacred precincts.[1] A male deity may claim that it is *he* who opens and closes the womb (Gen. 20.18; 29.1; 30.22; 1 Sam. 1.5-6; Isa. 66.9), but perhaps our mothers knew better and had the conviction to act upon that knowledge regardless of the consequences. While the late textual evidence of *De Syria dea* and Herodotus commonly used to reconstruct a fertility cult in Israel *remains* questionable,[2] to say the least, recent archaeological and literary reconstructions of the 'popular' religion of Israel are suggestive, if nothing else.[3] We need not explain away the Deuteronomistic Historian's hatred of the apostasy and heterodoxy of the women of Israel and Judah as simple misogyny and xenophobic propaganda. Perhaps those notices of women and queens leading their husbands astray are a potent testimony to the force of women's religious beliefs and practices, a force the text denigrates as trivial and outlandish but fears as powerful. Perhaps Gomer was a 'harlot' and proud of it. What would we find out about the meaning of harlotry if we could hear *her* voice instead of the male author who construes meaning for her?

The sad fact is that, if we restrict ourselves only to the biblical text and its point of view, we will never have access to the voices it has silenced. Inserting ourselves into the voids in the text will never be an approved historical-critical exercise, but it can be balm to the sore soul which has been dragged backwards through the shards of patriarchal language and metaphor one too many times. I found after completing my work on Hosea that I could not find peace or consider the project whole

1. S. Davies, 'The Canaanite-Hebrew Goddess', in C. Olson (ed.), *The Book of the Goddess: Past and Present* (New York: Crossroad, 1985), pp. 68-79.

2. Herodotus I, 199; *De Syria dea* 6. See Wolff's excursus on 'The Sex Cult', p. 14 (citation in my 'Hosea' article).

3. See, for example, S.M. Olyan, *Asherah and the Cult of Yahweh in Israel* (SBLMS, 34; Atlanta: Scholars Press, 1988), and S. Ackerman, ' "And the Women Knead Dough": The Worship of the Queen of Heaven in Sixth-Century Judah', in Day (ed.), *Gender and Difference*, pp. 109-24, both of which contain extensive bibliographies.

until I had given voice to the silenced, abused wife, harlot or not, who so shapes its structure and message yet remains in the shadows. As poet and artist, I decided to let Gomer speak, and lending her my voice, I found a powerful one.

A personal note is required to make sense of the prose 'set-up' for Gomer's 'Proceedings of an Alternative Covenant'. Since I modeled Gomer's oracle after Hosea's, which itself is a combination of 'covenant law-suit', divorce proceedings and salvation oracle, I also included a similar introduction and conclusion. This inclusio reflects the situation in my own life at the time it was written, just as Hosea's presumably does. In the absence of the ability to afford meaningful health care, my husband took a job as a corporate safety consultant to the nuclear power industry, an act which plunged our household into all the exigencies of a long-distance, 'commuter marriage'. Like Hosea's oracle, mine also imagines a new covenant that brings peace and healing to the land, and to hearts torn apart by distance and the ethical 'harlotries' faced by most adults in our capitalist society. Like the original covenant in the wilderness, this one is also made possible by a radical re-visioning of the divine and its relationship to the created world.

Proceedings of an Alternative Covenant: 'Gomer's' Testimony

Now when the word of the Lord stopped pestering this woman, circumstances said, 'Go, have a commuter marriage, for this land goes back and forth looking for reality, and finds none.' So this woman loved a man who always left, and he produced an investment fund, and gave it to her, and she named it 'Radiation', for she said, 'Great evil was done to the land, that I might go about in style.' And again she took him back when he returned with his laundry, and he produced a mutual fund, and she called it 'Not-Trusted', for she said, 'I love you, but how can I trust a transient[1] lover?' And after that, for tax purposes, he produced a certificate of deposit, and gave it to her. And she called its name 'Not-My-Money', for her heart said, 'I exist this

---

1. A 'transient' is also an unexplained power surge in a nuclear power plant, which usually leads to the reactor tripping off line.

way by his sufferance; the only thing that is mine is my faith and
my pain and my hope in my work.' And she wondered, does
the 'One-Who-Is' have as little choice in loving as we do?

> Divorce, my daughters! Divorce your tradition,
>> for its god is not a true mate,
>> and why should you stay his whore?
>
> Oh, they have had
>> their grain
>> and their wine
>> and their oil
> on your back,
>> from *your* cleft,
> until you cried out, broken,
> 'Let me instead be godless,
> for it will be better for me then
>> than it is now!'
> And you never knew
>> that it was from 'She-In-You'
>> that there came
>> the grain and the wine and the oil
>
> 'So, behold,' says your Maker,
> 'I will nurse you at my own breast.
> I am "She-Who-Inhabits-Your-Wilderness".
>> and you will answer me
>> as on the day of your birth,
> and you will not call me "Father" or "Son"
> but "Mother!", "Sister!", "Lover!"... "Ehyeh!"...[1]
> and we will again be as one.
> And on that day, I will set you free from your leading strings, and
> I will loose you from your bondage, and you will not say "My
> husband", but you shall say, "My friend"! And I shall banish the
> missile from the silo, and rinse contamination from the land, and I
> will liberate the beasts of the field and the birds of the air and the
> fish of the sea, and the creeping things of the earth. I will unbind
> them from your dominion into consciousness and responsibility
> and unity, and all the cosmos shall know itself One with Me,

---

1. The divine name revealed to Moses in Exod. 3.14 in its gender-
neutral form (first common singular). It may be read as existential, 'I am',
or as a causative form, 'I cause'.

and I shall make the torments of embodiment
the path to sure release',
> says the Power-That-Causes.

And on that day,
> the skies will answer the furrows,
> and the furrows will answer the hands,
> and the hands will tend the bellies,
> so that no *nepes* shall hunger again.

And I will say to 'Radiation',
> 'You are purified!';
and to 'Not-Trusted',
> 'I *will* trust you';
and to 'Not-My-Money',
> 'Your wages are as my wages';
and their maker will say,
> 'I have known the One through your eyes,
> and your visions are as my visions.
> Your dreams are as my dreams,
> for we both serve the land.'

THE FEMALE BODY, THE BODY POLITIC AND THE LAND: A SOCIOPOLITICAL READING OF HOSEA 1–2

Alice A. Keefe

Introduction

In the final decades of the northern kingdom, in an era of social crisis and political upheaval, the prophet Hosea gave graphic expression to the meaning of his times by depicting the nation Israel as a faithless wife, or as the text puts it, as an *'ēšet z^enûnîm* ('woman of fornications') bearing *yaldê z^enûnîm* ('children of fornications'). This metaphor is highly problematic from a feminist perspective, not simply because it lends scriptural authority to the structures of patriarchal marriage, but more critically because it seems to express a dualistic and gendered religious vision within which female sexuality becomes the symbol of sin and all that is 'other' to the meaning of the sacred within biblical religion.

This analysis of Hosea's use of female sexual imagery begins with the assumption that this woman's adultery ought to be understood as a metaphor for apostasy, specifically Israel's participation in a Canaanite or syncretistic 'fertility cult'. The woman's lovers are identified as the *b^e'ālîm*, the fertility deities of Canaan who embody the powers of regeneration of life immanent in nature. Within this cult, sexual rituals in imitation of the *hieros gamos* served to ensure the renewal of the earth's fertility. By labelling such worship fornication, Hosea seeks to repudiate a religiosity which locates the divine as immanent within nature and to recall Israel to its covenantal relationship with 'her' true 'husband' Yahweh, the transcendent god of history.

Feminist biblical scholars have largely accepted this equation between adultery and religious apostasy as their framework for the interpretation of Hosea's female sexual imagery, but have reversed the valuations which usually inform the discussion. Instead of lauding Hosea's attack on fertility religion as a theological accomplishment, feminist scholars indict Hosea for his role in advancing the patriarchal character of the Western religious traditions. The point is not simply that his metaphor legitimates a social structure within which males possess rights of control over female sexuality. More, the gender assignments of the metaphor, in which male is to God as female is to sinful humanity, in conjunction with the denigration of the female body as a symbol of sin, serve to enact and express a dualistic split between the spiritual (gendered as male) and material (gendered as female) spheres of human experience.[1] In response to such dualistic and incipiently misogynistic constructions, some feminist scholars have sought to resurrect this execrated fertility cult as a form of goddess religion within which the sacrality of the body, nature and the feminine was affirmed and celebrated.[2]

Hosea will always be a disturbing text for feminist readers because of its patriarchal presumptions (see for instance Weems).[3] However, the conclusion that Hosea's female sexual imagery inscribes a dualistic worldview demands critical reexamination given the manner in which this conclusion has been conditioned by a set of androcentric and theological assumptions, which are themselves already predicated upon dualist ways of thinking about gender imagery and religious meanings. Through a hermeneutical critique and revisioning of our approach to Hosea, this study will propose that Hosea's imagery of female sexual transgression does not refer to Israel's

1. T.D. Setel, 'Prophets and Pornography: Female Sexual Imagery in Hosea', in L.M. Russell (ed.), *Feminist Interpretation of the Bible* (Philadelphia: Westminster Press, 1985), p. 92.

2. H. Balz-Cochois, 'Gomer oder die Macht der Astarte: Versuch einer feministischen Interpretation von Hos 1–4', *EvT* 42 (1982), pp. 37-65; F. van Dijk-Hemmes, 'The Imagination of Power and the Power of Imagination: An Intertextual Analysis of Two Biblical Love Songs, The Song of Songs and Hosea 2', *JSOT* 44 (1989), pp. 85-86; reprinted in A. Brenner (ed.), *A Feminist Companion to the Song of Songs* (The Feminist Companion to the Bible, 1; Sheffield: Sheffield Academic Press, 1993).

3. R. Weems, 'Gomer: Victim of Violence or Victim of Metaphor?', *Semeia* 47 (1989), pp. 87-104.

apostasy in a supposed fertility cult, but to the meaning and condition of Israelite society and polity in the mid to late eighth century.

As will be argued below, the popular thesis concerning a syncretistic fertility cult in eighth-century Israel does not rest on any firm textual or extratextual evidence, but rather may be traced to the biases of a theological agenda within which Canaanite religion is gendered as the seductive and degenerate 'other' against which biblical religion defines itself. Rather than reading Hosea against the background of these androcentric constructions, this study will read Hosea's female sexual imagery in light of the repeated association of sexual transgression and social violence in the biblical narratives. This intertextual clue suggests that Hosea's language about Israel as an '*ēšet z*^e*nûnîm* functioned rhetorically as a commentary upon the pressing sociopolitical conflicts of Hosea's time.

These conflicts coalesce around the economic and political policies of the monarchical establishment during and subsequent to the reign of Jeroboam II. During these decades, Israel and Judah's joint control over the vital trading routes which traversed Palestine opened lucrative opportunities for profit in interregional trade. To exploit this economic potential, the royal house and its allied elite pursued strategies of land accumulation and the commercialization of agriculture.[1] Under royal directive, large areas of the countryside were devoted to specialization in one or two 'cash crops', viviculture in the hills and grain in the lowlands;[2] the resultant efficiency in agricultural production generated grain, wine and oil in abundance for export trade in exchange for luxury goods and military hardware. While an elite

---

1. These royal policies, their social consequences and the prophetic response to them are explored from a socio-scientific perspective in many recent studies including D.N. Premnath, 'Latifundialization and Isaiah 5.8-10', *JSOT* 40 (1988), pp. 49-60; B. Lang, 'The Social Organization of Peasant Poverty in Biblical Israel', *JSOT* 24 (1982), pp. 47-63; M. Chaney, 'Bitter Bounty: The Dynamics of Political Economy Critiqued by Eighth-Century Prophets', in R.L. Stivers (ed.), *Reformed Faith and Economics* (Lanham, MD: University Press of America, 1989), pp. 15-30; and J.A. Dearman, *Property Rights in the Eighth-Century Prophets: The Conflict and its Background* (Atlanta: Scholars Press, 1988).

2. Chaney, 'Bitter Bounty', p. 19.

sector of the population reaped great profits, these processes of latifundialization[1] came at the cost of the dispossession and impoverishment of increasing numbers of highland families whose lands, by customary law, were supposed to be inalienable.[2]

It is well known that Hosea's prophetic contemporaries, Micah, Isaiah and Amos, were immediately concerned with the rampant injustice, judicial corruption and oppression of the poor which accompanied the eighth-century boom in agribusiness. But the relevance of these issues for the interpretation of Hosea's marriage metaphor has been obscured through the operation of a theologically determined methodological approach which presupposes that spirit and matter are dual and, consequently, that religious meanings may float free from the human involvement with the material and social conditions of life. The commonplace dichotomy which is drawn between Amos's concern for social issues and Hosea's concern for cultic issues depends upon this dualistic assumption that religion and

1.   The term 'latifundialization,' familiar within social economic theory, describes a process of systematic shifts in land use and ownership, within which small farms, dedicated to diversified subsistence agriculture, are increasingly absorbed into large 'latifundia' or agrarian estates, dedicated to the production of one or more cash crops. Such a process of economic development is contingent upon the opening of trading networks and the rise of consumer desire for the luxury goods which then become available. The transition from a subsistence agrarian economy to a trade-based market economy typically results in increasing wealth for a shrinking number of landowners, and increasing poverty for the dispossessed peasantry (Premnath, 'Latifundialization'; Lang, 'Social Organization'; Chaney, 'Bitter Bounty').

2.   In ancient Israel, rights to particular fields were held within the patrilineage, with inheritance passing from father to son. The sale or transfer of these patrimonial lands outside of the immediate kinship group was prohibited (see Lev. 25.23; 1 Kgs 21.3; Ruth 4.1-8). For a thorough discussion of property rights in ancient Israel and the response of the eighth-century prophets to elite infringement upon these rights, see Dearman, *Property Rights*. Wright also provides a helpful introduction to the issue, with emphasis upon the theological dimensions of laws of land inalienability (C. Wright, *God's People in God's Land: Family, Land, and Property in the Old Testament* [Grand Rapids, MI: Eerdmans, 1990], pp. 55-65).

society inhabit two separate spheres of human activity. It then becomes possible to interpret a text which purportedly deals with the proceeds of cultic issues without sustained reference to its economic, social or political contexts.

The alternative to a theological idealism is usually a sociological reductionism which subsumes cultic or sacral concerns to epiphenomena, supporting and reflecting the structures of social organization, as if society existed apart from the religious language which it manipulates. But as the discipline of *religions-wissenschaft* teaches us, religion is neither autonomous from nor merely derivative of social processes and material conditions. In response to theological idealism, we must say that religion is not about entities other than the world, but is about a *mode of orientation* in the world; it is about the constitution of worlds of meaning out of the raw stuff of the material, geographical and historical givens and processes that press upon human life in any particular time and place.[1] Therefore we cannot speak about Hosea's theology apart from the realities of Hosea's world. In response to reductionism, we must question whether we can even speak about society per se prior to or apart from that society's symbolic or sacral foundation upon which the bonds of shared identity and meaning are established. Without these points it is difficult to perceive the deeper religious and social issues undergirding Hosea's discourse.

The religious orientation of the early Israelites had been rooted in the structure of the *bêt 'āb* ('the house of the father' or 'lineage'[2]), the relationship of these *bātê 'ab* to their patrimonial lands and, further, a system of exchange, credit and mutual solidarity based upon the bonds of kinship and proximity. These relationships, within which these highland people organized themselves, signified their exchanges and related themselves to their land, constituted the essential matrix of religious meaning

1. This understanding of religion is indebted to Charles H. Long, for whom religion is a matter of orientation, 'that is, how one comes to terms with the ultimate significance of one's place in the world' (C.H. Long, *Significations: Signs, Symbols, and Images in the Interpretation of Religion* [Philadelphia: Fortress Press, 1986], p. 7).

2. L. Stager, 'The Archaeology of the Family in Ancient Israel', *BASOR* 260 (1985), p. 22.

in early Israel.[1] However, under the monarchy, as Israel's clan- and village-based subsistence economy was being progressively transformed into a commercial economy driven by interregional trade, this traditional social and sacral matrix was profoundly disrupted. The commodification of the processes of production and exchange and the rupture in the intimate relationships between household and land brought about by widespread dis- possessions and latifundialization meant the loss of all that had served to define and maintain the particular self-understanding and religious orientation of this community. Thus the crisis of Hosea's time was not simply a social crisis, but a religious crisis in which the constitutive meaning and identity of this community was rapidly disintegrating. This sense of cultural crisis and dislocation was further intensified by rampant corruption and violence within the royal administration, such that the public cult, whose meaning was bound up with that of the nation and its king, had become profane.

Reading Hosea 1–2[2] in light of this context, this paper will

---

1. This religious orientation to lineage and land was most clearly manifest in the beliefs and practices of ancestor worship (H.C. Brichto, 'Kin, Cult, Land and the Afterlife—A Biblical Complex', *HUCA* 64 [1973], pp. 1- 54; E. Bloch-Smith, *Judahite Burial Practices and Beliefs about the Dead* [JSOTSup, 123; Sheffield: JSOT Press, 1992]). The dead were a powerful source of blessings and protection for their descendants if buried properly within the family tomb and worshipped as custom demanded. The burial of the dead within the patrimonial holdings legitimated and ensured the family's perpetual claim to the land. Further, rituals of sacrifice to the dead, obligatory for all members of the *mišpāhâ* ('clan'), served to fortify and sacralize clan solidarities (1 Sam. 20.6, 29; Bloch-Smith, *Judahite Burial Practices*, p. 124). The presence of the ancestor's bones in the soil sealed and sacralized the intimate relationship between the *bêt 'āb* and its land and fostered the bonds of fidelity between lineage members. This religious complex linking 'kin, cult and land' (Brichto, 'Kin, Cult, Land') was no foreign accretion, but an 'integral part of social organization' in ancient Israel which persisted through the monarchical period (Bloch-Smith, *Judahite Burial Practices*, p. 124).

2. This study will limit its analysis of Hosea's use of female sexual imagery to chs. 1–2, to the exclusion of ch. 3. There are two motives behind this decision. The first is stylistic: Hos. 1–2 constitutes an integral literary unit bounded by reference to the children's symbolic names. Attention to Jezreel in particular will provide an important clue for the reading of the

show how Hosea's language about female fornication and the disintegration of one family unit offers a powerful and evocative metonym for this situation of socio-religious crisis. From this perspective, it appears that Hosea's trope is not really a marriage metaphor at all, but a family metaphor, which draws upon the centrality of the family in traditional Israelite life as a way of speaking to the disintegration and impending destruction of that way of life brought about by the self-aggrandizing practices of Israel's elite establishment.

The Case of the Missing Fertility Cult

An imagination of Canaanite religion as a morally degenerate and sexually obsessed fertility cult has long conditioned the interpretation of Hosea's sexual imagery. Primary features of this syncretistic cult supposedly included worship of the rain god Baal and the Canaanite goddesses of 'sex and fecundity', deities who signified the divinization of the life-giving forces of procreation and regeneration immanent in nature, its seasonal cycles and the body. Ritual sex acts within this cult were aimed at ensuring fertility through acts of sympathetic magic in imitation of the *hieros gamos* between the rain god Baal and his consort, the earth goddess, who embodied the numinous power of fertility in the land. Described in this way, Canaan's worship of copulating deities who embody the seasonal repetitions and power of nature appears diametrically opposed to Yahwistic faith, which imagines a singular deity who stands above nature's rhythm as its creator and Lord.

Reading Hosea in this context, the fornications of the *'ēšet z^enûnîm* appear as a seemingly obvious sign for Israel's apostasy. As Gomer chases her lovers, so Israel pursues these

whole. The second motive is strategic. Hos. 3.1 is the only place in Hosea where the woman's lovers are explicitly identified with 'other gods'. Any mystery in the metaphor is here eliminated with a clear equation: adultery equals apostasy. It may be that a move from metaphor to allegory is the work of a redactor within the Deuteronomistic school. But without venturing any redactional theories, this study claims the hermeneutical liberty to read Hos. 1–2 without any a priori closure concerning how its sexual imagery must be read.

nature deities, forgetting Yahweh and renouncing the commitments of covenantal faith.[1] Commentators explain that the faithless wife Israel has committed a grave theological error in believing that it is the *bᵉ'ālîm* who give to her 'the grain, the wine and the oil' (v. 6); rather, the text proclaims that it is Israel's true 'husband' Yahweh who is the transcendent source of all abundance (v. 10a). Therefore the renewal of the earth's fertility must depend not upon rituals of sympathetic magic, but upon moral action in obedience to Yahweh's covenant.

This interpretation has served well within the theological project of defining the superiority and uniqueness of biblical religion over and against all competitors. Thus few have seriously challenged the conclusion of the biblical theologians that the great point of Hosea's discourse is to reject the Canaanite notion of sex as a sacred mystery and to assert the transcendence of God over nature. However, despite its appeal, none of the key elements of the fertility cult thesis—popular Baal worship, the *hieros gamos* between Baal and the earth goddess, or the practice of sacred prostitution—can be substantiated by reference to the textual or extra-textual sources from eighth-century Syria-Palestine.

1. Many interpreters argue further that Gomer's fornications actually took place within the context of the sex cult, such that her adultery becomes not only a figurative sign, but also a literal instance of Israel's apostasy. For example, Wolff proposed that the practice of sacred prostitution within the fertility cult took the form of bridal rites, in which young women consecrated their wombs to the fertility deities by offering up their virginity to a passing stranger. For Wolff, '"the whore" Gomer was probably no exception in her own day; rather, she was simply one of many Israelite women who had submitted to the bridal rites customary among the Canaanites' (H.W. Wolff, *Hosea* [trans. G. Stansell; Philadelphia: Fortress Press, 1974], p. xxii). Mays offered another version, arguing that the *'ēšet zᵉnûnîm* whom Hosea was to marry was a cultic official, who regularly performed sexual rituals at the shrines as part of her ritual duties (J.L. Mays, *Hosea: A Commentary* [OTL; Philadelphia: Westminster Press, 1969], p. 26). Although Andersen and Freedman acknowledged that neither of these proposals could be substantiated, they nevertheless also affirmed that 'everything points to her [Gomer's] promiscuity as participation in the ritual sex acts of the Baal cult' (F.I. Andersen and D.N. Freedman, *Hosea* [AB, 24; Garden City, NY: Doubleday, 1980], p. 166).

First, outside of Hosea's own scattered references to Baal or the $b^{e'}\bar{a}l\hat{i}m$, we have scant confirmation from any other biblical text for rampant Baal worship in eighth-century Israel.[1] Neither Amos, Micah nor Isaiah appears to be troubled by Israelite worship of Baal or the $b^{e'}\bar{a}l\hat{i}m$, nor do they seem to be aware of any widespread moral degeneration, which is assumed to be a consequence of Israel's engagement with the sex cult. The book of Kings also offers little evidence of syncretistic Baal worship in Israel, apart from the politically motivated foreign imports of the Omrids in the ninth century. Jezebel's Baal (1 Kgs 16.31-32; 18) was clearly no mere fertility deity, but the Baal or lord of Tyre, whose temple in Samaria gave sacral expression to Israel's lucrative alliance with Tyre. Only 2 Kgs 17.15-17 claims that polytheistic practices predicated the fall of Israel, yet this formulaic catalogue of cultic offenses is unsupported by other texts and stands out as an exilic addition to Kings. The extant epigraphic evidence also fails to witness to rampant polytheistic practice or Baal worship in eighth-century Israel.[2]

More serious than the lack of evidence for widespread Baal worship in ancient Israel is the failure of the 'sacred prostitution' hypothesis. The scholarly assumption that sexual rituals were a prominent feature of Canaanite religion rests primarily upon the dubious and second-hand testimony of classical writers such as Herodotus, fortified by a process of circular reasoning that can be nowhere independently substantiated.[3] Herodotus's

---

1.   J.H. Hayes, 'Hosea's Baals and Lovers: Religion or Politics?', paper delivered at the AAR/SBL Annual Meeting in New Orleans, 1990.

2.   Tigay's study (J.F. Tigay, *You Shall Have No Other Gods: Israelite Religion in Light of Hebrew Inscriptions* [Atlanta: Scholars Press, 1986]) of the onomasticon (records of personal names) from eighth- and seventh-century Israel and Judah reveals that Hosea's compatriots did not often name their children after deities other than Yahweh. If religious beliefs are reflected in the names people bear, then there is little warrant here to suggest that the worship of foreign gods or goddesses had made strong inroads in eighth-century Israel. Tigay's survey of other epigraphic evidence indicative of religious loyalties, such as salutations, votive inscriptions and prayers for blessings, also indicates that 'deities other than Yahweh were not widely regarded by Israelites as sources of beneficence, blessing, protection and justice' (p. 37).

3.   The assumption concerning the prevalence of ritual sex in the ancient

descriptions of ancient Mesopotamia were motivated by a desire to demonstrate the inferior and barbaric character of Semitic cultures and their pagan religions in contrast to the glory of Greece. As Robert Oden[1] has argued, the willingness of modern, historically trained biblical scholars to rely upon such dubious testimony is indicative of a shared impetus to affirm the superiority of one culture through a description of the sexual debauchery of another.

Furthermore, our extant sources from Bronze and Iron Age Canaan reveal no trace of any mythological text concerning a *hieros gamos* between Baal and an earth goddess.[2] This putative mythologem, in which the fertility of the earth depends upon the intercourse of the rain god and the mother earth, was supposedly the basis of the Canaanite sex rituals. But at Ugarit, Baal does not even seemed to have enjoyed the company of a regular consort, and his connection with the earth's fertility seems to depend less upon his sexual activity than upon his cosmic struggles with the personified forces of chaos, particularly Mot ('death'). Also, the earth goddess or mother goddess who is supposed to serve as Baal's consort in this *hieros gamos* is nowhere in evidence in the materials from Ugarit.[3]

Near East has profoundly conditioned our understanding of religion and sexual meanings in ancient Israel. Yet although the extant evidence for such practices is clearly deficient, it is only in the last decade that the sacred prostitution hypothesis has received sustained and critical examination. See: R. Oden, *The Bible Without Theology: The Theological Tradition and Alternatives to It* (San Francisco: Harper & Row, 1987), pp. 131-53; S. Hooks, 'Sacred Prostitution in Israel and the Ancient Near East' (PhD dissertation; Hebrew Union College, 1985); J.G. Westenholtz, 'Tamar, *Qedeša, Qadištu,* and Sacred Prostitution in Mesopotamia', *HTR* 82.3 (1989), pp. 245-65; and T. Frymer-Kensky, *In the Wake of the Goddesses: Women, Culture, and the Biblical Transformation of Pagan Myth* (New York: The Free Press, 1992), pp. 199-202, all of whom find no substantive evidence to support the thesis that sacred prostitution was practiced in the ancient Near East in the first or second millennium BCE.

1. *The Bible Without Theology*, pp. 131-53.

2. E.J. Adler, 'The Background for the Metaphor of Covenant as Marriage in the Hebrew Bible' (PhD dissertation; Berkeley: University of California, 1990), pp. 130-44.

3. None of the goddesses who are known to us from Bronze Age Canaan was primarily associated with the earth. J.A. Hackett ('Can a Sexist

Those scholars who assume a mythologem of the fertile earth as a goddess do not cite any sources to support their position.

The widespread assumption that there was such an earth goddess, divine source of the earth's fertility, is telling, as it helps to expose the androcentric determinants which underlie the imagination of Canaanite religion as fertility religion. The predilection of the male scholarly guild to imagine any and all Canaanite goddesses as fertility goddesses[1] serves to support an imagination of Canaan's fertility cult as essentially a goddess cult. Albright's view that sacred prostitution was 'an almost invariable concomitant of the cult of the Phoenician and Syrian Goddess, whatever her personal name'[2] is representative of a general tendency to label the generic fertility goddesses of Canaan as the source of the licentious practices of the fertility

Model Liberate Us? Ancient Near Eastern Fertility Goddesses', *JFSR* 5 [1989], p. 69) demonstrates this point in regard to each of the most prominent goddesses of Canaan. Asherah is the consort of El and mother of the gods. As such, she is associated with fertility, but not specifically with agricultural growth; rather, she is a marine deity, her favorite epithet being 'lady of the sea'. Anat is characterized primarily by her association with warfare and the hunt; while Anat does copulate with her brother, Baal, she can no more be referred to as an earth mother than can Yahweh, who incorporates many of her attributes. Astarte's name indicates her origin as an astral deity. In her dissertation, Adler ('Covenant as Marriage', pp. 130-44) also surveys all the lesser known goddesses of Canaan, but can find no likely candidate for the role of an earth goddess, consort of Baal, in the extant texts.

1.   See Hackett, 'Sexist Model', and P.L. Day, 'Why is Anat a Warrior and a Hunter' (in D. Jobling, P.L. Day and G.T. Sheppard [eds.], *The Bible and the Politics of Exegesis* [Cleveland: Pilgrim Press, 1991], pp. 141-46) for the manner in which the goddesses of Canaan are automatically characterized as 'fertility' goddesses within the androcentric traditions of biblical scholarship. As Hackett explains, even though the Ras Shamra texts clearly show Baal and El to be the Canaanite deities who are most immediately concerned with agricultural and human fertility respectively, the scholarly literature speaks of Baal as a 'storm' god and El as the 'chief' of the pantheon, while reserving the 'fertility' epithet as a singular description for the female deities of Canaan, whose association with this function is much more tangential (Hackett, 'Sexist Model', p. 74).

2.   W.F. Albright, *Archaeology and the Religion of Israel* (Baltimore: Johns Hopkins University Press, 2nd edn, 1946), p. 75.

cult.[1] As these divine 'courtesans' are axiomatically linked with the sacralization of the natural and (illicit) sex,[2] it becomes safe to assume, as Albright does, that the 'erotic aspect of their cult must have sunk to extremely sordid depths of social degradation'.[3] In opposition to this 'voluptuous and dissolute' fertility cult,[4] which is gendered in such feminine terms, stands faith in Yahweh, the god of history and ethics, whose masculinity in Hosea's metaphor is by no means arbitrary, as Klaus Koch explains, but is deliberately so conceived in contrast with this other power, which is 'conceived of in feminine terms'.[5]

The depiction of fertility religion as essentially feminine religion is further reinforced by the widespread assumption that the sacred prostitutes of the fertility cult were predominantly female. This is the case even though the biblical text refers to both *qādēš* and *qᵉdēšâ* (Deut. 23.17), terms which are translated as male and female 'cult prostitutes'.[6] Mays, for example, in his

1. For a more recent example of the same conflation of the fertility cult with goddess worship, see S.H. Dresner, who describes the 'central divinities' of the pagan fertility cult as 'power-hungry goddesses' ('The Return of Paganism', *Midstream* June/July 1988, p. 32). Cf. the critique of this view offered by Frymer-Kensky (*Wake of the Goddesses*).

2. As these fertility goddesses are further characterized as consorts or sacred courtesans, terms which tend to denote sexual partnerships outside of marriage, scholars imply that there is something illegitimate or illicit about their sexual activity (Day, 'Anat', pp. 141-42). These overtones of illegitimate sexuality attached to the goddesses then resonate with the depiction of their cult, in which extra-marital sex was supposedly the order of the day.

3. Albright, *Archaeology and the Religion of Israel*, p. 77.

4. Budde 1899, as cited by Oden, *The Bible Without Theology*, p. 136.

5. K. Koch, *The Prophets. I. The Assyrian Period* (trans. M. Kohl; Philadelphia: Fortress Press, 1983), pp. 82-83.

6. These terms *qādēš* and *qᵉdēšâ* clearly refer to some kind of proscribed cultic official, but there is no compelling reason to assume that their ritual duties included sex acts (Hooks, 'Sacred Prostitution', pp. 164-87). References to these cultic personnel in 1 Kgs 15.11, 22.47 and 2 Kgs. 23.7 give little indication as to their identity or function. The identification of these cultic personnel as cultic prostitutes is based largely upon three passages where these terms appear in parallel with or in substitution for *zônâ* (a common prostitute; Gen. 38.15, 21-22; Deut. 23.17-18; Hos. 4.14). But the logic of this conclusion is arbitrary. Given the conventional

description of sacred prostitutes, refers only to the feminine plural term qᵉdēšôt.[1] Where the male qādēš elicit discussion, they are often assumed to be 'sodomites'.[2] Rarely does male hetero-sexual activity emerge in these discussions as intrinsically associated with the meaning of Canaanite religion.

As Canaanite religion is imagined as a sensual and tempting 'other', teeming with fertility goddesses and the female sacred prostitutes who serve them, we find that it is not just the sacralization of sexuality in general, but of *female* sexuality in particular which marks the meaning of a mode of immanental sacrality against which biblical theology defines itself. The gender polarities of Western culture, which automatically associate femininity with materiality and immanence, and masculinity with spirit and transcendence, have served to validate and reify theology's

representation of proscribed worship as *znh* ('to act as a prostitute'), it would not be surprising to find ritual officiants of proscribed worship pejoratively termed whores (C. Bucher, 'The Origin and Meaning of ZNH Terminology in the Book of Hosea' [PhD dissertation; Claremont Graduate School, 1988], p. 91). This usage could have quickly found its way into common parlance, such that qᵉdēšâ may have served as a synonym for zônâ, as in Gen. 38. If cultic prostitution was actually practised in ancient Israel, and if these terms did indeed refer to cultic prostitutes, it is surprising that Hos. 4.14 is the only text in the prophetic corpus which makes reference to qādēš, qᵉdēšâ, qᵉdēšîm or qᵉdēšôt.

Hos. 4.14 is commonly cited as a prooftext for the thesis that rituals of sacred prostitution were prevalent in ancient Israel: 'for the men themselves go aside with harlots, and sacrifice with cult prostitutes'. But in this passage, there are no verbs indicating sexual activity. Andersen and Freedman suggest that the verb *prd*, translated 'go aside' in the RSV, may mean 'to divide' as in the division of the sacrificial meat between the worshippers and the priests (*Hosea*, p. 370). Thus the reference is to the normal practice of the sacrificial ritual, but here the priests are polemically characterized as 'whores', in keeping with the anti-clerical tone of the preceding passages (vv. 4-13).

1.   Even while admitting that 'the cult of Baal involved both men and women', Mays goes on to explain that in these rites, 'the men lay with sacred prostitutes, and the women as devotees of Baal possibly made themselves available to male worshippers to receive fertility through the cult' (*Hosea*, p. 25). Thus the male participants are worshippers; it is the women who serve as sacred prostitutes.

2.   Albright, *Archaeology and the Religion of Israel*, p. 159.

polarization between Canaan's fertility religion and Israel's ethical monotheism. Female sexuality as an icon for immanental sacrality is linked with Canaanite religion as the inferior yet 'seductive' other which must be resisted and excluded in the process of defining the superiority of the biblical tradition. Rather than seeking to lift up and celebrate the negated pole of a dichotomy which is itself already a construction of male 'fears and fantasies',[1] it is perhaps better to reject these androcentric formulations altogether, and work to rethink the religious situation in eighth-century Syria-Palestine anew.

It is clear that this entire dualistic and gendered figuration of Israel versus Canaan can no longer be sustained in light of more sophisticated analyses of ancient Near Eastern religions and the relationship of Israel to them.[2] Also, the traditional model of cultural contestation upon which the fertility cult thesis rests must now be seen as highly suspect in that it naively relies upon an antiquated paradigm of Israel as an invading force which conquered Canaan and then succumbed to its 'foreign' influence. As socio-scientific research leads us to understand the *emergence* of Israel as a movement of indigenous peoples within Canaan,[3]

1.   Hackett, 'Sexist Model', p. 68.

2.   For discussion and critique of the theological biases which assume and then defend the absolute uniqueness of Israel through the construction of such oppositions as 'myth versus history', see, for example, J.J.M. Roberts, 'Myth versus History: Relaying the Comparative Foundations', *CBQ* 38 (1976), pp. 1-13; H.W.F. Saggs, *The Encounter with the Divine in Mesopotamia and Israel* (London: Athlone Press, 1978); and D. Hillers, 'Analyzing the Abominable: Our Understanding of Canaanite Religion', *JQR* 75.3 (1985), pp. 253-69.

3.   This paradigm shift was pioneered by G.E. Mendenhall ('The Hebrew Conquest of Palestine', *BA* [1962], pp. 66-87) and followed by N. Gottwald (*The Tribes of Yahweh: A Sociology of the Religion of Liberated Israel, 1250-1050 BCE* [Maryknoll, NY: Orbis Books, 1979]), who proposed that the Israelites were not foreign invaders but indigenous peasants who revolted against the oppressive political structures of the Canaanite city states. While their critique of older models of Israel's origins have proven influential, their 'peasants' revolt' hypothesis has been widely questioned (see for example N.P. Lemche, *Early Israel: Anthropological and Historical Studies on Israelite Society before the Monarchy* [Leiden: Brill, 1985]). Alternative views offered by R.B. Coote and K. Whitelam (*The Emergence of Early Israel in Historical Perspective* [The Social World of Biblical Antiquity, 5;

we must revise our approach to ancient Israelite religion, such that continuity with Canaanite religion rather than discontinuity becomes our basic presupposition.[1] From this perspective, a paradigm of opposition between Canaan's fertility cult and ethical Yahwism gives way to a more realistic vision of the religion of monarchical Israel as a 'classical West Asiatic religion, the basic structure of which recurs from Mesopotamia to Northern Syria and Palestine'.[2]

Sheffield: Almond Press, 1987]) and Lemche see the origins of Israel as a less dramatic and rather inevitable consequence of a widespread political and economic collapse at the close of the Bronze Age, which prompted widespread flight from Canaan's lowlands in favor of the more agriculturally marginal highlands. For a review of recent debate in this field, see J.D. Martin, 'Israel as a Tribal Society', in R.E. Clements (ed.), *The World of Ancient Israel: Sociological, Anthropological and Political Perspectives* (Cambridge: Cambridge University Press, 1989), pp. 95-118.

1.   So M. Coogan, who stresses that for methodological purposes it is essential to consider Israelite religion as a species of Canaanite religion, and not as a foreign import subject to corruption and degeneration. There are distinctive qualities to Israel's religion, but these must be examined from a perspective which first situates the emergence of those qualities from within a Canaanite matrix of religious belief and practice ('Canaanite Origins and Lineage: Reflections on the Religion of Ancient Israel', in P.D. Miller *et al.* [eds.], *Ancient Israelite Religion* [Philadelphia: Fortress Press, 1987], pp. 115-16). For recent scholarship on ancient Israelite religion from this perspective, see especially Miller *et al.* (eds.), *Ancient Israelite Religion*; N.P. Lemche, *Ancient Israel: A New History of Israelite Society* (Biblical Seminar, 5; Sheffield: JSOT Press, 1988), pp. 197-257; and E.W. Nicholson, 'Israelite Religion in the Pre-Exilic Period: A Debate Renewed', in J.D. Martin and P.R. Davies (eds.), *A Word in Season* (JSOTSup, 42; Sheffield: JSOT Press, 1986).

2.   See Lemche, *Ancient Israel*, p. 239. The biblical self-presentation to the contrary stems largely from the exilic period, when the Deuteronomistic writers responded to the threat of cultural assimilation and ethnic dissolution through the construction of a national myth of origins which defined the boundaries of Israelite identity in opposition to the lures of a foreign (that is, Canaanite) culture (E.T. Mullen, *Narrative History and Ethnic Boundaries: The Deuteronomistic Historian and the Creation of Israelite National Identity* [Atlanta: Scholars Press, 1993]). While the influence of Deuteronomistic interests in the transmission of Hosea's oracles must be acknowledged, these interests should not wholly determine the manner in which we read Hosea's female sexual imagery. Rather, attention to the

In Iron Age Israel as in all the states of Syria-Palestine, religion was a national and territorial phenomenon, integrally related to the meaning of the nation and the structures of its power. The nation was the territory of the god, administered by his vice-regent or 'son' the king, whose power to rule was ideologically grounded in his control over the deity's cult. The Yahweh cults in Israel and Judah were organs of their respective national governments, each of which not only served to lend sacral legitimacy to the state, but also functioned practically as part of its administrative structure. As G.W. Ahlström argued at length, the national cult of Yahweh, complete with its temples, shrines and priests, was an integral component of and support for the royal administration in Israel and Judah.[1]

Persisting alongside of the official cultus in Israel were other long-standing (that is, 'Canaanite') beliefs and practices which were oriented not to the power of the state, but to the welfare and continuance of the family or clan. The fertility of fields, flocks and families was a primary concern at this level of Israelite life, such that the power of fertility was experienced as hierophanic. In Israel, this religious orientation to fertility was expressed both at the domestic level in the female figurines in the household shrines,[2] and at the public cult sites, where *'ăšerîm*

commonalities between Israel and its neighbors is more illuminating for explicating the concerns of the eighth-century prophet.

1.   G.W. Ahlström, *Royal Administration and National Religion in Ancient Palestine* (Studies in the History of the Ancient Near East, 1; Leiden: Brill, 1982).

2.   The distribution of these terracota female figurines which are found in abundance from the eighth century onwards at a frequency of roughly one per household in Judean and Israelite sites suggests to J. Holladay that they probably served as the central feature of the household shrine ('Religion in Israel and Judah under the Monarchy: An Explicitly Archaeo-logical Approach', in Miller *et al* [eds.], *Ancient Israelite Religion*, p. 278). The religious significance of these female figurines in the monarchical period is disputed. Some scholars contend that these were household icons of an Israelite goddess, most probably Asherah, designed to enhance fertility (Coogan, 'Canaanite Origins', p. 119; Holladay, 'Religion in Israel and Judah', p. 278). Others find this explanation implausible because, in distinction from the iconic Canaanite statues, these figurines bear no con-ventional symbols of divinity nor any inscriptions to indicate a definitive

were planted, wooden poles named after the goddess Asherah and modelled after the tree of life, which was one of her symbols.[1] This popular reverence for the power of fertility, modelled in the sacred female form and in the sacred tree, was a pervasive and indigenous religious response to the precarious conditions of life within this arid land. If one wishes to speak of a fertility cult in Hosea's Israel, then these feminine religious forms, that is the *'ªšerîm* at the cult sites, the domestic figurines and possibly also the worship of Asherah herself,[2] would have

identity (M. Tadmor, 'Female Cult Figurines in Late Canaan and Early Israel: Archaeological Evidence', in T. Ishida [ed.], *Studies in the Period of David and Solomon and Other Essays* [Winona Lake, IN: Eisenbrauns, 1982], pp. 170-71; J.B. Pritchard, *Palestinian Figurines in Relation to Certain Goddesses Known through Literature* [New Haven: American Oriental Society, 1943], p. 86). Rather than representing a goddess, Pritchard found it more likely that the figurines functioned as talismans to promote fertility. Also taking the latter position, Frymer-Kensky suggests that these feminine forms functioned as a kind of 'visual metaphor, which show in seeable and touchable form that which is most desired. In other words, they are a kind of tangible prayer for fertility and nourishment' (*Wake of the Goddesses*, p. 159). Whether as talisman or as goddess, it is clear that these figurines functioned as symbols for a religious concern with fertility.

1.   See S.M. Olyan, *Asherah and the Cult of Yahweh in Israel* (Atlanta: Scholars Press, 1988) for a full treatment of the asherim cult objects and the goddess Asherah in the Hebrew Bible, and see Frymer-Kensky (*Wake of the Goddesses*, pp. 153-61) for discussion of the symbolic links between female sexual imagery, trees and the power of fertility. That the sacred tree, ancient Near Eastern symbol of the power of life, fertility and regeneration, was a symbol for Asherah is suggested by R. Hestrin in her studies of the Ta'anach cult stand ('The Cult Stand from Ta'anach and its Religious Background', in E. Lipinski [ed.], *Phoenicia and the East Mediterranean in the First Millennium BC* [Studia Phoenicia, 5; Leuven: Peeters, 1987, pp. 61-77) and the Lachish Ewer ('The Lachish Ewer and the Ashera', *IEJ* 37.4 [1987], pp. 212-23). This symbolic complex of tree/woman/fertility is also visible in the 'pillar-based' female figurines, whose pillared and gently flaring lower half intimates the shape of a tree trunk, such that each figurine perhaps resembles 'a kind of tree with breasts' (Frymer-Kensky, *Wake of the Goddesses*, p. 160). A suggestive comparison is found in an image from New Kingdom Egypt in which a tree extends a breast to give suck to the Pharaoh (see sketch in Hestrin, 'Ta'anach', p. 70).

2.   The eighth-century inscriptions from Kuntillet 'Ajrud which invoke the blessings of 'Yahweh and his Asherah' have suggested to many

been its most obvious manifestations.[1] One would think that if a religious concern with fertility were the prime foil of Hosea's polemic, then these feminine icons of the sacred would have been obvious targets. Yet nowhere does Hosea refer to any of these.[2]

scholars that the goddess Asherah herself may have been worshipped in monarchical Israel alongside of Yahweh (for example W. Dever, 'Ashera, Consort of Yahweh? New Evidence from Kuntillet 'Ajrud', *BASOR* 255 [1984], pp. 21-38; Olyan, *Asherah*). Others argue that rather than signifying a distinct deity, her name was more of a feminine hypostasis of the effective presence of Yahweh, perhaps derivative from the cult objects themselves (P.K. McCarter, 'Aspects of the Religion of the Israelite Monarchy: Biblical and Epigraphic Data', in Miller *et al.* [eds.], *Ancient Israelite Religion*, pp. 146-49; see also discussion in M.S. Smith, *The Early History of God* [New York: Harper & Row, 1990], pp. 88-94). This academic debate remains unresolved but, in any event, at the level of popular practice, such distinctions may well have disintegrated. An illuminating analogy may be made to religious practices and beliefs concerning the Mother of God within Roman Catholicism. Although Roman Catholics understand and affirm the orthodox position that Mary is not divine but only an intercessor, prayers and piety in relation to Mary clearly invest her with divine status.

1.   Here we see that the generative female body did offer a symbol for the power of fertility in ancient Israel, but in ways that are quite distinct from the scholarly conflation of Canaanite religion and feminine religion. In this symbolic complex, the power of fertility is manifest not in illicit coital intercourse performed by divine courtesans or sacred harlots, but in the female body itself, particularly in the life-sustaining breast. The female figurines and the asherim were not foreign accretions, but were accepted dimensions of the Yahwistic cult until the 'reform' movements of the seventh century BCE. Furthermore, it was not only female sexuality that symbolized the power of fertility in Palestine; for instance, the bull was a prominent masculine symbol of the power of fertility manifest in the male deities El, Baal and Yahweh.

2.   Attempts to discover veiled references to the Canaanite goddesses or the *'ašerîm* in Hosea have not been convincing. Wellhausen's emendation of Hos. 14.8aβ (Heb. 14.9aβ) to read 'I am his [Ephraim's] Anat and his Asherah' has not been widely accepted (see Olyan, *Asherah*, p. 21; Wolff, *Hosea*, p. 233; cf. J. Day, 'A Case of Inner Scriptural Interpretation', *JTS* 31 [1980], pp. 314-15). It is sometimes suggested that 'the thing of wood' of which the people inquire (Hos. 4.12) might refer to the wooden asherah (Day, 'Interpretation', p. 315; Wolff, *Hosea*, p. 84), but there is insufficient support for this reading; the term in question, *'ēs*, appearing in parallel with *maqlô* ('his staff'), probably also refers to some kind of rod or stick used for

Rather, in chs. 4–14, Hosea repeatedly and explicitly attacks Israel's official cultus as the symbol of and support for the power of Israel's corrupt royal administration. Israel's sanctuaries, priests, sacrificial rituals and icons are condemned as idolatrous, corrupt and doomed for destruction along with the elite structures of power which they sanctify.[1] Israel's sins are political, and the cultic references are most often metonymic, as in Hosea's condemnation of the Bethel icon as the 'calf of Samaria' (8.6), in reference to the royal city whose power it undergirds.

The dominance of the fertility cult thesis does not finally rest upon any pervasive evidence but upon the projection of the gender polarities of Western culture onto the interpretation of Hosea's female sexual imagery. Within the Western androcentric

---

divination (Andersen and Freedman, *Hosea*, pp. 365-66; Olyan, *Asherah*, pp. 19-20). Olyan's review of the texts in question leads him to conclude that there is no direct condemnation of or allusion to the asherim or Asherah in Hosea (*Asherah*, pp. 19-21).

Further, the idols and images which Hosea decries should not be identified with the female figurines of the domestic cult. These idols and images are most often condemned in the context of a critique of practices at the public altars (4.17-19; 11.2; 13.2) or within the national cult (8.4-5). There is nothing to suggest that Hosea has any interest in the rituals or practices of domestic religion or that these images and idols are feminine in their appearance.

1.   See, for example, Hos. 8.4-6, where condemnation of idol making parallels the condemnation of the kings and princes who were set up without Yahweh's knowledge. Rulers and idols are linked together; both are creations of falsity, made by humans and not God. See also Hos. 10.7-8a, where oracles concerning the death of the king and the destruction of the high places are conjoined; the monarchy and its sanctuaries will fall together, for they are coordinate realities. The sanctuaries are polemically characterized in 10.8a as the high places of '*āven* ('iniquity') because of their close ties to the royal government. To assume that this 'iniquity' concerns matters of exclusively religious concern, that is, sexual rituals for fertility deities, reflects a naivety concerning the symbiotic relationship between the national cult and the national government. Again, in Hos. 10.14b-15, Bethel (MT) will be destroyed because of its 'wickedness', and so too shall the king of Israel 'be utterly cut off'. Priests too, as part of the state's chain of power, are called to judgment along with the 'house of the king' and the 'house of Israel' (5.1), and are linked to acts of violence and villainy (6.9).

imagination, the female body is linked inextricably with nature, the passions, sin, sexuality, and all that is foreign or tempting. Thus female sexuality is assumed *naturally* to serve as an obvious sign for the immanental religious meanings of Canaan's sexualized nature worship. Reading Hosea's *'ēšet zᵉnûnîm* within this framework, it appears axiomatic that her fornications represent Israel's infatuation with a sexualized nature religion.

Sexual Transgression and Social Violence

To reread Hosea's sexual imagery it is necessary to extricate ourselves from the dualistic framework of the Western androcentric imagination, and consider how sexual imagery, and particularly female sexual imagery, functions within the symbolic order of ancient Israelite society and literature. In a society that defines itself through a 'proper' (here specifically a patriarchal) order of sexual relations, textual images of the sexual transgression of women (including both rape and adultery) figure the disintegration of societal bonds. Not only in the prophets, but throughout the biblical narratives, one persistently finds a rendering of societal and political issues through stories of sexual encounters, licit and illicit. One might point to David's court history, where stories of the sexual appropriation of women and the political appropriation of power are inextricably intertwined;[1] or to the thrice repeated wife-sister tales, where anxiety about the nation's vulnerability to stronger powers is expressed in stories of the matriarch being taken sexually by foreign rulers.[2] Even more pointedly, the thrice repeated conjunction of rape and war in the biblical narratives (Gen. 34, Judg. 19, 2 Sam. 13) suggests the presence of a literary convention in which the female body figures the social body, such that the sexual violence of rape serves as a

---

1. R. Schwartz, 'Adultery in the House of David: The Metanarrative of Biblical Scholarship and the Narratives of the Bible', *Semeia* 54 (1991), pp. 35-56; A. Berlin, *Poetics and the Interpretation of Biblical Narrative* (Sheffield: Almond Press, 1983), pp. 23-33.

2. J.G. Williams, *Women Recounted: Narrative Thinking and the God of Israel* (Sheffield: Almond Press, 1982), p. 47.

metonym for internecine violence.[1] Judges 19 depicts the brutal gang rape of an unnamed woman whose body is then dismembered into twelve pieces; the story offers a gruesome commentary upon the civil war among the twelve tribes of Israel which immediately follows (Judg. 20–21). The same juxtaposition of sexual violence and social violence is evident in the narrative connections between Dinah's 'humbling' and her brothers' bloody assault upon the Shechemites (Gen. 34); and between Amnon's rape of Princess Tamar and Absalom's rebellion (2 Sam. 13–19), underscoring again the political or social symbolism in episodes of sexual transgression which one finds throughout the Hebrew Bible.

These intertextual clues suggest the hypothesis that in the book of Hosea imagery of female sexual transgression serves as a metaphoric locus through which issues of societal disintegration and violence are given expression. The brief exploration of this hypothesis which follows is offered not with the desire to establish a new 'correct' reading of the text, but in order to demonstrate that the hermeneutical closure which has hitherto surrounded the interpretation of Hosea's sexual imagery is not a necessary reflex of the text but an arbitrary limitation imposed by failure to appreciate the social connotations of the sexual language in the Hebrew Bible.

The political and social connotations of Hosea's sexual language are clearly visible throughout chs. 4–14, where fornication or harlotry serves as a leitmotif in the context of an extended critique of Israel's royal administration and supporting cultic institutions.[2] Most pointedly, in Hos. 8.9, the prophet

1. A.A. Keefe, 'Rapes of Women/Wars of Men', forthcoming in *Semeia*.
2. This point is typically obscured, as commentators operate under the assumption that the metaphorical use of *znh* terminology in Hosea must refer to cultic apostasy. But there is no warrant for this assumption. The semantic range of the metaphorical uses of the root *znh* includes not only religious apostasy, but also other forms of faithlessness to or rebellion against Yahweh (Num. 14.33; 15.39; Ps. 73.27). Hosea's contemporary Isaiah proclaims that Jerusalem has become a harlot (*zônâ*); her sin is not apostasy but injustice, graft, thievery, murder and neglect of orphans and widows (Isa. 1.21-23). Elsewhere, *znh* terminology is employed to describe the treacherous political and commercial activities of Tyre and Nineveh (Isa. 23.15-17; Nah. 3.1-7). Thus when Hosea proclaims that Israel has

accuses Ephraim of hiring 'lovers' among the nations, such that illicit sex becomes a trope for the forging of international treaties. Following this and other clues, Gale Yee and John Hayes have independently suggested that the lovers of Hosea 2 are not fertility gods but Israel's foreign allies and trading partners;[1] this identification finds support elsewhere in the prophetic literature where 'lovers' is deployed more explicitly as a metaphor for Israel's supposed allies (for example Jer. 4.11;

'played the harlot' and 'loved a harlot's hire upon all threshing floors' (9.1) there is no reason why this text should be interpreted as referring to Baal worship (see for example Wolff, *Hosea*, p. 154). Rather, the setting at the threshing floor suggests a reference to corrupt economic practices in connection with the harvest. So too, while Wolff assumes that 'the spirit of harlotry' which possesses Ephraim (5.3) must refer to the people's 'total apostasy' (*Hosea*, p. 99), Hosea himself explains that this condition of harlotry is defined by *ma'l‘lêhem* ('their deeds') which 'do not permit them to return to their God' (5.4); the same term *ma'l‘lêhem* is used elsewhere by Hosea to refer more explicitly to acts of violence and corruption within royal circles (7.2; 9.15). The greatest concentration of harlotry imagery is found in ch. 4, where the 'harlotry' of the priests and the people is related to their rejection of the knowledge of God. The object of such 'knowledge' is not simply correct worship, but righteousness, such that its absence results in sins of violence and deception (4.1-2). There is no reason to assume that the characterization of the cult as harlotrous implies the presence of apostate rituals but, rather, like Amos, Hosea insists that sacrifice to Yahweh, in the absence of *ḥesed* ('steadfast love') and righteousness, is vacuous and hypocritical (Hos. 6.6; cf. Amos 5.21-24). For a discussion of Hos. 4.14, see above.

1.   Yee's identification of the lovers as Israel's allies and trading partners follows from her redactional analysis in which all of those passages which make reference to Baal, the *b‘'ālîm* or 'other gods' are assigned to subsequent stages of the tradition. She proposes that the 'harlotrous' activity of the northern kingdom was for the prophet political in nature, not cultic (G. Yee, *Composition and Tradition in the Book of Hosea: A Redaction-Critical Investigation* [Atlanta: Scholars Press, 1987], pp. 305-306). Hayes bases his suggestion on the conventional use of 'lovers' as a trope for vassals or treaty partners within ancient Near Eastern suzerain-vassal treaty language (J.H. Hayes, 'Hosea's Baals and Lovers: Religion or Politics?', paper presented to the AAR/SBL Annual Meeting, New Orleans, 1990). A biblical example of the idiom is found in 1 Kings where an envoy from Tyre speaking to Solomon describes King Hiram as 'a lover of David' (1 Kgs 5.1), thus professing Tyre to be an ally and treaty partner.

22.20-22; Lam. 1.2; Ezek. 23.5-21). Baruch Halpern pushes the point further by situating Hosea's references to the $b^e\check{a}l\hat{\imath}m$ in the context of ancient Near Eastern theopolitics, in which a singular national god and his cult undergirded the meaning and power of that state.[1] The $b^e\check{a}l\hat{\imath}m$ were no fertility deities, but the high gods of their respective state cults, signifying particular historical and cultural structures of power and production. The issue evoked in the image of chasing after such lovers or $b^e\check{a}l\hat{\imath}m$ then does not involve a conflict between a sexualized fertility cult and an ethical Yahwism, but the situation of Israel among the nations. From this perspective, adultery as a metaphor has to do with Hosea's critique of Israel's foreign maneuvering, which elsewhere he attacks more directly (5.13; 7.11; 12.1).

An alternative approach to the meaning of the $b^e\check{a}l\hat{\imath}m$ in Hosea is to be found in the symbolic correlation between Baal and particular structures of economic and social, as well as political, organization. Baal, at Ugarit and elsewhere, was a god of rain, but that does not mean he was simply a fertility deity. Agricultural production always takes place in relation to particular structures of social power, land ownership and the distribution of produce; therefore, the rain god who brings agricultural abundance is also implicated in these structures. This tradition of thinking about Baal begins with Robertson Smith;[2] and is continued by Gary Anderson, who argues that 'Baal was inextricably tied to the growth of agriculture and the accumulation of tillable land by the ruling elite'.[3] In the same vein, Robert and Mary Coote call Baal the 'patron of commercial agriculture under royal control and conspicuous consumption of trade commodities',[4] whose cult gained importance in the context of the boom in agribusiness enjoyed by Israel during the Omrid

---

1.   B. Halpern, '"Brisker Pipes than Poetry": The Development of Israelite Monotheism', in J. Neusner *et al.* (eds.), *Judaic Perspectives on Ancient Israel* (Philadelphia: Fortress Press, 1987), pp. 93-94.

2.   W. Robertson Smith, *The Religion of the Semites* (New York: Meridian Books, 2nd edn, 1956).

3.   G.A. Anderson, *Sacrifices and Offerings in Ancient Israel: Studies in their Social and Political Importance* (Atlanta: Scholars Press, 1987), p. 20.

4.   R.B. Coote and M.P. Coote, *Power, Politics, and the Making of the Bible: An Introduction* (Minneapolis: Fortress Press, 1990), p. 43.

dynasty and then under Jeroboam II. Worship of this 'god of commerce' was therefore tied to the latifundial structures of land ownership which had come to dominate the hills of Ephraim in Hosea's time.[1] In this view, to chase after lovers becomes a metaphor for Israel's embracing forms of social organization based on latifundial agriculture. Such socio-economic structures are in Hosea's eyes foreign and antithetical to traditional forms of social organization and sacral meaning based upon the control of the *bêt 'āb* over its patrimonial lands.

These two readings of Israel's lovers, the political and the economic, are complementary, given that political alignments were integral to elite strategies of profiteering; a commercial economy was necessarily an international economy in which goods flowed back and forth across national borders. Neither the image of apostasy nor that of adultery ought to be read literally; rather, the worship of other gods and fornication with other lovers serve as alternating and intersecting tropes for inappropriate alliances or commercial 'intercourse', and point towards the situation of Israel in the midst of a booming international market economy, in which the body of the nation, that is the social body, is politically and economically deeply implicated in structures of exchange and trade with other powers.

The desire of the *'ēšet zᵉnûnîm*, the woman of fornications, is for her lovers because, as she says, it is they 'who give me my bread and my water, my wool and my flax, my oil and my drink' (v. 2.5b [Heb. 7b]), while the aggrieved husband laments that she does not remember that it was he—Yahweh—who 'gave her the grain, the wine, and the oil', which now he threatens to take back in their seasons (v. 8a [Heb. 10a]). Within the fertility cult thesis, the woman's mistake is theological, as she attributes the power of fertility to gods immanent in nature and subject to ritual manipulation, whereas in fact the power rests in the hands of the one transcendent Lord of history. But this theological interpretation divorces the prophet's rhetoric from the specific meanings which grain, wine, oil and other agri-cultural products carried in this particular socioeconomic

1. Coote and Coote, *Power, Politics, and the Making of the Bible*, pp. 49-50.

context. The issue of the religious meaning attached to fertility in eighth-century Israel cannot be adequately discussed apart from the recognition that commercialized agribusiness had come to dominate the terraced slopes of the Palestinian highlands, and the fruits of the land were in the hands of an urban elite. The grain, wine and oil were the 'commodities of choice'[1] within a burgeoning market economy based on international trade; the woman's desire for these and other goods reflects the desire of the powerful and wealthy for the profits and pleasures which this trade produced.

For Hosea, Israel has become an *'ēšet z*e*nûnîm*—a woman or wife of fornications. The image is incongruous, since the root of *z*e*nûnîm, znh*, does not ordinarily describe the adulterous activity of a married woman, but the fornications of a single woman, most frequently a prostitute.[2] The trope thus combines the image of adultery, that is the sex act as betrayal of a fundamental societal bond, and the image of prostitution, that is the sex act as performed for the sake of profit. Both resonances, of betrayal and profiteering, are appropriately descriptive of the situation in Israel as Hosea views it.

We know that the lively export trade in the grain, the wine and the oil had ushered in an era of prosperity and luxury for Israel's landowning class and elite establishment in the eighth century. But as many have argued, this prosperity for some came at the cost of impoverishment for many others, as increasing numbers of small landowning families were dispossessed from their patrimonial lands which were then absorbed into large estates dedicated to commercialized

1.   D. Hopkins, 'The Dynamics of Agriculture in Monarchical Israel', in K.H. Richards (ed.), *Society of Biblical Literature Seminar Papers 1983* (Chico, CA: Scholars Press, 1983), p. 196.

2.   The common term for adultery, that is the violation of a husband's sexual rights over his wife, is *n'p*. It is therefore somewhat surprising that Hosea avoids use of this term in the articulation of his 'marriage' metaphor, preferring derivatives of the root *znh*, which usually refer to sexual activity which does not transgress the marriage bond (P. Bird, '"To Play the Harlot": An Inquiry into an Old Testament Metaphor', in P.L. Day [ed.], *Gender and Difference in Ancient Israel* [Minneapolis: Fortress Press, 1989], p. 77; Adler, 'Covenant as Marriage', p. 309).

agriculture.[1] Such dispossessions, whether managed legally or illegally,[2] constituted a betrayal of traditional highland law, which forbade the sale of patrimonial lands outside of the family lineage.

Amos addresses the shifting socioeconomic conditions of Israelite life with direct accusations regarding the corruption of justice and the situation of the poor. But Hosea's rhetoric is not focused upon the suffering of individuals, but upon another consequence of latifundialization, the disintegration of traditional structures of Israelite identity and meaning. The religious orientation of these highland people, that is, the world of meaning and value which they inhabited, was bound up in the

1. The causal relationships between the commercialization of agriculture and the dispossession and impoverishment of the Israelite peasantry are persuasively explored by Chaney ('Bitter Bounty'), B. Lang ('The Social Organization of Peasant Poverty in Biblical Israel', *JSOT* 24 [1982], pp. 47-63) and Premnath ('Latifundialization'), among others. Cf. M. Silver (*Prophets and Markets: The Political Economy of Ancient Israel* [Boston and The Hague: Kluwer-Nijhoff, 1983]), who argues that the transition to cash cropping and a trade-dependent market economy raised the standard of living of the average Israelite. But Silver's analysis ignores the shifting patterns of social stratification which were integral to the development of an economy dependent upon international trade (Chaney, 'Bitter Bounty', p. 18). While agricultural production increased on the more efficient latifundial estates, the yield from peasant labor was siphoned off for urban consumption and export trade.

2. See discussion by J.A. Dearman (*Property Rights in Eighth-Century Prophets: The Conflict and its Background* [Atlanta: Scholars Press, 1988], pp. 63-77), who suggests that the conservative, lineage-based system of land tenure did not necessarily enjoy legal protection under civil law in the monarchical state. The practice of land inalienability is indigenous to social contexts where subsistence agriculture and family-centered modes of production predominate; with the transition to a commercial economy, socio-economic pressures would favor laws in which land could be treated as a capital resource, available for sale. Thus against Alt and others who attribute the commodification of land in Israel to Canaanite influences, Dearman argues that these conflicts over property rights were more likely rooted in 'competing social institutions and economic goals within Israelite society' (*Property Rights*, p. 74). It may be that Israelite royal law permitted the alienation of patrimonial lands on 'legal grounds for such a reason as indebtedness even though there must have been community pressure to prevent it' (*Property Rights*, p. 74).

structures of the *bêt 'āb*, whose integrity in turn rested upon control of its patrimonial lands, by which its sustenance was ensured; and in its control of female sexuality, by which its perpetuation over the generations was ensured.[1] In this context, a prophetic metaphor regarding a man's loss of sexual control would resonate with the anxieties of Israel's many less powerful *bātē 'āb* concerning the loss of control of their land. The prophet thus gives expression to the meaning of the contemporary situation in which elite strategies of economic development had rendered financially inevitable the alienation of ancestral lands.

In this light, it is necessary to look again at Hosea's parabolic self-representation as one who takes to himself 'a woman of fornications and children of fornications' (1.2b). Theological reflection on the trope assumes the marriage as an allegory for the covenant; the husband's pain at his wife's betrayal and his forgiveness of her become a model of divine pathos and grace. In this view, the children are somewhat extraneous to the allegory. However, the parallelism between the two terms—*'ēšet zᵉnûnîm* and *yaldê zᵉnûnîm*—and the lack of an intervening verb suggest that the children of harlotry are as much a key to the meaning of the trope as the mother's activity.[2] Indeed the children, with their symbolic names, offer leitmotifs binding together the whole of Hosea 1–2. The meaning of Israel is carried not only by the mother, but also by the children,

1.   For a fuller discussion of the manner in which the *bêt 'āb* served as the symbolic foundation for the meaning of Israel as a whole, see C. Wright, *God's People in God's Land: Family, Land, and Property in the Old Testament* (Grand Rapids: Eerdmans, 1990). Wright proposes that the theological meaning of Israel as a community of Yahweh was 'earthed and rooted in the socio-economic fabric of the kinship structure and their land tenure, and it was this fabric which was being dissolved by the acids of debt, dispossession, and latifundism' in the eighth century (*God's People*, p. 109). The abuse of political, economic and juridical power by the elite classes was therefore not simply a 'symptom' of Israel's spiritual degeneracy as some assume; these processes of land accumulation and dispossession 'constituted in themselves, in fact, a major "virus" which threatened the stability of society and *thereby also* the relationship with Yahweh' (*God's People*, p. 109).

2.   Bird, 'To Play the Harlot', p. 80.

'Jezreel', 'Not Pitied' and 'Not My People'. This trope then is not really a marriage metaphor, but a *family* metaphor. It is a parable of a *bêt 'āb* irrevocably disrupted; the point is reiterated later in ch. 5 in Hosea's ominous declaration that 'they have borne alien children' (5.7). In a social system in which the patrilineal family formed the essential social unit and sacral locus of Israelite society, and in which the integrity of this unit rested upon the assurance of paternal legitimacy, Hosea's imagery of a fornicating wife and her illegitimate children signifies the disintegration and end of that society.

The trope is thoroughly patriarchal, but does not rest on the stereotypical association of female sexuality with sin or evil so familiar in later Jewish and Christian symbolism. Rather, for Hosea's world, at stake in female sexuality is female fertility, and the continuity of the 'house of the father' in legitimate patrilineal succession. Thus the imagery of wifely fornication leads immediately to the children of fornication. The house of Israel is now a house full of *yaldê z^enûnîm*, alien children; Israel has become alien unto itself.

Of the children's names, most evocative and perplexing is that of the first-born son, Jezreel, which sounds so hauntingly like Israel, first-born son of Yahweh. Jezreel is a polyvalent trope— at once a royal city, and so a synecdoche for the royal house; and a fertile valley, indeed the most abundant breadbasket of Israel. Further, the name itself is a pun: Jezreel means 'God sows', which is a good name for such rich farmlands; but carries the double entendre of God sowing destruction, as he warns in the naming oracle: 'for yet in a little while I will punish the house of Jehu for the blood of Jezreel, and I will put an end to the kingdom of the house of Israel' (1.4).

The import of the 'blood of Jezreel' can hardly be explained within a hermeneutics of apostasy for, according to the book of Kings, this blood was spilled in the context of Jehu's victory over the apostate Omrids and their Phoenician Baal cult (2 Kgs 9–10). Rather, in Hosea's mouth Jezreel functions as a political slogan, recalling the copious 'blood of Jezreel' which Jehu spilled in the establishment of his dynasty as an emblem for the degeneracy of the present political order. This prediction of the fall of Jehu's dynasty might insist that we situate this oracle prior to 745 BCE, were it not for the striking parallel between Jehu's accession by regicide and the political situation in Israel after Jeroboam II's death, which was marked by a series of royal assassinations. The violence by which Jehu overthrew the Omrids seemed to be reaping its karma in Hosea's own time, to the effect that the monarchy was unstable and vacillating in its alliances in a time when the Assyrian threat required far-sighted leadership. Thus Jezreel as a rhetorical device names the degenerate, blood-soaked royal house as the first-born 'son of fornication'; in other words, these kings are bastards.[1]

A related interpretive possibility connects the name Jezreel with the story of King Ahab's appropriation of Naboath's vineyard (1 Kgs 21), which, while originally circulated as propaganda against Omrid oppression, could as well have served as a vehicle of protest in Hosea's time against similar policies of monarchical land grabbing. The evocation of Jezreel links this seat of royal power to the matter of the stolen land and the fate of the nation; Hosea thus squarely lays the blame for the current crisis at the foot of the throne.[2]

---

1.   See also Hos. 7.4-7, where Hosea more directly expresses his judgment upon a political situation in which the kingship had become a revolving door of bloodshed. Here again, a metaphor of sexual transgression (this time male sexual transgression) gives force to the condemnation: 'They are all adulterers...all of them are hot as an oven, and they devour their rulers' (7.4, 7a).

2.   It is important to emphasize that the economic system in eighth-century Israel was not a nascent free-market economy; rather it was a 'command economy' under royal directive (Chaney, 'Bitter Bounty'). Much, if not all, of the commerce and trade was initiated and controlled by the crown, which used the profits not only to support an opulent royal establishment, but also for the purchase of additional national insurance in the form of military hardware. Those who controlled large estates did so by virtue of a monarchical land-grant system, in which royal servants and officials received land-grants and taxation privileges from the crown in return for their loyalty and continued support (Dearman, *Property Rights*, pp. 108-27). A certain percentage of the taxed yield would of course go to the crown. Also, the king himself directly controlled estates so large that they required a minor bureaucracy to administer them; 1 Chron. 27.25-31 illustrates this point in regards to the situation in Judah. A 'command economy' differs from capitalism in that the distribution and flow of wealth are determined more by the decisions of the royal administration than by the

The agricultural connotations carried by the name Jezreel are also evident in the rendering of Jezreel's mother, as in the opening oracle where the wayward wife of God is 'the *land* which fornicates mightily away from God' (1.2c). The identity between the woman and the fertile land is suggested again in ch. 2 when the husband's threat to strip his wife naked fades into images of drought and desolation upon the land; the divine husband says he shall 'make her like a wilderness, and set her like a parched land, and slay her with thirst' (2.3b [Heb. 2.5b]). Now the *land* is to become barren for the land itself has committed fornication and become guilty of betrayal, accepting seeds sown in it to yield an adulterous bounty that is not of Israel and for Israel, but is to be given to others.

In Hosea, the woman's body is the social body, but she is also at once the land, now sown for others, and the first fruit of her adulterous womb, Jezreel, whose name sounds so much like Israel, evokes the royal house and the violence and corruption which had become endemic there. The female body, the body politic and the fertile land intertwine in a dense symbolic complex that yields no unambiguous correspondences, but which evokes the reality of the contemporary situation as one of betrayal, bloodshed and 'adulterous' political and commercial liaisons.

For Hosea, female sexuality was not a sign for what was 'other' or foreign, as it is in the minds of Hosea's modern interpreters; rather, like the land, the fertile female body was a locus and symbol for the life and meaning of the social body in its continuity across the generations. In this setting, Hosea's imagery of Israel as the woman/land, who sells her body to multiple lovers and bears alien children, is no allegory for apostasy, but a symbol of the death of the nation.

forces of supply and demand (G. Lenski, *Human Societies: A Macrolevel Introduction to Sociology* [New York: McGraw-Hill, 1970], pp. 263-72). The royal house and its retainers were therefore the ones ultimately responsible for the social evils of Hosea's time.

Conclusion

Hosea was an angry man. But he was not angry because the people of Israel sought ritual assurance that their fields and their bodies would be fruitful. Rather, Hosea was angry because elite strategies of land accumulation and coordinate power politics had transgressed and profaned the sacred nexus of relationship among and between the people and their land. The transformation to a market economy, within which land, produce and people had been commodified, constituted a religious crisis concerning the meaning and identity of this people. Hosea's metaphor of the nation as a woman of fornications bearing children of fornications bespeaks his contemporary situation, in which the realities of intra-societal violence and the transgression of traditional communal values had irreparably ruptured the order of the world as known by these people.

The space limitations of this article do not allow for a sustained explication and defense of the thesis that Hosea's female sexual imagery carries socioeconomic and political connotations. However, I hope to have demonstrated that the traditional interpretation of adultery as a trope for apostasy is neither necessary nor even adequate to account for Hosea's use of female sexual imagery. The general consensus that Hosea's great point is to define an opposition between sex and the sacred is less a function of the text itself than a function of an interpretative approach which is, at the outset, burdened by implicitly dualistic modes of thinking about sex, gender and religion.

If one follows the path charted by this article, it appears in the end quite ironic that Hosea is understood as the champion of a dualistic religious vision, in which spiritual meanings are elevated above and opposed to the human involvement in materiality and corporeality. For at stake in Hosea's discourse is the loss of the sacred as it was manifest in the relationship of the people to the land and its produce, that is, in their relationship to the materiality of their existence. Read in this context, Hosea's dark and disturbing language of female sexuality does not symbolize an otherness that must be rejected, but points to that which was most essential to the meaning of his world and which has now been lost.

BOXING GOMER:
CONTROLLING THE DEVIANT WOMAN IN HOSEA 1–3

Yvonne Sherwood

In the thirteenth-century Conradin manuscript, the story of Hosea and Gomer's controversial marriage is illuminated in a particular way. Hosea—icon of grace and male supremacy—inclines his head to bless his prodigal wife, while Gomer, demure and coy, gratefully receives his blessing. The illustration catches the eye and controls the interpretation: it borders the text ideologically, as well as physically, by setting the parameters in which acceptable readings must operate. In this paper, I argue that androcentric commentary has illuminated (shed light on) the text from its own perspective, and has boxed Gomer in with words, to restrain her pernicious influence on the reader.

The consensus of commentary appears to be that Gomer desecrates the holy text, by breaking the rules of patriarchy and combining the roles of promiscuous woman[1] and wife (and,

---

1. In this paper I shall translate the phrase אשׁה זנוּנים variously as 'promiscuous woman', 'prostitute' and 'woman of harlotry' in order to do justice to Gomer's ambiguous status in the text. Following Phyllis Bird, I assume that the stem *znh* refers, more widely than *n'p*, to all pre- or extra-marital intercourse, and that the abstract plural noun points to habitual behaviour and inclination rather than profession. However, as Bird also observes, Hosea is the first text to develop the term figuratively, and broadens its usage in two ways. First, it uses it to include a sense of betrayal, usually limited to *n'p* since the woman is promiscuous away from (מאחרי) her husband. Secondly, it blurs the role of the אשׁה זנוּנים with that of the professional prostitute, since in ch. 2 the 'wife of harlotry' receives presents for her services. Though 'promiscuous woman' probably does most justice to the literal denotative sense, 'woman of harlotry' and 'prostitute' are incuded in the connotative sense. In using all three terms interchangeably, I want to reflect the way in which patriarchy does not

even more audaciously, prophet's wife). It is generally considered that Yahweh's command that Hosea take a 'wife of harlotry' is something of a divine *faux pas*, but since Yahweh cannot be fallible, the commentators' discomfort works itself out in the treatment, or erasure, of the difficult woman. As the infamous problem area of the text, Gomer is treated, not in the sense of objective detachment, but in the sense of remedying or doctoring her to give her a new, religiously marketable image. The woman is the object of the male gaze and is shaped by his desires: one commentator beautifies her physically as a 'rustic beauty of northern Israel';[1] another beautifies her morally, as an angel with a 'long overdue halo'.[2]

Attempts to remove or improve Gomer are so ingenious and creative that they seem to have more in common with midrashic storytelling than with the quasi-scientific objective ideal. A detailed analysis of male *readings* exposes the myth, as Esther Fuchs puts it, of the 'objective phallacy',[3] the fallacious distinction between commentary and reading, objective androcentricism and subjective feminism, in which the first term is privileged and the second subordinated. This study attempts to deconstruct this hierarchy, by showing that the difference between androcentric and feminist readings lies not in their inventiveness but in their self-consciousness about that inventiveness, and their status. For the privilege given to traditional readings depends on their relationship to the reading community rather than to the text, and androcentric readings are validated by tradition and by a dominant interpretive community. It is not just a case, as one feminist critic puts it, of 'canonical

discriminate between the three roles in this text, and to underline in the strongest possible terms, the perceived threat of Gomer's sexuality. See P. Bird, '"To Play the Harlot": An Enquiry into an Old Testament Metaphor', in P.L. Day (ed.), *Gender and Difference in Ancient Israel* (Minneapolis: Fortress Press, 1989), pp. 75-94.

1. T.K. Cheyne, *Hosea, with Notes and Introduction* (Cambridge: Cambridge University Press, 1887), p. 14.

2. L.W. Batten, 'Hosea's Message and Marriage', *JBL* 48 (1929), p. 257.

3. E. Fuchs, 'Contemporary Biblical Literary Criticism: The Objective Phallacy', in V.L. Tollers and J. Maier (eds.), *Mappings of the Biblical Terrain: The Bible as Text* (Bucknell Review; London and Toronto: Bucknell University Press, 1990), pp. 134-42.

texts' passing into the culture 'tagged with a patriarchal interpretation...[and] validated by what the Institution of Reading has understood'.[1] Rather the readings themselves assume a canonical status, and appear so 'naturally' connected to the text that even feminist readers find it difficult completely to disentangle themselves from their pervasive and 'orthodox' assumptions.[2]

One of the most common distinctions made between feminist and androcentric readings of biblical texts is that whereas the story and character of the male protagonist is clearly outlined, the woman's story is made up of silences, omissions and lacunae. This leads to the assumption, expressed by feminists and non-feminists, that the male reader reads with the text, and the feminist reader, in constructing the female's story, reads outside it, between the lines, or 'against the grain'.[3] While this distinction is helpful, it needs to be qualified: patriarchal readings may reinscribe the ideology of the text, but are no more faithful or legitimate in terms of detail. In Hosea, as much imagination is needed to construct an androcentric view of the domestic situation as to construct a feminist one, because the human is eclipsed by the divine, and both characters function as visual aids in

1. A. Munich, 'Notorious Signs, Feminist Criticism and Literary Tradition', in G. Greene and C. Kahn (eds.), *Making a Difference: Feminist Literary Criticism* (London: Methuen, 1985), p. 251.

2. The canonical status of male readings was demonstrated in a discussion in *The Independent* last year. In a rare example of Hosea in the news, Daphne Hampson described the text as 'a piece of pornographic literature: God, who is good and faithful, being compared to the (male) prophet, while that which is fickle—Israel—is captured by the imagery of a (female) prostitute described in lewd language' (D. Hampson, 'Christianity Will Always Be a Male Religion', *The Independent*, 15 November 1992). Instantly the dominant male reading reasserted itself, and one reader's response, published the next day, argued that Hampson did not do the 'great Israelite prophet' justice since she 'fail[ed] to make clear that Hosea loved his fickle wife and could not bear to see her destroyed by the inevitable results of her wayward behaviour' (A.A. Macintosh, *The Independent*, 16 November 1992). Though both Hampson and Macintosh were interpreting creatively, Macintosh seemed not to realize that he was doing so, and wrote with the confidence and authority of one who has tradition on his side.

3. J.C. Exum, *Fragmented Women: Feminist Subversions of Biblical Narratives* (JSOTSup, 163; Sheffield: JSOT Press, 1993), p. 11.

Yahweh's cosmic morality play. Textual fidelity is an illusion created by ideological mimicry: there is no more evidence to support the idea of 'a man wounded in his deepest feelings through an ill-fated marriage that saddened his life and coloured his thought'[1] than to identify Gomer, as some feminist critics are beginning to do, with the subversive power of female Canaanite deities.[2] Even commentators who automatically side with the prophet also concede that 'the book...has extremely little help to give us about the prophet himself':[3] comically, J. Paterson, who seems to be privy to Hosea's sexual secrets, his beliefs and his life-story also admits that 'the one fact the prophet tells us concerning himself is that he married *Gomer bat Diblayim* who bore him three children and was guilty of marital infidelity'.[4] In claiming that as much information is given about Gomer as about Hosea, I am not trying covertly to redeem Hosea as a non-patriarchal text, or to displace all culpability from text to interpretation, since to say that a text sides with one character and that a text gives more information about one character is to say two completely different things. Gomer and Hosea are equal in one sense only, in the scanty information that is given about them, and the text remains, as Marie-Theres Wacker so aptly put it, 'a "right strawy epistle" for the *Woman's Bible*'.[5]

The politics of 'objectivity' is a politics of exclusion: as Esther

1.   C.H. Toy, 'Note on Hos. 1–3', *JBL* 32 (1913), p. 77.
2.   For examples of this type of approach, see H. Balz-Cochois, 'Gomer oder die Macht der Astarte: Versuch einer feministischen Interpretation von Hos. 1–4', *EvT* 42 (1982), pp. 37-65; M.-T. Wacker, 'Frau-Sexus-Macht: Eine feministische Relecture des Hoseabuches', in *Der Gott der Männer und Frauen: Theol. z. Zeit* 2 (Düsseldorf: Patmos, 1987), pp. 101-25.
3.   G. von Rad, *Old Testament Theology. II. The Theology of Israel's Prophetic Traditions* (trans. D.M.G. Stalker; Edinburgh: Oliver & Boyd, 1965), p. 138.
4.   J. Paterson, 'Hosea', in F.C. Grant and H.H. Rowley (eds.), *A Dictionary of the Bible* (Edinburgh: T. & T. Clark, 2nd edn, 1963), p. 397. Among other things, they deduce from this scanty information that Hosea 'sublimated' his 'sex instinct' into love for God and humanity, that he married a woman who was initially pure but disappointed him, and that 'he discovered the gospel buried deep in...his suffering' and so became 'essentially an evangelist, a prophet of grace'.
5.   Wacker, 'Frau-Sexus-Macht', p. 102.

Fuchs points out, the 'choral harmony' between 'authoritative narrators' and 'objective critics', father texts and faithful sons,[1] creates a strong sense of cosy reciprocity and mutual affirmation that reinforces female marginality and unquestioningly perpetuates patriarchal values. The illusion of closeness to the text, ideological solidarity posturing as 'objectivity', is enhanced by the style of traditional commentary: the way in which the male critic subordinates himself to the text, and patiently examines each verse in sequence, suggests that he is subordinated to the master-text, and governed by it alone. 'Objectivity' is a political word that implies superiority, validity and privileged contact with reality but, once the spell of 'objectivity' is broken, what remains is an underlying sense of 'legitimacy', made explicit in the work of Meir Sternberg. Sternberg's much-criticized claim, that there are 'legitimate' and 'illegitimate' ways of filling gaps,[2] only elaborates on the latent assumption of many readings— that sons are the true, hoped-for heirs of the biblical text and women the less-desired offspring, and that inventions used to read against the ideology of the text are somehow more 'subjective' than inventions used to support it.

In this paper I seek to explore male solidarity, among readers and between readers and the text, but also to expose the subjectivity of androcentric readings. Disturbed by Gomer, the text urges control of the deviant woman, and demands that she be boxed in, hemmed in by thorn bushes, and surrounded by walls.[3] The way in which all male readings, as diverse as the Midrash and twentieth-century Christian commentary, are intent on taming the *tame* underlines their unity with one another and with the text, but at the same time deconstructs the distinction between androcentricism and feminism because it shows that traditional readers as well as feminists can be 'resisting readers'[4] and resist elements of the text that displease them. Ironically, androcentric readers repeat the ideology of the

1. Fuchs, 'The Objective Phallacy', p. 138.
2. M. Sternberg, *The Poetics of Biblical Narrative: Ideological Literature and the Drama of Reading* (Bloomington: Indiana University Press, 1985), p. 188.
3. Hos. 2.6 (RSV).
4. J. Fetterley, *The Resisting Reader: A Feminist Approach to American Fiction* (Bloomington: Indiana University Press, 1978).

text, that the woman must be tamed, specifically by adamantly resisting, avoiding or rewriting the statement that Hosea and Yahweh associate themselves with such a woman. This paper begins with an examination of four ancient and four modern strategies for coping with a difficult woman, and then moves on to consider the effect of this dubious critical legacy on a contemporary feminist re-reading.

Strategies for Coping with a Difficult Woman

Midrash Rabbah: From 'Promiscuous Woman' to 'Lethargic Queen'
Midrash Rabbah, a kind of rabbinic reader-response, creates three surrogate stories for Hosea's marriage, one of which could appropriately be called 'The Tale of the Lethargic Queen'.[1] The plot is basically as follows. Servants overhear a king lavishly praising his wife, and imagine her to be the perfect woman, but are then surprised to see her 'looking disreputable, her house untidy, the beds not made'. The story ends with a moral exhortation to all negligent wives, and by inference all slothful servants of Yahweh: 'If he lavishes such praise on her when she is *disreputable*, how much more when she is at her *best!*' The story softens and domesticates the disturbing original by changing the wife of harlotry into a wife of lethargy. According to Proverbs, the antithesis of the good wife who 'works with willing hands' to spin wool and flax is 'the adulteress with her smooth words', whose lips drip with honey and whose speech is smoother than oil.[2] Presumably, an intermediate version of the evil woman is the negation of the good woman, whose house is untidy and her beds not made. From the stock of images of pernicious womanhood, the Midrash selects the milder figure, and the audaciously bad wife is restyled as simply less than satisfactory.

Targum Jonathan: Diblayim (Two Figs) into Fig Leaves
A midrashic rule of thumb would seem to be: whenever a prostitute crosses your path, circumnavigate her as widely as possible. The rabbis seem to be of the same persuasion as Judah,

1.   *Num. R.* 2.15.
2.   Prov. 31.13; 2.16.

who, according to Midrash Rabbah, would have avoided Tamar altogether, had not an angel of the Lord appeared on the scene, and proleptically hinted that the presence of the prostitute was, regrettably, a key factor in the birth of the next generation.[1] Targum Jonathan does not simply swerve to avoid the offensive woman, but erases her altogether. With a subtle change in pointing, the targumist alters the strange dual form *Diblayim* to a derivative of 'fig', *d^ebēlâ*, and reduces the offensive woman to the inoffensive whisper of falling fig-leaves. Hos. 1.2-3 in the More Refined Version reads as follows:

> The beginning of the word of the Lord with Hosea: and the Lord said to Hosea, 'Go and prophesy against the inhabitants of an idolatrous city, who continue to sin. For the inhabitants of the land surely go away from the worship of the Lord'. So he went and prophesied concerning them that, if they repented, they would be forgiven; but if not they would fall as the leaves of the fig-tree fall.[2]

As in Eden, fig leaves are used as a cover-up and Gomer bat Diblayim is concealed by the phrase 'as the leaves of the fig tree fall'. The Targum replaces conception with concepts, and sex and children with a philosophical encounter between justice and iniquity, so pressing a startlingly physical text into the mould of conventionality.

The Babylonian Talmud: Manhandling Gomer's Image

In *Pesaḥim*, the prophet is recast as a foolish 'old man', a Polonius-type figure, who has not learnt his lines or his function properly, and who is given a wife of harlotry partly as punishment, and partly as part of a private re-education programme. When the Holy One approached Hosea and accused his people of sinning, the text is quite clear that the prophet *'should* have replied "These are thy children...extend thy mercy to them"',[3] but instead he ineptly and rather tactlessly suggested that the Holy One find himself another nation. By making Hosea the object of a joke, the text reduces his status until he deserves

1. *Gen. R.* 85.8.
2. K.J. Cathcart and R.P. Gordon, *The Aramaic Bible. XIV. The Targum of the Minor Prophets* (Edinburgh: T. & T. Clark, 1989).
3. *Pes.* 87a-b.

such a woman, so that the embarrassment of his marriage is perceived as apt retaliation on the part of the exasperated deity.

Though divinely ordained, the marriage of a prophet with a 'wife of harlotry' is hardly what we would expect from a 'marriage made in heaven', and the Talmud counteracts the implied unfairness of Yahweh in arranging such a bad marriage for his man. Interestingly, to my knowledge, it is the only text to solve the problem with adjustments to Hosea's character, rather than Gomer's,[1] and since the redemption of the text no longer depends on improving Gomer's image, this frees the rabbis to fantasize about the precise extent of her sexual depravity. The name *Gomer-bat-Diblayim* is passed around the interpretive circle, and variously manhandled:

> '*Gomer*': Rab said, [That intimates] that all satisfied their lust [*gômerîm*] on her; 'the daughter of Diblayim': [a woman of] ill fame [*dibbâ*] and the daughter of a woman of ill fame [*dibbâ*]. Samuel said: [It means] she was as sweet in everyone's mouth as a cake of figs [*dᵉbēlâ*]. While R. Johanan interpreted: [It means] they all trod upon her as a cake of figs [is trodden].[2]

'Gomer' is passed around from man to man and becomes the plaything of wordplay, as every possible dimension of her name is exploited. The text foregrounds the tension of the male response to the promiscuous woman, for the same consciousness that perceives her as a liability (more suited to a clown than a prophet) also revels in her erotic potential. The combination of censure and exploitation still characterizes social and religious responses to the promiscuous woman, and commentators have continued to add their own allegorical innuendoes to the rabbis'

---

1. The only other text I have discovered that is prepared to sacrifice Hosea's reputation in order to redeem the text is a letter from Peter Damian to his bishops warning them not to imitate the very unbishoplike Hosea. According to Damian, Hosea broke the law regarding appropriate wives for priests (Lev. 21.13-15), and having delighted in the 'wickedly soothing caresses' of an improper woman, reaped disaster as signified in the auspicious names of his children. P. Damian, 'Letter 59', in T.P. Halton (ed.), *The Fathers of the Church: Medieval Continuation*. II. *Peter Damian, Letters 31-60* (trans. O.J. Blum; Washington: Catholic University of America Press, 1990), pp. 394-403.

2. *Pes.* 87a-b.

images of fig-like succulence, and unlimited sexual power. In the 'male fantasies of commentators',[1] as one feminist critic puts it, Gomer has been perceived as the 'two-figged kitchen maid',[2] a cheap women who can be purchased for two cakes of figs, the woman who is complete (*gmr*) in her beauty or her depravity,[3] and the 'vile strumpet of the Baalim'[4] whose name was vocalized using the pointing of *bošet*, shame.[5] No hyperbole is out of bounds: critics smirk at her, as 'something of an expert in the erotic arts',[6] and condemn her, for falling into the ultimate debasement of the abyss of prostitution,[7] ironically depicting her 'unrestrained and lustful character'[8] in descriptions that are themselves unrestrained.

Ibn Ezra and John Calvin: The Prostitute in Parenthesis
Eager to restrain the subversive influence of a promiscuous woman on a supposedly moral text, commentators struggle to consign her to various forms of non-reality. Ibn Ezra, a staunch advocate of *peshat* or simple interpretation, is embarrassed by the pernicious woman into imitating uncircumcised scholars, and committing what he regards as the sin of allegory. He calls his interpretation dream rather than allegory, but the effect is the same.[9] Because he pronounces marriage and conception

1. Wacker, 'Frau-Sexus-Macht', p. 110.
2. E. Nestle, 'Miszellen', *ZAW* 29 (1909), pp. 233-41, and W. Baumgartner, 'Miszellen', *ZAW* 33 (1913), p. 78.
3. J. Burroughs, *An Exposition of the Prophecy of Hosea* (Edinburgh: James Nichol, 1643), p. 9.
4. Paterson, 'Hosea', p. 397.
5. W. Rudolph, *Hosea* (KAT, 13.1; Gütersloh: Gerd Mohn, 1966), p. 49ff.
6. A. van Selms, 'Hosea and Canticles', *OTWSA* 7.8 (1964–1965), pp. 88-89.
7. L. Bouyer, *La Bible et l'évangile* (Paris: 1951), p. 66.
8. Wacker, 'Frau-Sexus-Macht', p. 110.
9. Just like allegory, Ibn Ezra's dream ushers the reader into a series of one-to-one correspondences, in which, for example, the phrase 'and she bore a son' refers to the generation following Jeroboam, the son of Joash, the conception of a daughter, *Lô' Rûḥāmâ*, refers to the following generation, and the reference to the birth of *Lô' 'Ammî* means that 'the exiled tribes begot children in Israel'. See A. Lipshitz, *The Commentary of Rabbi Abraham Ibn Ezra on Hosea* (New York: Sepher-Hermon Press, 1988), pp. 21-22.

incomprehensible, he consigns all and especially the אשׁת זנונים to a 'vision of prophecy or a dream of the night'.[1] Every time that Gomer or implied intercourse is mentioned, he reasserts the dream framework: 'So he went and took the woman mentioned above. All this he perceived as a vision.'[2] Gomer is only mentioned elliptically, as the 'woman mentioned above', and even in name she is determinedly avoided.

John Calvin also places the woman in parenthesis, and consigns her to the realm of quasi-reality using the medium of the stage. Like Ibn Ezra he avoids the pernicious influence of the woman as person or even as name, and in his presentation the prophet takes part in a one-man stage show, with no other living participants. The play begins surrealistically, as Hosea brings a pile of putrefying figs onto the stage, which he then 'names for his wife'.[3] Yet anxious that even this act of erasure has not completely reformed the text Calvin, like Ibn Ezra, constantly interposes with a parenthetical 'let the reader understand' as soon as marriage, conception and birth are mentioned. When Hosea declares that he has married 'a wife habituated to adulteries and whoredoms', Calvin adds 'the whole people knew that he had done no such thing'.[4] When this wife conceives, he is quick to emphasize her non-existence: 'It now follows the wife conceived—the imaginary one, the wife as represented and exhibited'.[5]

Twentieth-Century Midrashim

Modern critical commentary tends to consider itself superior to stories, figs and other such fanciful notions. As Hans Frei has argued in *The Eclipse of Biblical Narrative*,[6] under the terms of historical criticism the question of the text's validity came to

1. Lipshitz, *Ibn Ezra on Hosea*, p. 7.
2. Lipshitz, *Ibn Ezra on Hosea*, p. 21.
3. J. Calvin, *Commentaries on the Twelve Minor Prophets*. I. *Hosea* (trans. J. Owen; Edinburgh: Edinburgh Printing Company, 1846), p. 48.
4. Calvin, *Hosea*, p. 45.
5. Calvin, *Hosea*, p. 48.
6. H. Frei, *The Eclipse of Biblical Narrative* (London: Yale University Press, 1980).

depend on proving the text's historical authenticity. Yet ironically, proving the validity of Hos. 1.2 has always depended on affirming its *non*-historicity, and twentieth-century accounts of Hosea's marriage are not qualitatively different from their ancient counterparts. In this section I want to look how the 'modern-myth makers',[1] as H.L. Ginsberg calls them, or twentieth-century midrashim, have compiled their own creative *gemara*, a cluster of colourful stories around the edges of the text. I shall examine four strategies, romance, hagiography, metaphor and redaction criticism; all of which strive to improve the harlot (like the Midrash) or remove her (like the Targum), so struggling to insist that the Lord did *not* say to Hosea, 'go take a wife of harlotry'.

Romance, or Gomer the Beloved

My first example of twentieth-century *'aggādâ* is the poignant tale of star-crossed lovers, a kind of scholarly station bookshop romance conceived, most flamboyantly, by T.K. Cheyne, and retold here in his own words.

As a northern prophet, Cheyne's Hosea was affected 'by the genial moods of nature in the north' and had an 'expansive, childlike character'.[2] The exquisite love poem which we know as the Song of Songs affected him deeply, and in it he read of the 'rustic beauties of northern Israel', beautiful not only in their 'external attractions', but also in their 'gentle and noble womanly virtues'.[3] He fell in love and, in Gomer-bat-Diblayim, he thought he had found a 'bride like the Shulamite of his favourite poem'.[4] She betrayed him, but he pursued her, so following the pull of 'heart-logic'[5]—a compulsion which the critic, and his many successors, seem to share. Carried away on a tide of romanticism, critics suspend all critical judgment, and the figure of the prostitute seems to make a fool of them. Like babbling fools in front of a beautiful woman, they compete in

1. H.L. Ginsberg, 'Hosea', *EncJud*, VIII, p. 1012.
2. T.K. Cheyne, *Hosea, with Notes and Introduction* (Cambridge: Cambridge University Press, 1887), p. 10.
3. Cheyne, *Hosea*, pp. 14-15.
4. Cheyne, *Hosea*, p. 20.
5. Cheyne, *Hosea*, p. 19.

descriptions of just how beautiful she was and how much Hosea loved her, and most extremely, O.R. Sellers resorted to the words of the song 'I've found my sweetheart Sally' to convey the depths of Hosea's love: 'What she has been, what she has done, I never care to know, because to me she'll always be as pure as driven snow'.[1]

Male critics cannot find words enough to express their solidarity with Hosea the victim: G.A.F. Knight strained the sentence, as well as the facts, in writing of 'poor, dejected, spurned and broken-hearted Hosea';[2] George Farr judged that the prophet had 'suffered far more poignantly than Job';[3] while G.W. Ewald, equating Hosea the man and Hosea the text, maintained that the text is so disjointed because it breaks itself up into sobs.[4] Supported by such eminent figures as Wellhausen, W.R. Harper, and W. Robertson Smith, the 'tragic story of Hosea's sin-blasted home'[5] has achieved canonical status, and S.L. Brown, in his introduction to his 1932 commentary, found no reason to question the now naturalized story. Undeterred by the lack of information, critics have formed a kind of Nicene Creed about the life of Hosea. Brown explains that

> These chapters describe how his marriage to a woman who he greatly loved and the breaking up of his home through his wife's adultery led the prophet to understand more fully than before the heinousness of Israel's apostasy and the depth of Yahweh's love for his people.[6]

In an article by George Farr, the story becomes an item of faith, recited like a creed: 'We believe,' wrote Farr, 'that there was

---

1. O.R. Sellers, 'Hosea's Motives', *AJSL* 41 (1924–25), p. 244.

2. G.A.F. Knight, *Hosea: Introduction and Commentary* (London: SCM Press, 1960), p. 25.

3. G. Farr, 'The Concept of Grace in the Book of Hosea', *ZAW* 70 (1958), p. 103.

4. G.W. Ewald, *Commentary on the Prophets of the Old Testament.* I. *Joel, Amos, Hosea and Zechariah* (trans. J.F. Smith; London: Williams & Norgate, 1875), p. 218.

5. W.E. Crane, 'The Prophecy of Hosea', *BSac* 89 (1932), p. 481.

6. S.L. Brown, *The Book of Hosea with Introduction and Notes* (London: Methuen, 1932), p. 1.

only one woman in Hosea's life; she was truly his wife and the marriage was originally for love...'[1]

Hagiography, or Gomer the Saint

The love story makes the text more palatable: despite the violence of ch. 2, Hosea becomes a figure of grace, and a fore-runner of Christ. H.H. Rowley, for example, appeals to the epistle to the Hebrews, and claims that, like 'Another', Hosea 'learned obedience through the things he suffered'.[2] The story of 'Gomer the Saint' also takes its precedent from Hebrews in the sense that Gomer gets the Rahab treatment, and is restyled as an exemplary figure in a catalogue of faith. If the first story is that of the forgiven and chastened harlot, the second is paradoxically that of the *chaste* harlot, an oxymoron which originates with Jerome, who argued, impossibly but adamantly, that 'The prophet did not lose his chastity because he was joined to a harlot, but that the harlot gained a chastity she did not have previously'.[3] The same combination of determination and impossibility is found in L.W. Batten's 1928 address to the (then) Society of Biblical Literature and Exegesis in which he approached the confessedly difficult task of 'put[ting] a bit of a long overdue halo about the head of one heretofore adjudged worthy of stoning for her sins'.[4] Like Christ he attempted to redeem the woman caught in adultery by restraining the stones of her critics, but grace does not translate to scholarship very well, and his magnanimity forced him into logical impasses. Batten argued, for example, that Hosea's use of images of adultery proves that he had a high sense of marital fidelity, which he would 'naturally' have learned from his wife,[5] and like Jerome he attempted to compensate for his less than compelling

1. Farr, 'Concept of Grace', p. 100.
2. H.H. Rowley, 'The Marriage of Hosea', in *Men of God: Studies in Old Testament History and Prophecy* (London: Nelson, 1963), p. 97.
3. Jerome, *Commentaria in Osee Prophetam*, 25: 823, cit. H.C. Oswald, *Luther's Works*. XVIII. *Lectures on the Minor Prophets* (St Louis, MO: Concordia, 1975), p. 3.
4. Batten, 'Message', p. 257.
5. Batten, 'Message', p. 262.

logic with absolute phrases such as 'naturally',[1] 'I think we would all agree',[2] and 'Beyond reasonable doubt'.[3] In the absence of evidence—Gomer left no diaries, and there were no eyewitnesses—his argument is ridiculously unequivocal, and his one-sided and defensive reading appears to be as much a reaction against what Milton termed 'this whore pluralitie' as against whoredom itself. His conclusion emphasizes the potentially unlimited power of the reader as the judge's hammer comes down with absolute certainty: 'The court is all-powerful,' he pronounces, 'and finds a verdict easy: the charge against Gomer is dismissed. Next case.'[4]

Batten's article is a particularly extreme example of the imposition of the critical will on the text. The female is shaped by the male, the Hebrew text is Christianized and moralized, the text is coerced by the powerful reader, and ambiguity bows to the critical demand for univocality. In each case, the weaker capitulates to the stronger and the dominant ideology triumphs. Batten is not the only critic to take this stance: Leroy Waterman enthusiastically defends Gomer in a string of hyperbole, and maintains that she was 'not a woman who meant to be bad, or was conscious of being bad', but was a 'brave woman, a devoted woman, yes, and a true-hearted woman too'.[5] Even a meticulous scholar such as H.W. Wolff cannot resist an at least partial redemption of the promiscuous woman, with all the logical problems that involves. For Wolff, it means abandoning his rigorous standards of historical scholarship, and arguing, against the evidence, for Canaanite bridal initiation rites. He does not absolve Gomer completely but provides *mitigating* circumstances, arguing that Gomer was not 'an especially wicked exception' but merely an 'average, modern Israelite woman'.[6] In the revision of Gomer as a thoroughly modern miss, Wolff appears to be acting sacrificially on behalf of the text

---

1. Batten, 'Message', p. 262.
2. Batten, 'Message', p. 262.
3. Batten, 'Message', p. 272.
4. Batten, 'Message', p. 275.
5. L. Waterman, 'The Marriage of Hosea', *JBL* 37 (1918), p. 201.
6. H.W. Wolff, *Hosea* (trans. G. Stansell; Philadelphia: Fortress Press, 1974), p. 15.

and transgressing his own standards, so that Yahweh and Hosea will not be found transgressing theirs.

Escape by Metaphor

There are two main ways in which metaphor is used to dilute Gomer's offence: stressing that harlotry is only a metaphor for idolatry, and emphasizing Gomer's role as a metaphor for Israel. Using the first method, Gomer-bat-Diblayim becomes a woman of *idolatry*, rather than a woman of *harlotry*: as J. Coppens argues she is *only* a prostitute in the 'religious, metonymic sense of the word'.[1] Yet Coppens also betrays the fact that this conclusion was preordained by his own expectations, numbering himself among 'those of us who are of the opinion that *Gomer's reputation must be improved...*'[2] The metaphorical option seems to act as a safety net for those who *cannot* read the text literally. There is a necessity in operation: Coppens writes '*Il faut blanchir Gomer*'—we *must* whiten Gomer.[3]

The second way of whitening, or whitewashing the text, is related to the first, and stresses Gomer's role as a substitute for the nation. Because Israel is elsewhere portrayed as a child with his parent, critics insist that Gomer must be originally childlike and innocent and therefore must be a virgin at the point of her marriage. Because Gomer and the child describe the same tenor—Israel—the assumption is that they are equivalent: interestingly though the nation is also described as a stubborn heifer, half-baked bread and a crooked merchant, and no attempt is made to harmonize these images. My suspicion is that altering Gomer to fit the tenor Israel is a foil for altering her to fit the moral requirements of a biblical text: conveniently, with a little metaphorical remanoeuvring, I.H. Eybers rejoices to find that all 'ethical objection' 'disappears entirely'.[4] As in Coppens's article an imperative is in operation: A.B. Davidson, in the first edition of *A Dictionary of the Bible*, argues that Gomer cannot already be a 'sinner' because this 'does not suit the symbolism', and is a

1. J. Coppens, 'L'histoire matrimoniale d'Osée', *BBB* 1 (1950), pp. 39-40.
2. Coppens, 'L'histoire', p. 43.
3. Coppens, 'L'histoire', p. 43.
4. I.H. Eybers, 'The Matrimonial Life of Hosea', *OTWSA* 7.8 (1964–65), p. 20.

sense which 'the words cannot bear'.[1] For 'words' and 'symbolism' substitute 'commentator': perhaps it is a sense which does not suit the commentator, and which he cannot bear. Norman Snaith writes: 'If the allegory is to be complete, *we need a Gomer who* is at first faithful and later becomes unfaithful'.[2] The tell-tale phrase 'we need a Gomer who' implies that there are potentially many versions of Gomer, and that they are selected, like models from a catalogue, to serve a particular textual look.

Redaction Criticism: From Moral to Textual Corruption

Just as the Midrash deftly circumnavigates the image of the prostitute, so modern critics make deliberate detours in order to deflect the reader's attention away from the problematic woman. G.A.F. Knight makes much of the phrase 'so he went' and praises Hosea's obedience, without confronting the dilemma of what Hosea went to do,[3] while Walter Vogels obscures the moral dilemma with praise, and applauds the prophet for his consistency in living out his own sermon illustration.[4]

Redaction criticism, while it has had some useful suggestions to make concerning Judean editing of the text, has sanctioned this glossing with the aura of objective methodology. Invoking redaction criticism, a respected methodology, as their witness, critics such as W.R. Harper, L.W. Batten and H. Birkeland,[5] as well as their more recent successors, have elided the phrase 'of

1. A.B. Davidson, 'Hosea', in J. Hastings (ed.), *A Dictionary of the Bible* (Edinburgh: T. & T. Clark, 1904), p. 421. The second edition rectified this evasion by deliberately confronting the 'sordid, solid facts'; Paterson, 'Hosea', p. 398.

2. N. H. Snaith, *Amos, Hosea, and Micah* (London: Epworth Press, 1959), p. 53; my italics.

3. Knight, *Hosea*, pp. 41-42.

4. W. Vogels, 'Osée-Gomer car et comme Yahweh Israël, Os 1-3', NRT 103 (1981), pp. 722-23.

5. W.R. Harper, *A Critical and Exegetical Commentary on Amos and Hosea* (Edinburgh: T. & T. Clark, 1905); Batten, 'Message'; H. Birkeland, *Zum Hebräischen Traditionswesen: Die Komposition der Prophetischen Bücher des Altes Testament* (Oslo: Jacob Dybwad, 1938).

whoredoms' as, in Batten's words, a 'clumsy gloss'.[1] This has allowed them, conveniently, to ascribe the seeming *moral* corruption of the text to *textual* corruption, and rather like those who protest that Gomer became harlotrous, to keep the wife in her original pure form, without the harlotries which, they claim, were added later.

The problem with redaction criticism is that it can look suspiciously like editing. The critic can effectively place in the hands of redactors 1, 2 and 3 the editorial changes that *he* would like to make. The redactionist's scissors are potentially all-powerful, and he can cut and paste the text until its ideology is a reprint of his own. The danger of the theoretical Ur-text is that it can become a repository for all the critic's ideals, and anything which does not fit this ideal vision can be described as a 'later addition'. As one early critic, who was well before his time, put it in a critique of W.R. Harper:

> All the passages which have been...excised have the same fault in the eyes of the modern radical critic, viz. that they contradict his cherished theories. This is their crime and excision is their punishment.[2]

From Male to Female Reading Strategies

Though chronologically and culturally diverse, a male readership is united in its protest about the difficult woman, and four major strategies for coping with her begin to emerge. She is *contained*, and her pernicious effect diluted or mitigated; the threat of her is *erased*; she is *humiliated*; or she is forcibly *improved*, in varying degrees, as 'wife of lethargy', redacted 'wife' or martyr. Comparing commentary and text suggests that the faithful sons, like henchmen, are in fact carrying out the threats of the father text, issued against the uncooperative woman in Hosea 2. Yahweh/Hosea threaten to contain her by 'hedg[ing] up her way with thorns, and build[ing] a wall against her';[3] commentary boxes her in with words, and consigns her to a dream, a play or a parenthesis, designed to keep her from

1. Batten, 'Message', p. 265.
2. M. Scott, *The Message of Hosea* (New York: Macmillan, 1921), p. 22.
3. Hos. 2.6 (RSV).

influencing and spoiling a male-scripted 'reality'. The text threatens to erase her, by slaying her with thirst;[1] critics invent all sorts of ingenious ways of spiriting Gomer out of the text, awkwardly allegorizing to replace her with piles of figs or fig leaves. The text threatens to humiliate her by stripping her in the sight of her lovers:[2] commentary humiliates her by associating her name with 'shame' and, like the text, titillates as it humiliates, in excessive fantasies about the precise extent of her depravity. The text is obsessed with returning her to innocence, with making her respond 'as in the days of her youth':[3] critics use metaphor to insist that Gomer was youthful and innocent, and forcibly remove her harlotries by redaction.

Like the text, commentary shapes Gomer according to the desires of a violent and stringent purism: remade according to narrow definitions, she must either become a woman in white with golden 'halo', the subservient female icon of patriarchy, or she must fit the only alternative definition, as completely depraved whore. Male critics tend to empathize with Yahweh/Hosea's insistence that the woman must be pressed into moral conformity, and can be even more forceful than the text in their demands for reformation. Just as Hosea was supposedly caught up into Yahweh's emotions,[4] they are caught up into the text's, so creating a trinity of sympathy which unites against the female. L. Bouyer sympathizes with a love that 'would not tolerate any stain in his beloved', and that 'could not resign itself' to the fact of Gomer's harlotry: his feeling and the prophet's become curiously entangled as he insists that Hosea wanted her 'pure, as on the first day of her marriage', and needed to give her a 'new and unalterable virginity'.[5] Reinforcing the distinction between ideological affinity and objective fidelity to the text, many critics perpetuate the text's ideology—that men can issue ultimatums about how their brides must look and behave—specifically *by* denying the detail. Like the prophet, they find themselves unable to resign themselves

1. Hos. 2.3.
2. Hos. 2.10.
3. Hos. 2.3, 15.
4. Von Rad, *The Theology of Israel's Prophetic Traditions*, p. 140.
5. Bouyer, *La Bible et l'évangile*, p. 66.

to the wife of harlotry, which leads them specifically to resist the text in its offensive declaration that the prophet deliberately took for his wife a blemished woman.

In the text as in commentary, a strong negative reaction against the deviant woman inadvertently implies the threat of her potential power. Beneath the surface level of repulsion and censure lies fascination and *need*: Yahweh and Hosea need a 'woman of harlotry' as a visual aid for their symbolic message, and ironically censure her for the harlotry they have requested.[1] By enlisting and denouncing the woman on the same basis—promiscuity—the text expresses, on a symbolic, displaced level, the ambiguous response of patriarchal society to the prostitute. Commentary is even more overt in its mixed responses, and even as it censures her, betrays its need of her, as the seduced imagination fantasizes about Gomer's fig-like succulence, and the precise extent of her sexual prowess. The overtly sexual woman has the power to embarrass and intimidate and, in their hasty attempts to look away, scholars become clumsy and awkward and even, embarrassingly, break their own rules, like Ibn Ezra or H.W. Wolff.

The insistence on Gomer's silence betrays the greatest fear, the fear of hearing the woman's point of view. Stringent censorship suggests that, if her voice were heard, it would subvert and seriously jeopardize the patriarchal perspective. As in all aspects of its treatment of Gomer, commentary is only following the directions of the text, a text which outlaws her opinion and only allows her voice to be 'heard' through the filter of reported speech and male polemic.[2] Ironically, the male speaker can only imagine a perfect reconciliation scene by erasing Gomer's voice and autonomy, and scripting her: 'Then she shall say, "I will go after my first husband, for it was better with me then than now"...And there she shall answer as in the days of her youth...and in that day you will call me "my

---

1. It is interesting that most commentators tend to underplay the fact that Yahweh requests and needs a 'woman of harlotry' by rewriting the order of the story. According to most commentators, Hosea married a woman who later became promiscuous, and Yahweh/Hosea cleverly adapted this unfortunate fact to good purposes in their moral drama.

2. Hos. 2. 5, 12.

husband"'.[1] Reconciliation scenes with only one protagonist are not very convincing, and add to the dominant impression that only by restraining the female can patriarchy achieve what it wants. Gomer is forbidden to speak so that she cannot spoil the narrative, but the tactic works against itself, because censored voices are always the most intriguing.

In contrast to the conventional tableau of grace, Hosea 1–3 can also be read as a tableau of patriarchy, the establishment of a system by the systematic exclusion, entrapment and repression of the female will. The threat of the 'woman of harlotry' is that of the countervoice, the opposite which, if listened to, threatens to relativize and subvert the absolute and univocal main/male perspective. Reading the gaps in a different (but equally legitimate) way provides clues as to why Gomer is so feared, and why she must be excluded from the happy-ever-after, if there is to be one. For though we are given very few details about her, each one constitutes a threat and an act of resistance to patriarchal absolutes. As 'wife of harlotry' she conflates mutual exclusives and breaks patriarchal taboos, and the birth of three children in succession[2] betrays a fear of the unmitigated power of procreation. Unlike her barren and assimilated sisters, Sarah, Rebekah, Rachel and Hannah, Gomer represents uncensored, unrestricted woman, who is dealt with in the course of the narrative rather than prior to it, in her presentation. The majority of women in the Hebrew Bible are already tamed before we encounter them—that is, they are infertile and dependent on Yahweh's will. Gomer is dependent neither on Yahweh nor her husband for conception, and becomes a rare and fearful spectre of autonomous female sexuality.[3] Though Hosea intervenes and calls her children 'Not Loved', she weans (and presumably suckles) them,[4] so placing a question mark in the margin of the curse. Physically, she expresses her resistance

---

1. Hos. 2. 7, 15, 16.
2. Hos. 1. 3-9.
3. For an excellent discussion of how the Hebrew Bible dissociates women and the power of procreation, see E. Fuchs, 'The Literary Characterization of Mothers and Sexual Politics in the Hebrew Bible', *Semeia* 46 (1989), pp. 151-66.
4. Hos. 1.8.

by running away, expressing dissatisfaction with her husband by pursuing other, more attractive offers.

Whereas most texts present the woman as already assimilated, Hosea 1–3 is intriguing because it dramatizes the battle of wills, albeit from a one-sided perspective. Just as androcentric criticism instinctively perpetuates and affirms the male perspective, so the woman reading the biblical text can unite with the woman in the biblical text, and extrapolate from the glimpses of defiance to perpetuate her disturbing influence. Norman Snaith makes Gomer according to his need, and it is the feminist critic's prerogative to make her according to hers. According to Mary Ann Tolbert, the 'profoundly liberating dynamic of the feminist movement' is the freedom to proclaim a feminist perspective as 'legitimate' rather than 'marginal and deviant as patriarchy would have it';[1] but, even when reading is stripped of polemical claims to 'objectivity', and reduced to the lowest common denominator of need, this process can be easier in theory than in practice. For women as well as men have been taught to see the male perspective as normal and legitimate; or, as J. Fetterly puts it: 'Though one of the most persistent of literary stereotypes is the castrating bitch, the cultural reality is not the emasculation of men by women but the immasculation of women by men'.[2] A brief examination of Helgard Balz-Cochois's essay on Gomer's power shows how the resisting reader sides with the resisting character but, even as she threatens to 'blow up' scholarly theology[3] by 'redeeming (Gomer) from silence',[4] she shows signs of being intimidated by the pervasive ideology she seeks to oppose.

Balz-Cochois's provocative reading of Gomer's story begins defiantly: confronting those who may condemn her 'sub-jectivity' she argues that the role of her poetic story is to counter the romantic fables of the past, and only shows as much sympathy towards Gomer as scholars have shown towards her

---

1. M.A. Tolbert, 'Protestant Feminists and the Bible: On the Horns of a Dilemma', in A. Bach (ed.), *The Pleasure of Her Text: Feminist Readings of Biblical and Historical Texts* (Philadelphia: Trinity Press International, 1990), p. 5.

2. Fetterley, *The Resisting Reader*, p. xx.

3. Balz-Cochois, 'Gomer', pp. 37-65 (38).

4. Balz-Cochois, 'Gomer', p. 51.

husband.[1] If she contravenes historical critical standards then, she maintains, she is simply following the tradition of Hosean scholarship, but although her romantic invention is less extreme than that of T.K. Cheyne, in practice it is far more tentative and apologetic. Having successfully demolished the alliance between androcentric readings and objectivity, she still appears to be haunted by her own marginality and a pervasive sense of transgression. Following the model of Hegelian dialectic, she presents a thesis, which is Hosea's point of view, and an antithesis, which is Gomer's. Notably her antithesis is far more self-conscious about its subjectivity, and flanked with paragraphs of methodological apologetic. In complete opposition to the univocal absolutism of L.W. Batten, Balz-Cochois constantly relativizes her own position, arguing against herself that her exegesis is 'risky',[2] and conceding that 'feminist freedom' may be perceived as 'methodological weakness'.[3] As she tells Gomer's story, she breaks off to self-consciously renew her poetic licence or, as she puts it, take a particularly deep breath of poetic freedom.[4] Her joke, in a reflex of self-depreciation, reintroduces the notion of androcentric legitimacy by implying that her feminist antithesis is somehow less valid, and to be taken less seriously. Paradoxically, Balz-Cochois simultaneously debunks and protects the objective ideal, and endorses, even as she resists, the views of those who oppose her. Her somewhat bashful reading is an excellent example of the tensions experienced by the feminist scholar, schooled in patriarchal values, and taught seductive, androcentric stories. As Jane Miller confesses in her provocatively titled *Seductions*:

> I was, and still am, seduced by men's systematic and exhaustive claims on our meanings and our realities through their occupation of everything which is thought of not as male, but simply as human. That sort of seduction even extends to aspects of feminism; for feminism has been shaped by the need to earn a place for itself within politics, within the academy and its disciplines,

1. Balz-Cochois, 'Gomer', p. 54.
2. Balz-Cochois, 'Gomer', p. 58.
3. Balz-Cochois, 'Gomer', p. 46.
4. Balz-Cochois, 'Gomer', p. 53.

within 'common sense' accounts of what is allowed as reasonable.[1]

If Balz-Cochois's defence of Gomer's story is interesting, its content is even more so, since, like the woman who envisions her, Gomer simultaneously deconstructs and affirms patriarchal prejudices. On one hand, she threatens and relativizes the dominant point of view—she worships Astarte, counters biblical prejudices about Canaanite culture, and perceives Hosea as eccentric, and Yahwism as essentially uninteresting and irredeemably male. She personifies the disturbing power of female sexuality perceived as 'holy, right and good',[2] and yet she also affirms patriarchy's worst parodies of woman as irrational and trivial. Without questioning the motives of her male predecessors, Balz-Cochois subordinates herself to the androcentric tradition that attempts to redeem Gomer, and extrapolating from Wolff's dubious argument that she is good, but misled, she builds a character who is well-meaning, reliant on her senses and not given to serious thought. When Hosea forbids her to attend a cult festival, she does not go defiantly, of her own accord, but because the neighbours come to call for her. When Hosea pursues her and gives a sermon to the rebellious people, some laugh, some are vexed, but Gomer does not know what to think, and does not want to think at all but simply to enjoy the feast. Even when imprisoned, she does not experience anger at injustice, but rather a shallow regret that she can no longer participate in the 'lovely festivals'.[3] Ironically, Balz-Cochois's rereading of Gomer is rather like traditional androcentric readings of Gertrude, Hamlet's mother, as a 'soft animal creature...very dull and very shallow...[who] loved to be happy in a good-humoured, sensual fashion'[4]—a view vehemently countered by Carolyn Heilbrun in an essay that set

1. J. Miller, *Seductions: Studies in Reading and Culture* (London: Virago, 1990), p. 1.

2. Balz-Cochois, 'Gomer', p. 48.

3. Balz-Cochois, 'Gomer', pp. 51-53.

4. A.C. Bradley, *Shakespearean Tragedy* (New York: Macmillan, 1949), p. 167.

a precedent for reconsidering 'images of women' in critical traditions, as well in texts.[1]

Although plurality is the hallmark of feminist criticism, and there is no one true description of Gomer-bat-Diblayim, feminist readings, like androcentric readings, must be carefully scrutinized to see whose needs they are subordinated to. The two aspects, plurality and criticism, are not incompatible: reconsidering the myth of Eros and Psyche, Rachel Blau DuPlessis confessed 'I make my Psyche from my need. And when others need a different Psyche, let them make it', but, at the same time, reacted strongly against a reading that argued that Psyche becomes truly feminine when she chooses beauty over knowledge: 'I say, I needed this, you needed that. I say: I do not believe your interpretation'.[2] Like Blau DuPlessis, I find it disturbing when female characters are redeemed with appeals to the eternal feminine, to beauty, sensuousness, irresponsibility or irrationality, particularly when that redemption is effected by a female reader. Nor is Balz-Cochois the only critic to subscribe to, even as she opposes, patriarchal values: Renita J. Weems radically redefines Gomer as a 'sexually victimized woman' and a 'pawn in a match between Hosea (Yahweh) and her lovers (other gods)' but at the same time describes her as 'stubborn and recalcitrant' and 'erroneous', ultimately siding with 'Hosea the betrayed husband', who 'does not wish to humiliate her, though he will if he must'.[3] The challenge is to avoid patriarchal

1.   C.G. Heilbrun, 'The Character of Hamlet's Mother', in *Hamlet's Mother and Other Women: Feminist Essays on Literature* (London: The Women's Press, 1991), pp. 9-17.

2.   R. Blau DuPlessis, 'Psyche, or Wholeness', *Massachusetts Review* (Spring 1979), pp. 77-96.

3.   R.J. Weems, 'Gomer: Victim of Violence or Victim of Metaphor?', *Semeia* 47 (1989), pp. 96-97. For other feminist interpretations of Gomer's, as opposed to Hosea's, marriage, see T.D. Setel, 'Prophets and Pornography: Female Sexual Imagery in Hosea', in L.M. Russell (ed.), *Feminist Interpretations of the Bible* (Oxford: Basil Blackwell, 1985), pp. 86-95; M.J. Winn Leith, 'Verse and Reverse: The Transformation of the Woman, Israel in Hos. 1-3', in P.L. Day (ed.) *Gender and Difference in Ancient Israel* (Minneapolis: Fortress Press, 1989), pp. 95-108; F. van Dijk-Hemmes, 'The Imagination of Power and the Power of Imagination', *JSOT* 44 (1989), pp. 75-88; reprinted in A. Brenner (ed.), *A Feminist Companion to the Song of*

encapsulations of femininity, and to break the convention by which 'identity is what you can say you are according to what they say you can be'.[1] Yet while women are ideally equipped to read against the ideological grain, the ability to perceive alternative points of view can potentially work against them. As Barbara Johnson put it, 'women are all trained to be deconstructors' since 'they are socialized to see more than one point of view at a time', but this potentially revolutionary ability is also the root of the 'self-repression or ambiguation'[2] perfectly illustrated in Balz-Cochois's self-depreciating apologetic. The power of feminist biblical criticism is that women are in an ideal position to uncover hidden stories, and to release silent female characters into readability: the danger is that because the 'other' point of view they are socialized to see is not their own, attempts to read against the grain can go partly against the dominant voice of the narrative and partly, instinctively, against their own desires.

Songs (The Feminist Companion to the Bible, 1; Sheffield: Sheffield Academic Press, 1993), pp. 156-170.

1. J. Johnston, *Lesbian Nation: The Feminist Solution* (New York: Simon & Schuster, 1973), p. 68.

2. B. Johnson, 'Interview', in I. Salusinszky (ed.), *Criticism and Society* (London and New York: Methuen, 1987), pp. 169-70.

GOD IS TO ISRAEL AS HUSBAND IS TO WIFE:
THE METAPHORIC BATTERING OF HOSEA'S WIFE

Naomi Graetz

Reading a Haftara (an additional reading from the Prophets) after the weekly reading of the Torah (the Pentateuch) is a time-honored custom among Jews, although the origin of the custom is obscure. The rabbis who initiated the custom may have wanted to make a religious statement that the writings of the Prophets, not only the Torah, are also divinely inspired.[1] Perhaps it also fit the philosophy of the Pharisaic approach: seeing the Torah as an open, fluid text, subject to constant scrutiny and interpretation. At a time when the reading of the Five Books of Moses took between two and a half to three and a half years to complete, the Haftara simply consisted of several random verses, not necessarily related to the weekly portion.[2] Later, when the weekly portion became standardized, the Haftara also became fixed. It served, among other things, as a sort of internal commentary on, or an elucidation of, the Torah portion itself.

An example of this is the Haftara accompanying the first portion of the book of Numbers. The opening chapter of Numbers, *bemmidbar* ('in the wilderness'), is a census of the Israelites during the wilderness period. The Haftara, from ch. 2 of the book of Hosea, refers to 'the multitudes of the people who are as the sands of the sea'. Hosea's message is that the people no longer listen to God's word (*dābār*) and, if they do not shape up, they will be in danger of entering a spiritual wilderness

---

1. See the blessings surrounding the Haftara reading.
2. For detailed information on the Haftara tradition see J. Jacobs, 'Triennial Cycle', *JewEnc*, XII, pp. 254-57; L.I. Rabinowitz, 'Haftarah', *EncJud*, XI, pp. 1342-45. Both entries have excellent bibliographies.

(*midbār*). However, when (and if) the people of Israel will again be faithful to him (as they were during the period of the wilderness, *bammidbār*), he will renew his covenant with them. Hosea speaks for God and says:

> Assuredly, I will speak coaxingly to her
> And lead her through the wilderness (*midbār*)
> And speak (*dibbartî*) to her tenderly (Hos. 2.16)

There is an integral connection made by the associative word-play of the root *dbr* and *midbār*, which has to do with God's word and the wilderness. The wordplay echoes important themes and serves as a rhetorical device which unites and connects the Haftara from the book of Hosea with the Torah portion from the book of Numbers.

The Marriage Metaphor

Hosea was an eighth-century BCE prophet who, most commentators[1] believe, addressed himself to the Northern Kingdom of Israel. This kingdom, according to the Bible, was destined to be exiled because of its sins. Hosea describes God's relationship to Israel in metaphorical terms as a marriage. According to Gershon Cohen, such a marriage metaphor is not found in the literature of any other ancient religion beside Israel's. He writes, 'The Hebrew God alone was spoken of as the lover and husband of His people, and only the house of Israel spoke of itself as the bride of the Almighty'.[2] Hosea's protagonist is himself, the husband who casts out his wife for

---

1. We know next to nothing of Hosea ben Beeri's background, lineage or locality—only the name of his father. Those who study the book have difficulties dating it and identifying people, places and events. It was common practice among some scholars to remove references to Judah in this book, since the consensus among scholars is that Hosea's audience is Israel and not Judah. See the 'Introduction' in F.I. Andersen and D.N. Freedman, *Hosea: A Commentary and New Translation* (AB, 24; Garden City, NY: Doubleday, 1980), pp. 31-77, for a detailed background to this book.

2. G. Cohen, 'The Song of Songs and the Jewish Religious Mentality', in *Studies in the Variety of Rabbinic Cultures* (Philadelphia: Jewish Publication Society, 1991), p. 6.

being unfaithful to him and then takes her back—with the understanding that 'she' will behave herself.

According to Harold Fisch,

> Hosea more than any other book of the Bible...gives us God's side of the relationship. It is dominated by the first-person mode of address as God himself cries out, cajoles, reprimands, mourns and debates with himself... Hosea gives us fundamentally 'the prophet's reflection of, or participation in, the divine pathos', as that pathos is directed toward man,[1]

who in this case is depicted as woman.

According to Benjamin Scolnic, who paraphrases Gershon Cohen,

> God, not Baal, is Israel's husband and lover... Since a wife's loyalty to her husband must be absolute and unwavering, it is a powerful analogy to the complete loyalty that God demands of the Israelites. The covenant between God and Israel made at Mount Sinai is a marriage; idolatry, which breaks the covenant, is adultery.[2]

God orders Hosea to marry Gomer daughter of Diblaim, a promiscuous woman (*'ēšet zᵉnûnîm*)[3] who, metaphorically speaking, is Israel, while Hosea is placed in the position of God. God/Hosea punishes Gomer/Israel for committing adultery/ worshipping other gods. However, because of 'his' great love for 'her', and 'his' commitment to the covenant of marriage, 'he' begs 'her' to come back and restores 'her' to 'her' former state. Thus we have a male prophet, who represents a male God. Gershon Cohen writes,

---

1. H. Fisch, 'Hosea: A Poetics of Violence', in *Poetry with a Purpose* (Bloomington: Indiana University Press, 1990), p. 141. Fisch calls our attention to A.J. Heschel, *The Prophets* (Philadelphia: Jewish Publication Society, 1962), p. 27.

2. B. Scolnic, 'Bible Battering', *Conservative Judaism* 45 (1992), p. 43.

3. See P. Bird, '"To Play the Harlot": An Inquiry into an Old Testament Metaphor', in P.L. Day (ed.) *Gender and Difference in Ancient Israel* (Minneapolis: Fortress Press, 1989), pp. 75-94. Bird writes, 'Although the underlying metaphor is that of marriage, the use of *znh* rather than *n'p* serves to emphasize promiscuity rather than infidelity, "wantonness" rather than violation of marriage contract or covenant' (p. 80).

> The Bible unquestionably affirmed the masculinity of God and spoke of Him graphically as the husband... By proclaiming His masculinity...Judaism affirmed His reality and...potency... To such a person one could proclaim fealty, submission and love.[1]

This God, however, threatens the people for not worshipping him exclusively. Though presumably the entire community, male and female alike, sins against God, the prophet has chosen to describe the people of Israel exclusively in terms of imagery which is feminine.

The standard interpretations of Hosea sympathize with the husband who has put up with so much from this fickle woman, and who desperately promises his wife everything if only she will return to him. The midrash depicts the relationship between God and his people in a poignant manner.

> After [Hosea's wife] had borne him several children, God suddenly put the question to him: 'Why followest thou not the example of thy teacher Moses, who denied himself the joys of family life after his call to prophecy?' Hosea replied: 'I can neither send my wife away nor divorce her, for she has borne me children.' 'If, now,' said God to him, 'thou who hast a wife of whose honesty thou art so uncertain that thou canst not even be sure that her children are thine, and yet thou canst not separate from her, how, then, can I separate Myself from Israel, from My children, the children of My elect, Abraham, Isaac, and Jacob!'[2]

God is here seen as all-forgiving, and the husband who cannot separate himself from his wife is the model after which Hosea is expected to pattern himself. In *Numbers Rabbah* there are several fables which depict God as a king who is angry with his wife, or as a father who is angry with his son. In these stories there are 'happy endings': the king buys his wife some jewelry and they presumably kiss and make up, despite his previous statements that he will divorce her; the father scolds his son for not going to school and then afterwards invites him to dine with him.[3]

1.   Cohen, 'The Song of Songs', p. 15.

2.   *b. Pes.* 87a-b as related by L. Ginzberg, *The Legends of the Jews* (Philadelphia: Jewish Publication Society, 1968), IV, pp. 260-61.

3.   *Num. R.* 2.15, pp. 51-52. All English translations are from H. Freedman and M. Simon (eds.), *Midrash Rabbah* (London: Soncino Press, 1983).

If we disregard the sympathetic overtones in the midrash and read between the lines of Hosea, we see that in the biblical text the 'poignant relationship' is achieved at a price. We see it well in a midrash from *Exodus Rabbah* which compares God to a wife-beater. It is on the verse 'If thou lend money to any of my people' (Exod. 22.24). It describes how after Israel was driven from Jerusalem, their enemies said that God had no desire for his people. Jeremiah asked God if it was true that he had rejected his children:

> 'Hast Thou utterly rejected Judah? Hath Thy soul loathed Zion? Why hast Thou smitten us, and there is no healing for us?' (Jer. 14.19) It can be compared to a man who was beating his wife. Her best friend asked him: 'How long will you go on beating her? If your desire is to drive her out [of life], then keep on beating her till she dies; but if you do not wish her [to die], then why do you keep on beating her?' His reply was: 'I will not divorce my wife even if my entire palace becomes a ruin.' This is what Jeremiah said to God: 'If Thy desire be to drive us out [of this world], then smite us till we die.' As it says, 'Thou canst not have utterly rejected us, and be exceedingly wroth against us! [Lam. 5.22], but if this is not [Thy desire], then 'Why hast Thou smitten us, and there is no healing for us?' God replied: 'I will not banish Israel, even if I destroy my world', as it says, 'Thus saith the Lord: If heaven above can be measured...then will I also cast off all the seed of Israel, etc.' [Jer. 31.37].[1]

This midrash depicts an emotional bond that has developed between God and his people which has resulted in Israel's being gradually taken prisoner by a pathological courtship.

The psychiatrist Judith Herman, in her recent book, *Trauma and Recovery*,[2] describes a woman who becomes involved with a batterer and interprets his attention as a sign of love. The woman minimizes and excuses his behavior, because she cares for him. To avoid staying in this relationship she will have to fight his protestations that 'just one more sacrifice, one more proof of her love, will end the violence and save the relationship'.[3] Herman

---

1. *Exod. R.* on *Mishpatim* 31.10, pp. 388-89. Thanks to Howard Adelman for bringing this midrash to my attention.
2. J. Herman, *Trauma and Recovery: The Aftermath of Violence from Domestic Abuse to Political Terror* (New York: Basic Books, 1992).
3. Herman, *Trauma and Recovery*, p. 83.

writes that most women are entrapped by the batterer because he appeals to 'her most cherished values. It is not surprising, therefore, that battered women are often persuaded to return after trying to flee from their abusers.'[1] This is the relationship expressed by Jeremiah according to the midrash.

Turning back to Hosea, we see that our text details very explicitly a case of domestic abuse. We see this in the punitive measures Hosea plans to take. In v. 5, God/Hosea threatens to

> strip her naked and leave her
> as on the day she was born;
> And I will make her like a wilderness,
> render her like desert land,
> and let her die of thirst (Hos. 2.5).

In v. 8, God/Hosea threatens to

> hedge up her roads with thorns
> and raise walls against her.

In v. 11 God/Hosea says he will humiliate her by taking back

> My new grain in its time
> and My new wine in its season,
> And I will snatch away My wool
> and My linen that serve to cover her nakedness.

If this depicts the real state of Hosea/God's and Gomer/ Israel's relationship we have here a very troubled marriage. Gale A. Yee, in the new *Women's Bible Commentary*, writes that 'Chapter two pushes the marriage metaphor to dangerous limits, whereby [God's] legitimate punishment of Israel for breach of covenant is figuratively described as threats of violence against the wife.'[2] Hosea begins with the threats to strip her naked. These threats escalate, with the children being abused by association with the mother's shamelessness. The next thing he does is to isolate his wife from her lovers by 'building a wall against her', so that she is totally dependent on her husband. Then he withholds food from her and publicly

---

1. Herman, *Trauma and Recovery*, p. 83.
2. 'Hosea', in C.A. Newsom and S.H. Ringe (eds.), *The Women's Bible Commentary* (Louisville, KY: Westminster Press, 1992), p. 199.

humiliates her by uncovering her nakedness.[1]

Benjamin Scolnic's reaction to Hosea 2 is as follows:

> I don't mean to pretend that this isn't rough stuff. But we must remember that this really is a metaphor understood...by the Israelites *as a metaphor*... I will not hide behind the notion that since this is all 'just a metaphor' or polemic against Baal-worship, we don't have to take the words themselves seriously. But there is never a chance that any of the things threatened here will be carried out.[2]

However, F.I. Andersen and D.N. Freedman, the commentators on Hosea in the Anchor Bible series, are not so sure that Hosea's threats are benign. They hint that God's threats of death in Hos. 2.5 (see above) might have been carried out when the people betrayed God:[3]

> That is why I hacked them with my prophets;
> I killed them with the words of my mouth.
> My judgment goes forth like the sun (Hos. 6.5).

Scolnic, however, minimizes these threats, viewing them as an act of prophetic desperation. These threats, he writes, are 'about love, not wife-battering. They are about forgiveness, not punishment... [The perspective is] of a man who has the right too...strip her, humiliate her, etc., but doesn't and, instead, seeks reconciliation.'[4] Is Scolnic correct in arguing that this is just some mild form of verbal abuse? Again, the commentators of the Anchor Bible disagree. They write, 'the passage expresses

---

1.   I. Pardes, in *Countertraditions in the Bible* (Cambridge, MA: Harvard University Press, 1992), writes, 'To further understand the sin and punishment, one needs to bear in mind that "uncovering the nakedness" is a biblical expression designating illicit sexual relations (from incest to adultery). Conversely, "covering the nakedness", as is evident in both Hosea 2.11 and Ezekiel 16.8, is a synonym for marriage' (p. 134).

2.   Scolnic, 'Bible-Battering', pp. 47-48. Scolnic's article was written as a response and companion piece to my article 'The Haftorah Tradition and the Metaphoric Battering of Hosea's Wife', *Conservative Judaism* 45 (1992), pp. 29-42, which is an earlier version of this article.

3.   Andersen and Freedman write about Hos. 2.5 that 'A fourth possible stage, death, threatened in v. 5, is apparently never reached (but see 6.5)' (*Hosea*, p. 129).

4.   Scolnic, 'Bible-Battering', p. 48.

both an ardent will to reconciliation and an indignant determination to use coercive or punitive measures to correct or even to destroy her'.[1]

One can argue that by using the marriage metaphor we are allowed to glimpse the compassionate side of God.[2] Because of the intimate relationship, God is more accessible to his people. Not only do we have descriptions of an intimate relationship with God but we also have allusions to the idyllic, pre-expulsion relationship of equality between God and humanity.[3]

> In that day, I will make a covenant for them with the beasts of the field, the birds of the air, and the creeping things of the ground... And I will espouse you with faithfulness; then you shall know (*yāda‘*) God intimately (Hos. 2.20-21).

However, unlike the relationship between Adam and Eve, the relationship between God and Israel is one sided. God would like the uncomplicated pre-expulsion relationship, before the people 'knew' (*yāda‘*) about choice. God promises the returning nation an intimate covenantal relationship with him despite the fact that knowledge (*da‘at*) was the reason Adam and Eve were punished.

Jeremiah, too, depicts a God who loved his young, eager, naive Israel, yet turns on his people when 'she' grows up and wants some independence. When God decides to espouse Israel forever with faithfulness, it is so that the people will 'know' (*yāda‘*) only God. If Israel wants to know more than just God, if she wants to take fruit from the tree again, the implication is that she will again be expelled from the Garden of Eden, stripped naked and left as on the day 'she' was created—with nothing (Hos. 2.5). God is telling Israel/Gomer that she can either be intimate with him (her husband) or with other gods/ lovers but not with both of them at the same time. She can have

---

1. Andersen and Freedman, *Hosea*, p. 128.
2. We can only guess what the marriage metaphor meant in Hosea's day. We, however, see how it came to be used and abused in later generations.
3. In Gen. 1.27 male and female are created in one act. I do not agree with Trible's 'depatriarchalizing' of Gen. 2–3. See P. Trible, 'Depatriarchalizing in Biblical Interpretation', in E. Koltun (ed.), *The Jewish Woman: New Perspectives* (New York: Schocken Books, 1976), pp. 217-40.

knowledge of good and evil from him or from others. If she chooses others, he will destroy her. So despite the potential glimpse of a compassionate God, he is accessible to his people only on his own terms.[1]

Finally, one can argue as Scolnic does, that this 'really is a metaphor', that is, the marriage metaphor is 'only a metaphor' and the motif of sexual violence is *'only* a theme of the metaphor'. H.L. Ginsberg, in his articles on Hosea,[2] has pointed out that Hosea's important innovation is the 'husband and wife allegory'.

> The doctrine of God's jealousy and His insistence that His covenant partner Israel worship no other gods beside Him [is a] factor favorable to the birth of such an allegory... This, however, was heavily outweighed by a horror of associating sexuality with God, and only the need of the...hour overcame this inhibition to the extent of giving rise to the wife metaphor, or allegory...[3]

In his discussion of the commentators on Hosea, Ginsberg writes that the rabbis of the Talmud 'accepted literally the divine command to Hosea to marry a prostitute',[4] and that Rashi was still satisfied with such a view. But Ginsberg's sympathy is clearly with Ibn Ezra, Kimhi and Maimonides, who

---

1.   It is worthwhile comparing the book of Hosea to the Song of Songs, which is probably the only completely non-sexist account of a relationship between a man and a woman in the Bible. There are echoes of this relationship in Hos. 2.9. Van Dijk-Hemmes argues that there is an intertextual relationship between the two texts and that if we 're-place the "quotations" back into the love-songs from which they were borrowed, the vision of the woman in this text is restored'. To see how she develops this idea see F. van Dijk-Hemmes, 'The Imagination of Power and the Power of Imagination: An Intertextual Analysis of Two Biblical Love Songs: The Song of Songs and Hosea 2', *JSOT* 44 (1990), p. 86; reprinted in A. Brenner (ed.), *A Feminist Companion to the Song of Songs* (The Feminist Companion to the Bible, 1; Sheffield: Sheffield Academic Press, 1993), p. 169.

2.   H.L. Ginsberg, 'Studies in Hosea 1–3', in M. Haran (ed.), *Yehezkel Kaufmann Jubilee Volume* (Jerusalem: Magnes Press, 1960), pp. 50-69 of the English Section; *JBL* 80 (1961), pp. 339-47; and 'Hosea, Book of', *EncJud*, VIII, pp. 1010-25.

3.   Ginsberg, 'Hosea, Book of', p. 1016.

4.   Ginsberg, 'Hosea, Book of', p. 1011.

maintained that the story was 'but accounts of prophetic visions'.[1] Even if we accept Ginsberg's view that the book of Hosea is not a real description of a husband–wife relationship but *only* a metaphorical, allegorical vision, that does not mean that such metaphoric imagery has no power, no force. As many have pointed out, it is no longer possible to argue that a metaphor is less for being a metaphor. On the contrary, metaphor has power over people's minds and hearts. As Lakoff and Turner write,

> Far from being merely a matter of words, metaphor is a matter of thought—all kinds of thought... [It] is part of the way members of a culture have of conceptualizing their experience... For the same reasons that schemas and metaphors give us power to conceptualize and reason, so they have power over us. Anything that we rely on constantly, unconsciously, and automatically is so much part of us that it cannot be easily resisted, in large measure because it is barely even noticed. To the extent that we use a conceptual schema or a conceptual metaphor, we accept its validity. Consequently, when someone else uses it, we are predisposed to accept its validity. For this reason, conventionalized schemas and metaphors have *persuasive* power over us.[2]

One of the side effects of thinking metaphorically is that we often disregard the differences between the two dissimilar objects being compared. One source of metaphor's power lies precisely in that we tend to lose sight of the fact that it is 'just' a metaphor. What this means in our case, writes Renita J. Weems, is that 'God is no longer *like* a husband; God *is* a husband'. If 'God's covenant with Israel is like a marriage...then a husband's physical punishment against his wife is as warranted as God's punishment of Israel'.[3]

---

1. Ginsberg, 'Hosea, Book of', p. 1012.
2. G. Lakoff and M. Turner, *More than Cool Reason: A Field Guide to Poetic Metaphor* (Chicago: University of Chicago Press, 1989), pp. xi, 9, 63.
3. R.J. Weems, 'Gomer: Victim of Violence or Victim of Metaphor?', *Semeia* 47 (1989), p. 100. She is quoting S. McFague, *Metaphorical Theology* (Philadelphia: Fortress Press, 1982).

Dangerous Assumptions

Let us turn to two rabbis who use similar metaphors in their midrashim: one classic and one contemporary. The first example appears in a midrash which connects the Torah portion of Numbers to the Haftara from the book of Hosea.

> R. Hanina said, Only in ignorance could one think that what He meant by saying 'I will not be to you' was that He would not be to you for a God. That is certainly not so; what then does, 'and I will not be to you' mean? That even though you would not be My people and would seek to separate yourselves from Me, yet 'I will not be to you'; My mind still will not be the same as yours, but *in spite of yourselves you will be My people*... As I live, saith the Lord God, surely *with a mighty hand, and with an outstretched arm, and with fury poured out, will I be king over you* (Ezek. 20.33).[1]

One can look at this extraordinary proclamation in two ways: (1) positively, as a sign of God's devotion; no matter what the people do, he still loves them; or (2) negatively, as a sign of mental illness. There is no mutual consent. This is all against 'her' (the people's) will. There has been no discussion, no ending of mutual recriminations. 'He' does not recognize the writing on the wall. 'She' does not want 'him', she has had it with 'him'; sick of 'his' mighty hand, outstretched arm and fury. She has decided to leave him, but he refuses to face facts. To him marriage means 'I will espouse you to me forever', even if it does not work out. She feels she has no option, that she is trapped in the marriage.

Now let us turn to Rabbi Shlomo Riskin, who writes a weekly column for *The Jerusalem Post*.[2] His midrash is on the Song of Songs, traditionally considered to be an allegorical depiction of the mutual love of God and Israel:

> When God knocks in the middle of the night, He wants the Jewish people to let Him in and end their long exile... But the nation answers...that it is too difficult to dirty oneself by joining

---

1. *Num. R.* 2.16 (p. 53 in Freedman and Simon).
2. The *Post* is the only daily English-language newspaper in Israel. Riskin's weekly column 'Shabbat Shalom' appears in the popular overseas edition as well.

God in His Land, stepping into the 'mud' of a struggling country... Rejected, God removes His hand from the latch... Only then does the nation grasp the significance of her hesitation and her innards begin to turn as she rises to open the door. Unfortunately, her actions, because she is *smothered in perfume*, are dull and heavy, her arms and fingers *dripping with cold cream* and *Chanel No. 5*. By the time the latch is opened, God is gone, and she goes on searching desperately everywhere for her beloved [italics mine].[1]

Here Riskin, in his reading of the Song of Songs, has chosen to use the metaphor of a sinning woman to depict the entire nation (both men and women!) which does not heed God's call to settle in the land of Israel. He does this without being in the least cognizant of the anti-female bias of the metaphor. The ancient metaphor—God as male and the sinning people as female—is alive and well in present-day rabbinical thinking.

Harold Fisch, another contemporary writer, uses the prooftext of Hos. 11.7-8 to keep this bias alive:

And my people are bent
On turning away from me...
But how can I give you up, O Ephraim?
How shall I surrender thee, O Israel?

Writing as a literary critic, he states that

paradoxically we discover God's unconditional love only through the negating of it... Through the language of denial, God's *over-mastering love* is manifested. It cannot be overcome, nor can the name Ammi (my people) be eradicated [emphasis mine].[2]

I find this imagery and way of thinking reminiscent of John Donne's famous Holy Sonnet 14.

Batter my heart, three person'd God; for you
As yet but knock, breathe, shine, and seek to mend.
Take me to you, imprison me, for I,
Except you enthrall me, never shall be free,
Nor ever chaste, except you ravish me.

Both the prophet and Donne accept the assumption that God is an aggressive, domineering being who is master over his

1. *The Jerusalem Post*, Friday 13 April 1990.
2. Fisch, 'Hosea: A Poetics of Violence', p. 145.

passive, female, adoring people. There is a need to eradicate the self through an intense sexual relationship. The implication is that in order to find God one must sacrifice one's sense of selfhood.[1]

But this type of thinking is dangerous both to women and to society in general. I argue, along with other feminist commentators,[2] that the language of Hosea and the other prophets and rabbis who use 'objectified female sexuality as a symbol of evil'[3] has had damaging effects on women. Women who read of God's relationship with Israel through the prism of a misogynist male prophet or rabbinical commentator, and have religious sensibilities, are forced to identify against themselves.[4]

---

1.   This message is familiar to women.

2.   See M.I. Gruber, 'The Motherhood of God in Second Isaiah', *RB* 3 (1983), pp. 251-59 (also in *idem, The Motherhood of God and Other Studies* [South Florida Studies in the History of Judaism, 57; Atlanta, GA: Scholars Press, 1992], pp. 3-15).

3.   T.D. Setel, 'Prophets and Pornography: Female Sexual Imagery in Hosea', in L. Russell (ed.) *Feminist Interpretation of the Bible* (Philadelphia: Westminster Press, 1985), p. 86. Tikva Frymer-Kensky recognizes the problematic nature of our text and the marriage metaphor but is not willing to accept that the negative portrayal of Israel-as-wife rises from misogyny. She writes that except for Ecclesiastes, 'there are no overt anti-woman statements in the Hebrew Bible... [although] the depiction of the Wanton City-woman is the most truly negative portrayal of any female in the Bible' ('The Wanton Wife of God', in *In the Wake of the Goddesses* [New York: The Free Press, 1992], p. 150). But she stresses that the prophets' anger is directed against the people (city) and not the women. She admits, however, that 'the intensity of these passages and their sexual fantasies of nymphomania and revenge seem to be fueled by unconscious fear and rage' (p. 150).

4.   Gruber ('The Motherhood of God', p. 358) writes that Jeremiah and Ezekiel 'intimated that in the religion of Israel maleness is a positive value...while femaleness is a negative value with which divinity refuses to identify itself'. Frymer-Kensky ('The Wanton Wife', p. 152) writes that 'the marital metaphor reveals the dramatic inner core of monotheism: the awesome solo mastery of God brings humans into direct unadulterated contact with supreme power...in this relationship, the people stand directly before and with God... There is only us and God'. Clearly the relationship is awesome, but to the battered wife/people, there is something frightening about there being no buffer or intercessor between us and a God who is depicted as a vengeful husband.

Fokkelien van Dijk-Hemmes asks the salient question:

> Why is Israel, first the land but then also the nation, represented in the image of a faithless wife, a harlot and not in the image of e.g. a rapist? This would have been more justified when we look at Israel's misdeeds which YHWH/Hosea points out in the following 4.1–5.7… And beyond that, it is the men who are held responsible for social and religious abuses; it is the priests who mislead the people (4.4-6) and the fathers who force their daughters to play the harlot (4.13-14).[1]

Why did it not occur to Riskin to say that 'Israel was too busy fiddling with his computers or tinkering with his cars or watching football on the Sabbath to have time to pay attention to God'?

The problem is that the ancient metaphors of marriage, in order to emphasize God's love, take for granted the patriarchal view of women's subservient role. They represent God's punishment of Israel as justice. According to Ilana Pardes, God's severe response to Israel is 'almost moderate, given her ingratitude. One is expected to take pity on God for having to play such a violent role, for having to suffer so for the sake of Law and Order.'[2] Prophets and rabbis should not be enshrining the legal subordination of women in metaphor.[3] In my view, love, punishment and subservience are not compatible concepts.

Why should this concern us at all, since presumably the metaphor *only* expresses the social reality of the biblical period? In fact one can argue that understanding 'the historical setting of prophetic texts may provide a perspective of "moral realism" which allows them to be read as sacred writing'.[4] However, the argument for a historical setting recedes if we realize that because of the sanctification of Hosea 2 in a fixed Haftara, it plays a role in perpetuating biblical patriarchalism into our own day. Because of its morally flawed allegory, the message of the prophets can be understood as permitting husbands to abuse

1. Van Dijk-Hemmes, 'The Imagination of Power', p. 85.
2. Pardes, *Countertraditions*, p. 136.
3. J. Plaskow, *Standing Again at Sinai: Judaism from a Feminist Perspective* (San Francisco: Harper & Row, 1990), p.6.
4. Setel, 'Prophets and Pornography', p. 95.

their wives psychologically and physically.[1]

An argument for the continuance of this fixed Haftara in the tradition might be its so-called 'happy end'. If we examine God's declaration of love to 'his' people superficially, it appears to be a monogamous declaration by God to his formerly faithless people. Hos. 2.16-22 goes as follows:

> I will speak coaxingly to her
> and lead her through the wilderness
> and speak to her tenderly...
> There she shall respond as in the days of her youth, when she
> came up from the land of Egypt.
> And in that day—declares the Lord—
> you will call [Me] *'îšî* [husband],
> and no more will you call Me *ba'alî*.
> For I will remove
> the names of the Baalim from her mouth,
> and they shall nevermore be mentioned by name.
>
> In that day, I will make a covenant for them with the beasts of the
> field, the birds of the air, and the creeping things of the ground; I
> will also banish bow, sword, and war from the land. Thus I will let
> them lie down in safety.
>
> And I will espouse you forever:
> I will espouse you with righteousness and justice,
> and with goodness and mercy,
> and I will espouse you with faithfulness;
> Then you shall be devoted to (*yād'at 'et*) the Lord.

One might claim that in a polytheistic society, the assumption of total faithfulness on God's part and the demand of faithfulness to a single God on the people's part was revolutionary. The prophet's use of the marriage metaphor, 'You will call [Me] *'îšî* [my man/husband]', is a new vision of a God who will not tolerate a polygamous association. 'And no more will you call me *ba'alî* [my husband/lord/master]. For I will remove the names

---

1. See Plaskow, *Standing Again*, p. 6. See also Gruber, 'Motherhood of God', who concludes his article by saying: 'a religion which seeks to convey the Teaching of God who is above and beyond both sexes cannot succeed in conveying that Teaching if it seeks to do so in a manner which implies that a positive-divine value is attached only to one of the two sexes' (p. 35).

of the Baalim [pagan gods]...'[1] The monogamous aspect of marriage on the part of the husband is clearly unusual, but it still does not address the problematics involved in monogamy when one side controls the other.

Mary Joan Winn Leith argues that

> The rejected form of address, Ba'al, implies not only a different deity, but also a different, more dominating relationship... God's new title, 'husband' ['*îšî*], signals a new beginning, a new betrothal, and a (re)new(ed) covenant, whose inauguration sounds strikingly like a (re)creation of the world.[2]

But there is a terrible assumption here in Leith's argument. Israel has to *suffer* in order to be entitled to this new betrothal. 'She' has to be battered into submission in order to kiss and make up at the end. She has to agree to be on the receiving end of her husband's jealousy. The premise is that a woman has no other choice but to remain in such a marriage. True, God is very generous to Israel. He promises to espouse her forever with righteousness, justice, goodness, mercy and faithfulness. But despite the potential for a new model of a relationship between God and Israel, it is not a model of real reciprocity. It is based on suffering and the assumption that Israel will submit to God's will. Hosea, however, rejoices in this transformation and in the 'ordeal [which] has fit the woman for a new, enhanced relationship with God'.[3]

The reader who is caught up in this joyous new betrothal and renewed covenant overlooks the fact that this joyous reconciliation between God and Israel follows the exact pattern that battered wives know so well. Israel is physically and psychologically punished, abused and then seduced into remaining in the covenant by tender words and caresses. The religious images may be as beautiful and profound as Leith has pointed out but, as Yee writes,

---

1.   There is a double entendre here, since Baal can also be understood to mean 'husband'.

2.   M.J.W. Leith, 'Verse and Reverse: The Transformation of the Woman, Israel, in Hosea 1–3', in Day (ed.), *Gender and Difference*, p. 101.

3.   Leith, 'Verse and Reverse', p. 103.

> studies have shown that many wives remain in abusive relation-
> ships because periods of mistreatment are often followed by
> intervals of kindness and generosity. This ambivalent strategy
> reinforces the wife's dependence on the husband. During periods
> of kindness, her fears are temporarily eased so that she decides to
> remain in the relationship; then the cycle of abuse begins again.[1]

God is not suggesting a full-fledged partnership, despite his declarations. Hosea's portrayal of Israel as a sinning woman returning abjectly to the open arms of her husband who graciously accepts her—after her great suffering, and providing she repents—has limited the potential of the relationship. Thus, the prophet's marriage metaphor is problematic. It makes its theological point at the expense of women and contracts rather than expands the potential of partnership.

One might argue that Jewish tradition did try to expand the potential. This can be seen in the assumption that Jewish males gain sensitivity from their obligation to recite the concluding phrases from the Haftara when they put on their *tefillin* (phylacteries) every morning.

> And I will espouse you forever:
> I will espouse you with righteousness and justice,
> and with goodness and mercy,
> and I will espouse you with faithfulness;
> Then you shall be devoted to (*yāda'at 'et*) the Lord (Hos. 2.21-2).

What does it mean to daily identify with a woman's position? For that is what the male does. The male wraps the bands of the *tefillin* around his middle finger—almost like a wedding ring. He repeats the words God says to his bride. He affirms and reaffirms his binding relationship with God. Clearly God is binding himself to Israel as a groom binds himself to his bride. The male who puts on *tefillin* identifies with the bride. Since the male (identifying with the female) is in a subservient relationship to God in this daily rerun of the ritual of marriage, does he gain any insight from this experience which forces him to subconsciously reverse roles? Can this ritual act be a basis for re-interpreting Hosea?

---

1.   Yee, 'Hosea', p. 200.

Reinterpreting Hosea

There are two midrashim which shed light on this question. One of them, a midrash on a verse from *Parashat Ekeb* (Deut. 7.12), looks promising as a basis for reinterpretation. This midrash connects the covenant between God and Abraham with the marriage of a king and a noble woman who brings two valuable gems into the house. In this partnership type of relationship she brings gems and he also brings gems. When she loses the gems, he takes away his. When she finds them, he restores his and decrees that,

> a crown should be made of both sets of gems and that it should be placed on the head of the noble lady... God too set up corresponding to them two gems, namely, loving kindness and mercy... Israel lost theirs... God thereupon took away His...And after Israel have restored theirs and God has given back His, God will say, 'Let both pairs be made into a crown and be placed on the head of Israel,' as it is said, 'And I will betroth thee unto Me, yea, I will betroth thee unto Me in righteousness and in justice, and in loving kindness, and in compassion. And I will betroth thee unto Me in faithfulness; and thou shalt know the Lord' (Hos. 2.21).[1]

The greater context of this midrash is that of the book of Deuteronomy. In this book Israel is constantly being berated and threatened by God. If Israel behaves as God demands, Israel will be treated well. If Israel strays from the narrow path, Israel will be punished. However, the rabbis have made a tremendous conceptual leap forward by allowing us to infer from the relationship that God has with Abraham the potential relationship of partnership that a man can have with his wife.[2]

However, in another less promising midrash which connects the passage 'For the Lord your God is a consuming fire, an impassioned God, *'ēl qannā"* (Deut. 4.24) with the passage 'I will espouse you with faithfulness' (Hos. 2.21), we have a different kind of relationship: God as a jealous husband. In contrast to

---

1. *Deut. R. (Ekeb)* 3.7 (pp. 75-76 in Freedman and Simon).
2. Thanks to Michael Graetz for bringing the midrash to my attention and discussing its meaning with me.

those who merit '*ôlām habbā*'—the next world—are those who are consumed by a great fire. The rabbis ask: how do we know that God is jealous? The answer is: just as a husband is jealous of his wife, so is the God of Israel.[1]

Thus, the use of the *tefillin* ritual could become a means of reinterpreting the Haftara from Hosea only if it is accompanied by specific interpretation.

Reforming the Haftara Readings

What can be done to address the problem of women's subordination, yet remain within the bounds of the tradition?

The easiest approach is simply to dissociate ourselves from the text with a disclaimer such as, 'This was the way women were seen in ancient times; this way of continuing to view women is dangerous and we *of course* do not view women as subordinate to men, as sexual objects to be vilified'. We should not continue to honor this tradition. Today, there can never be extenuating circumstances that encourage violence in a marriage.

Another option is to take a second look at the tradition, with a view to reforming the present fixed cycle of Haftara portions, by choosing other prophetic passages in place of offensive ones.

When the sages introduced the additional readings and when the weekly Torah portion was fluid, *any* reading could suffice to fulfil the requirement of the blessing of reading from *nᵉbî'êy hā'emet wāṣedeq* ('prophets of truth and righteousness'). Later, when haftarot (the additional portions) were codified, that is, were associated with particular weekly portions, the haftara also served the purpose of interpreting the Torah, of being a sort of first-line midrash on the portion. As with so much else, what started out as fluid is now fixed, virtually codified. Thus, although the custom of fixed haftarot exists, we have ample precedent to change the readings completely.

Theological Implications

It is almost a truism to speak of God as having the power and authority to control and possess. However, it is theologically

---

1. *Tanhuma*, Parashat ṣaw 14.1.

debatable whether God wants to use this power to interfere in our lives. Unfortunately, the prophets persisted in representing God as having and wanting the same authority to control and possess that a husband has traditionally had over his wife. In an ideal marriage, in which there is a relationship of equality, a wife should not have to submit to her husband's authority.

The purpose of the metaphor is to enhance acceptance of God's relationship with Israel. But that can only be the case in a society in which the marriage metaphor is acceptable to men and women. When the marriage metaphor is a priori unacceptable to men and women of a particular society then it no longer serves as an acceptable mode of thought concerning God's relationship to Israel.

It is difficult, perhaps impossible, to sustain a metaphoric relationship that implies a double standard. We need new metaphors—perhaps to be inspired by the Song of Songs.[1] Scolnic objects to my thesis that we need alternative haftarot, arguing that 'dropping a haftorah is not the Jewish way...certainly [it is] not the Conservative Jewish approach'.[2] I disagree. Today, when the ideal of marriage has shifted to a more congenial ideal of partnership, the classic, ancient metaphors in the haftarot describing the relationship between God and his people have proved to be limited, misleading and repugnant.

1. Pardes contrasts the patriarchal marital model in Hosea with the antipatriarchal model of love in the Song of Songs. She writes that the Songs of Songs 'could be made to function as a countervoice to the misogynist prophetic degradation of the nation. It could offer an inspiring consolation in its emphasis on reciprocity. For once the relationship of God and His bride relies on mutual courting, mutual attraction, and mutual admiration, there is more room for hope that redemption is within reach' (*Countertraditions*, p. 127). However, she also takes issue with Phyllis Trible, 'Depatriarchalizing'.
2. Scolnic, 'Bible-Battering', pp. 52-53.

Fantasy and the Displacement of Pleasure: Hosea 2.4-17*

Francis Landy

The principal problems in Hosea 2 are: (1) how to reconcile—if one can—the violence and obsessiveness of the first part of the chapter with the blissful tour de force of the second; (2) how it interacts with the framing parable in chs. 1 and 3; and (3) how it functions as a microcosm, a *mise en abyme*, of the book as a whole.

The feminist critique of the chapter is by now well established: that it robs the woman of her voice and her point of view, that it objectifies and degrades her. We can build on that critique, not only by a detailed reading of the text, but by asking where the author stands, if 'he'[1] is the speaker or the addressee, what the relationship is in the text of mystification and discovery, desire and knowledge; to see beneath the male control, undercut by uncertainty, revisions and impossibility, a desire for surrender of power, knowledge and discourse. This will not breach the exclusivity of the male fantasy, but note that, as repeatedly in Hosea, it is also a fantasy of the transfer of gender, of slippage between male and female personae. This can be illustrated at the end of the chapter where the male child, Jezreel, is suddenly feminized. Since Jezreel is etymologically correlated with the divine seed, God's insemination of the earth is also 'his' surrender to it.

---

*   From F. Landy, *Hosea* (Readings; Sheffield: Sheffield Academic Press, forthcoming).

1.   I put 'he' in inverted commas to distinguish, at least this once, the biological gender of the presumably male author from his symbolic gender.

The first part of the chapter (vv. 4-15)[1] is a repeated fantasy of desolation and sexual exposure. The distancing parable frames the inner dynamic of God's jealousy, rage and cruelty. But it also frames by visions of reconciliation, marked by the transformation of the children's names in vv. 1-3 and 24-25. The continuity between God's speeches in vv. 3 and 4, and their matching imperatives—'Say...', 'Strive...'—suggests that from the far future he turns to present alienation, that his acknowledgment of kinship and love for his children, reflected in their words to each other, is undercut by their immediate predicament, as agents of familial strife, and by doubts about their legitimacy. Inciting the children is, however, a displacement of his own quarrel. That it is transparently a delaying tactic, a mirror for his own contention, is evident from their silence; the only words we hear are his. Another form of displacement is that which renders the fantasy hypothetical, by introducing it with 'lest' (v. 5); only if the children's strife does not succeed will it come into effect. Both are rationalizations that distance the fantasy from himself; the children are screens or ventriloquists whose intercession will avert punishment. In the next section (vv. 7-9) children and hypothesis disappear. Instead, God proposes to bring about the woman's return through preventive measures. Blocking her path with thorns may parallel the fantasy of exposure or preempt it; at any rate, it is justified as a means of rehabilitation. This line of thought is abandoned; in the last section (vv. 10-15) the fantasy is unmediated by preventive measure or postponement.

Repetition is characteristic of obsession; the same scenario recurs, with greater or lesser aesthetic or ethical revision. In our section, the masks are progressively stripped away; this may be either a Freudian 'working through' or typical of a sadistic process, in which the expenditure of violence leads to an access of love. Symptomatic of obsessiveness is its hypertrophic language: the long lists, the extended verses, the insistence of the repeated imperative 'Strive', the punning focus on particular

---

1. Many English versions have a verse numbering that is slightly different from the Hebrew text. In these, 2.4 = 2.2, 2.5 = 2.3, and so on. I have retained the Hebrew verse numbering, however, since there are translations, such as the NJPS, which follow it.

phonemes, whose elaboration suggests either a single underlying thought or the baroque pressure to generate as many
permutations as possible.[1]

The fantasy is complex, overdetermined and pornographic in
that, as Setel says, it depicts women's sexual shame.[2] The infu-
sion of violence into sexuality is not, however, primarily or only
a means of excitation. Chapter 2 belongs to the literature of
sexual disgust in which desire appears only spectrally, as a
revenant, and in reverse. Exposing the woman's nakedness to
the gaze of her lovers is doubly voyeuristic; the viewer sees her
through the eyes of others, and participates vicariously in their
pleasure. However, the sight renders the lovers impotent: 'no
man shall deliver her from my hand' (v. 12). The object of desire
becomes undesirable, *nablût*, both 'contemptible' and 'foolish'.
The jealous husband paradoxically acts as pander, but only to
nullify the sexual transaction, to divest the woman of cultural
and social significance. She becomes a sign of the libidinal body;
the word *nablût*, 'folly' or 'shame', at least metonymically refers
to her genitalia and associates them with folly, contempt and
cosmic disorder.[3] The body, imagined as anarchic and subversive, is nevertheless passive, subject to the look of the surrounding males. Vision is a means of appropriation, of immense
symbolic resonance, as the rhetoric of striptease, advertising
and so on shows. The underlying fantasy, then, is of gang-rape,

1. *te'enatah*, 'her fig tree', in v. 14 is compressed three words later into
etnah, 'a [harlot's] hire'. Another example is the extraordinary concatena-
tion of 'n' and 'p' sounds in: *wᵉtāsēr zᵉNûNēhā miPPānēhā wᵉNaᵃPûpēhā
mibbēn šādēhā PeN 'aPšîṭeNNā...*, 'that she should remove her harlotries
from her face and her adulteries from between her breasts, lest I strip her
bare' (vv. 4-5).

2. T.D. Setel, 'Prophets and Pornography: Female Sexual Imagery in
Hosea', in L. Russell (ed.), *Feminist Interpretations of the Bible* (Philadelphia:
Westminster Press, 1985), pp. 86-95.

3. The word *nablût* occurs in the Hebrew Bible only here and is subject
to extensive discussion. For *nablût* as a metonymy for the genitalia see
H.W. Wolff, *Hosea* (Hermeneia; Philadelphia: Fortress Press, 1974), p. 31,
and D. Stuart, *Hosea–Jonah* (WBC; Waco, TX: Word Books, 1987). For the
proposal that *nablût* is a term for cosmic disorder, see R. Murray, *The
Cosmic Covenant: Biblical Themes of Justice, Peace and the Integrity of Creation*
(London: Sheed & Ward, 1992), p. 47.

the woman encircled by predators. The fantasy, however, is reversed: the sight turns back on the seers and taunts them with their incapacity to claim her. The husband, in exhibiting his wife, simultaneously discards her and asserts his prerogative over her.

The exposure of the woman is the prelude to her devastation, related in vv. 5 and 14. Predation is climactically embodied in the wild beasts that consume 'them'—vine and fig tree, but also Israel—at the end of v. 14. The wild beasts are displaced figures for God as executioners of his will: the identification becomes closer later in the book, when God adopts feral imagery for himself (5.14; 13.7-8). In 5.14 God, a metaphorical lion, boasts that 'none can deliver' from him, as does the husband in v. 12. Their rapacity converges with the desolation God brings in the first part of the verse. Verse 5 combines imagery of exposure with dessication. There is a reversal both from adulthood to infancy, since the woman is as naked 'as on the day of her birth', and from life to death. Death by thirst and drought negate her role as the source of life and sustenance, perceived through the prism of her breasts in v. 4. One may note a similar fantasy in the case of the woman suspected of adultery in Numbers 5, whose womb and thigh wither if she is guilty.

Verses 5 and 14 somewhat schematically match and oppose each other. In v. 5, God's threat to make Israel 'like a wilderness' is coupled in v. 14 with his intention to make it 'as a forest',[1] two antithetical margins of culture. The vision in v. 5 in passive, the woman abandoned and parched, while that in v. 14 is active, ravaging by wild beasts. Moreover, in v. 5 there is a fantasy of infancy, immediately succeeded in v. 6 by YHWH's rejection of his children. The baby is not merely helpless, but a precultural being; reducing the woman to its condition ejects her from the symbolic—social and linguistic—order to pure animality, as does the exposure of her body in v. 12. But it also infuses the fantasy of sexual exposure with the far more terrible one of the exposure of children. Lasciviousness and sexual disgust supervene on infanticide.

---

1.   The parallel is perhaps clearer in Hebrew than in English, since the verbal forms used are identical: *weʿśamtîhā kammidbar* (v. 5) and *weʿśamtîm leyaʿar* (v. 14).

The husband is motivated by jealousy, which turns love into anti-love, rendered more intolerable by the memory of the love that has been defiled. Jealousy extenuates his vindictiveness; he is not intrinsically hateful, the common wisdom goes, but driven to it by circumstances. Circumstances, however, license a pre-existing reservoir of repressed thoughts. Of these the most important is the belief that woman, archetypally the mother, will always let one down, and the present betrayal merely confirms this inherent unreliability; and that aggression, impelled by greed, hatred and envy, is therefore justified. That the woman, from being a source of succour, becomes a desert is the germinal fantasy in v. 5; that she is torn to pieces is that of v. 14. The transfer from breasts (v. 4) to infant (v. 5) suggests a projection, an exchange of identity between mother and child. This is amplified in v. 5, in which the abandoned child turns the mother into a figure of abandonment. One is reminded of those children who, according to Donald Winnicott, are deprived of their mothers' presence for too long and, in despair, abandon them.[1]

The two fantasies, of abandonment and aggression, are mutually dependent in that the rage is provoked by frustration and, in turn, results in rejection. At the same time, they are incompatible since the woman is both absent, dying of neglect, and available for laceration. For that reason, perhaps, they are separated by the span of the passage. Contradictory and complementary, they enact the metaphorical play of likeness and difference, the resistance of the imagination to a single construction. The satisfactions of violence breach yet leave intact the narcissistic space outlined by the presence/absence of the mourned mother/lover in which the child fears death by exposure, reflected in the sexual sphere by the cross-currents of sadism, isolation and sterility.

Another element is introduced by the metaphor of blocking the woman's path with thorns in v. 8. This is a prelude to her subjection to her lovers' gaze in v. 12. As O'Connor shows, a non sequitur intervenes between prevention of access to them and humiliation before them.[2] The logical obstacle is not only a

1.   D. Winnicott, *Playing and Reality* (London: Routledge & Kegan Paul, 1991), pp. 112-13.
2.   M.P. O'Connor, 'The Pseudo-Sorites in Hebrew Verse', in

sign of resistance to and rationalization of the underlying fantasy, but also contributes an additional scenario of the woman's suffering. At this point the passage comes closest to pornography, in the sense of the inscription of women's shame for the sake of male pleasure. It feeds off the woman's desperation and frustration, gratifying the man both with the vision of female desire and the assertion of his power; this may be combined, voyeuristically, with hatred and envy that the desire is not for himself. The thorns, in particular, suggest cruelty and presage entrapment by the gaze of the lovers in v. 12. The sadistic fantasy relies on the pain of the woman, on imagining her consciousness; one notes the care with which God puts words in her mouth, projects himself into her speaking and acting. For this reason, the 'story' can never culminate in her destruction; it ritualistically exorcises the hatred on which it draws, to which it alludes. The erotic cover is evoked only to be displaced. Underneath the hint of perversion (or diversion), toying with the woman, tormented by the memory of desire and the wish to punish, are the nullification of the sexual transaction through exposure and the complex metamorphoses suggested by the superimposed images of rape and bestial voracity. If the one scene conceives of the woman stripped of her humanity, surrounded by hunters, the other turns the hunters into animals. They, symbolically, clothe themselves in their victim; nothing suggests more clearly the contagion of destruction: making the woman into a wilderness and consuming her reflects their desolation and fear of dissolution.

The erotic substratum of the text, its reversal of the language of love, is more poignant because of its echoes of the Song of Songs. These are particularly evident in vv. 8-9, and contribute to the sexual suggestiveness of those verses. In Song 3.1-4, the woman seeks her lover through the city at night, encountering watchmen before she eventually finds him; the phrase 'I sought him and did not find him' is repeated at the end of vv. 1 and 2. In Hos. 2.8-9 we find the same pair of verbs, 'seeking' and 'finding'; the phrase 'she will not find' likewise occurs at the end

E.W. Conrad and E.G. Newing (eds.), *A Ready Scribe: Perspectives on Language and Text. Essays in Honor of Francis I. Anderson's Sixtieth Birthday* (Winona Lake, IN: Eisenbrauns, 1987), p. 243.

of the clause. In Song 5.2-7, a variant of 3.1-4, the phrase 'I sought him and did not find him' appears too (5.6). Here, however, the watchmen beat and strip the woman. In both texts, Song of Songs and Hosea, the woman's search for her lover, contravening social propriety, is invested with erotic anticipation, intensified by frustration: she represents the amorous body. In both, she suffers humiliation. However, they are from opposite perspectives. Whereas in Hosea the voice is male and articulates a fantasy that passes from the sadistic game to voyeuristic exposure, in the Song of Songs it is female and expresses her outrage; we do not know what the watchmen feel, and the ordeal permits the celebration of the beauty of the woman's lover and thus of her own eros (Song 5.10-16).

Another difference is that in Hosea the woman's speech contradicts appearances: the pornographic gratification of witnessing her love-sickness is undercut by her confessedly economic motives. She will go after her lovers, because they provide her with sustenance, according to v. 7; she determines, in v. 9, to return to YHWH because he was a better investment. As Fokkelien van Dijk-Hemmes shows,[1] economic dependence is a powerful instrument of male control and rhetoric; women do not have libidos, or at least not libidos that count, but merely know where their interest lies. Since they are not genuinely sexual beings, they can be subsumed by male fantasy. The woman then corroborates her whorishness by being mercenary, and is subject both to the man's resentment and his will. More important, however, necessity provides a potential counter-argument to the passage's polemic: that the woman is compelled by ignorance and destitution, not by lust. If she genuinely does not know that YHWH is her benefactor (v. 10) and suffers from amnesia (v. 15), her guilt is extenuated. The counter-argument is developed in ch. 4, where the people perish 'without knowledge' (4.5), because the priests have been negligent of their duty. On the other hand, daughters and brides are granted

---

1. F. van Dijk-Hemmes, 'The Imagination of Power and the Power of Imagination: An Intertextual Analysis of Two Biblical Love Songs—The Song of Songs and Hosea 2', *JSOT* 44 (1989), pp. 75-88; repr. in A. Brenner (ed.), *A Feminist Companion to the Song of Songs* (The Feminist Companion to the Bible, 1; Sheffield: Sheffield Academic Press, 1993), pp. 156-70; p. 82.

immunity, in a curious inversion of the double standard, because their sexual liaisons follow men's bad example.

The Song of Songs is a much more pervasive presence in this passage than has been previously recognized,[1] not so much on the surface of the text as in its basic imagery. Whether one is dealing with the genre of love poetry, an early forerunner of the Song of Songs, or simply serendipity is impossible to determine, since the Song of Songs itself was probably composed much later. In any case, the invective in Hosea is directed against a valorization of love and the world represented most comprehensively by the Song of Songs. In Song 1.13, the woman's lover lies between her breasts like a sachet of myrrh; in Hosea (2.4) this is replaced by the signs of her adultery. In the Song of Songs, the birth of the lovers is an epiphany: the woman was 'splendid to the one who gave her birth' (6.9), the man is awakened to love and to life in a birth scene under an apple tree, full of cosmic significance (8.5). In Hosea, being reduced to one's birth state is evidence of utter dehumanization and nakedness is the subject of shame instead of celebration, as in the Song of Songs. In Hosea the wilderness is a sign of the woman's desolation and death by thirst; in the Song of Songs it is the place of the lovers' tryst, associated with exotic spices and sights (Song 1.14; 3.6; 8.5). In Song 4.8 the woman is invited to come down from Lebanon, the home of wild beasts; here, wild beasts threaten devastation.

Like Hosea, the Song of Songs exposes the woman to the sight of others, the 'lovers' and 'friends'[2] who are urged to 'eat' and 'drink' in the garden of love in 5.1 and, in particular, the spectators who elicit her return in 7.1[3] so that they may 'gaze' at her. In contrast to Hosea, however, their vision is positive; the voices must at least concur with that of the male lover in the descriptive catalogue of her beauty in 7.2-7. Like the woman in Hosea, the Song of Songs woman is metaphorically

---

1. Apart from in two previous studies: van Dijk-Hemmes, 'The Imagination of Power'; and A. van Selmes, 'Hosea and Canticles', *OTSWA* 7.8 (1964–65), pp. 85-89.

2. This may be obscured in translations; for instance NRSV substitutes 'with love' for 'lovers'.

3. 6.13 in English translations.

correlated with the land of Israel;[1] the description fragments the body into part-objects, each one of which develops a life of its own and is interconnected with the others in complex ways. The metaphorical process *simultaneously* splits and recombines, resulting in a total vision of the world, integrated and transformed through love. In Hosea, the sexual metaphor provides similar opportunities for the vision of recreation. However, fragmentation and integration are projected *successively* into the text, rendering problematic their logical cohesion: are they simply juxtaposed, is the transformation an act of will? The denial of the sexual relationship at the beginning of the passage ('For she is not my wife and I am not her husband') implicitly cancels out all its associated couplings, the entire interaction of God and Israel. It thus becomes a metaphor for the failure of the metaphorical process, just as in the Song of Songs the union of lovers is the sign of its success: the work of the poem corresponds to their discourse. The failure of metaphor, however, can only be communicated through metaphor, which thus subverts itself. Further, the denial is countermanded by YHWH's assumption of marital authority over the woman and by the woman's acknowledgment in v. 9, as well as by the framing narrative.

There is another contrast, another way in which the metaphor in Hosea is suspect. We know that the Song of Songs has its literal meaning, actually refers to the love of lovers. The reference of the metaphor in Hosea is quite opaque. It may refer to the exclusiveness of the cult, sacrificial communion as analogous to sexual communion, or to the transfer of moral qualities—loyalty, compassion and the like—as an equivalent to seminal fluids, as v. 22 might suggest, or to fertilization of the earth, corresponding to the imagery of 'sowing' and 'answering' in vv. 23-25. Betrothal may or may not mean consummation. If the passage accuses Israel of a category mistake—YHWH is its husband, not Baal—it propagates the Baalization YHWH it denounces.[2] The

1. This metaphorical dimension is too pervasive to require illustration; it is particularly evident in 7.2-7.
2. For this interpretation see, for example, H. Fisch, 'Hosea: A Poetics of Violence', in *Poetry with a Purpose: Biblical Poetics and Interpretation* (Bloomington and Indianapolis: Indiana University Press, 1988), pp. 147-48;

'wife' may be land or people; the identification is alternatively assumed by the text and abandoned by it.[1] The metaphor may accordingly be interpreted in various ways, none of which is decisive.

If the 'wife' is Israel, then it comprises both genders. The literal negation of the bond between 'my people' and 'I am' in 1.9 is transposed to the metaphorical one between 'husband' and 'wife' in v. 4. But this is hardly innocent. The supplementation, or mystification, is also a displacement: the male-dominated Israelite society is characterized as female. God is the supreme patriarch before whom all the men are women: the relation of male to female is that of God to humanity. But the metaphor is meaningless; the shift in gender of the men corresponds to no social or sacred reality. Their classification as 'women' is not reflected in their behaviour or in their self-perception. Its sole function, indeed, is to activate the contrast between wife and whore as a metaphor for their faithlessness, to compound their vilification with misogyny, even if only in drag. However, the transfer from male to female serves also to foreground, to render visible, women as social actors. We catch glimpses of women's normal life, especially cultic life, in the indictment that fuels YHWH's fantasy, in prospective nostalgia for the complacent present. It may be, as Phyllis Bird suggests,[2] that women are especially implicated in the accusation of sexual perfidy: that while the polemic is ostensibly against Israel, male and female, and lacks overt sexual content on the level of denotation, in fact it connotes women as preeminent vehicles of estrangement, so that a polemic against Israel easily becomes one against women.

In that case, the identification of her lovers is also in question. In v. 15, the lovers are parallel to the Baalim whose days YHWH

Wolff, *Hosea*, p. 34; H. Balz-Cochois, *Gomer: Der Hohenkult-Israels im Selbstverständnis der Volksfrommigkeit* (Frankfurt: Peter Lang, 1982). Whitt, at the cost of some radical textual excision, holds that the 'wife' is Asherah (W.D. Whitt, 'The Divorce of Yahweh and Asherah in Hos. 2.4-7, 12ff.', *SJOT* 6 [1992], pp. 31-67).

1.   For an accurate account of this, see J. Jeremias, *Der Prophet Hosea* (ATD; Göttingen: Vandenhoeck & Ruprecht, rev. edn, 1983), pp. 41-42.

2.   P. Bird, ' "To Play the Harlot": An Inquiry into Old Testament Metaphor', in P.L. Day (ed.), *Gender and Difference in Ancient Israel* (Minneapolis: Fortress Press, 1989), p. 82.

will visit, and in v. 10 YHWH's gifts of silver and gold are dedicated to Baal's image. The lovers whom Israel credits with the sustenance are likewise easily decoded as indigenous gods who are responsible for her fertility. There may be some reference to foreign powers, as elsewhere in the book. But the transfer from metaphorical to real women, the focus on women as exemplars of Israel's cultic perversity, will also direct our attention to their real lovers whose licentiousness at festivals is condemned in 4.12-14. If the lovers are not only Baalim but Israelite men, they participate in the scapegoating of the woman who, as Israel, represents themselves. The men are then ambiguous: as literally male and figuratively feminine, they are invited by YHWH to a parody of male bonding, whose victims they are. Literal and metaphorical domains mutually interact in that the actual affairs of Israelite men and women give rise to, and are encouraged by, their metaphorical promiscuity. At the same time, the collapse of the metaphorical into the literal threatens the distinctions on which metaphor is based. The intensity and detail with which the passage is elaborated are proportionate to its tendency to fragment. The repetition of the argument is not only a sign of obsessiveness, but of a wish to integrate discordance, to achieve reconciliation.

Verse 16 is the turning point, introduced by yet another 'Therefore'. As many commentators remark, the logical connection is surprising: nothing prepares us for the indictment to be followed by anything other than punishment. David Clines[1] argues that the three 'therefore's (vv. 8, 11, 16) represent alternatives of which only the last is truly viable if Israel, and thus God's enterprise, is to survive. There is, however, a direct continuation with the previous section. Verse 15 ends, 'and me she forgot, says YHWH'. Her forgetfulness annuls her history as the domain of memory, as well as providing potential extenuation. God, in turn, revokes history and takes her back to the beginning.

But is this possible? God supposes that through reversing time he can erase the memory of his violence, that he too can

1. D.J.A. Clines, 'Hosea 2: Structure and Interpretation', in E.A. Livingstone (ed.), *Studia Biblica 1978, I: Papers on Old Testament and Related Themes* (JSOTSup, 11; Sheffield: JSOT Press, 1979), p. 99.

make a new beginning. However, in practice return to the wilderness can only mean the end of Israel's political existence in the land, hence the death and exile that the book portends. It is coterminous with the deadly wilderness that Israel becomes in v. 5; the place of devastation and thirst is also the scene of romantic fulfilment. The two aspects of the figure of the mother are now divided: the land and the people. Only by leaving the land can Israel reliquish its identification with the land and its *mésalliance* with its indigenous gods. Only thus can it be exclusively YHWH's. In the romance, the children disappear: the woman returns to a prenuptial condition, marked by freedom from social responsibility and prurience, beyond birth and conception, before the entrance into the land and history. The wilderness, as Leith[1] has argued, is a liminal space, in between stages of life and geopolitical entities; she compares our chapter to a rite of initiation in which the transition from one state to another is marked by symbolic death and the suspension of social norms. The wilderness is the place of barrenness and death, but also of a new birth and the passage from chaos to order. The woman then passes through the fantasied death of v. 5 as a prelude to her initiation into marriage, her affirmation as a sexual person.

YHWH's desire may be construed in various ways: as an attempt at reparation, as the jealous person's desire for a lost love, as the sadist's longing for intimacy. Either the excitation of violence is transposed into that of sexuality, or the exhaustion of violence permits or provides an excuse for tenderness. Whereas in v. 5 the wilderness juxtaposed images of birth and death, in v. 17 birth, associated with the exodus as well as the wilderness, is metaphorically aligned with sexual awakening, as in the Song of Songs. The two images of the wilderness are both discontinuous and concurrent. Since the reality of exile is dissimulated by the romance, nostalgic regress to the beginning coincides with the end of Israel's political history, with the death of the kingdom. If one of the principal problems of the chapter is how to reconcile its beginning and its end, the violence and obsessiveness of the first part with the blissful transformation of the

---

1.   M.J. Leith, 'Verse and Reverse: The Transformation of the Woman, Israel in Hosea 1–3', in Day (ed.), *Gender and Difference*, pp. 95-108.

second, its rhetoric and structure support both their integral connection and their disjunction. On the one hand, the second half reverses the first: the children, from being rejected as 'children of promiscuity', are acknowledged as 'my people'; compassion replaces lack of compassion; disavowal of marital status is redressed by betrothal; forgetfulness is transferred from YHWH to the Baalim, and concomitantly ignorance of YHWH's gifts becomes knowledge of YHWH himself. Beasts are no longer destructive, since YHWH establishes a covenant with them. On the other hand, the unexpectedness of the change, the incommensurability of the two parts, is marked by the threefold repetition of 'on that day' (vv. 18, 20, 23), corresponding to the threefold repetition of 'therefore' (vv. 8, 11, 16). In both cases, repetition imposes simultaneity on the sequence. 'On that day' suggests a radical transformation of reality, an entirely new temporal order: the collapse of so many events into one day both lengthens it indefinitely and separates it from everything that precedes it. 'On that day' in prophetic writings is a formula for the new age the prophet heralds. Moreover, each event accomplishes a resolution of narrative tensions, the conclusion of the story which is also world history. The indefinitely long day verges on the infinity suggested by YHWH's betrothal to Israel 'for ever' (v. 21). Each time 'on that day' recurs, it announces a new divine initiative, an unforeseen supervention on human affairs. That they all occur on the same day marks them coeval, so that they become variants of each other, different aspects of the same picture.

'Says the Lord' in v. 15 is followed by 'Therefore' at the beginning of v. 16. Together they function as a hinge that both separates and connects the two halves of the chapter. The two temporal planes then interlock; the transformative journey into the wilderness coincides, as we have seen, with death and dispossession. The phrase 'on that day' otherwise occurs in Hosea only in 1.5, in the context of the breach of Israel's military power. Whether it is identical with the 'day' of ch. 2 is imponderable. At any rate, the formula associates the threshold of destruction with the advent of the new era. That it does not occur elsewhere broaches the question of whether ch. 2 is a microcosm of the rest of the book which repeats the trajectory from destruction to restoration, the divine vacillation between condemnation and compassion. 'On that day' demarcates a time that is or is not coterminous with that of the conclusion in ch. 14; it potentially disrupts integration of 2.16-25 into the book's structure.

In v. 16 YHWH allures the woman and takes her into the wilderness; there he speaks to her heart. The word for 'allure' may refer to seduction (for example Exod. 2.20), deception and, in the case of YHWH, to the entrapment of prophets and kings with misleading vaticination. Here, however, it loses the negative connotations familiar, for example, from Proverbs. Seduction may be an unusual pastime for YHWH. Nevertheless, it associates him not only with the paramours of the first part of the chapter, but also with the lovers of the Song of Songs. As in the Song of Songs, the lovers go from the wilderness to settled land. It is the matrix of their speech, where the woman awakens her lover at the place his mother bore him (Song 8.5); now, in Hosea, it is the woman who is brought back to her beginning, to the 'days of her youth'. YHWH persuades through speaking 'to her heart': it is less the content of the speech that matters than its appeal to her sensory and effective faculties. As in the Song of Songs, language seduces indirectly, through imaginative and sensual richness. It seeks to lift the inhibitions society imposes on young women. In other words, it counteracts the symbolic order that language itself constitutes. The words are a sign of the sexual male body, the nudity that society and its texts usually conceal; they elicit an equally expressive response. The word for 'allure' (Heb. *pth*) recurs in Hosea in 7.11, where Ephraim is a foolish (*pôtêh*) dove courting the great powers; YHWH thus takes advantage of its amorous susceptibility. In the Song of Songs the woman is, metaphorically, a dove whose voice her lover cultivates (Song 2.14). The desire for the woman's speech is the first breach in the closed circle of the male fantasy; it opens the possibility of a dialogue, albeit from within the fantasy, that will disrupt its exclusivity. The word for 'wilderness' (Heb. *midbar*) puns on that for 'I will speak' (Heb. *weaddibbartî*) that immediately follows it. The two are opposites: the wilderness is the world of silence in which the speech of her lover is the only thing that is heard. The transformation of silence into speech is equivalent, on the sexual plane, to the poetic celebration of nakedness. It is followed immediately by another transformation, of the wilderness into vineyards: 'I will give her thence her vineyards' (v. 17). It is unclear whether the vineyards are conflated with the wilderness—so the detail 'thence' might suggest—or whether they contrast the desert and settled land, exile and return. At any rate, they are opposites. Vineyards are associated with Dionysiac intoxication, hence with the pleasures of the first half of the chapter. This leads in turn to another transformation, of the valley of Achor to the Gate of Hope. The valley of Achor was the site of the first sacrilege on Israel's entrance into the land (Josh. 7.24, 26). The eeriness of the wilderness, its combination of dread and miracle, denaturizes it. All that sustains Israel in this waste is the divine word. The matrix is paradoxically a hostile environment, where Israel is not at home. Intertextually, the divine speech would presumably correspond to the Torah that God gave to Israel in the wilderness, the Torah whose infringement he castigates.

HOSEA 1–3, GENESIS 1–4 AND MASCULIST INTERPRETATION*

John Goldingay

As far as I know masculist interpretation of Scripture does not exist; indeed its birthing may be premature. By masculist interpretation I mean something different from male interpretation, which is simply what everyone did until twenty years ago.[1] That was interpretation undertaken mostly by males of texts which were written mostly by males, without the possibility occurring to anyone that this might limit or skew what the interpreter saw. Feminist interpretation drew attention to all that and asked what might become visible in texts when women read them as women rather than as honorary men. Masculist interpretation is parasitic on feminist interpretation; it is by definition post-feminist. It asks what might become visible in texts when they are read in conscious awareness of maleness. Arguably, at least, masculist interpretation of course need not be limited to males any more than feminist interpretation need be limited to females, but in this piece I write as a man seeking to be self-aware as a man.

A passage such as Hosea 1–3 provides an obvious context for the raising of this question. This is not merely because there seems no prospect of coming to agreement on an understanding of these chapters on a historical-critical basis (for example on

* A paper due to be published in *HBT* 16.2 (1994) or 17.1 (1995), slightly expanded in the light of the discussion at the seminar on feminist interpretation at the Edinburgh meeting of the Society for Old Testament Study, July 1994.

1. But see for example the opening chapters in E. Schüssler Fiorenza (ed.), *Searching the Scriptures. I. A Feminist Introduction* (New York: Crossroad, 1993; London: SCM Press, 1994) for the earlier history of feminist interpretation.

questions of the literary relationships between the chapters and the historical relationships between the events they refer to and between the female figures who appear),[1] though that is so. It is because whatever the answers to these questions, the text is overtly an expression of a distinctively male experience, and it is this experience which is then a base from which an understanding of God is expressed. There is of course a feminist literature which illumines Hosea 1–3,[2] but a masculist interpretation will have a different starting point and perspective, even if possibly a complementary one. If feminist interpretation uses women's experience as an aid in gaining illumination on the text's own concerns, including its implications for the nature of God, and in discovering its affirmation and challenge regarding what it means to be women (and men), masculist interpretation uses men's experience for parallel ends.

The feminist literature on Hosea 1–3 raises telling questions about the male prophet, his God, and their attitude to their partners, and a 'masculist interpretation' could be taken to be a means of avoiding those, a means of subverting the feminist agenda, evading the challenge to patriarchy and androcentrism, and reinstating male interpretation in new man-ish guise (it is for this reason that its birthing may be premature). That is not my desire. A masculist interpretation does not replace a feminist one; further, the masculist interpretation of Hosea 1–3 which follows is not the only possible one (it is a conservative one, to begin with, more Phyllis Trible than Mieke Bal or Cheryl Exum). But my hope is that something like masculist interpretation might help me to handle the theological implications of the androcentric, patriarchal aspect to Scripture, and help me come to terms with myself as a man in such a way that I may be able to change and thus respond to the feminist critique. To be

---

1.   See recently G.I. Davies, *Hosea* (London: Marshall, Morgan & Scott; Grand Rapids: Eerdmans, 1992), and *Hosea* (OTG; Sheffield: JSOT Press, 1992).

2.   See, for example, T.D. Setel, 'Prophets and Pornography: Female Sexual Imagery in Hosea', in L.M. Russell (ed.), *Feminist Interpretation of the Bible* (Philadelphia: Westminster Press, 1985), pp. 86-95; R.J. Weems, 'Gomer: Victim of Violence or Victim of Metaphor?', in K.G. Cannon and E. Schüssler Fiorenza (eds.), *Interpretation for Liberation* (*Semeia* 47 [1989]), pp. 87-104.

post-feminist is to build on feminism, but not to attempt to leave it behind.

Masculinity and Genesis 1–4

So what is masculinity? The opening chapters of Genesis point to three particular features of maleness which both resonate with the experience of many men and women today and also seem of prima facie relevance to the interpretation of Hosea 1–3. They thus make Genesis 1–4 a suggestive text to put alongside Hosea 1–3. First, men discover who they are by setting themselves over against women. It is when the man sees the woman that he knows who he is. It is enough to make him leave father and mother and want to live with her. Of course he then finds that his relationship with this wonderful creature gets him into dead trouble. For a man, at least, there is thus a tragic ambiguity about the man–woman relationship. Women are our making: we are lonely or dissatisfied or incomplete without them, as they do not seem to be without us (part of the background may lie in the fact that a girl's first relationship is with a person of her own sex, a boy's with a person of the opposite sex).[1] But women are also our downfall: not necessarily for reasons to do with them, but for reasons to do with us. All this is not confined to the marriage relationship. For men there can in general be a spark about their relationships with women which can be particularly creative and in which they can find themselves, though there is also the potential for big trouble not least because men may find it more difficult to avoid falling in love with women colleagues and friends than vice versa (the 'When Harry Met Sally' syndrome).

A second feature of masculinity which is reflected in the opening chapters of Genesis is that men are responsible. They rule. They have authority. To judge from Gen. 1.26-28 this is not how God meant it to be, because authority was designed to be shared by men and women, but to judge from Genesis 3 it is

---

1. Cf. V. Saiving Goldstein's classic discussion of this distinction between the sexes in 'The Human Situation: A Feminine View', *JR* 40 (1960), pp. 100-12; reprinted in C.P. Christ and J. Plaskow (eds.), *Womanspirit Rising* (San Francisco: Harper, 1979), pp. 25-42.

how it came to be. For a man that, too, has an ambiguity about it. There is great fulfilment to be gained from the exercise of responsibility, of power, and much good that can come from it, but there is also stress and temptation attached to it, and potential for evil.

A third feature of masculinity is relative physical strength, aggressiveness and the capacity for violence, perhaps the inclination to violence. When the Bible first speaks of sin, in Genesis 4, what it speaks of is violence. Cain's response to disappointment with God's reaction to him is anger, and that is when sin is couching like a demon at his door (?; Gen. 4.7). He spurns the challenge to utilize his strength and aggressiveness to defeat this demon and instead turns them onto Abel. Henceforth Cain himself expects to live in fear of the cycle of violence he has initiated. He is a master who will be outdone by his pupils, as is illustrated in the chilling prosody of his great-great-great-grandson who is proud to multiply Cain's violence (Gen. 4.23). Yet even male strength, aggressiveness and violence are matters of ambiguity and tragedy, and not merely sin. A petite feminist I know says that one thing she appreciates about men is that they are bigger than she is; they can reach things she cannot, for instance. Our aggressiveness can be a means of achievement, for the sake of others and not just for ourselves as individuals (or for our sex). In general, our strength, our aggressiveness and our capacity for violence are gifts which can be used on behalf of the weak, but they can easily become our sin.

Male sexuality, responsibility or power, and strength or violence might be able to form a holy trinity; they can certainly form an unholy one. Indeed, each of the three possible combinations of these three features of masculinity suggests an oppression or a burden. Men have commonly had to be responsible for the sexual relationship, and that becomes a problem for us as men ('Why should I always have to take the initiative?') as well as for women ('Why do I have to sit here and wait?'). We have been able to combine sex and violence, and have often done so; in general, it is men who commit rape. In other areas, too, we assume it is natural to exercise responsibility by force; in general, it is men who fight wars.

Masculinity and Hosea 1–3

What happens when one reads the opening chapters of Hosea in the light of their being a male text? In their very preamble (1.1) we are introduced to a man identified by his relationship with his father, and with five monarchs who are all male. It is mostly men who get the positive opportunity to exercise power in Israel (an exception such as Athaliah in 2 Kgs 11 proves the rule by behaving with the violence of an honorary man), and who thus also bear the burden of guilt for the people's failure, which is commonly attributed to the leadership's failure.

When we come to the material that relates to Hosea's relationship with a woman or women and to Yahweh's analogous relationship with Israel, we begin with the assumption that the man is also responsible for the sexual relationship. It is he who has to take the initiative in wooing, and in wooing again. The ambiguity of a man's relationship with a woman comes out very clearly in the material. The relationship is characterized by love and pain; it is capable of bringing both great joy and great hurt. If most singers of blues, soul and rock are men, and most of their songs are about the pain their relationships with women have brought them, then Hosea is their patron prophet. The potential for joy makes a man want to reach out as Hosea does, the potential for pain and rejection makes him want to lash out, an instinct only just under the surface in chs. 2 and 3.[1] A man to whom his wife is unfaithful is torn between violence and love (see for example Hos. 2.4-5 and 16-17 [2-3 and 14-15]). The unholy trinity are all at work.

All three features of a man's relationship with a woman reappear in the relationship Hosea attributes to Yahweh. The male prophet thinks of God as in the position of a man with a man's instincts.

First, Yahweh is incomplete without Israel as men are incomplete without women. It is he who seeks her, not she who seeks him (I usually avoid the gendered language, but here it is appropriate). The climax to his word of rejection is that she ceases to be his people and he ceases to be her God (1.9); it is a

---

1. On Hos. 2 see Weems, 'Gomer'.

calamity for both. The climax to his indictment of her is that she forgets him (2.15 [13]); to be forgotten is to be treated as a non-person, to cease to be. The climax of his vision of a blissful future is that she should once again say 'You are my God' (2.30 [28]). Yahweh's self-knowledge depends on his relationship with Israel. Who is Yahweh if Yahweh ceases to be 'the holy one of Israel', to use Isaiah's phrase (Isa. 1.4)?

All this is particularly interesting given that Hosea, like other prophets, declines to find sexuality within the Godhead itself. Unlike other Middle Eastern deities, Yahweh has no heavenly wife or lover. The male prophet thus finds ways both of connecting God with and of disconnecting God from sexuality with its ambiguity. To connect God with it is to affirm that God is in touch with this fundamental aspect of male being with that potential for joy and hurt. To disconnect God from it is to deny that God is affected by its negative aspect with the possible implication that its tragedy, failure, pain, and rejection are ultimate realities.

Secondly, Yahweh takes the initiative in the relationship. In general, the male prophet resembles other contributors to the Hebrew Bible in picturing God as bearing a man's lonely responsibility for the world and for history. Admittedly it may also be noted that the Hebrew Bible does picture God as fairly laid-back about this responsibility. Yahweh has no trouble delegating and does not mind being sidelined. No doubt Yahweh can afford to take the long view in the confidence of seeing off whole sequences of uncooperative Israelite generations. As is the case with Yahweh and sexuality, though in a different way, the portrait of Yahweh as one exercising responsibility thus both reflects the nature of male experience and addresses it by offering an alternative model.

An implication of this way of looking at the gender-related element in the Bible's portrayal of God is that the Bible's emphasis on grace turns out to be from a male perspective. It is a feminist commonplace that men sin by acting, women by failing to act, another difference which may have a background in girls' forming their first relationship with a person of their own sex (from whom they do not need to differentiate themselves by taking identity-forming action) and boys' forming their first relationship with a person of the opposite sex (from whom they need to differentiate themselves by taking identity-forming action).[1] In stressing God's activity in gracious initiative, the male prophet tells men what they need to hear. Everything does not depend on us; there is some responsibility being exercised on a higher plane. This provides us with another reason to be more laid-back than we might be inclined to be.

Admittedly, subsequent insights in Hosea may deconstruct this suggestion. My colleague Gillian Cooper points out to me that in ch. 11 it is the powerlessness of Yahweh that speaks (she adds that this might explain part of Hosea's attractiveness for feminist interpreters, who otherwise are relatively little drawn to the prophets). Yahweh is caught between love and judgment with no way out. 'When God speaks through Hosea, we hear the voice of the parent, seeing the child rushing towards his downfall, and utterly powerless to do anything to stop it... God has taken the risk of letting the children go, and cannot step in and sort out their mess for them', though God never gives up on them.[2] A man, then, is beguiled into trusting God as possessing the all-powerfulness that he himself often seems expected to manifest, but cannot. He is in due course drawn on to accept the discovery that even God does not possess this quality, but models the ability to live without it.

Thirdly, the male prophet portrays Yahweh as involved in the violence which is a characteristic of maleness (see the references to Hos. 2 above). Yahweh had commissioned Jehu for the bloody coup d'état to which he was in any case inclined (2 Kgs 9–10). Now Yahweh declares the intention to punish Jehu for it (Hos. 1.4). The punishment will affect not merely the man but his entire household. One theological implication of such passages may be the conviction that Yahweh is willing to be compromised rather than stay unstained in an aseptic environment, if this is the inevitable price of being involved in history in its ambiguity. The story and the prophecy about Jehu also point to a further element in this attribution of violence to

1.   See Saiving Goldstein, 'The Human Situation'.
2.   G.A. Cooper, 'God's Gamble: Hosea 11.1-9', *Third Way* 15.8 (1993), p. 20. I am grateful to Ms Cooper for the encouragement to write and to persevere with this paper.

Yahweh. John Barton has suggested that prophets did not first analyse the moral nature of their society and then infer that Yahweh must act in judgment. Rather they first became aware that calamity was imminent and then looked at society and inferred the reasons.[1] Perhaps, then, the male prophets' pre-occupation with divine violence reflects a desire that violence be explained as much as a desire that violence be inflicted. They did not invent the violent calamities; they did invent the explanations of them. Perhaps male ambiguity about violence finds expression here: we are both attracted to it and afraid of it within ourselves. We need to feel that it is under control. Perhaps male awareness of responsibility for the world also finds further expression here: it is important to men that someone is in control, that things are not out of hand. In this connection, too, we can cope with violence if there is some logic to it.

As with sexuality, the male prophet both links Yahweh with violence and distances Yahweh from it. There is no violence within the Godhead, as there is among other Middle Eastern deities, but there is violence in God's relationship with the world. If men see God as involved in violence, this might (at least in theory) have the potential to protect the world a little from male violence; violence is God's business, not men's (cf. Lev. 19.18; Deut. 32.35; taken up in Rom. 12.19). Yet even while portraying God's exercise of violence on human beings, the biblical passages presuppose that God is not at ease with violence, that violence does not have the last word.

The prophets' descriptions of God will reflect the personalities and (for example) the sex of the writers. Divine revelation comes via the human personality; it is because human beings are made in God's image that they can speak of God in a way which reflects who they are as human beings. But it is only when we have men and women together that we have the divine image represented, and all this therefore suggests that (for instance) male insights on God which emerge from the Bible have to be complemented by female ones. But then I would think that, being a man.

---

1. J. Barton, 'History and Rhetoric in the Prophets', in M. Warner (ed.), *The Bible as Rhetoric* (London and New York: Routledge, 1990), pp. 53-55.

MARITAL FIDELITY AND INTIMACY: A VIEW FROM HOSEA 4*

Mayer I. Gruber

In her highly significant book *In the Wake of the Goddesses*[1] Tikva Frymer-Kensky writes: 'The transformation in thought brought about by biblical monotheism did not address sexuality. The Bible focuses on sexual behavior as a form of social behavior, but never incorporates sexuality into its vision of humanity or its relations with the divine.'[2] Frymer-Kensky goes on to explain that

> ancient pagan religion also portrayed the sexual impulse as a goddess of sexual attraction. Male gods, figures of potency, can express sexual activity: they cannot fully express sexual attraction in a predominantly heterosexual, androcentric society. The figure of Inanna/Ishtar provides a way to conceptualize the erotic impulse, a vocabulary to celebrate its presence, an image with which to comprehend the human experience of sexual desire. Sexual desire comes from the presence of Ishtar. When she is absent,
>
> > The Bull springs not upon the cow,
> > the ass does not inseminate the Jenny.
> > The man lies down in his (own) chamber
> > The woman lies down on her side.
>
> Sexuality was part of the divine realm, most specifically of the female divine. Even when other functions of goddesses were absorbed by male gods, sexuality could not be absorbed into male divinity. Ishtar remained the representative and divine

* This article is expanded from a lecture presented in the Solomon Goldman Lecture Series at the Spertus Institute of Judaica in Chicago, November 20 1994.

1. T. Frymer-Kensky, *In the Wake of the Goddesses* (New York: Free Press, 1992).

2. Frymer-Kensky, *Goddesses*, pp. 187-88.

patron of sexual attraction and activity. All of this religious dimension of sexuality disappears in biblical monotheism.[1]

Frymer-Kensky concludes her chapter called 'Sex in the Bible' with the assertion that 'the Bible's lack of discussion of the dynamics and implications of sex creates a tension within the biblical system. There is a vacuum in an essential area of human concern.'[2] In fact, as we shall see, the biblical prophets have a very clear vision of sexuality—but a radically different vision of sexuality than that which is embodied in the goddess Ishtar, who represents the dream of many a male to this day: unprotected sex with a female who spreads no life-threatening diseases, never gets pregnant, never demands marriage,[3] and allows both partners to delude themselves into thinking that genital tension and its release constitute intimacy.

This delusion, which is the classic description of the sexually active teenager,[4] has been shared throughout the generations by men and women of all ages, including men and women bound by and faithful to the bonds of matrimony, and who—reaching out to touch someone—never get beyond feeling each other to sharing each other's feelings and supporting each other emotionally.[5]

1.   Frymer-Kensky, *Goddesses*, pp. 187-88.

2.   *Goddesses*, p. 198.

3.   For the description of Inanna, the Sumerian counterpart of the Assyro-Babylonian Ishtar, as unattached female see Frymer-Kensky, *Goddesses*, pp. 25-29. Concerning the complexity of Ishtar/Inanna see, however, R. Harris, 'Inanna-Ishtar as Paradox and a Coincidence of Opposites', *History of Religions* 30 (1991), pp. 261-78.

4.   Cf. L. Dash, *When Children Want Children* (New York: William Morrow, 1989).

5.   J. Byng-Hall, 'Resolving Distance Conflicts', in A.S. Gurman (ed.), *Casebook of Marital Therapy* (New York and London: Guilford, 1985), p. 1, writes as follows: 'An adequate marriage can be described in this way. A creative marriage is one in which fresh discoveries are made in the to and fro of daily contact. In the safe, familiar warm setting of intimacy, two imaginations fire each other off to find new experiences of each other. When separate, each can be independent, although exploration may be fostered by an inner imaginary dialogue with a spouse who, it can reliably be anticipated, will be interested. An ongoing sharing of some of the new ideas can bring freshness into the intimacy, thus rejuvenating the relationship. An increasing depth of both intimacy and autonomy can then develop

Throughout the generations, in their desire to reach out and touch someone, married men and women who have been denied access to the hearts of their spouses often seek a paramour, of whom they say, 'He/she understands me. My spouse does not.'[1] Quite as often a spouse imagines that his or her non-cheating life partner is unfaithful. In many cases mutual respect and trust can be restored by proper counseling or therapy. Herbert C. Brichto's classic study of the rite of the bitter waters in Numbers 5 argues most convincingly that this elaborate rite, far from being an ordeal to expose the guilt of an unfaithful wife, is in fact a means of restoring the husband's faith and confidence in the innocence of a wife, who has been all too faithful to an aloof husband; whereas he may find it hard to believe that she could not have been seeking elsewhere the emotional support he has long denied her.[2]

This brings us to the fourth chapter of the book of Hosea or, to be more precise, Hos. 4.10-19. In the New Jewish Version of

with each phase complementing and adding to the other.' See also M. Edwards and E. Hoover, *The Challenge of Being Single* (New York: New American Library, 1975), pp. 166-67: 'It... comes as a big (and disappointing) surprise for people to learn that physical intimacy does not mean emotional intimacy. Instant intimacy is usually involved in a one-night stand, but it can also be involved in a longer relationship that typically seems to start bogging down whenever the partners leave the bedroom. The reason behind this syndrome is that some people fear emotional intimacy far more than they fear sex, and they use sex as a replacement for intimacy. Real intimacy involves two people getting to know each other by exploring thoughts, feelings, ideas, and it takes a lot of time and talking for this to happen. It isn't easy to achieve real intimacy, and since it is so much easier to hop into bed, many people settle for the illusion of intimacy which sex can beguilingly provide—for a time'.

1.   See E.M. Brown, *Patterns of Infidelity and their Treatment* (Frontiers in Couples and Family Therapy, 3; New York: Bronner/Mazel, 1991), p. 16; 'Marital infidelity is... an inefficient joint venture by a couple to transfuse life into their marriage'. See also p. 20: 'Affairs... are sexy, but they have little to do with sex—and a lot to do with keeping anger, fear and emptiness at bay'.

2.   See H.C. Brichto, 'The Case of the Soṭah and a Reconsideration of Biblical "Law"', *HUCA* 46 (1975), pp. 55-70.

the Hebrew Scriptures[1] is found a rare departure from the gibberish which passes for a translation of the passage in other English versions. Prepared by H.L. Ginsberg, editor of the New Jewish Version, this brilliantly original translation of the book of Hosea has yet to be provided with a commentary that will explain the scientific basis of its departure from the standard and the hackneyed and the banal in its attempt to convey to the modern English reader what Hosea actually said. However, Ginsberg left us with some laconic notes in the entry 'Hosea' in the *Encyclopedia Judaica*,[2] in the margin of the JPS *Tanakh* (1985)[3] and especially in an article called 'Lexicographical Notes'.[4]

We shall see that Hosea in Ginsberg's translation provides us with a biblical view of sexuality and marriage far more noble and ennobling than that of the sexually active teenager represented by Ishtar: 'Truly they shall eat, but not be sated; They shall swill, but not be satisfied, Because they have forsaken the LORD to practice lechery' (Hos. 4.10). In his improved translation of this verse Ginsberg has incorporated three very important insights, of which he spells out in his notes only two, assuming that the first of these three insights is self-explanatory. According to the rules of biblical poetry, we should expect that if the first clause speaks of eating, the second clause would speak of drinking—as in Prov. 9.4: 'Come eat of my bread and drink of the wine I have poured'; or Qoh. 9.7: 'Go eat your bread in joy and drink your wine in gladness'.

Taking for granted that the two verbs *'ākᵉlû* and *hiznû* must refer respectively to eating and drinking. Ginsberg finds proof that *hiznû* means 'drink to excess' in v. 18 of our chapter, which he translates, 'They drink to excess—their liquor turns against them'. Further proof that v. 10 refers to 'drinking' is found in the use at the end of that verse of the verb *yiprōṣû*, which means 'to be full of liquid', a usage of the verb *pāraṣ* found also in Prov. 3.10, which reads as follows:

1.   *Tanakh: A New Translation of the Holy Scriptures* (Philadelphia: Jewish Publication Society, 1985).

2.   H.L. Ginsberg, 'Hosea, Book of', *EncJud*, VIII, pp. 1019-20.

3.   *Tanakh*, pp. 985-87.

4.   H.L. Ginsberg, 'Lexicographical Notes', in *Hebräische Wortforschung* (VTSup, 16; Leiden: Brill, 1967), pp. 73-75.

Your barns will be filled with grain
Your vats will be full of (*yiprōṣû*) new wine.[1]

Hos. 4.10 thus introduces us to a description of festival celebrations in which people overeat and drink too much liquor—the sort of thing that happens at many a New Year's Eve party—and which often leads to what is described at the end of v. 10 and the beginning of v. 11 with the words *lišmōr zᵉnût*, 'to practice lechery'. Granted that in our standard Hebrew text the infinitive *lišmōr* and its object *zenût*, 'lechery', are found in distinct verses, most modern interpreters (including NRSV and Ginsberg) go back to the tradition embodied in the very oldest translation of Hebrew Scripture, the Septuagint, and understand here: 'They have forsaken the LORD to devote themselves to fornication'. Now here is a classic example of prophetic hyperbole.

We have all heard of the young Jewish single person who takes the *tefillin* along for the morning prayers after the night of non-marital sex. So where is the unfaithfulness? This is precisely the prophet's innovation. Consensual extra-marital sex between two single adults may not violate any law found in Leviticus 18 or 20. However, such a substitute for marital intimacy is not all we are meant to be. It is not the fullest representation of the divine image within us. So, in a manner typical of the prophets of the eighth century BCE, Hosea says that such a celebration of the festival of new wine,[2] where drinking leads to sexual license, is no less than a rejection of God.

Heschel writes, 'To us...exploiting the poor is slight; to the prophets a disaster'.[3] In the same vein Hosea tells us that a little extra-marital sex is no less than apostasy. An exaggeration if you will; but exaggeration which contains in it the potential to raise up marital sex to an expression of the intimacy which Hosea 1–2 and Jeremiah and Ezekiel and, of course, the classic commentaries on Song of Songs rightly compare to the proper

1. Ginsberg, 'Lexicographical Notes', pp. 73-74.
2. If Ginsberg is correct in understanding *tirôš* to mean 'festival of new wine', it is reasonable to suggest that this term may refer to the festival of the 15th of the month of Ab, which inaugurates the season of vintage, and which is described in *Ta'an.* 5.8.
3. A.J. Heschel, *The Prophets* (New York: Harper & Row, 1962), p. 4.

intimacy of the religious devotee to his or her God.[1]

The picture of a festival celebration leading to fornication is continued in the remainder of vv. 11-12, which Ginsberg translates as follows:

> Wine and new wine destroy the mind of my people
> It consults its stick, Its rod directs it!
> A lecherous impulse has made them go wrong,
> And they have strayed from submission to their God.

Ginsberg in his inimitable way points out that the expression 'wine and new wine' in v. 11 reminds him of the expression 'new grain and new wine' referring to the names of two festivals found in similar descriptions of orgiastic behavior in Hos. 7.14 and Hos. 9.1-2.[2]

In any case, we are talking here (in 4.11) not just about the wine but about a spirit of levity associated with a festival celebration and exacerbated by the drinking in excess of wine, which *yiqqah lēb*. Ginsberg translates, 'destroy the mind'. In fact, the Hebrew word *lēb* refers to the seat of both the intellect and the emotions. Hosea, speaking in the name of God, says that imbibing of wine leads, as we all know, to loss of control over both one's intellect and one's emotions so that one confuses purely physical intimacy with true intimacy, of which one of the most beautiful expressions can be sexual. This obfuscation is rightly called 'taking away the *lēb*', that is the power of intellect and emotions to govern one's behavior. So what happens when people lose their senses and in any relationship—even in marriage—confuse physical intimacy with the real thing?

The answer to this question is found in v. 12: 'It consults its stick, Its rod directs it'. Granted that stick and rod are two words for the same thing, to what is reference made here? Ginsberg here restored the pristine message of Hosea, long obscured by generations of biblical scholars, who saw here a

---

1. See, for example, Jer. 2.2; Ezek. 16.8.

2. Ginsberg, ('Lexicographical Notes', p. 74) holds that the correct reading in Hos. 4.11 is not *yayín*, 'wine', but *dāgān*, 'new grain', a festival which according to Ginsberg is mentioned also in Hos. 7.14; 9.1-2; and Ps. 4.8. This festival may well correspond to the barley harvest festival observed 'on the morrow of the Sabbath' and described in Lev. 23.9-14.

reference to wooden idols,[1] pointing out that the Hebrew terms *'ēs* and *maqleh* are in this passage, like the Arabic term *qadib*, the German *Rute* and in many instances of Latin *virga* and Syriac *qanya*, euphemisms for the male sex organ.[2] And so we have here in Hosea the description of a dialogue between a man and his sexual apparatus—to which there are ample analogies in the modern practice of sex therapy.[3] In this dialogue the man inquires of his sex organ what he should do and his sex organ tells him what to do. There are parallels to what is described here in several recent motion pictures such as 'Blink', where one character says to another 'You are thinking with your dick'.

It can also be pointed out that in Hosea's description of a dialogue between a man and his sex organ we have, possibly, the earliest reference to what feminist biblical scholarship calls 'phallocentric thinking'. Used as a pejorative for what might also be called politically incorrect thinking, the term 'phallocentric thinking' refers to an attitude of mind characteristic of all too many males who look upon every woman as no more than a sexual object.

Reinforcing what he has said in v. 10, namely that confusing physical intimacy with true intimacy is tantamount to apostasy, the prophet, again speaking in the name of God, declares in v. 12: 'For a lecherous spirit has led him [i.e., the Israelite male] astray so that they [i.e., the Israelite males collectively] have strayed from loyalty to their God'. In this verse we truly see the artistry of Hosea—who, like every great prophet of Israel, was a brilliant poet. We began with v. 10, in which we had the verb *hiznû*, 'they drank in excess'. We moved on to v. 11, where we found the noun *zᵉnût* meaning 'fornication, extra-marital sex', and we have arrived at v. 12 where a spirit of *zᵉnût*, 'fornication', brought about a situation in which *wayyiznû mitaḥat 'ᵉlōhêhem*, 'they strayed from their God'. Clearly, Hosea employs the literary technique uncovered and named by Martin Buber: *leitmotif*. Buber refers to the use of a single word or

1. Contrast F.I. Andersen and D.N. Freedman, *Hosea* (AB, 24; Garden City, NY: Doubleday, 1980), pp. 365-66.
2. Ginsberg, 'Lexicographical Notes', p. 74.
3. Personal communication from psychoanalyst Robert Galatzer-Levy, MD.

homonyms with distinct meanings.[1] The underlying message here is that wine leads to fornication, which is tantamount to apostasy. An intimate relationship of dialogue with the prophetic text or speech will enable the audience to decode the message, return to God, avoid fornication and restructure the festival celebration—so that it leads to true intimacy and serves as a worthy tribute to God's bounty in providing grapes and grain.

We have arrived now at vv. 13-14, my treatment of which[2] inspired me to seek the message abiding in vv. 10-12. Here is Ginsberg's rendering of vv. 13-14:

> They sacrifice on the mountaintops
> And offer on the hills
> Under oaks, poplars and terebinths
> Whose shade is so pleasant
> That is why their daughters fornicate
> And their daughters-in-law commit adultery.
> I will not punish their daughters for fornicating
> Nor their daughters-in-law for committing adultery;
> For they themselves turn aside with whores
> And sacrifice with prostitutes,
> And a people that is without sense must stumble.

In the standard modern English translations the word here translated 'prostitutes', Hebrew *qᵉdēšôt*, is often rendered 'temple prostitutes'.[3] Expanding upon Rashi's comment at Deut. 23.18, I have demonstrated that the term *qᵉdēšāh*, like its Akkadian analogue *ḫarimtu*, literally means 'set apart' and refers to a prostitute; and that there is no evidence in the Bible or in any other text from the ancient Near East for cultic prostitution.[4] Cultic prostitution is a scholarly myth according to which chance sexual encounters were perceived as fructifying the earth

---

1. M. Buber and F. Rosenzweig, *Die Schrift and ihre Verdeutschung* (Berlin: Schocken Books, 1936), pp. 226-38.

2. M.I. Gruber, 'The *qādēš* in the Book of Kings and in Other Sources', *Tarbiz* 52 (1983), pp. 167-76 (in Hebrew); 'The Hebrew *qᵉdēšāh* and her Canaanite and Akkadian Cognates', *UF* 18 (1986), pp. 133-48 (repr. in *idem*, *The Motherhood of God and Other Studies* [South Florida Studies in the History of Judaism, 57; Atlanta: Scholars Press, 1992], pp. 17-47); 'The *qᵉdēšāh*— What was her Function?', *Beersheva* 3 (1988), pp. 45-51 (in Hebrew).

3. See for example, NRSV.

4. M.I. Gruber 'The *qᵉdēšâh*', and 'The *qādēš*' (English and Hebrew).

and providing us with grain and grapes and olives.[1] One of the by-products of this scholarly myth is the widely held belief that extra-marital sex which is not part of a fertility cult is accepted and encouraged in the Bible. In this day of epidemic disease it is tragic that outdated pseudo-scholarship still gives, as it were, biblical sanction to chance sexual encounter as a substitute for intimacy.

Since I have already demonstrated elsewhere that *q^edēšôt* is simply a synonym for *zônôt*, 'prostitutes', we are free now to deal with the underlying message of vv. 13-14. There are two basic ideas here: (1) that sacrificial worship at outdoor rural shrines leads to licentious behavior, which is reprehensible; (2) that faithfulness in marriage is demanded equally from husbands and wives. Employing prophetic hyperbole, Hosea brings home the essence of true marital intimacy when he suggests that—contrary to the common reading of Leviticus and Numbers and Deuteronomy—unfaithful women shall go unpunished and enjoy divine protection so long as their husbands do not clean up their own act, confine their sexual activity to their lawfully wedded wives and teach their sons to do likewise.

It is highly worthy of note that the Mishnah and the Babylonian Talmud canonize Hosea's vision of a single standard for both sexes. The Mishnah boldly states in *Soṭ.* 5.1, 'As the bitter waters test her innocence or guilt so do the bitter waters test his innocence or guilt'.

The full implications of this egalitarian Mishnah are worked out in *b. Soṭ.* 28a. Elsewhere in the Mishnah it is stated (*Soṭ.* 9.9), 'When adulterers became many the rite of the bitter water ceased, and R. Johanan b. Zakkai abolished it, for it is written, "I will not punish your daughters when they commit fornication nor your daughters-in-law when they commit adultery, for they themselves go aside with prostitutes"'.

Perhaps our prophet is a feminist. Perhaps by giving divine sanction to woman's imitation of man's unfaithfulness—a blatant violation of legal norms accepted throughout the ancient Near East—our prophets and later the rabbis attempt to bring home to men the untenability of their own behavior and attitudes.

---

1. Frymer-Kensky, *Goddesses*, pp. 199-202.

We must remember that the book of Hosea is part of the almost lost literature of the Northern Kingdom. Some of this literature was rescued, preserved and edited by the academy set up by King Hezekiah (see Prov. 25.1). Believing that they were divinely inspired the members—prophets if you will—of the Hezekian Academy allowed themselves to intersperse the book of Hosea with what are called the Judaite glosses, in which the prophecies of rebuke spoken in the eighth century BCE in the Northern Kingdom would serve to encourage continued good behavior in the Southern Kingdom.[1] Typical of these glosses are the words 'Let Judah not incur guilt' in the middle of Hos. 4.15. Without the gloss, the original message of Hosea reads as follows, again in Ginsberg's translation: 'If you are a lecher,[2] Israel, do not come to Gilgal, do not make pilgrimage to Beth-aven, and do not swear by the LORD'. In effect, Hosea says, speaking in the name of God, if you Israelite men will continue to be unfaithful to your wives and engage in physical intimacy outside of marital intimacy, please do not come to my temples and please do not claim me as your God. Hosea's words are reminiscent of Isa. 1.12-13, 'Trample my courts no more'. It is God's proper response to behavior which has already been referred to in vv. 10-12 as Israel's rejection of God. If they have rejected God, they should stay home from the temple until their behavior reflects their acceptance of divine sovereignty, and all that acceptance should imply in terms of the proper behavior of an Israelite man to his wife and to women in general.

Skipping over v. 16, which is fully explained in note o in the JPS *Tanakh* (p. 987) and v. 17a, which Ginsberg has discussed at length in 'Lexicographical Notes',[3] we shall look briefly at the clauses of vv. 18 and 19: 'Disgrace is the gift, which the wind is bringing. They shall garner shame from their sacrifices'. Here Hosea concludes his address with the warning that the just reward for sacrifices offered up by men whose festival

---

1. See Ginsberg, 'Hosea', pp. 1016, 1024; the historicity of the Hezekiah academy has been called into question by M. Carasik, 'Who Were the "Men of Hezekiah" (Proverbs xxv 1)?', *VT* 44 (1994), pp. 289-300.

2. Heb. *zōnēh*, the masculine counterpart of *zōnāh*, 'harlot'; the masculine form is attested only here, in Hos. 4.15.

3. Ginsberg, 'Lexicographical Notes', pp. 73-74.

celebration includes fornication is not blessing but punishment.

Thus we see that Hosea 4 castigates men who are unfaithful to their wives, seeking intimacy elsewhere, instead of seeking help to create true intimacy in their marriages. Moreover, we have seen that the Bible in Hosea 4 goes out of its way to defend the women who, in response to the misbehavior of more than one generation of men in their families, themselves seek intimacy outside the bond of marriage as a last resort; or, if you will, enact a desperate cry for help—a cry for help which finds a more than sympathetic ear in the Mishnah and Talmud.

What is the other side of the coin—the abiding message of what a marriage should be according to Hebrew Scripture? This, of course, is found in the words of the last of the prophets, Malachi. In 2.15 he says, 'Do not be unfaithful to the wife of your youth'. In v. 14 Malachi explains what is the proper relationship between a man and the wife of his youth: $w^e h\hat{\imath}$' $h^a bert^e k\bar{a}$ w^e'$\bar{e}\check{s}et$ $b^e r\hat{\imath}t^e k\bar{a}$, 'She is your friend and the woman with whom you have covenanted'.[1]

$h^a bert^e k\bar{a}$ means 'your friend', your intimate companion to whom you open your heart and who opens her heart to you. Such a relationship is the basis for the physical intimacy which follows, and requires that physical intimacy be limited to this very special relationship of loving companions. Thus Malachi, the last of the prophets, likewise reminds us that a wife (or a husband) is first and foremost the most intimate friend that a person ever has—you do not betray that person's trust (and today especially we must add her physical well-being)—and you do your utmost not to engage in intimate physical contact with her or with anyone else except as the highest physical expression of an emotional and intellectual bond between two loving companions. 'If you can do that,' Hosea says, speaking in the name of God, 'You can come to my Temple and present your offerings and you can swear by my name.' That is just some of what Hebrew Scripture has to say about marital intimacy and fidelity.

---

1. G.P. Hugenberger, *Marriage as a Covenant* (VTSup, 52; Leiden: Brill, 1994), surveys and analyzes virtually every reasonable interpretation of Mal. 2.14 and its surrounding context from antiquity to the present day. For possible and probable meanings of the term 'covenant' in Mal. 2.14 readers are referred to Hugenberger's book.

I WILL DESTROY YOUR MOTHER:
THE OBLITERATION OF A CULTIC ROLE IN HOSEA 4.4-6

Margaret S. Odell

In Hos. 4.4-6, a figure who is identified as the priest's mother is condemned along with him and a prophet for failing to instruct the people in the knowledge of God. The mention of both the prophet and the mother has proven to be something of a crux for interpreters of this passage, since this is the only passage in Hosea in which a *nābî'* is either linked with a priest or condemned, and the allusion to the mother seems to disrupt the parallelism of priest and prophet.

Usually the difficulties are attributed to the complex redactional history of the unit, and solutions rest on deleting or emending one or the other references. For example, since H.W. Wolff understood the mention of the prophet in 4.5 to reflect the practice of cult prophecy in the southern kingdom and not Hosea's apparent self-identification with the prophets of northern Israel, he treated the mention of the prophet as a later Judean redaction.[1] Although the reference to the mother has not been so easily dismissed, it has been at least as difficult to explain.[2] While some have emended the text,[3] others have

---

1. H.W. Wolff, 'Hoseas Geistige Heimat', in *Gesammelte Studien zum alten Testament* (Munich: Chr. Kaiser Verlag, 1964), pp. 241-43; *Hosea: A Commentary on the Book of Hosea* (Hermeneia; Philadelphia: Fortress Press, 1974), pp. 77-78.

2. Cf. K. Budde, 'Zu Text und Auslegung des Buches Hosea', *JBL* 45 (1926), p. 285.

3. Budde, 'Hosea', p. 285; M.J. Buss, *The Prophetic Word of Hosea: A Morphological Study* (BZAW, 111; Berlin: Töpelmann, 1969), p. 11; A. Malamat, '*Ummatum* in Old Babylonian Texts and its Ugaritic and Biblical Counterparts', *UF* 11 (1979), pp. 534-35.

assumed that she is the priest's biological mother, and interpretations have tended to explain her inclusion in the judgment as a comprehensive denunciation of the priestly dynasty.[1]

These solutions to the puzzle of Hos. 4.4-5 have tended to oversimplify the problems of reconstructing the cult in northern Israel. As far as the mother is concerned, exegetical inquiry has been dominated by the assumption that the expression 'your mother' can have only a familial connotation; thus exegetes draw parallels with priests' *wives* (Amos 7.17) and *Judean* queen mothers (Jer. 22.26).[2] The assumption appears to reflect a cultural bias on the part of exegetes, a bias which is illustrated nicely by the conjectures of Andersen and Freedman on this problem. They begin their discussion of Hos. 4.5 by noting, 'It is hard to see how a prophet and the priest's mother come into the picture'.[3] However, they go on to posit a public, cultic role for the prophet but a private type of influence for the mother. Thus they suggest that the prophet was a 'major cult functionary' while the mother 'presumably...exerted a baleful influence on the life and career of her son'.[4]

In view of the problems inherent in the above-mentioned efforts to identify the mother, a re-evaluation of the evidence seems warranted. This study will argue that the mother of Hos. 4.5 is not the biological mother of the priest but rather a cultic official whose activities are reflected in the oracle against the mother in ch. 2. As a 'mother' in the cult, her role is to lead in the festal celebrations of the gifts of God. Although there is little evidence for the role itself, the obliteration of the role does have its reflex in the controversy narrative concerning Moses, Miriam and Aaron in Numbers 12. It will be concluded that the

1. N. Lohfink, 'Zu Text und Form von Os 4,4-6', *Bib* 42 (1961), pp. 301-31; Wolff, *Hosea*, p. 78; G.I. Davies, *Hosea* (NCB; Grand Rapids: Eerdmans, 1992), pp. 118-19; J. Jeremias, *Der Prophet Hosea übersetzt und erklärt* (ATD, 24.1; Göttingen: Vandenhoeck & Ruprecht, 1983), p. 66; cf. J.R. Lundbom, 'Contentious Priests and Contentious People', *VT* 36 (1986), p. 57.

2. Wolff, *Hosea*, p. 78; J.L. Mayes, *Hosea: A Commentary* (OTL; Philadelphia: Westminster Press, 1969); p. 68, and others.

3. F.I. Andersen and D.N. Freedman, *Hosea: A New Translation with Introduction and Commentary* (AB, 24; Garden City, NY: Doubleday, 1980), p. 380.

4. Andersen and Freedman, *Hosea*, p. 351.

biblical evidence for a cultic role of 'mother' exists not so much in its vitality and persistence but in its suppression.

The Mother as a Cultic Official

None of the above interpretations had considered the possibility that the mother's relationship to the priest is of a formal, cultic nature. The term 'father' is used of both priests and prophets in northern Israelite narratives (Judg. 17.10, 18.19; 2 Kgs 2.12, 6.21, 13.14);[1] thus it seems reasonable to suggest that a female cult leader would carry the corresponding honorific 'mother'. Admittedly, the evidence for this usage is slim. The term 'mother in Israel' occurs only twice (Judg. 5.7; 2 Sam. 20.19). Only one of these usages, the designation of Deborah as a mother in Israel, can be argued to have a cultic connotation.[2] Other evidence of female participation in the cult does not corroborate the use of 'mother' as a formal title.[3]

In Hosea, the term 'mother' also occurs in 2.4, when Hosea appeals to an unnamed party to bring a lawsuit against his or her mother: 'Contend with your mother, contend; for she is not my wife, and I am not her husband'. Junker and Yee have noted a connection between the usage of 'mother' in chs. 2 and 4 and have suggested that in both cases the mother symbolizes Israel.[4]

---

1. For priests, cf. A. Cody, *A History of Old Testament Priesthood* (AnBib, 35; Rome: Pontifical Biblical Institute, 1969), pp. 52-54.

2. In 2 Sam. 20.19, 'ēm occurs in a hendiadys: 'îr wᵉ'ēm. While it seems possible to argue that in 2 Sam. 20 the wise woman of the narrative is referring to herself along with the city, the expression 'îr wᵉ'ēm is more likely a reference to the city and its clan (Malamat, *'Ummatum'*, pp. 526-36).

3. For a summary and evaluation of biblical evidence of female participation in the cult, see P. Bird, 'The Place of Women in Ancient Israelite Cultus', in P.D. Miller, Jr, P.D. Hanson and S.D. McBride (eds.), *Ancient Israelite Religion: Essays in Honor of Frank Moore Cross* (Philadelphia: Fortress Press, 1987), pp. 397-419, esp. p. 404.

4. H. Junker, 'Textkritische, formkritische und traditionsgeschichtliche Untersuchung zu Os 4,1-10', *BZ* 4 (1960), p. 170; G.A. Yee, *Composition and Tradition in the Book of Hosea: A Redaction-Critical Investigation* (SBLDS, 102; Atlanta: Scholars Press, 1987), p. 264. Cf. also M. DeRoche, 'Structure, Rhetoric, and Meaning in Hosea 4:4-10', *VT* 33 (1983), p. 191; Lundbom, 'Contentious Priests', p. 59; and J.J. Schmitt, 'The Wife of God in Hosea 2', *BR* 34 (1989), pp. 5-18.

However, a symbolic interpretation, which seems appropriate for the oracle of ch. 2, disrupts the parallellism of 4.4-5, where the mother appears to be an individual standing alongside the priest and the prophet. If there is a connection between the usage of 'mother' in 2.4 and 4.5, a more concrete interpretation of the term should be considered.

Exegetes normally interpret the literal meaning of 'mother' in Hos. 2.4 familially, as a reference to Gomer's role as the mother of Hosea's children. Consequently, the term does not play a significant role in the interpretation of the woman's involvement in the cult. Instead, these activities are interpreted in light of terms which occur elsewhere in Hosea. Two such terms have dominated the interpretation of the woman's cultic activities: the designation of Hosea's bride as an *'ēšet z^enûnîm* (1.2), and the reference to *q^edēšôt* in 4.14. While the former term may simply suggest a woman who is predisposed to *znh*, or participating in sexual intercourse outside of marriage, exegetes tend to associate it with the latter term, which is usually understood to refer to a cult prostitute.[1] It is then assumed that the woman is a devotee of the Baal cults and participates in some form of cultic sexual activity. The question then revolves around the nature of her participation: was she an official or an ordinary lay participant? Mays had argued that the woman was a cult prostitute;[2] however, others have pointed out the difficulties with such an interpretation. A typical reservation is expressed by Andersen and Freedman:

> One of our main difficulties in interpreting many details in the Book of Hosea is our ignorance of Gomer's status in this regard—whether she was attached to the Baal cult as a worshiper, like any other laywoman who attended the shrines, or whether she was appointed to perform sacred functions in the temples.[3]

Their discussion implies that there are only two possibilities: either Gomer was a cult prostitute, or she was an ordinary lay participant in comparable cultic sexual activities. In either case,

---

1. Cf. Mays, *Hosea*, pp. 25-26.
2. Mays, *Hosea*, pp. 25-26.
3. Andersen and Freedman, *Hosea*, p. 161.

two features of her cultic involvement are highlighted: she is involved in the Baal cult, and that involvement is of a sexual nature.

In this discussion of the woman's cultic involvement, the term 'mother' has proven to be functionally irrelevant. Because it has been interpreted as a familial term, it has been understood simply as a link between the account of Hosea's marriage in ch. 1 and the oracle of ch. 2. That link, in turn, leads exegetes to interpret ch. 2 in light of the description of Gomer as an 'ēšet z^enûnîm (1.2). In addition, it is assumed that the root *znh* indicates the nature of her activity in the cult. Critical efforts to define the woman's participation in the cult thus reflect a preoccupation with defining possible sexual activity. The question of cult leadership is set aside, since evidence along these lines is scant, especially when one looks for evidence of leadership roles of a cultic sexual nature.[1]

As an alternative to earlier efforts to define the mother's cultic role in terms of her participation in the Baal cult, I would suggest that we define her role within the framework of a Baalized Yahweh cult. The issue would not be whether the woman participated in an alien cult, but the extent to which her role contributed to the syncretization of the worship of Baal and Yahweh. That the woman is involved in cultic ritual is beyond doubt; however, it has not been sufficiently noted that the description of her activities in ch. 2 combines features of Yahweh and Baal worship. Her jewelry indicates her participation in the Baal cults and perhaps also an identification with the goddess (2.4, 15).[2] However, she observes not only the feast days of the Baals but also the traditional Yahwistic festivals, new moons and Sabbaths (2.13, 16; cf. Exod. 23.12, 16-17).[3] In addition, she alternates between her search for her 'lovers' and her first 'husband' (2.7, 9).[4]

---

1.   For a critique of such reconstructions of cultic sexual activity in Hosea, see C. Bucher, 'The Origin and Meaning of ZNH Terminology in the Book of Hosea' (PhD Dissertation, Claremont Graduate School, 1988), ch. 1.

2   Andersen and Freedman, *Hosea*, pp. 224-25, 260-61; Wolff, *Hosea*, pp. 33-34.

3.   Andersen and Freedman, *Hosea*, p. 250; and Wolff, *Hosea*, p. 38.

4.   Andersen and Freedman, *Hosea*, p. 239.

But the question which remains unresolved is the level of her involvement: does she participate as a layperson, or does she exercise a leadership role? That question can be resolved, I think, by taking seriously her designation as mother. As a mother, she plays a role comparable to that of the priest in ch. 4. This comparability has been obscured by the literary context, in which the reader is led to interpret the oracle of ch. 2 in light of chs. 1 and 3. Despite this literary framework, the oracle itself is a separate unit.[1] In fact, where ch. 2 differs significantly from the literary framework provided by chs. 1 and 3, it is similar both in structure and content to the oracle against the priest in ch. 4.[2] The oracles in both chs. 2 and 4 are extended critiques of cultic behaviour, the former involving that of the mother, the latter that of the priest. Both oracles contain *rîb* terminology (2.4; 4.4); both hold particular individuals responsible for the failings of the people; and finally, the children in both chapters symbolize the people for whom the priest and the mother are responsible (2.4, 6; 4.6).

These similarities suggest that the mother of ch. 2 was understood as a leader and not simply a lay participant in the cult. Two features within ch. 2 further confirm the suggestion that the mother performs the role of a cult leader. First, although Hosea has denigrated her search for the gifts of the land as the desperate, self-serving behavior of a prostitute, she performs a role similar to that of the Levite whom Micah had hired to be a 'father and priest' (Judg. 17.10-11; cf. 18.19; the verse suggests that the notion of 'priest' was defined by the notion of fatherhood). What such fatherhood meant for the narrator of Judges is conveyed by Micah's remark once he has secured the Levite's services: 'Now I know that Yahweh will cause it to go well with me' (Judg. 17.13). A priest/father ensures blessings for his son; similarly, the mother in Hosea seeks good things from her gods:

> For she has said, I will go after my lovers, who give me my bread, and my water, my wool and my flax, my oil and my drink (Hos. 2.7).

---

1. For redaction-critical analyses of Hos. 1–3, see Yee, *Composition and Tradition*, pp. 51-130; and L. Ruppert, 'Erwagungen zur Komposition and Redaktionsgeschichte von Hosea 1-3', *BZ* 26 (1982), pp. 208-23.

2. Yee, *Composition and Tradition*, pp. 265-67.

The primary function of the mother of Hosea 2 and the priest/ father in Judges 17 is the same, to secure blessings from the gods.[1]

The notion that Miriam may be considered a cultic leader has been further developed by Gerald Janzen. Although Janzen agrees with Burns that Miriam's role is of a cultic nature, he suggests that Miriam's leadership is more comprehensive than Burns has implied. Where Burns sees Miriam as a leader of women (cf. Exod. 15.20), Janzen argues that Miriam initiates the cultic response at the sea and thus leads all of the people, whose response is reflected in Moses' song in 15.1.[2] The significance of Miriam's leadership is developed in Janzen's next point. He argues that Miriam's song, which should be understood as a God-given response to the event and thus part of the event itself, makes the salvific meaning of the event accessible to the observers: 'What the song does is to focus the meaning of the event through words that are part of the event'.[3] Finally, though he does not belabor this point, Janzen understands the narrative portrayal of Miriam to reflect the characteristic role of women in worship, as those who proclaim the glad tidings of God's mighty acts (cf. Ps. 68.12).[4] Miriam thus stands in the narrative as a prototype of a cultic leader who proclaims and thus interprets and makes the mighty acts of Yahweh available to the people as salvation. In fact, Janzen considers her role in the narrative as 'definitely Yahwistic cultic leadership'.[5]

Secondly, with respect to her praise for these gifts, the mother resembles Miriam and Deborah, who lead the people in hymnic celebrations of the mighty acts of God (Judg. 5; Exod. 15.20-21). That such hymnic celebrations reflect formal ritual has recently

1. Cf. Cody, *Old Testament Priesthood*, p. 28.
2. J.G. Janzen, 'Song of Moses, Song of Miriam: Who is Seconding Whom?', *CBQ* 54.2 (1992), pp. 215-16; reprinted in A. Brenner (ed.), *A Feminist Companion to Exodus to Deuteronomy* (A Feminist Companion to the Bible, 6; Sheffield: Sheffield Academic Press, 1994), pp. 187-99. Cf. also R.J. Burns, *Has the Lord Indeed Spoken Only through Moses? A Study of the Biblical Portrait of Miriam* (SBLDS, 84; Atlanta: Scholars Press, 1987), pp. 12-13 n. 4.
3. Janzen, 'Song of Moses, Song of Miriam', p. 218.
4. Janzen, 'Song of Moses, Song of Miriam', pp. 217-18.
5. Janzen, 'Song of Moses, Song of Miriam', p. 220.

been suggested by Rita Burns in her study of the biblical Miriam traditions. Burns notes that, even though Miriam is called a prophet in Exod. 15.20, her song in Exod. 15.21 is hymnic, not oracular in character. In addition, she suggests that Miriam's actions of taking up the tambourine and leading the women in dancing reflect ritual recreations of the divine warrior's victory. Miriam's role is thus more priestly than prophetic, since it is concerned with cultic ritual celebration, not with oracular communication.[1]

The actions of the mother in Hosea 2 parody this normative activity. Like Miriam, the mother in Hosea 2 celebrates the gifts of the gods, and her festivals are marked by mirth and rejoicing (2.13). She sings hymns of thanksgiving; but on her lips they are perversions of the Yahwistic hymns, since they thank the Baals for gifts that Yahweh has given: 'I will go after my lovers, who give me my bread and my water, my wool and my flax, my oil and my drink' (2.7). Andersen and Freedman have suggested that the mention of bread and water in this hymn reflects old formulations which encapsulated the mighty acts of God. They note, 'One such ascription, which goes back to the Wilderness period (Exod. 16:29; cf. Deut. 8:18), calls Yahweh *notēn leḥem*, "giver of bread" (Pss 136:25; 146:7; etc.)'. They conclude that the woman's song is to be understood as a countercreed and denial of Yahwistic faith.[2] However, it may be better to regard the song as an illustration of the kind of syncretism that became possible in her ritual celebrations. The gifts of Baal and Yahweh became associated with one another; and in the process, the distinct identities of the gods became obscured.

In all of these actions, then, the woman performs functions that can be likened to those of other women who figured prominently in Israelite worship. Where the priest instructs the people in the knowledge of God and offers sacrifices in their behalf (4.6, 8), the role of the mother is to lead in the festal celebrations and give thanks for the gifts of the land. That is precisely what she does in ch. 2. The problem is that she sings praises to Baal, not to Yahweh.

---

1. Burns, *Has the Lord Indeed Spoken Only through Moses?*, pp. 46-48.
2. Andersen and Freedman, *Hosea*, p. 231.

None of these activities necessarily implies cultic sexual activity. As noted earlier, such theories have depended on two things: the correlation of the terms *'ēšet zᵉnûnîm* (1.2) and *qᵉdēšôt* (4.14), and the assumption that the verb root *znh* had both metaphorical and literal connotations in Hosea. However, some exegetes have called for greater caution in the treatment of *znh* terminology in Hosea. Noting that the literal use of *znh* nearly always involves female subjects, Christina Bucher has argued that the verb root *znh* should be interpreted metaphorically, since Hosea tends to use the verb with masculine subjects.[1] She cautions against the assumption that Israel's apostasy also involved cultic sexual activity.

Exegetes have also become more cautious in their translation of the term *qᵉdēšâ* as 'cult prostitute'. For the Akkadian equivalent, *qadištu*, there is no evidence of cultic sexual activity, while there is an abundance of evidence that the *qadištu* performed other cultic functions, including chanting, presenting offerings, eating the leftovers of sacrifices, and performing purification rituals of healing.[2] Although the biblical evidence is more ambiguous, Ringgren has pointed out that no reference to the *qᵉdēšâ* or to her male counterpart the *qādēš* unequivocally describes cultic sexual activity.[3] Ringgren suggests that even Hos. 4.14, which would appear to be the most unambiguous indication that the *qᵉdēšâ* was involved in cultic sexual activity, requires some interpretive caution. He notes that although the *qᵉdēšôt* (lit., 'devoted ones') appear in synonymous parallelism with *zônôt* ('prostitutes'), their activities are different: the men 'go aside' with the prostitutes, while they offer sacrifices with the *qᵉdēšôt*. Because of this difference, Ringgren refrains from concluding that the verse unequivocally depicts the *qᵉdēšâ* as engaged in cultic sexual activity.

If the activities of the mother are interpreted within the framework of a Baalized Yahweh cult, her *zᵉnût* would be understood

1. Hos. 4.10, 11, 12, 14, 18; 5.3; 9.10.
2. M.I. Gruber, 'Hebrew *qᵉdēšāh* and her Canaanite and Akkadian Cognates', *UF* 18 (1986), pp. 138-45. Cf. also Gruber in this volume.
3. H. Ringgren, '*qādēš*', in H.-J. Fabry and H. Ringgren (eds.), *Theologisches Worterbuch zum alten Testament* (Stuttgart: Kohlhammer, 1989), IV, pp. 1200-1201.

metaphorically. The role of mother as singer and leader in the festal celebrations is rooted in Yahwism. However, under her leadership, the worship of Baal and the worship of Yahweh have become confused, and the unique blessings of Yahweh are not recognized: 'She did not know that it was I who gave her the grain, the wine, and the oil' (Hos. 2.8). Her failure is therefore comparable to the failure of the priest, who had rejected the knowledge of God. In the priest's case, 'knowledge' was rooted in Torah decisions concerning covenant law (Hos. 4.2, 6); in the case of the mother, 'knowledge' was rooted in the celebrations of the blessings of God.[1]

The Obliteration of the Mother

In the preceding discussion, I have argued that the mother of ch. 2 can be identified as a cult official. I have emphasized her similarity to Miriam in order to highlight the potential normativity of her role. This interpretation has at least two implications. First, it becomes possible to interpret the mother's $z^e n \hat{u} t$ in metaphorical terms as a perversion of her normative role. Her role in the cult has deep roots in the Yahwistic traditions. That it has become associated with Baal worship is undeniable; but what is important is that the role of the 'mother' was early associated with Yahweh worship. She is not a cult prostitute but, rather, an official whose responsibilities can be defined by analogy with Miriam, whose song in Exod. 15.20-21 quite possibly reflects the cult practice of commemorating the mighty acts of Yahweh.

Secondly, one may suggest that Hosea's judgment of the mother be brought back in line with his judgment of the priest. In the current literary framework of Hosea 1–3, the mother has come to symbolize all that is wrong with Israelite worship. The failure of the Israelite cult is identified as idolatry; and the metaphor of marriage and adultery is employed as a comprehensive critique of Israel's failure to acknowledge Yahweh as its God. However, Hosea condemned not only the mother, but all of the officials within the Israelite cult. That the mother should

1. Cf. E.J. Fisher, 'Cultic Prostitution in the Ancient Near East? A Reassessment', *BTB* 6 (1976), pp. 225-36.

be viewed as only part of the problem is suggested by Hosea's condemnation of the priest, prophet and mother in 4.4-5. Hosea condemns not only idolatry, but all of the developments within the Aaronide cult.[1] The mother, the leader of the celebrations, leads her children astray as she confuses the gifts of Yahweh with the gifts of Baal. But the priest fails in the instruction of Torah (4.4-6) and consequently profits from the worshipers' sin offerings (4.7-10).[2] Finally, prophetic oracles delivered within the cult only add to the confusion (4.12; cf. 9.7-9). In Hosea's view, the contamination of the Yahweh cult is extensive. Since every form of divine–human mediation is corrupt, all of the Aaronide mediators must be held accountable.

The full range of Hosea's concerns may be mirrored in the controversy narrative of Numbers 12, in which Miriam and Aaron are pitted against Moses. Coats has suggested that such narratives as Numbers 12 reflect conflicts within a late, established cult hierarchy which have been retrojected onto the wilderness traditions.[3] While Coats's suggestion has been generally accepted, the precise nature and origin of the conflict represented by the final form of Numbers 12 remains a matter of some scholarly debate. Coats gives the narrative a post-exilic date, while others posit J or E origins for the narrative.[4] What may be more important than the date is the situation reflected in the narrative, in which the respective roles of Aaron, Moses and Miriam must be redefined.[5]

In its present form, the narrative is a conflation of two controversies, both involving Miriam, each reflecting different

1.   Wolff, 'Hoseas Geistige Heimat', pp. 232-50.
2.   Buss, *The Prophetic Word of Hosea*, pp. 89-90.
3.   G.W. Coats, *Rebellion in the Wilderness: The Murmuring Motif in the Wilderness Traditions of the Old Testament* (Nashville: Abingdon Press, 1968), pp. 261-64.
4.   Coats, *Rebellion in the Wilderness*, pp. 263-64; M.L. Newman, Jr, *The People of the Covenant: A Study of Israel from Moses to the Monarchy* (New York: Abingdon Press, 1962), p. 63 n 41; M. Noth, *Numbers: A Commentary* (OTL; Philadelphia: Westminster Press, 1968), pp. 92-93; R.R. Wilson, *Prophecy and Society in Ancient Israel* (Philadelphia: Fortress Press, 1980), p. 156.
5.   Cf. R.P. Carroll, 'Rebellion and Dissent in Ancient Israelite Society', *ZAW* 89 (1977), p. 190.

dimensions of her role.[1] In itself, the conflation of stories about
Miriam indicates not only her prominence in the wilderness
traditions but also a situation in which a range of issues concerning female participation in the cult had been dealt with in narratives about her. In one of the stories (Num. 12.1, 10-15),
Miriam's role as a spokeswoman for the community is
highlighted when she rebukes Moses for his marriage to a
Cushite woman. Her punishment of leprosy removes her from
community life and public participation. In the second story
(Num. 12.2-9), Miriam is paired with Aaron as a prophet, and
the two speak out against Moses' unique claim to oracular
authority (12.2-9). The dispute is resolved at the tent of meeting
by means of an oracle which reasserts the superiority of God's
self-disclosure to Moses. This story does not necessarily end in
punishment. In itself, it simply subordinates Miriam and Aaron's
revelatory experience to that of Moses.

Burns has suggested that the conflict in Num. 12.2-9 is best
defined as a clash between the levitical and Aaronide priestly
houses over competing claims to oracular authority. Her delin-
eation of the dispute makes it possible to see the similarity
between this narrative and the issues presented in Hosea:
Hosea, standing in the levitical tradition, initiates a controversy
against the priest, prophet and mother, three officials of the
Aaronide cult. Numbers 12 contains a counter-charge: Miriam
and Aaron, the eponyms of the Aaronide cult, bring a charge
against Moses, the founder of the levitical tradition.

In its final form, Numbers 12 reflects the eventual outcome of
the controversy. Miriam's leprosy and subsequent exclusion
from the community, originally a punishment for her speaking
out against Moses' marriage, is now understood as punishment
for her challenge to Moses' oracular authority. Aaron, who had
joined Miriam in making this challenge, appears not to be
punished but rather continues to function as priest, as indicated
by his intercession for Miriam. Incongruous as this ending now
appears, the narrative describes a delimitation of roles which

---

1.   Much of what follows is indebted to the analysis by Burns, *Has the
Lord Indeed Spoken Only through Moses*, pp. 48-77.

had at one time existed in the Aaronide cult. At the beginning of the narrative, these roles included all those suggested in Hosea's indictment of the priest in 4.4-5: priest, as suggested by Aaron's role as intercessor in Num. 12.13-14; prophet, as represented by Miriam and Aaron's claim that God had spoken to them as well as to Moses; and mother, signified by Miriam's prominence in the narrative. By the end of the narrative, Aaron speaks only as priest and not as prophet, and Miriam speaks not at all. Thus the narrative indicates the outcome of the controversy between the levitical and Aaronide houses. Even though Aaron continues to function as priest, his role is now severely truncated. He may intercede for the people, but he may not communicate God's word to them. That role is now reserved for prophets 'like Moses', that is, prophets standing in the levitical tradition.

In the process of restricting the cultic functions of the house of Aaron, roles which had been performed by women are simply excised. In Numbers 12, those functions include the authority to speak on behalf of both the people and God. Eventually, all such functions for women disappeared from the cult. Numbers 12 legitimates the change in cultic structure by focusing on Miriam's marginalization.[1] Once claiming to speak on behalf of both the community and God, she now speaks not at all.

Similarly, in Hosea, redactional reshaping obscures and then obliterates the cultic role of the mother. As I noted above, the oracle denouncing the cultic activity of the mother in ch. 2 is structurally similar to the oracle condemning the priest in ch. 4. On its own, the oracle in ch. 2 describes the cultic failures of the mother. Her failures are described metaphorically as $z^e n\hat{u}t$; she sought out other lovers besides her first husband, Yahweh.

The literary framework of Hosea 1 and 3 concretizes the metaphor. As Yee has noted, the account of Hosea's marriage in ch. 1 now provides an interpretive framework which shapes our

---

1. For a study of Miriam's marginalization in the literary tradition, see P. Trible, 'Bringing Miriam out of the Shadows', *BR* 5 (1989), pp. 14-25, 34; reprinted in Brenner (ed.), *A Feminist Companion to Exodus to Deuteronomy*, pp. 166-86.

understanding of the oracles in ch. 2;[1] consequently, the
mother's cultic activities become increasingly associated with
Gomer's sexual infidelities.[2] Yee has pointed out that the
purpose of this literary structuring is to develop fully the
imagery of marriage and adultery as metaphors for Israel's relationship to God. However, one consequence of the redactional
structuring is that the oracle condemning the mother's cultic
abuses has become isolated from the oracle condemning comparable abuses of the priest in ch. 4. Thus the mother is no longer
viewed either as an active leader in the cult or as a colleague of
the priest; nor is her $z^e n\hat{u}t$ seen as part of a larger complex of
problems. Rather, she is viewed from within the confines of
Hosea's marriage and, as a symbol, she carries the full weight of
the condemnation of the cult. Once venerated as one who led
the community in its praises, then condemned by the oracle in
ch. 2, the mother is now presented by the literary structure of
Hosea 1-3 as an *'ēšet $z^e n\hat{u}n\hat{i}m$*, a wayward, incorrigible wife. As
the metaphor of harlotry is developed, her role as a leader thus
disappears from view.

At the beginning of this essay, I noted the difficulty many
exegetes have faced as they sought to explain the appearance of
the mother alongside the priest and prophet in Hos. 4.4-5. I
have argued that the mother was a cultic functionary, a colleague of the priest and prophet. The evidence for
reconstructing this role has been sparse; but such evidence as
there is reflects a process of delimiting roles within the Aaronide
cult. Even though the role of the mother has disappeared, hints
concerning the suppression of the role remain; thus there is
more evidence for the eradication of the role than for the role
itself. From the hints that are left behind, one can surmise that
Hosea's prophecy, 'I will destroy your mother', marked at least
one important occasion in the struggle to eliminate women from
the cult.

---

1. Yee, *Composition and Tradition*, pp. 63, 103-104.
2. H.H. Rowley, 'The Marriage of Hosea', *BJRL* 39 (1956), p. 222.

GOD AS MOTHER IN HOSEA 11*

Helen Schüngel-Straumann

1. *Introduction*

God-talk is and remains a central focus of theology, and it is an abiding problem for theologians to offer a credible description, representation, or proclamation of God in the face of a world that is, to a great degree, indifferent to the whole matter. This is all the more true of the Old Testament imagery for God because the manifold variety of that imagery is not even recognized by many people, while others contrast the wrathful God of the Old Testament with the loving God of the New, and still others simply dismiss the God of the Old Testament as hopelessly male and patriarchal.

But we are not the first generation to find God-talk difficult. It was not very different for Hosea, a prophet who found himself in a Canaanite culture with a plethora of goddesses and gods and a cultic practice to match. He was engaged in a tense struggle with these local deities representing the personified forces of nature. For the people, especially the ordinary farmers, they were more appealing and more tangible than YHWH, the God of Israel. Where the majority of the population was engaged in agriculture, practical questions took precedence: who gives rain and makes the land fertile, so that it will produce the food needed for sustenance? The question at issue was not theoretical monotheism, which is such a lively topic for discussion in Old Testament scholarship at the present time,[1] but

* Originally published as 'Gott als Mutter in Hos. 11', *Tübinger Theologische Quartalschrift* 166 (1986), pp. 119-34. Translated by L.M. Maloney.
1. For this discussion see, for example, O. Keel (ed.), *Monotheismus im Alten Israel und seiner Umwelt* (BibB, 14; Freiburg, 1980); B. Lang (ed.), *Der*

rather the question of *what kind* of God this YHWH is, and *how* he relates to Israel.

The text from the prophet Hosea whose presentation of God is to be investigated here is not peripheral, but central to the Old Testament: it is a crucial statement. In my opinion, the centrality and importance of this text has not always received adequate recognition in Old Testament scholarship or in Christian theology. This may be due to the way in which this chapter has previously been interpreted: namely, on the basis of a strongly Christian and trinitarian idea of God.

2. The Image of God in Hosea 11

Provisional Translation[1]

1 When Israel was young, I loved him;
out of Egypt I called my son.
2 But when I called them
they ran from me,
they sacrificed to the Baals,
and they sent up incense to images.
3 But it was I who nursed Ephraim,
taking him in my arms.
Yet they did not understand
that it was I who took care of them.

· *einzige Gott: Die Geburt des Biblischen Monotheismus* (Munich, 1981); E. Haag (ed.), *Gott der einzige: Zur Entstehung des Monotheismus in Israel* (QD, 104; Freiburg, 1985).

1. This translation follows the Hebrew text as closely as possible; it is not meant to be used as it stands in practical contexts, such as the liturgy. For reasons of space, not all the difficult points in the text will be individually treated in detail; for such treatment, see the apparatus in the commentaries. Reference will be made primarily to the four most-used commentaries in German. In recent years the book of Hosea has been treated by commentators both for the broader public and for more scholarly circles by A. Deissler, *Hosea* (Die Neue Echter Bibel, 4.8; 1981); J. Jeremias, *Hosea* (ATD, 24.1; Göttingen: Vandenhoeck & Ruprecht, 1983); W. Rudolph, *Hosea* (KAT, 13.1; Gütersloh: Gerd Mohn, 1966); H.W. Wolff, *Hosea* (BKAT, 14.1; Neukirchen–Vluyn: Neukirchener Verlag, 3rd edn, 1976); ET *Hosea: A Commentary on the Book of the Prophet Hosea* (trans. G. Stansell; ed. P.D. Hanson; Hermeneia; Philadelphia: Westminster Press, 1974). Citations in the text are from the English edition.

4   I drew them with cords of humanity,
    with bands of love.
    And I was for them like those
    who take a nursling to the breast,
    and I bowed down to him
    in order to give him suck.
5   He must return to Egypt,
    and Assyria will be his king,
    because they refused to return.
6   And the sword will rage in their cities
    and root out their idle chatterers,
    and they will have to reap
    what they themselves have sown.
7   But my people is bent on turning away from me:
    They call out to Baal,
    but he will never bring them up!
8   How can I give you up, O Ephraim?
    How can I hand you over, O Israel?
    How can I give you up like Admah?
    How can I treat you like Zeboiim?
    My heart recoils against me,
    my womb is utterly inflamed within me.
9   I cannot execute my burning wrath,
    nor can I utterly change (what is within me), so as to
        destroy Ephraim!
    For I am God
    and not a man,
    holy in your midst,
    and I do not come to destroy.
10 ...
11 Then they shall come trembling like birds from Egypt,
    and like doves from the land of Assyria.
    And I will return them to their homes.

[The words of YHWH].

A Note on Method
The text selected is a clearly defined unit. Hosea 11 begins a
new section, and there is not a single key-word linking it to the
preceding section, 10.9-15. It opens with a historical-theological
retrospect. In ch. 12 we find another new beginning without
reference to ch. 11, but containing a series of discrete prophetic
sayings. Thus Hosea 11 is a separate block whose theme and set

of connected key-words reveals it as a closed and integral unit. Only v. 10, on the basis of its style and content, diverges from this internal unity.[1]

In its form and genre, Hosea 11 is a historical-theological lament, couched entirely in the 'I' form. YHWH, the God of Israel, speaks in the first person throughout. Only v. 10, already mentioned, forms an exception: there YHWH is referred to in the third person.

The most striking of the special characteristics of the language are found in the four parallelisms. Almost all the verses are strongly rhythmic and consist of one or more *parallelism membrorum*. Among the familiar motifs and traditions employed are, in the first place, the theologoumenon of the exodus from Egypt, as well as a series of allusions to the divine command-ments in the decalogue.

The *Sitz im Leben* of this text can best be sought in the prophet's intimate circle of disciples, where these words were collected and elaborated even beyond the time of the collapse of the northern kingdom. Hosea himself, though he may well have seen it coming, probably did not witness the destruction of the capital Samaria and the deportation of the population in 722–721 BCE. The words in ch. 11 are from the prophet's later period and can be regarded as the quintessence of a painful and mature prophetic life.

Hosea 11 is an absolutely *authentic* text, and undeniably stems from this eighth-century prophet. In spite of its linguistic dif-ficulties, its often original and clever images, and the relatively complicated history of its transmission, which often leaves room for a variety of possible translations, we can clearly see that this is one of the most significant theological texts from the northern kingdom of Israel.[2] The certainty that these words come from

---

1. This verse is regarded by most commentators, by reference to Amos 1.2 and other similar passages, as a late insertion; for that reason it will play no further part in the interpretation here. Both stylistically and metrically, it is quite different from the rest of the chapter.

2. Hosea is the only writing prophet from the northern kingdom. It is true that Amos also appeared there, but he came from the southern king-dom of Judah. Hosea, by contrast, was a *native* of northern Israel in his origins, his world of ideas, and his theological thinking. For that reason, his

Hosea himself makes it especially important to illuminate the text from a new, and perhaps previously unrecognized angle.

The clearest caesura lies between vv. 7 and 8: therefore, in what follows the text will be treated in two sections, namely vv. 1-7 and vv. 8-11, although still shorter units could also be discerned.

Hosea 11.1-7

This section speaks of God's care for Israel, Israel's reaction, and the consequences.

From the beginning, when YHWH called Israel out of Egypt, this God had done nothing but assist his people. But YHWH's good deeds were met with an incomprehensible reaction on the part of the people: ingratitude and apostasy. This history is rehearsed in three stages of reflection, each of which describes YHWH's caring acts and Israel's negative reaction. The starting point and basis is YHWH's positive declaration: 'When Israel was young, I loved him; out of Egypt I called my son'.[1] Verse 2 recounts the first negative reaction: the people set themselves in active opposition to the call of their God by turning to the service of Baals and idols. The next recollection of YHWH's good works in v. 3a is followed by Israel's second negative reaction in v. 3b, this time in a more passive formulation: 'Yet they did not *understand*...' The verb *yāda'* expresses more properly a practical knowledge by way of the senses than an intellectual

---

world of ideas is different in many ways from that of the better-known southern kingdom, and his language is often difficult to understand. Therefore images that at first seem alienating should not be too facilely compared to ideas stemming from Judah and Jerusalem.

1.   The LXX has a plural here, possibly to smooth over the difficulties resulting from the fact that v. 2 continues immediately in the plural. Hos. 11 shifts repeatedly from singular to plural, which can be interpreted as reflecting a focus at one time on the people as a whole, and then again on individual members. E. Zenger ('"Durch Menschen zog ich sie..." [Hos. 11.4]: Beobachtungen zum Verständnis des prophetischen Amtes im Hoseabuch', in L. Ruppert, P. Weimar and E. Zenger [eds.], *Künder des Wortes: Beiträge zur Theologie der Propheten* [Würzburg, 1982], pp. 183-201) distinguishes singular and plural strata in Hos. 11, with the plural stratum showing an interest in the prophets. According to Zenger, it is the prophets who have 'drawn' Israel with bands of love (v. 4).

apprehension; it expresses the idea that Israel *refuses* to acknowledge the practical, concrete experience it has of this YHWH.

Verse 4 again presents YHWH's acts in three verbs describing care and concern, and this is followed by Israel's third and last negative reaction in v. 5, now formulated in a final and definitive statement: '...because they refused to return'. This expression of final obduracy is contained within the proclamation of punishment in vv. 5-7, showing that the defeats Israel has experienced in war, and ultimately its exile by the Assyrians, are the consequence of wrong behaviour. This is the well-earned punishment for faithless Israel, a punishment Israel has brought upon itself. The first part of ch. 11 concludes with the negative judgment that Israel is tenacious in its apostasy. In contrast to YHWH, Baal is described at the end as one who cannot help the people.

In line with the theme I have chosen, I will now begin by examining the individual statements about YHWH's behaviour in this first section. How is God's treatment of Israel described? The verbs are particularly important, because they show how much care YHWH has exercised toward this people.

In v. 1 two very common, but basic verbs are employed: 'love' ('*āhab*)[1] and 'call' (*qāra'*). The key word 'Egypt' that appears here would have evoked immediately, in every hearer, the memory of Israel's rescue from slavery and the confession of faith: 'YHWH led Israel out of Egypt'.

---

1.   The verb '*āhab*, most frequently used for love between husband and wife, but also for that of parents and children, friends, and so on, corresponds generally to the broader meaning of 'love' in English. Like its most frequent antonym, 'hate' (*śn'*), it is not founded in an abstraction, but reveals in its basic structure an emotional excitement arising out of physical feeling. What is described by '*āhab* is passionate longing for another, the desire to be close to the other not only in an 'interior' or spiritual sense, but physically. This does not mean that the concept expresses only or especially a sexual aspect, for which Hebrew has another, *yāda'*. Its emphasis lies on the *feeling* of love. (On this, cf. G. Wallis, ''*āhab*', *TDOT*, I, pp. 99-118.) The root appears again in v. 4, and again it speaks of an action of YHWH. Hosea may be the first person, historically speaking, who applied this word expressly to YHWH's love for his people. Before Hosea, it could not be said that YHWH *loved* Israel.

When Israel was still very small, YHWH began to love it. Thus it was not Israel's doing. The basis for this love resides with YHWH alone. With the second verb, *qāra'* ('call', also in the sense of vocation, for example in the case of the prophets), God expressly establishes a personal relationship. Usually, it is one of higher station who calls, and expects that the other will respond. These first two verbs establish YHWH's personal relationship to Israel: thus far, Israel does nothing at all.

Verse 3, with its emphatic, even oath-like *'ānokî* ('But it is I', or 'but it was I'), begins a listing based on three verbs, all referring to the way one deals with an infant, a nursling.

tirgaltî is usually regarded as a rare form, a *tiph'el* with the meaning of a *hiphil*,[1] containing the root *rgl* ('foot'). Then it would mean 'teach to walk', as a tiny child is taught to walk by putting one foot in front of the other, laboriously taking its first steps. But the verb is not found with this meaning anywhere else in the Old Testament, and this sense is postulated only for this verse in Hosea. In Arabic, the root *rǧl* means 'suck, nurse'.[2] If we translate the verse as 'Yet it was I who nursed Ephraim, taking (Heb. *lqḥ*) him in my arms', the result is a logical sequence: the infant is embraced and taken up to be nursed.[3]

1.   Thus Wolff, *Hosea*, p. 191; Rudolph, *Hosea*, pp. 208-209; and others.
2.   Rudolph (*Hosea*, p. 209) expressly notes this, but thinks that it is 'rather unlikely with a masculine subject, despite Num. 11.12'. Here pre-judgment governs the interpretation! Moreover, Jerome and the Vulgate translated with *nutricius*, which can mean 'the one who brings up', but the same word is used for 'nurse, feed'. In any case, Jerome saw a different connection here than most modern interpreters find! For the history of interpretation, including medieval Jewish readings, see especially the old commentary by A. Wünsche, *Der Prophet Hosea übersetzt und erklärt* (Leipzig, 1868).
3.   This would also obviate the problem suggested by Rudolph's commentary, namely that 'one cannot teach children to walk by taking them in one's arms. There must therefore be two different actions described here, teaching to walk and..holding in the arms' (Rudolph, *Hosea*, p. 209). Further possibilities are discussed: perhaps 'the arms are those of the children, and the father holds them by the arms as he teaches them to walk (thus, e.g., Luther)'. But the matter is not so complicated. It is far simpler if we translate the root in its older meaning of 'suck, nurse', for a nursling must be taken into one's arms, and then we have a logical sequence of events, without any need to change the text!

In this context, we should also note that 'teaching to walk' is often understood far too narrowly in the sense of our modern culture. In earlier times no special significance was attached to this action; it was something children learned by themselves. Besides, it is not vitally important, and therefore it is out of place here, where the text is listing all the things YHWH has done to insure the people's *survival*. On the other hand, the child's nursing is highly important. Without it, no infant could survive in ancient times, and when we reflect that children were nursed for two or three years, such a statement is what we would expect in terms of the imagery that has been chosen here.

After the 'nursing' and 'taking in the arms' follow a third verb, *rāpa'* (heal). This word is used for dressing wounds, but also in a more general sense of 'caring' or 'nurturing'.[1]

In this way, we find a single coherent and logical sequence in the text if we are careful to hold fast to the imagery that the prophet apparently had in mind, namely that the infant is to be nursed, and, for that purpose, is taken in its mother's arms. Of course it is cared for, and nurtured, and even healed when that becomes necessary.

The interpretation of v. 4, probably the most difficult part of this first section to understand, depends on whether one reads *'l* as 'nursling' (*'ûl*) or 'yoke' (*'ôl*); the Hebrew consonants are the same in either case. Many commentators claim that Hosea is using a second image at this point; thus YHWH would be comparing his care for Israel with the way an intelligent farmer treats animals, not abusing them but easing the yoke on their necks, lifting it now and again. But no matter how familiar the image of ploughing oxen may be in Hosea (Hos. 4.16, or 10.11), with this reading we cannot explain the second part of v. 4, which talks of 'giving to eat' and 'bending down'.

---

1.   H.J. Stoebe remarks that dressing wounds, sores and injuries is frequently used as an image for the wretched situation of the people. Lack of attention can be fatal. 'We may also add Hos. 11.3 to this list, although here *rp'* does not quite fit the preceding image of fatherly care' (*Hosea* [THAT, II; Munich: Chr. Kaiser Verlag], p. 807). To begin with, it is amazing how Stoebe can speak almost in passing of 'fatherly care', but also how little attention he gives to the concrete context!

For this reason, I prefer to read this consonantal sequence as '*ûl*, 'nursling', and I believe that the prophet is continuing to hold consistently to a single image.[1] The first part of the verse, 'I drew them with cords of humanity, with bands of love', expresses the idea that YHWH's task of bringing up Israel is done with care, 'humanely'. The root *'āhab* also makes a direct terminological reference back to v. 1, and to the loving deed of YHWH that is the basis for all the rest.[2]

In v. 4b *wā'ehyê*, 'I am', or 'I was', repeats anew that God lifts up the child. Most commentaries translate *lehyēhem* with 'cheeks', but it would be more correct to write 'breasts',[3] which would also explain the plural! Hosea uses an extremely difficult construction here ('I was like those who...'). The prophet is clearly making an effort to avoid a particular kind of terminology, and thus does not use either 'father' or 'mother'.[4] Hosea is apparently making an effort to avoid the word 'mother', although at this point it is really inevitable. The second verb here is from the root *nṭh* (bow, bend down, stoop, Heb. *wᵉ'aṭ*). To lift up the nursling (*rmm*, cf. also v. 7), YHWH must bend down, apparently in order to give suck to the child.[5] There

1. Thus also Wolff, *Hosea*, p. 191 (following Sellin, Buber, and others). Cf. also Isa. 49.15; 65.20!
2. Cf. my earlier note on this term. For Zenger ('Durch Menschen'), these bands refer to the prophets.
3. Cf. for example, Ruth 4.16! According to *KB*, I, p. 30 this describes the 'lower, external anterior side of the human body, where one places favorite persons, animals, children'. For women, that means the breasts. Rudolph (*Hosea*, p. 210) introduces this suggestion by a reference to van Honacker and H.G. May, but rejects it because for him 'the image of the child has already been dropped in v. 4a'. As I will show, the image of the child or infant persists through the whole first section of the text, vv. 1-7.
4. Some versions, such as the German *Einheitsübersetzung* (an ecumenical translation) use the word 'parents', although this has been bracketed in the revised edition. The term is not present in the Hebrew text at all, and it would be difficult to fit into the picture. How could two people press an infant to their cheeks, and which ones? But if we decide for 'breasts', not only does the plural present no problem, but we also have an explanation of why the prophet is making such heavy weather of the language at this point.
5. Following the suggestion of *BHS* and most commentaries, I shift the *lô'* from the beginning of v. 5 to the end of v. 4 and read it as a dative pronoun ('fed *him*'). Cf., for example, the extensive textual annotations in

could not be a more vivid image of nursing an infant. None of the commentators denies that the text speaks of 'feeding', and the statement it makes is unmistakable, since infants do not 'eat'. They are fed, that is, nursed.

It also seems to me worthy of note that this group of three motherly and caring activities of YHWH is introduced by the verb *hyh*. This verb, standing in the emphatic first position, is certainly a deliberate play on the divine name YHWH: '*I am* like those...'. A literal translation would be: 'And yet I was there for them like those who raise a tiny infant to their breasts...'. Hebrew speakers would inevitably hear the divine name YHWH in this. Hosea's theology of the name in 1.9 shows that he was familiar with such wordplays. While the passage under consideration says that YHWH was *there*, in the sense of being caring and helpful, that very thing is negated in Hos. 1.9: 'You are not my people—and I am no longer *'ehyê* for you' (i.e. no longer YHWH in the sense of 'there for you').

The meaning of God's name, YHWH, God's helpful 'being there', is thus graphically described in the first section of Hosea 11 in tangible, concrete images.[1] The various historical stages through which Israel passed under YHWH's guidance (exodus, desert wandering and so on) are not dressed up in majestic words, but are described in modest imagery drawn from daily life. Hosea can also use a different style. In ch. 13 he speaks baldly, but in 11.1-4 he employs imagery from the world of infants to show how God makes life possible, protects and shields it like a mother bringing up her child.

It is true that the prophet never expressly calls YHWH 'mother'. In his time that would have been too open to misunderstanding, for Hosea was engaged in a bitter struggle with Canaanite fertility gods, and in particular the goddesses who, in practical terms, probably played a more important role than the male gods. But all the activities listed in vv. 1-4 were, in Hosea's time, the exclusive province of mothers. On the other hand, nowhere in the text does Hosea directly call his God 'father'. He even resorts to extraordinarily complex language

Rudolph, *Hosea*, p. 110. The LXX translates that way as well.

1.   On this, cf. my article 'Überlegungen zum Jahwe-Namen in den Gottesgeboten des Dekalogs', *TZ* 38 (1982), pp. 496-506.

when his concern is to avoid clear terminology (cf. especially the discussion of v. 4b above). That can only mean that Hosea deliberately avoids the terms 'father' and 'mother' when describing YHWH's tender, motherly behaviour. Therefore it is at the very least astonishing how universally the newer commentaries, in interpreting this chapter, speak of the father–son relationship, and of fatherly love and care. Not once do they even raise a question about this kind of language, or make it a topic of discussion![1]

We thus find a unanimous picture: the entire literature on Hosea 11 speaks from the outset and without exception of a father, fatherly love, and *nothing else*. It seems as if the idea of a father–son relationship is so solidly in place that there is not even the beginning of an attempt to question it. But in my opinion this interpretation, no matter how widespread, cannot be derived from the text itself.

1.   Wolff says in the introduction to his interpretation, 'The traditions from Israel's earliest times, transposed into the metaphor of *fatherly love*, stand prominently in the foreground' (*Hosea*, p. 195; emphasis supplied), and he writes regarding v. 1, 'Yahweh's love for helpless young Israel was demonstrated not only by his deliverance of him from Egypt, but at the same time by his "call", as a father calls "his son"' (*Hosea*, pp. 197-98). Similarly, Rudolph writes, 'YHWH loves pitiful Israel as a father loves his son, and the first act by which he demonstrates his fatherly love is the Exodus...' (*Hosea*, p. 214). Jeremias speaks of Hosea's use of the image of the father–son relationship (*Hosea*, p. 140); Hosea is said to be concerned 'solely with the care of a father for the child that is still unable to care for itself...' (p. 141). Only Deissler speaks of 'fatherly, or rather parental love as a model for comparison' (*Hosea*, p. 50), probably because this commentary is based on the *Einheitsübersetzung*, which uses the word 'parents' in this verse. However, in the commentary that follows, Deissler also refers only to the 'fundamental act of fatherly love' or the 'fatherly call to a life-filled communion with YHWH' (pp. 50-51). In the literature apart from the commentaries we find the same situation: as examples, let me mention U. Winter, *Frau und Göttin: Exegetische und ikonographische Studien zum weiblichen Gottesbild im Alten Israel und in dessen Umwelt* (OBO, 53; Göttingen: Vandenhoeck & Ruprecht, 1983), who refers to Hos. 11 on p. 633 and sees in 11.1-4 early election of Israel described as 'paternal love for a child (a son)'. See also D. Kinet, *Ba'al und Jahwe: Ein Beitrag zur Theologie des Hoseabuches* (Frankfurt, 1977), pp. 97, especially nn. 18-20; H. Ringgren, ''ab', *TDOT*, I, pp. 1-19, esp. pp. 17-18.

After the listing of YHWH's good actions, v. 5 presents an initial reversal in the text. Verses 5-7 enumerate the consequences that ungrateful Israel has brought upon itself. They are closely connected with the preceding verses both in content and in terminology. The key word 'Egypt' in v. 5 refers back to the initial verse, and the end of v. 5, 'because they refused to return', summarizes Israel's attitude with a finality that allows no more room for change. The prophet thus reveals the power of his language in a play on words with the root *šûb*, which is used as the first and last word in this significant v. 5, each time in a different sense. At the beginning it describes the return to Egypt, and thus the reversal of 'salvation history', while at the end it describes the people's refusal to turn back, to return to YHWH.

In v. 6 the concrete consequences of the self-imposed punishment are developed. The prophet speaks of his own present, in which the Assyrian king Shalmaneser V was plundering the cities of Samaria.[1] Hosea sees a theological connection between the refusal to turn back and the political situation, that is, the collapse that has occurred in his own time.[2]

Verse 7 closes the first part with various references in content and terminology to the preceding verses. What is new in this verse is the complaining, even wounded tone in YHWH's speech, beginning with 'but *my* people' and another variation on the root, *šûb*, as in v. 5; this time not in reference to a general 'turning back', but to a *personal* 'turning away from *me*', that is, from YHWH.[3] At the same time, although this speech allows the people no more room for manoeuvre, it still expresses YHWH's fidelity to Israel, which is designated by the suffix 'my'.[4] YHWH

---

1. Cf. Wolff, *Hosea*, p. 100.

2. The difficult expression in v. 6b, *mimmō ʿaṣôtêhem* (cf. the textual note in Rudolph, *Hosea*, p. 211) has the meaning of 'preparation' or 'judgment'. I translate freely, following Rudolph: 'They will have to reap what they have sown'. [The German idiom is literally: 'They will have to spoon up what they have crumbled'.—Tr.]

3. Cf. the textual note in Wolff, *Hosea*, p. 248.

4. It may be that the prophet's emotional attitude is also expressed here: he himself had to call his own child *lōʾ ʿammî* (Hos 1.9), but YHWH still (or again) calls his people *ʿammî*!

still has not separated himself entirely from this people; his personal feeling is very clear. It is possible that we already find indications here of the connection to the following section in vv. 8-11.

The section closes with the assertion that the people are calling on Baal;[1] but in contrast to YHWH, Baal cannot bring up (*yerômēm*) Israel.

The key word 'Baal' connects v. 7 with v. 2, while the root *rmm* links v. 7 with v. 4. This verb, which Isa. 1.2 also uses in a speech of YHWH for 'bringing up' children,[2] is clearly contrasted here with YHWH's efforts to bring up Israel, as detailed in vv. 1-4. (In light of the high infant mortality rate in biblical times, the language literally means to 'bring them through'). What YHWH does in love and care is denied of Baal, and not only *de facto*. It is not merely that Baal does not do it, but it is impossible for him; he *cannot* do it.

Thus the whole section, vv. 1-7, which began with the key word 'bring up', has a well-developed theme. We find here a single, logical idea and a single image:[3] YHWH brings up Israel and reaps ingratitude; Israel runs after Baal, although he cannot do this job of upbringing. The image of Israel as a child or infant is thus concluded only at v. 7.

Before we can draw further conclusions, we must consider the second part of Hosea 11, vv. 8-11.

Hosea 11.8-11

The major reversal in the text occurs between vv. 7 and 8. Not only is the new beginning in v. 8 highly significant, but at this point the speech of YHWH, which previously referred to Israel in the third person, shifts to direct discourse, and a very

1. I emend here by adding *'al* before *ba'al*. Cf. *BHS* as well as Wolff, *Hosea*, pp. 192-93, and others.

2. Originally Isa. 1.2b read: 'I bore children and brought them up (*rmm*), but they have rebelled against me...'. The statement, in its terminology and in its contrast between YHWH and faithless Israel, is very similar to Hos. 11.1-7.

3. This can only be denied if, like Rudolph, one sees the image of the infant as ending with v. 4a. He regards v. 7 as completely corrupt and arrives at a variety of purely hypothetical possible interpretations, none of which is persuasive.

passionate discourse at that. Here an emotional component in YHWH's self-reference comes to the fore; we may possibly see it as already hinted in v. 7, with the phrase '*my* people'.

This second section contains at least one major addition. As already mentioned, v. 10 falls outside the norm of ch. 11 both on the basis of its style and in its content. It is certainly the work of a later hand. Verse 11 presents more difficulty. If this last verse is assigned to Hosea, which is doubtful, we would find here, as in vv. 1-7, the *consequences* for Israel described as a reaction of YHWH, namely return from prison and restoration to the land. But we must set aside the question whether this sentence was at all possible, in this form, before the exile.

The formula of divine speech at the end of the chapter is certainly the work of a later hand. It concludes not only Hosea 11, but the greater collection that constitutes Hosea 4–11.

Beginning with v. 8, we are considering events that take place within YHWH's own self; nothing more is said about Israel's behaviour. In four lines, constructed as two parallel pairs, God asks four questions of himself and answers them at the end of the verse. Hosea is a master of language, and this kind of word-play is typical of him. Already in 6.4 God had posed the same kind of despairing questions:

> What shall I do with you, O Ephraim?
> What shall I do with you, O Judah?
> Your love (*ḥesed*) is like a morning cloud
> like the dew that goes away early.
> *Therefore* I have hewn them by the prophets...

Similarly, in 11.8 God, in this wrestling with himself, first poses a question in order to draw its consequences afterward:

> How can I give you up, O Ephraim?
> How can I hand you over, O Israel?
> How can I give you up like Admah?
> How can I treat you like Zeboyim?

But here the consequence is quite different from that in ch. 6. YHWH does not follow with punishment for *Israel* (which in v. 7 he still calls 'my people', in spite of its apostasy). Instead, the punishment in a sense is turned against YHWH himself, for his own heart rebels:

My heart turns against me
my remorse burns intensely.[1]

In the Old Testament the heart is not the seat of emotions, but primarily of decision-making and will-power. The word in the second line that is often translated as 'remorse' or 'compassion' comes from a root very rarely found in the Old Testament (*nhm*) which can mean, for example, 'to allow oneself to regret one's plans'. The idea of 'remorse' is utterly inappropriate to describe this situation, because it always contains an element of the notion that the thing regretted was reprehensible. But that is not the case here: the action God has announced, namely the destruction of Israel, was in the prophet's view only too well justified! Jeremias suggests that we should speak here of God's 'self-control...in order to make it clear that what is meant is a power that turns aside God's wrath from destruction and subdues it, *although* that wrath is all too well founded'.[2] But there is another possible reading. The Masoretic Text says literally:

My heart is turned against me,
kindled together are my compassions (*nihûmāy*, plural).

In place of this last word, J. Wellhausen proposed that we should read *rah*ᵃ*māy*,[3] which in fact was the reading of the old Syriac translations and of the Targum. This would require only the change of a single consonant in the Hebrew text, and we would have a smooth reading:

...my womb (*rehem*) is utterly inflamed within me.

The plural of this word, *rah*ᵃ*mîm*, which is usually translated as 'mercy', is frequently applied to God in the Old Testament.

It is fairly well known that *rah*ᵃ*mîm* ('love' or 'mercy') is derived from *rehem* ('womb'),[4] but Hosea 11 has never previously been

1. Wolff, *Hosea*, p. 193.
2. Jeremias, *Hosea*, p. 145.
3. J. Wellhausen, *Die Kleinen Propheten übersetzt und erklärt* (Berlin, 4th edn, 1963), p. 128.
4. Cf. H.J. Stoebe, '*rhm*', *THAT*, II, pp. 761ff. According to him, four fifths of all occurrences have YHWH as subject. *rhm* always refers to one more highly placed with respect to someone lesser. On this, see also P. Trible, *God and the Rhetoric of Sexuality* (Philadelphia: Westminster Press, 1978), p. 48; Winter, *Frau und Göttin*, p. 475.

examined in this connection. This way of reading gives us a very clear and logically constructed statement; the parallelism is more evident in this interpretation, which is by no means a new one. In addition, there is a very close and almost literal parallel in 1 Kgs 3.26. In the fable about the wisdom of Solomon, who gives the child to its rightful mother, it is said of the true mother that 'compassion for her son burned within her'. Therefore she says: 'Please, my lord, give her the living boy; certainly do not kill him'.[1]

I thus translate v. 8b in the Hosea text literally:

> My heart recoils against me,
> my womb is utterly inflamed (*kmr*) within me.

The placement of the words in the translation retains the Hebrew parallelism; we thus find a clear correspondence between 'heart' and 'womb', and between 'recoils' and 'is utterly inflamed'. Both lines describe a powerful, self-directed emotion within God's own self. In light of the emotion expressed in v. 1, where Israel is called 'my son', God is unable to carry out just punishment on this, his own flesh and blood, because the maternal emotions so powerfully described here, working within God himself, prevent him from doing so.

The consequence of this 'turmoil' within God is described in v. 9, which gives the reason for it all. This is the climax of the entire text, and deserves special attention. It begins with another parallelism. The usual translation runs something like,

> I cannot execute my burning wrath,
> I cannot again destroy Ephraim.

Both lines begin with the negative *lô'* ('I cannot'). There has been much discussion of the verb *šûb* ('turn back')[2] in the second line, and it is usually translated 'again'. But YHWH has not yet destroyed Israel!

---

1. Translation from the NRSV. Literally we read here, with the same verb as in Hosea (*kmr*, 'become hot, aroused', found only 4 times in the Old Testament): 'For her womb (*reḥem*) was enflamed toward her son...'.

2. Cf. Hosea's mastery of wordplay. As early as v. 5 (see above) he has already used the verb *šûb* in several variations.

The long discussion of whether this refers to a second destructive action of YHWH or not[1] need not be replicated here. It is much simpler to refer the verb to the preceding verse. The decision YHWH made in v. 8 will not be reversed again (*šûb*). God's internal turmoil and reversal of intention remains controlling. YHWH will not draw back from it again; thus, it seems better to read 9a as,

> I cannot utterly change (what is within me), so as to destroy Ephraim.

Verse 9b then presents the reasons for YHWH's unusual and unexpected action, and here we find ourselves at the climax of all the statements made in this chapter:

> For I am God (*kî 'el 'anôkî*)
> and not a man (*wᵉlô' 'îš*),
> holy in your midst (*bᵉqirbᵉkâ qādôš*),
> and I do not come to destroy.

Here four statements, rigidly parallel in construction, are juxtaposed: the first line in each pair is positive, the second negative.

In the first YHWH says of himself that he is *'ēl* (God, divine) and not *'îš* (a man, male). The statement is quite clear, and there are no textual variants. According to Wolff, the word *'ēl* in Hosea underscores the incomparable divinity of the God of Israel.[2] The solemnity of this first line, *kî 'ēl 'ānôkî*, recalls the formula by which God introduces himself in the decalogue, especially the emphatic *'ānôkî*, already solemnly placed in the first position in v. 3. God's being *'ēl* is contrasted with being *'îš*, and this is given as a reason for the revolution within God's heart that was just described. This requires further explanation.

God acts in this way because he is *'ēl* and not a man (*'îš*). We would expect a man to act logically, by executing his wrath and carrying out the plan of destruction he has made. YHWH here separates himself from the kind of action that would be logical for a 'man', from what is expected of males. When the translation reads: 'For I am God and not (a) man', we would expect exegetes to say something about this important contrast. Instead,

---

1. For example Wolff, *Hosea*, pp. 201-202.
2. Wolff, *Hosea*, p. xxv.

we find only general observations about human nature.[1] The word '*îš*, correctly translated as 'man', is simply generalized into 'human being' by the interpreters. But what is being described here is not ordinary *human* behaviour, but something that is specifically *masculine*. The newer commentaries present essentially the same picture.[2] None of them comments on what Hosea actually says regarding the '*îš*, the 'man' in a gender-specific sense, and not just the 'human being'.[3]

When Hosea wants to speak of the 'human being' or 'human behaviour' so as to include women, he has other words at his disposal, for example '*ādām*.[4] This more general term even

---

1.   '...that God proves himself to be God and the Holy One in Israel in that he, unlike men, is independent of his partner's actions. Remaining completely sovereign over his own actions, he is not compelled to react. The Holy One is the totally Other, who is "Lord of His own will, who does not execute the fierceness of his anger... in His decision He is independent and free. Holy means superior, almighty"' (Wolff, *Hosea*, p. 202; the inserted quotation is from L. Köhler, *Theologie des Alten Testaments* [Tübingen, 4th edn, 1966]; cf. the English translation by A.S. Todd, *Old Testament Theology* [Philadelphia: Westminster Press, 1957], p. 52).

2.   'YHWH cannot destroy Israel because he is God. For Hosea, God's real difference from human beings consists not in unapproachable eminence, but in victory over his righteous wrath, in his will to preserve those deserving of death from destruction. All analogies with human thought and action fail before this divine self-mastery' (Jeremias, *Hosea*, p. 46). Deissler translates '*îš*' as 'human being', and says of v. 9: 'Human rage is ordinarily translated immediately into deeds of vengeance. But God is "different". He is the "Wholly Other" (= holy), not only in his being, but also in his actions... Therefore he will not proceed to wrathful judgment' (*Hosea*, p. 52). Rudolph also translates 'human being': 'How can wrath and love coexist? It is possible because YHWH is God and not a human being... An enraged human being is carried away by his own wrath and hatred, and even parents who love their children are so irritated by stubbornness and impudence that they go too far in their anger. It is different with God. And what is so new and astonishing is that Hosea subsumes this side of YHWH under the concept of *qādôš*' (*Hosea*, p. 218).

3.   Hosea uses the word '*îš*' 10 times, most frequently in the sense of 'husband' (2.4, 9, 18; 3.3). The word can also mean 'anyone' (see 4.4; 2.12; 6.9). In Hos. 9.7 the expression '*îš* '*ᵉlōhîm* ('man of God') refers to the prophet himself, but on the lips of someone else.

4.   '*ādām* appears 4 times in Hosea. In 6.7 it appears to be a place name; 9.12 has it in the sense of 'childless' ('without people'). In Hos. 13.2 the

appears in ch. 11. In v. 4 YHWH, in giving an example of his 'humane' way of treating his people, speaks of the 'cords of humanity' with which he led stubborn Israel.[1] Having used the word *'ādām* (human) for his own way of behaving, he can scarcely distance himself from that very trait in the second section. Thus Hosea does not intend to contrast divine and *human* behaviour; for that he would have had to use a different terminology. Apparently he wants to describe the contradiction between *'ēl*-behaviour and *'îš*-behaviour. It is *masculine* attitudes that YHWH refuses to adopt, not those that are genuinely and universally human![2]

Parallel elements of the behaviour rejected by God in v. 9 are 'not being able to destroy' and 'not executing burning wrath'. If we refer back to v. 8, 'giving up' and 'handing over' are associated terms. Masculine behaviour would thus mean punishing without redress, allowing one's wrath to run its course, and carrying out a justice that would mean destruction for Israel. If this is the essence of *'îš*—justice, punishment, wrath, consequence—then YHWH's conduct is completely different: YHWH is *measurelessly* inconsequent or illogical.[3] YHWH is not concerned

prophet ridicules *people* for kissing calves: he is making fun of the cattle cult of Samaria, and women were probably more numerous among the worshippers of the bull than men. In this sentence, whose interpretation is in dispute, the word *'ādām* is at the end. It can be used for individuals or collectively. The fourth example is in Hos. 11.4!

1.   See the remarks on v. 4 above.

2.   The examples cited, of course, show how simple it is to equate the masculine with the universally human. But when a prophet speaks with such fine distinction at such a crucial point, the text requires a precise and differentiated interpretation.

3.   As an example of such logical masculine interpretation, although it has not been followed by anyone in recent literature, let me quote from the commentary by T.H. Robinson, *Hosea* (HAT, 1.14; Tübingen: Mohr, 2nd edn, 1954), p. 45: 'As a holy God, YHWH, to be true to his nature, must destroy Israel's cities just as he once destroyed Admah and Zeboyim. But it breaks his heart to impose this punishment. [His heart] urges him to let his people go free in spite of their sin (8). Human weakness by itself would have given in to such a rush of emotion and by its surrender would have betrayed the high moral principle YHWH represents. Precisely because he is God and not a human being, YHWH can resist the impulse to forgive, which is almost too strong for him, and can ruthlessly defend the cause of moral

with his pride, his self-concept, his rights, or masculine 'face-saving'. Instead, this YHWH is anxious to preserve his *relationship*, and this is a kind of behaviour that is much more frequently and more strongly ascribed to women than to men. This attitude of YHWH, who prefers to make himself vulnerable and sacrifice himself rather than have it happen to his beloved Israel, is founded in his being *'ēl* and in the concept of *qādôš*, terms that are also placed in parallel to each other. Here *qādôš* ('holy') does not refer to morality, but to a condition of being different, separated, something that also enables behaviour which is contrary to expectations.

But in order that this last term will not limit YHWH to a single concept, the prophet includes the opposite pole within the same line: 'in your midst'! If *qādôš* emphasizes distance, *bᵉqirbᵉkā* stresses nearness: this God of Hosea is caught in the tension between distance and closeness, between masculine and feminine behaviour. With all the variety with which Hosea describes his God, in his language he presses to the uttermost boundaries of what it was permissible to say in his time, and probably far beyond them.

The *concrete* consequence for Israel of this 'turmoil' within YHWH is their return to their own homes (v. 11). Hosea makes another wordplay with the verb *šûb* (return) and this time, in clear contrast to v. 5, uses it in a new and salvific sense. No longer *šûb* the apostasy of the people or their return to Egypt, nor is it recoil within God's heart (v. 9). Now it is 'coming home' ('trembling', because they are different now) and then coming to rest and being allowed to stay there.[1]

---

purity and holiness (9). His tight to do this is founded on the fact that he himself will suffer the most from it. The people struck down by the crushing blow is destroyed, but YHWH goes on living and must bear forever the burden of the unspeakable pain given to his heart by human sins and the catastrophe that follows. In short, there are things that are more terrible than destruction, and it was better for Israel to vanish utterly than to continue on the way that it had irrevocably chosen for itself.'

1.   *yšb hiphil*. It is possible that Hosea here uses the verb *šûb* again, since according to Gesenius we should presume the *hiphil* of *šûb* at this point.

3. *Summary: Observations and Conclusions*

The statements about God in Hosea 11 are not marginal comments. They are found within a central text. This is, in fact, a key text within the Old Testament. It is sometimes even described as the Old Testament 'gospel'.[1] Its images evidently have a special theological significance and power.

It is well known that the Bible often speaks of God anthropomorphically. But it frequently happens 'that God is represented in the OT not only anthropomorphically, but also andromorphically, i.e., as a male'.[2] However, this common opinion is not valid for Hosea 11. The prophet vehemently rejects such a masculine God-image. Hosea does not speak of his God andromorphically here, but *gynomorphically*. Although he avoids the word 'mother', he describes the everyday actions and behaviour of a mother bringing up an infant, and in the second section he depicts YHWH as a mother who cannot find it in her heart to subject this child to the punishment it deserves. How did a male prophet of YHWH arrive at such feminine and motherly statements about God?

When Hosea speaks of the Canaanite cult in ch. 11 he polemicizes primarily against Baal.[3] Baal is rejected especially because of his masculine and sexual aspect. Apparently Hosea is determined not to equate YHWH with natural forces, especially those characteristic of Baal. Therefore his God is not an *'îš*, namely not a masculine Baal. But the female gods are also rejected. If YHWH is not a Baal, he does not need a female partner. Female gods are not opposed because the prophet is anti-woman. There is a deeper reason: YHWH needs no *'ªšerâ* because he is not a Baal;

---

1. Cf., for example, G. von Rad, *Theologie des Alten Testaments* (Munich: Chr. Kaiser Verlag, 4th edn, 1965); ET *Old Testament Theology* (trans. D.M.G. Stalker; New York, 1962–65), II, p. 145; Deissler, *Hosea*, p. 52; Jeremias, *Hosea*, p. 139; Wolff, *Hosea*, pp. 203-204; A. Weiser, *Das Buch der zwölf kleinen Propheten* (ATD, 24; Göttingen: Vandenhoeck & Ruprecht, 5th edn, 1967), p. 84; and others.

2. N.P. Bratsiotis, *''îš'*, *TDOT*, I, pp. 222-35, at 232; similarly J. Kühlewein, *''îš'*, *THAT*, II, p. 135: 'Although in the OT YHWH is depicted as a *man*, it is only seldom and metaphorically that he is called *'îš'*.

3. The word is found in the plural in v. 2, and in the singular in v. 7.

he does not need a wife, because he is not an *'îš*.

Hosea is speaking at a time *before* the triumph of the dualism that splits female and male in such ominous fashion. Therefore he can use both male and female images and metaphors for God. The feminine can describe for him the whole fullness of divinity. The great goddesses of the ancient Orient were not female gods in the sense that they represented one aspect only. Instead, they represented a *totality* and were normative for everyone, both men and women. They cannot be set over against the male gods.[1]

YHWH *as mother* is a valid image of God for Hosea, and he uses it just as, elsewhere, he depicts YHWH as a jealous husband; at that point Israel (feminine) represents the unfaithful wife. Hosea loves to work with contrasting pairs. Whereas in the image of God as husband and Israel as unfaithful wife he distributes the male–female polarity in such a way that God is on the male and Israel on the female side, in Hosea 11 and elsewhere[2] we find that YHWH as mother is contrasted with her child, who is depicted as male ('youth', 'son', as in 11.1).

It seems that at the very end of his long and painful life and activity, Hosea had found that masculine images of God were of dubious validity. The metaphors of judge, king, hero and husband were no longer useful. In the desperate situation before the final collapse of the northern kingdom, the prophet resorts to images that are better adapted to express his last and deepest experiences with his YHWH, the God of Israel. Only in YHWH's motherly love can the prophet still find a chance for Israel. Some two hundred years later, after the collapse of the southern kingdom, we observe something similar. Deutero-Isaiah also uses feminine and maternal imagery to revive his people. He finds these images more appropriate for offering aid, hope and comfort in a time of catastrophe. This is not to say

---

1. Cf. for example R.R. Ruether, *Sexism and God-Talk: Toward a Feminist Theology* (Boston: Beacon Press, 1983), esp. ch. 2. 'Sexism and God-Language: Male and Female Images of the Divine', pp. 47-71: 'We should guard against concepts of divine androgyny that simply ratify on the divine level the patriarchal split of the masculine and the feminine' (p. 61).

2. Cf., for example. Hos. 13.8, where YHWH speaks of himself as a mother-bear whose cubs have been stolen.

that it is not legitimate to call on God as father, king or judge. But each of these titles is only *one* among many possibilities. It is not uniformity, but *variety* of symbolism and divine titles that serves to describe God adequately, because we cannot speak of God except in images. 'God the mother' can therefore express the prophetic or biblical experience of God just as well as 'God the father', as long as we keep in mind that *both* are images, and that neither aspect excludes the other. The divine shows itself with different faces and, according to the circumstances, it is sometimes the fatherly, and sometimes the motherly face of God that appears more helpful.

Biblical andromorphisms or gynomorphisms are often difficult to understand today. Is such a language of imagery perhaps provisional, and should it be recast into abstract and intellectual forms as quickly as possible? By no means! Hosea is not turning concepts of God into language; he is speaking out of *experience* that he cannot formulate except in graphic images.[1] The more concrete the images, the greater their power. The more abstract and intellectual an image of God becomes, the less effective it is; it pales and often no longer speaks to human beings. Against all types of one-sided spiritualization, we should cling to this graphic, drastic way of speaking, because the images say more thus than when they are dissolved into concepts.[2]

Our failure to understand the images any longer may be the very reason why the statements of Hosea 11, which involve so many superlatives, have not been more effective in subsequent years. As people have tried to systematize the images, they have lost their vividness. Interpreters as a group have worked on the basis of an androcentric Christian trinitarian doctrine and have conceived God in Hosea 11 from the outset as 'father'. The effect was to destroy the image. A mother cannot

1.   'Of course this is all very anthropomorphic, but I think that if Hosea had to explain himself in our conceptual language he would say that human theomorphism can only be preserved by the fact that God continues to be so anthromorphic' (M. Buber, *Der Glaube der Propheten* [Darmstadt, 2nd edn, 1984], p. 149).

2.   On this, see the remarks of J.G. Janzen, 'Metaphor and Reality in Hosea 11', *Semeia* 24 (1982), pp. 7-44.

be changed into a father with impunity.[1] When the utterly feminine and maternal imagery is pressed into a masculine mould, it loses its concrete expressive power.

The progressive patriarchalizing of the Christian image of God[2] has made it less and less possible, in successive years, to accept a female figure as a representation of the divine, something that was still easily possible in Hosea 11. People have generally been content to allow the (male) God a few maternal features, so that the underlying just and strict Father-God is enriched with some female and maternal characteristics and thus acquires a gentler overall image.

But the history of interpretation has had to deal not only with the image of God. It must also struggle with the image of humanity. The history of reception of the prophet Hosea shows how differently gender-motivated images have been adopted and reflected upon, even though in Hosea they stand together and have equal weight. Where God is on the masculine side—and this is always the positive, honorable role—the traditional statements are fully accepted. But when the masculine aspect is in the inferior position, namely as 'son' in the role of unfaithful Israel while YHWH takes the female part, the ideas have found practically no reception at all. Apparently, since interpretation has been practised almost exclusively by men, there has been a conscious or unconscious influence of the interpreters' own self-identification. 'God the mother' is almost entirely obscured in the tradition of reception and interpretation. Men identify themselves completely with the divine, and in the Christian tradition God is always thought of, implicitly or explicitly, as male, until 'both the concept of God and that of the human being as a spiritual entity...are onesidedly oriented to "patriarchal" primal images'. That ultimately brings us to the equation of God with

---

1. All the twists and turns in the explanation of the most concrete expressions in order to reinterpret them from motherly activities to those that could be predicated of a father have resulted in shattering the point of the text.

2. On this, see especially the interesting essay by F.K. Mayr, 'Patriarchalisches Gottesverständnis? Historische Erwägungen zur Trinitätslehre', *TQ* 152 (1972), pp. 224-55.

'father' and human being with 'man'.[1]

There are many biblical texts that contain other than patriarchal ideas—including Hosea 11. However, they are almost automatically read with this Christian pre-understanding and are thereby *diminished*. It is time to interpret them anew, from a feminist perspective.

TRACES OF THE GODDESS IN THE BOOK OF HOSEA*

Marie-Theres Wacker

1. *The Problem*

A major thrust of Christian feminist theology in Europe and
North America addresses the necessity for and appropriateness
of feminine metaphors in God-talk. If this concern were transposed to the area of biblical research, especially exegesis of the
Hebrew Bible, it would reveal two inherent aspects: on a textual
level, questions about the feminine metaphors in the speeches of
Israel's God as revealed in the biblical writings; on a historical
level, questions about the veneration of other deities alongside
YHWH, especially female deities. Such veneration generated
conflicts in ancient Israel; of that there can be no doubt. It is not
inconsequential that, in the 1980s in Germany, matriarchal feminists were led to counter-reading the Christian Old Testament
as a document of a once-living but later suppressed goddess-
religion.

In the discussions of these feminist-theological—or better,
thealogical—positions, I first became aware of what happens if
feminist theology is not sufficiently self-critical: it stumbles into
all sorts of hermeneutical traps, and one notable trap is a new
form of anti-Judaism: blaming Jews for the death of the goddess.[1] I hold it necessary to continue thinking and talking about

*   This is a revised and expanded version of an article in German,
forthcoming in W. Dietrich and M. Klopfenstein (eds.), *Ein Gott allein?
JHWH-Verehrung und biblischer Monotheismus im Kontext der israelitischen
und altorientalischen Religionsgeschichte* (Freiburg and Göttingen, 1994);
translated by L.R. Klein.
    1.   Cf. M.-T. Wacker, 'Matriarchale Bibelkritik—ein antijudaistisches
Konzept?', in L. Siegele-Wenschkewitz (ed.), *Verdrängte Vergangenheit, die
uns bedrängt* (Munich, 1988), pp. 181-242; *idem*, 'Feminist Theology and

this negative, anti-Jewish tradition in Christianity, especially in view of the growing racism and anti-Judaism in Germany. In any case, these false leads have not ended questions about goddess traditions in the Old Testament; what we need are reformulations of the questions or more precise formulations of what is asked, what is sought. In this sense—greater caution and increased precision in the questions put to a concrete text-complex of the Hebrew Bible—I would like to concentrate on the book of the prophet Hosea, the first of the so-called 'Minor Prophets'.

This biblical book is marked by a pronounced criticism of Israel's cult practice and by a conception of God which elicits specifically gender-influenced metaphors. According to recent studies in the history of religious trends in ancient Israel,[1] this book is held to be the oldest document of ancient Israel to give evidence of specific changes in the belief in God. These changes were perhaps already in evidence as early as the ninth century; however, with Hosea, the Northern Kingdom prophet of the eighth century, they gained voice and developed into a contentious and delimiting understanding of Israel's belief in God. The gold in the temples of Samaria and Bethel was not only glitter: in the book of Hosea, the golden calf of Samaria, a symbol of YHWH as Baal-god, was regarded as a symbol of the perverted knowledge of God and perverted ritual practice.

Because Baal seems to have a female consort, YHWH's being honoured as Baal raises the question of a female deity besides the God of Israel. Many older as well as recent commentaries maintain (if they even perceive the problem) that goddesses are included in the Baal-polemic of the book of Hosea.[2] To date, no

Anti-Judaism: The Status of the Discussion and the Context of the Problem in the FRG', *JFSR* 7.2 (1991), pp. 109-16; and J. Plaskow, 'Anti-Judaism in Feminist Christian Interpretation', in E. Schüssler-Fiorenza (ed.), *Searching the Scriptures. I. A Feminist Introduction* (New York: Crossroad, 1993), pp. 117-29.

1.   See particularly B. Lang, 'The Yahweh-Alone-Movement and the Making of Jewish Monotheism', in *Monotheism and the Prophetic Minority* (Sheffield: Almond Press, 1983), pp. 13-56.

2.   Cf. J. Wellhausen, *Die Kleinen Propheten* (Skizzen und Vorarbeiten, 5; repr.; Berlin, 4th edn, 1963), p. 101; H.-W. Wolff, *Dodekapropheton I. Hosea* (BKAT, 14.1; Neukirchen–Vluyn: Neukirchener Verlag, 3rd edn, 1976), p. 48

research has worked on the traces of a specific goddess-tradition in this biblical book, or collected the traces of a quarrel with such goddess traditions, or suggested an interpretive frame. These are the goals of the following comments. I would like to include, rather than exclude, a much-needed analysis of the text's formation history in order to develop a precise direction for the questions raised and the hypotheses formulated.[1]

2. Tracking the Traces

1. The Goddess in Text-Critical Conjecture

Because the book of Hosea offers a pronounced polemic against gods other than YHWH, it has been assumed that attacks against female deities must also be present in the text. This has occasionally excited text-critical conjectures wherein a goddess should be, so to speak, returned to the text. Such goddess rejuvenation by conjecture is to be seen especially in Hos. 4.18; 9.13; and 14.9.

'Groves of Asherah' or 'Image of God'? One passage, which is generally regarded as almost hopelessly corrupt and has generated almost unlimited conjectures (and translations) is Hos. 4.17-19.

17a	חבור עצבים אפרים	Ephraim is joined to idols:
17b	הניח־לו	let him alone.
18a	סר סבאם	Their drink is sour:
18b	הזנה הזנו	they have committed whoredom continually:

('Baal has become a collective term for Canaanite gods...since not even Asherah is mentioned beside him...' and J. Jeremias, *Der Prophet Hosea* (ATD, 24.1; Göttingen, 1983), p. 45 n. 11.

1. See especially the new approaches by G. Yee, *Tradition and Composition in the Book of Hosea* (SBLDS, 102; Atlanta: Scholars Press, 1987), and M. Nissinen, *Prophetie, Redaktion und Fortschreibung im Hoseabuch* (AOAT, 231; Neukirchen–Vluyn: Kevelaer, 1991), which—in my opinion correctly—describe the formation history of Hosea in terms of Deuteronomistic editorial reworking. In my first article on Hosea ('Weib-Sexus-Macht: Eine feministisch-theologische Relecture des Hoseabuches', in *idem.* [ed.], *Der Gott der Männer und die Frauen* [Düsseldorf: Patmos, 1987], pp. 101-25), I could not incorporate these approaches.

18c/d	אהבו הבו קלון מגניה	her rulers with shame do love, Give ye.
19a	צרר רוח אותה בכנפיה	The wind hath bound her up in her wings,
19b	ויבשו מזבחותם	and they shall be ashamed because of their sacrifices.[1]

Besides the imperative mood (v. 17b), which does not fit into its context, two further anomalies are especially striking. The feminine suffixes in v. 18d (מגניה, 'her shields') and v. 19a (בכנפיה, 'in her wings'/אותה, 'her') do not have clear textual references, and the meaning of the nominal construction קלון מגניה (v. 18d) is disputed.[2] Two interpretations are encountered in the literature, interpretations that, with assistance from text-critical conjectures, point to a goddess and her cult objects.

Harry Torczyner[3] attacks the text relatively energetically and succeeds in making a statement about Asherah gardens. 'Hosea ridicules the Asherahs to whom Israel sacrifices as "gardens", whose branches and leaves are taken by the wind'.[4] When speaking about 'gardens' Torczyner is less concerned with the goddess than with cult objects contradicting what Hosea considers acceptable in YHWH's cult. However, since he must assume a series of textual errors as well as corrections, his conjecture appears doubtful despite his interesting intuition.

Grace Emmerson[5] observes that the LXX renders הנח־לו ('let him!', v. 4.17b) as ἔτηκεν ἑαυτῷ σκάνδαλα ('he has set up for

---

1.   The translation given is that of the KJV, which is close to the Hebrew here.

2.   The RSV accords with the LXX in fully allowing the feminine forms to disappear and understands v. 18d comparatively (vv. 18c-19a: 'they love shame more than their glory / A wind has wrapped them in its wings...'); the KJV retains the feminine forms but allows their grammatical reference to remain open.

3.   H. Torczyner, 'Dunkle Bibelstellen', in *Festschrift K. Marti* (BZAW, 41; Berlin, 1925), pp. 274-80.

4.   More precisely, הנחלו קלון מגניהם   צררה רוח אותם בכנפיה ('Shame reaps he [Ephraim] from his gardens / the wind catches them in his wings...'; Torczyner, 'Dunkle Bibelstellen', p. 277). This interpretation warrants attention in that it may find support in Hos. 4.12 (the ridicule about the 'wood') and Isa. 1.31 (the polemic against 'gardens').

5.   G. Emmerson, 'A Fertility Goddess in Hosea IV 17-19?', *VT* 24 (1974), pp. 492-97.

himself traps/scandals'), thus adding the noun σκάνδαλα to the verb and pronoun offered by the MT. She suspects that an indication or even a name of a goddess may have fallen away behind the Hebrew הנח־לו. This denotation, which the Greek version would still have had available in its *Vorlage*, was found so 'scandalous' that it was translated by σκάνδαλα. Thus the feminine references in 4.18-19 are presumed to be to the original textual denotation of a goddess. In this way, Emmerson arrives at a text that reads:

> Ephraim has fellowship with idols; he has set up for himself [a goddess]. When their drink is gone, they engage in prostitution. They love the shame of her wantonness. The wind has bound her up in those skirts of hers, and they will be ashamed because of their sacrifices.[1]

Emmerson's assumption appears to resolve the question of the feminine forms. Of course, nothing is proven thereby.

Reference to Asherah? Already in 1867, Heinrich Ewald[2] attempted to regain a reference to Asherah in Hos. 9.13. This verse is, like Hos. 4.17-19, almost incomprehensible in the MT:

אפרים כאשר־ראיתי לצור	Ephraim, as I saw Tyre,
שתולה בנוה	is planted in a pleasant place
ואפרים להוציא	but Ephraim shall bring forth
אל־הרג בניו	his children to the murderer.[3]

Ewald extracts a reference to Asherah, written without a feminine ending, from the relative clause כאשר־ראיתי (as I saw), and derives a unified image:

> Ephraim is for me like Tyrian groves of lust, planted in a meadow and Ephraim should bring his sons there to be strangled.[4]

The advantage of this interpretation is that the feminine participle שתולה (planted) achieves a point of reference with the introduction of the 'Asherah'.

---

1. Emmerson, 'Fertility Goddess', p. 497.
2. H. Ewald, *Die Propheten des Alten Bundes*. I. *Hosea* (Stuttgart, 2nd edn, 1867), pp. 171-247, 227-30.
3. Translation mainly following the KJV which is close to the Hebrew text; the RSV follows the LXX.
4. Ewald, *Propheten*, I, p. 277.

While Ewald considered this noun as only a designation for a 'grove of lust', Henryk Samuel Nyberg[1] offered a similar conjecture which nevertheless seems to involve the goddess Asherah or at least a cult object pointing to her. Nyberg paraphrases Hos. 9.13:

> As when children were brought to the Asherah of Tyre,
> which was as planted in a meadow,
> thus is Ephraim in the process of bringing his children
> (in order) to be slaughtered before the Asherah.[2]

Nyberg obviously thinks of Hoseanic polemic against child sacrifice in the name of Asherah.

'I am his Anath and his Asherah...' The best known critical conjecture in the book of Hosea is certainly the one Julius Wellhausen introduced concerning Hos. 14.9,[3] a conjecture which has since been frequently adopted.[4] Wellhausen sought to improve the traditional reading of the MT (אני עניתי ואשרנו, 'It is I who answer and look after you'; 14.9b) through some slight modifications (אני ענתו ואשרתו, 'I am his Anath and his Asherah') and thereby reconstituted not one but two goddesses in the book of Hosea. If he was right, the God of Israel (through the mouth of his

1.   H.S. Nyberg, *Studien zum Hoseabuche* (Uppsala, 1935).

2.   Nyberg, *Studien*, p. 71. His literal translation of Hos. 9.13 reads: 'Ephraim is like the Asherah / who is a drama play for Tyre / planted on the meadow; / and Ephraim is ready to bring out / his children to the slaughterer' (p. 71).

3.   Wellhausen, *Kleine Propheten*, p. 134.

4.   For example, see B. Duhm, *Anmerkungen zu den Zwölf Propheten* (Giessen, 1911), pp. 42-43 (with the specially interesting note: 'perhaps, next to these great goddesses, the evergreen cypress takes the place of the tree gods; perhaps, however, the cypress also represents the great mother goddess to whom the peasants now hang clothes and such on the tree'; p. 43); cf. *idem, Die Zwölf Propheten: In den Versmassen der Urschrift* (Tübingen: Mohr, 1910), p. 47; E. Sellin, *Das Zwölfprophetenbuch* (Leipzig/Erlangen, 1922), pp. 105-106, 108; G. Fohrer, *Die Propheten des 8. Jahrhunderts* (Gütersloh, 1974), p. 89; M. Weinfeld, 'Kuntillet 'Ajrud Inscriptions and their Significance', *SEL* 1 (1984), pp. 121-30, pp. 122-23; most recently O. Loretz, '"Anat-Aschera (Hos. 14,9) und die Inschriften von Kuntillet 'Ajrud', *SEL* 6 (1989), pp. 57-65, and M. Dietrich and O. Loretz, *Jahwe und seine Aschera* (Ugarit.-Bibl. Literatur, 9; Münster, 1992), pp. 173-82.

prophet) describes himself here as Anath and Asherah to his people, as if God had incorporated the names and, thereby, the functions, even the reality of these goddesses.

Although, as Wilhelm Rudolph has put it, this conjecture may have been a 'monument of astuteness', it is, nevertheless, 'only with difficulty conceivable in the mouth of Hosea'.[1] Rudolph thereby attempts to articulate why 'the historical Hosea' was not able to use the name of a goddess. In contrast, I want to use Rudolph's quotation as refering to a textual feature of the biblical book of Hosea. In its original Hebrew, the text of this book is energized to an unusual degree by the ambiguities of sound and visual image of the written words, and thereby encodes a precise meaning more than disclosing that meaning. In such a text, unambiguous speech in the sense of direct naming of a goddess is not necessarily to be expected. Therefore, text-critical restoration of goddess names—as Ewald and Nyberg suggest—should be avoided.[2] It is more advantageous to seek traces of the goddess in implications and sound-play.

2. *The Goddess in Poetic Sound-Play*
Sound patterns, especially in Hos. 14.9 and 4.12,[3] hint of reference to a goddess.

---

1.   W. Rudolph, *Hosea* (KAT, 13.1; Gütersloh: Gerd Mohn, 1966), p. 249. Sellin, in the second edition of *Das Zwölfprophetenbuch* (1929; see p. 224) rescinded this conjecture, which he had accepted in the first edition in 1922.

2.   Textual criticism is, following Emmerson's example, at best able to offer evidence of textual gaps without being able to fill them in definitively.

3.   A. Deem, 'The Goddess Anath and some Biblical Hebrew Cruces', *JSS* 23 (1978), pp. 25-30, started from Hos. 2.16-17 in order to consider the etymology of the goddess name Anat as suitable for a love-goddess. In juridical contexts (like Deut. 21.14; 22.24, 29) and narrative as well as poetic texts (like Gen. 34.2; Judg. 19.24; 20.5; 2 Sam. 13.12, 14, 22, 31; Ezek. 22.11; Lam. 5.11) the D-stem of *'nh* means 'rape'. Therefore, according to Deem, one can postulate a basic stem which means 'free-wished' sexual love and is used in Hos. 2.17. Perhaps, however, the erotic overtones should not be exaggerated; cf. R. Mosis, 'Die Wiederherstellung Israels', in *idem* and R. Lothar (eds.), *Der Weg zum Menschen* (FS A. Deissler; Freiburg, 1989), pp. 110-33.

Hosea 14.9. Even if Wellhausen's presumptions go too far, it may be that the biblical formulation אֲנִי עֲנִיתִי וַאֲשׁוּרֶנּוּ ('It is I who answer and look after you') does suggest an awareness of sound play on the words 'Anath' and 'Asherah'. In order that such word-play have any sense at all, we must question whether, at the time of Hosea and afterwards, the names of these goddesses were known and used in Israel. Sources of reference to the name Anath are exceedingly scant:[1] with the exception of place names involving Anath—for example, Anatoth, birthplace of the prophet Jeremiah—and the origin of the judge Shamgar, described as son of Anath (Judg. 3.31), there is only the indication of the deity Anathyahu, from the Egyptian post-exilic military colony Elephantine. This deity was occasionally attributed to traditions going back to Israel's Northern Kingdom, but no proof for that is available.[2]

The situation is far more favorable for the name 'Asherah'.[3]

---

1.   Cf. in greater detail M.-T. Wacker, 'Gefährliche Erinnerungen', in *idem*. (ed.), *Theologie-feministisch* (Düsseldorf, 1988), pp. 42-52.

2.   Even if a seal from Samaria of the Iron II phase shows the goddess standing on a horse—a pictorial representation typical for Anath—this is not evidence that she was actually called 'Anath' at that time in Samaria. See G.A. Reisner *et al.*, *Harvard Excavations at Samaria* (Cambridge, MA: Harvard University Press, 1924), II, pl. 56, 3586, where this seal is curiously shown upside down.

3.   The Asherah literature of recent years has increased almost beyond grasp. Only a few articles can be mentioned: J. Day, 'Asherah in the Hebrew Bible and Northwest Semitic Literature', *JBL* 105 (1986), pp. 385-408; W. Dever, 'Asherah, Consort of Yahweh? New Evidence From Kuntillet 'Ajrud', *BASOR* 255 (1984), pp. 21-37; J. Hadley, 'The Khirbet el-Qom Inscription', *VT* 37 (1987), pp. 50-62; *idem*, 'Some Drawings and Inscriptions on Two Pithoi from Kuntillet 'Ajrud', *VT* 37 (1987), pp. 180-211; K. Koch, 'Aschera als Himmelskönigin in Jerusalem', *UF* 20 (1988), pp. 97-120; A. Lemaire, 'Les inscriptions de Khirbet el-Qôm et l'Ashérah de Jhwh', *RB* 84 (1977), pp. 595-60; Dietrich and Loretz, *Aschera*; Z. Meschel, 'Did Yahweh have a Consort? The New Religious Inscriptions from the Sinai', *BARev* 5 (1979), pp. 24-35; S. Schroer, *In Israel gab es Bilder* (OBO, 74; Freiburg and Göttingen, 1987), pp. 21-45; M. Smith, 'God Male and Female in the Old Testament: Yahweh and His "Asherah"', *TS* 48.2 (1987), pp. 333-40; M.-T. Wacker, 'Aschera oder die Ambivalenz des Weiblichen', in *idem* and E. Zenger (eds.), *Der eine Gott und die Göttin* (QD, 135; Freiburg: Herder, 1992), pp. 137-50, and Weinfeld, 'Kuntillet 'Ajrud'.

There are, after all, 40 mentions of Asherah in the Hebrew
Bible, and there are the famous blessing formulas of 'YHWH and
his Asherah' from Khirbet el-Qom and Kuntillet 'Ajrud, dated to
the eighth or seventh century BCE. At any rate, in the Hebrew
Bible Asherah is primarily known as a cult object, as the above
mentioned, older conjectures assume. But contemporary
exegetical discussion minimally tends to assume the transparency
of these cult objects and to acknowledge the goddess, believed
in and honoured, behind the objects. Perhaps a hearer (feminine
or masculine) from monarchic Israel could actually grasp a coded
reference to the name of the goddess Asherah. In any case, this
link between Hosea and other biblical books, particularly the
book of Kings with its polemics against Asherah, did not remain
hidden to the post-exilic scribes, who understood this prophet
in the context of the entire Hebrew Bible.

Hosea 4.12: The 'Elah (Terebinth/Goddess). The most notable and
clearest evidence of a goddess in the form of a word-play
appears in Hos. 4.12c-13d:

12c	כי רוח זנונים התעה
d	ויזנו מתחת אלהיהם
13a	על־ראשי ההרים יזבחו
b	ועל־הגבעות יקטרו
c	תחת אלון ולבנה ואלה
d	כי טוב צלה

12c	for a spirit of harlotry leads astray
d	and they are whoring from under their God
13a	on tops of the mountains they offer
b	and on the hills they burn incense
c	under oak, poplar and terebinth
d	for good is her shade.[1]

The double identification of place ('on the mountains'/'on the
hills'; v. 13a, b) is framed by another double indication marked
by the preposition 'under' (vv. 12d, 13c): they go away 'from
under' their God and place themselves 'under' the named trees
instead (the implied metaphors of power and domination have

---

1. My translation, following the Hebrew text as closely as possible.

been noted by Bird[1]). Finally, the two outside lines may, as Andersen and Freedman suggest,[2] be indications of a 'whoring spirit'—in v. 12c as a hidden allusion, so to speak *pars pro toto*—identified with a goddess. This gives the striking feminine suffix in v. 13d ('her' shadow) an indirect reference. On the other hand, the immediately preceding line (v. 13c) has a feminine reference stem, the tree, the אלה (terebinth). The name of this tree is a homonym with the feminine form of El, God—that is, Elah or Elat: goddess. Even if the word Elah never appears in the Hebrew Bible in the sense of goddess, it cannot be completely denied that the text, with its love for sound-play, makes use of this homonymy. We have another reason for evoking the goddess: a Late Bronze Age ewer from Lachish shows a stylized tree on top of which, in old Hebraic letters, the word אלה (goddess) appears.[3]

With this evidence, the discussion goes far afield with non-biblical, even non-textual materials: it involves pictorial objects now. With all possible methodological care, a correlation of pictorial and textual material may be permitted.[4]

3. *Iconic Representations of the Goddess*
Goddess iconography, especially as recently made accessible by the 'Freiburg School',[5] is of incalculable assistance in decoding the goddess motif in Hosea. For this purpose, the extensive material has to be counterchecked in two ways. On the one

1. See P. Bird, '"To Play the Harlot"', in P.L. Day (ed.), *Gender and Difference in Ancient Israel* (Minneapolis: Fortress Press, 1989), pp. 83-84.
2. F.I. Andersen and D.N. Freedman, *Hosea* (AB, 24; Garden City, NY: Doubleday, 1980), p. 366.
3. See R. Hestrin, 'The Lachish Ewer and the Asherah', *IEJ* 37 (1987), pp. 212-23; *idem*, 'Understanding Asherah', *BARev* 17.5 (1991), pp. 50-59; and, most recently, O. Keel and C. Uehlinger, *Göttinnen, Götter und Gottessymbole* (QD, 134; Freiburg: Herder, 1992), p. 80.
4. Methodology certainly has to respect the fact that iconography presents its own 'discourse'. One has to be careful of shortcuts when relating texts and images to each other.
5. See especially U. Winter, *Frau und Göttin* (OBO, 53; Freiburg and Göttingen, 1983); Schroer, *Bilder*; *idem*, 'Die Zweiggöttin in Israel/Palästina', in M. Küchler and C. Uehlinger (eds.), *Jerusalem* (FS O. Keel and H. Keel-Leu; NTOA, 6; Freiburg, 1987), pp. 201-25; Keel and Uehlinger, *Göttinnen*.

hand, one must take into consideration what iconographic evidence has been found that corresponds to the text of Hosea; on the other hand, one has to focus mainly on those pictorial remains which, according to archaeological stratigraphy, belong to Hosea's temporal and spatial environs.[1]

Shields of the Goddess? First of all, I allude to an example of a fruitless attempt to bring a goddess icon into consideration. Nyberg[2] suggested an interpretation of Hos. 4.18c-d as referring to a goddess. This time, he came to grips with the texual problems by grammatical qualification (as is his usual method), not by textual-critical intervention. Defining the nominal conjunction קלון מגניה as a paratactical relative clause, and reading this clause as object of the preceding verb, he produced the following translation: 'they love (intensely) (her) whose shields are shame'.[3] For Nyberg, the supposed relative clause furnishes proof of a goddess whose iconographical identity is marked by shields.[4]

Of course Nyberg's assumption is utterly dependent upon iconographical evidence of a goddess armed with shields. Such evidence has not been submitted to date. The image-motif of a woman with a disc, several examples of which were also found in Hosea's Samaria,[5] appear to support Nyberg's claims at first glance. However, investigations by Silvia Schroer, Christoph Uehlinger and Carol Meyers tend to interpret the disc as bread

---

1.   In addition to the books identified in the foregoing note, Reisner's two volumes (*Samaria*) and J.W. Crowfoot *et al.*, *Samaria-Sebaste*. II. *The Ivories* (London, 1938); III. *The Objects* (London, 1957) are very helpful.

2.   Nyberg, *Studien*, for Hos. 4.18.

3.   Nyberg, *Studien*, pp. 33-34 ('sie lieben [heftig] [die], deren Schilde Schande sind').

4.   G. Braulik, 'Die Ablehnung der Göttin Aschera in Israel', in Wacker and Zenger (eds.), *Der eine Gott und die Göttin*, pp. 106-36, 119-20, assimilates Nyberg's understanding with reference to an unpublished article by Norbert Lohfink. Andersen and Freedman (*Hosea*, pp. 76, 373) also adopt the idea, but with a different syntactical analysis of the Hebrew text.

5.   Cf. Keel and Uehlinger, *Göttinnen*, fig. 190e, p. 185.

or as a hand-drum.[1] The woman with the disc may well belong to a goddess cult, but Hos. 4.18 does not deal with this image.

The Goddess as Tree. An analysis of Hos. 4.12-13 is more rewarding. The homology Elah=tree/goddess, which may be found behind v. 4.13, is available as a concrete goddess image, that of the goddess as tree. On the above-mentioned Lachish ewer, tree images and identifying script are combined, but Silvia Schroer has shown with abundant material based purely on images that there is a relation between the female deity and the tree or branch motif in the ancient Near East.[2]

For Hosea and his time, the following development is striking: during the Late Bronze Age, a typical image of the divine is a naked goddess with caprids standing on a lion. Sometimes she has already been replaced by a tree. In contrast, in the Iron Age when Israel, from an archaeological point of view, was a recognizable entity for the first time, the female is most frequently replaced by a stylized tree, standing, as does the naked goddess, on a lion and flanked by caprids. In this regard, instructive examples are the second cult stand from Lachish and a pithos drawing from Kuntillet 'Ajrud.[3] From Samaria in the time of Hosea come two artifacts: a piece of ivory with a standing caprid, which could have belonged to a composition of 'tree with caprids',[4] and a seal showing humans before a tree, their hands raised in prayer.[5] All this evidence leaves it hardly doubtful that the tree metaphors of Hos. 4.13 actually are a

1. Schroer, *Bilder*, pp. 277-81; Keel and Uehlinger, *Göttinnen*, pp. 187-88; C. Meyers, 'Of Drums and Damsels', *BA* 45.1 (1991), pp. 16-27.

2. See Schroer, 'Zweiggöttin'.

3. See figures in Keel and Uehlinger, *Göttinnen*, no. 184, p. 179, and no. 219, p. 239.

4. See Crowfoot, *Ivories*, pl. 13.6.

5. Initially published by F. Zayadine, 'Une tombe du fer à Samarie-Sébaste', *RB* 75 (1968), pp. 562-85, p. 585 fig. 9.8; embraced by K. Jaroš, 'Die Motive der Heiligen Bäume und der Schlange in Gen 2-3', *ZAW* 92 (1980), pp. 204-15, p. 208 no. 7; see also the seal no. 4 from Tel el-Far'ah (North). For supplementary material see H. Keel-Leu, *Vorderasiatische Stempelsiegel* (OBO, 110; Freiburg and Göttingen: Herder, 1991), p. 67. Because caprids and lions are missing in this composition, the referential character of the tree to a feminine deity is admittedly less certain.

transparent reference to a currently believed and worshipped female deity.

The Goddess as Cow. A further area of goddess symbolism in the Iron Age is the cow-and-calf motif. A nice example originated, once more, in Kuntillet 'Ajrud. At Samaria, the image remains without documentation—which, of course, may be coincidental—but there is a small stamp seal from nearby Tel el Far'ah (North) showing this motif.[1]

In Hosea, the cow motif appears twice (Hos. 4.16 and 10.11),[2] both times without reference to God-talk but with allusion to Israel or Ephraim. Once negatively, once positively, these passages describe how YHWH enjoys having this cow under his direction. Is this the way Hosea conceived the relation of the feminine divine to the God of Israel? At any rate, as early as 1879 Karl August Reinhold Tötterman assumed that, 'Perhaps it is with regard to calf-service that the prophet compares Israel with a stubborn cow'.[3]

1. The drawing from Kuntillet 'Ajrud is reproduced in Keel and Uehlinger, *Göttinnen*, fig. 220, p. 241; for the stamp seal from Tel el-Far'ah (North) cf. R. de Vaux, 'Les fouilles de Tell el-Far'ah, près Naplouse', *RB* 53 (1951), pp. 541-89, 580-81. The only seal from Samaria showing a bovine (see Reisner, *Samaria*, II, pl. 56, 3980) does not belong to goddess iconography.

2. Andersen and Freedman (*Hosea*, p. 555) deem it possible that Hos. 10.5 with its *plurale majestatis* עגלות ('heifers') contains a hidden polemic against a goddess. I suspect, however, that the relevant term עגלות בית און conveys either a demeaning abstraction ('calf-thing' of Beth-Aven; read *ᵉglut* and see Jeremias, *Hosea*, p. 127) or an early—and equally polemical—form of what is later found in the Greek version of the Bible, namely the noun 'Baal' combined with the feminine article (η Βααλ; עגלה is then to be vocalized *ᵉglat*).

3. K.A.R. Tötterman, *Die Weissagungen Hoseas bis zur ersten assyrischen Deportation (I–VI,3): Nebst einem Commentar des Karäers Jephet ben Ali zu Hos. Cap. I–II,3* (Helsingfors, 1879), p. 70. One wonders what Rudolph (*Hosea*, p. 114) wants to stress when writing that Hos. 4.16 does not only speak about the stubborn work-animal, resistant to being fastened in a halter, but also: 'the cow does not want the bull to approach her and retreats from him. Only both actions together express Israel's obstinacy against his God.'

The Goddess in the Image of a Woman. Besides the named animal and plant forms of goddess symbols, further images of the goddess as a woman are to be observed in the period of Iron II B and C. Archaeological evidence shows that, starting with the eighth century BCE, houses and graves contained increasing quantities of small figures of a woman with a full skirt and bare breasts. Her arms were either hanging at her side or bent so that the hands support the breasts. The most plausible meaning of these so-called pillar figurines is that of a goddess icon in the family cult, a center of women's religion. According to the excavation reports, a series of such pillar figurines were brought to daylight at Samaria too,[1] which means that the goddess, presented as woman, must have played a significant role in the Samarian household cult.

In addition, Samaria has yielded a series of terracotta plaques depicting a sitting woman with a baby, apparently a *dea lactans*, a maternal goddess.[2] Like the pillar figurines, with their exaggerated breasts, the latter are differentiated from the naked goddess images of the earlier centuries, with their erotic ambience integrating the worlds of plants and animals: these plaques appear concentrated on maternal and nourishing functions.

On the other hand, it should be mentioned that among the ivories from Samaria—which certainly belong in the context of the court—is found a small depiction of the so-called 'Woman in the Window'.[3] This motif also hints at the goddess, in this instance as a love-goddess. The image, however, is limited to the head, particularly the face; as in the pillar figurines, where only the face is well defined. This reinforcing tendency of iconographic evidence—concentration on the maternal aspect, reduction of the erotic to the face—may be important for an adequate historical and biblical-theological judgment of how the book of Hosea deals with goddess traditions.

1. Reisner, *Samaria*, II, pl. 75; Crowfoot, *Ivories*, pl. XI.
2. See Crowfoot, *Objects*, pl. XII. 6-8; cf. Keel and Uehlinger, *Göttinnen*, p. 383.
3. See Crowfoot, *Ivories*, pl. XIII. 2; interpretations can be found in Winter, *Frau und Göttin*, pp. 296-301, and in Keel and Uehlinger, *Göttinnen*, pp. 225-26.

4. *The Goddess and Literary Roles of Women*

Whereas the above submits evidence concentrating on selective traces of goddess themes in Hosea, the following focuses on textual units which offer a systematic dispute with the believed-in power of the goddess, a dispute effected by using women's roles or, more precisely, women's roles as perceived in the text. Hosea 4, notably vv. 11-14; Hosea 11; Hosea 14, especially the last verses of the chapter; and, finally, Hos. 2.4-25 are of interest in this regard.

Women in the 'Shadow' of the Goddess. Hosea 4 can be read as one unified composition. The introductory verses 1-3 strike the basic tone of a dispute with Israel, and the two subsequent sections (4-10, 11-19) scourge Israel's failing relationship with God. Just as the emphasis in 4.4-10 is on the guilt of the priests, who keep the people in ignorance, the focus of 4.11-14 is on the consequences of that ignorance. The priests tolerate, even advance cults which, in the view of the prophet, lead to downfall, lead to nothing.

Hos. 4.11-14 is framed by two phrases (v. 11, v. 14e) which are similar in tone and content and which further parenthetically enclose the intervening verses. In this way, the structure of the text advises reading with a unified perspective: Hos. 4.11-14 paints a cult enterprise characterized as entirely misleading. The only differentiation of the misled people is according to feminine aspects. There are the daughters and brides or daughters-in-law, the whores and the 'hierodules' (*qᵉdēšôt*, קְדֵשׁוֹת). The daughters and daughters-in-law are accused of extra-marital sexuality; the 'hierodules' are named side-by-side with the whores and by this are included in the sexual activity of such women, even if their immediate function in this picture appears to be involvement in ritual sacrifice. The accusation is apparently directed toward a connection between cult and sexuality in the shadow of the goddess. Furthermore, if the designation of the *qᵉdēšôt* harbours a corresponding designation of the erotic goddess as Qudshu or Qedeshet, as evidenced in Late Bronze Age steles,[1] it would be an additional argument for the aura of

---

1. On these stelae see O. Keel, *Das Recht der Bilder gesehen zu werden* (OBO, 122; Freiburg and Göttingen: Herder, 1992), pp. 203-208. Cf. my

a goddess evoked in the text: the $q^e d\bar{e}\check{s}\hat{o}t$ were, so to speak, officially her representatives. The entire passage of Hos. 4.11-14 may accordingly be directed toward a criticism of a goddess cult[1] in which women and their—in the view of the critics—misled sexuality played a central role.[2]

Goddess motifs also appear recognizable, as suggested above, in Hos. 4.16-19. The entire chapter, after the introductory verses 1-3, seemingly juxtaposes a false YHWH cult (4.4-10) and disapproval of a goddess cult (4.11-14, 15-19) and reveals itself as a finely composed unity in two main parts.

YHWH in the Role of Mother Goddess. Hosea 11, an independent composition, depicts God's love for young Israel who nevertheless goes his own way and thereby encounters misfortune. God, however, cannot forget Israel and accommodates himself by an internal redirection of his own ways, culminating in the statement: 'For I am God, not אִישׁ (man/human/male)' (11.9).

considerations of the institution of the 'hierodules': M.-T. Wacker, 'Kosmisches Sakrament oder Verpfändung des Körpers?', in R. Jost *et al.* (eds.), *Auf Israel Hören* (Freiburg and Luzern: Herder, 1992), pp. 47-84.

1. As T.H. Robinson, 'Hosea bis Micha', in *idem* and F. Horst (eds.), *Die Zwölf Kleinen Propheten* (Tübingen: Möhr, 1938), p. 20, had already suspected.

2. There has not yet been a decision about what the actual cultic practices were in Hosea's time. H. Balz-Cochois, *Gomer* (Europäische Hochschulschriften, 23.191; Frankfurt: Peter Lang, 1982) conjectures, on the basis of her ten years' experience—as theologian in different African countries and as observer of African-Christian syncretism—that Hos. 4 could refer to a village festival orgy which includes the initiation of young girls. If, on the other hand, we perceive the text's war-mongering by powerful members of the people as a rationale, we may discern behind Hos. 4.11-14 a ritual staged by those in control over cult and government to provoke an increase in the birth rate, a ritual about which Hosea complains. This interpretation finds support in the discernible focus on mother-functions in the goddess iconography of Hosea's time and after. In any event, such claims about the historical backgrounds of a text must be proven by a thorough investigation of its formation history. In the meantime, I limit myself to the characteristic flow of the text itself, since its ironic polemic and simultaneously complaining diction are certainly not designed to describe the presupposed historical circumstances in an 'objective' manner.

This statement makes possible the redirection and return of Israel to God.

Helen Schüngel-Straumann[1] rekindled discussion about this text with her feminist theological thesis that Hosea 11 should be read as a sketch of gynocentric God-talk. In this reading, Hosea places an image of God as mother before his hearers. In my opinion, the text is not capable of maintaining a pure gynocentrism; instead, it is more concerned with conflict between the father-masculine and the mother-feminine aspects of God himself/herself. In this conflict, however—and Schüngel-Straumann is entirely correct in this regard—the mother-feminine has the last word[2]. In a slightly different way, Martti Nissinen has recently further developed the feminine dimensions of Hosea 11. He places the royal goddess Ishtar, of the New Assyrian Royal Oracles, at the side of the divinity of Hosea 11, and compares the two; in so doing, he thoroughly embeds the mother simile in a political context.[3]

The central metaphor for motherliness in Hosea 11 is the nourishing of the little boy: 'I bent toward him and gave him (something) to eat' (v. 4). Exactly this nourishing aspect, also prominent in the iconographic representation of the nursing mother, appears to be an important factor which further links the pillar figurines. Even the fruit-bearing tree between the caprids in Kuntillet 'Ajrud confirms the impression that at the time of Hosea the 'maternal' strongly dominated the divine feminine.[4] Hosea 11 is, it may be concluded, a text written

1. See H. Schüngel-Straumann's article in this volume, 'God as Mother in Hosea 11'.

2. Cf. M.-T. Wacker, 'Gott als Mutter?', *Concilium* 25 (1989), pp. 523-28. The article by O. Keel, 'JHWH in der Rolle der Muttergottheit', *Orientierung* 53 (1989), pp. 123-32, confirms the intuition of Schüngel-Straumann with reference to the role of YHWH in the flood-narrative. According to Keel, YHWH transforms himself from a manly-destructive to a motherly-protective divinity. Criticism by S. Kreuzer, 'Gott als Mutter?', *TQ* 169 (1989), pp. 123-32 is sometimes to the point but expressed in a style which admits limited sensitivity to the questions raised.

3. Nissinen, *Redaktion*, pp. 268-90.

4. In his interpretation of Hos. 11.4, Nissinen (*Redaktion*, pp. 290-94) points to the cow-and-calf motif, thus stressing anew the motherly-nourishing aspect of this passage.

against the background of Israel's increasing turn to the maternal, nourishing goddess; but the text itself returns to a feminine-maternal symbolism for God-talk. I can only suggest but not prove here that I consider this maternal symbolism of YHWH as stemming from an understanding of this god as El. As El, YHWH has paternal and maternal traits; as El, YHWH can meet the needs of those who search for feminine aspects of the divine.

YHWH 'as' Tree-Goddess. In the closing chapter of the book (Hos. 14.5-9) YHWH is compared to a greening tree (ברוש, cypress?) whose fruit benefits Ephraim-Israel. That the divine tree is described as ברוש has a stylistic basis: vv. 14.9a-d/b-c are chiastically related and, further, create a chiastic echo with each other.

a		אפרים מה־לי עוד לעצבים
b	אני עניתי ואשורנו	
c	אני כברוש רענן	
d		ממני פריך נמצא

a	O Ephraim, what have I to do with idols?
b	it is I who answer (you) and look after you
c	I am like an evergreen cypress
d	from me comes your fruit.[1]

The shadow motif, already encountered in Hos. 4.12, returns in v. 14.8. The meaning of 'shadow' is hardly exhausted with a purely functional explanation as 'giver of coolness'. Rather, the shadow appears to be another indication of a divine presence, as does the tree itself. Against the background of the disputed fascination with the tree goddess depicted in ch. 4, the borrowing of this metaphor in God-talk seems intentional here. With all due caution, by means of comparison, the symbol of the goddess is identified with the God of Israel. YHWH assumes characteristics of the tree goddess: her numinous presence as suggested by the shadow motif, and especially the nourishing aspect of her fruit.[2] Incidentally, Ephraim-Israel appears in the

---

1. According to RSV.
2. In addition to 4.12-13 and 14.9, a third reference to tree iconography may be discovered in Hos. 9.16. The verse paints the image of Ephraim as a cut-down tree. The word for 'fruit' (פרי) punningly refers to the name

paradisiacal picture that Hos. 14.5-9 paints: as the lily, webbed with God's dew; and as the grapevine—the wine itself, which fogs understanding and promotes the mis-directed cult—is transformed. In contrast to the manner of Hosea 4, this passage (Hos. 14.5-9), as Helgard Balz-Cochois has shown,[1] suggests that the God of Israel can integrate the fascination with the goddess in a positive way.

The Goddess Theme of Hosea 2. Hos. 2.4-25 is a long unified God-monologue, an argument between YHWH on the one hand and a feminine being on the other. This woman has the charac-teristics of a mother; at any rate, the beginning of the text calls her children as witnesses against her. She also has the attributes of a whore (or adultress) who holds fast to her clients or lovers (see esp. v. 2.7). With three references (vv. 2.8, 11, 16), the monologue points the way along which the woman should proceed, away from her lovers and only to YHWH. It is clear that this text can be read as an allegory of Israel's disturbed relationship with God. On this basis, the implication is that Israel must recognize YHWH alone.

Fokkelien van Dijk-Hemmes[2] posed the question: why was Israel's failure to recognize the uniqueness of YHWH presented as a woman, a mother who hangs on to her lovers? The most current exegetical answer is that the prophet's marriage experi-ence with an unfaithful woman imposed itself. In addition, a folk myth which involves the land as the bride of the land-god, Baal, is assumed as supplementary background inspiration. Van Dijk-Hemmes suggests an alternative approach: should not Israel's tendency toward a goddess, as concretely described in ch. 4, be

---

'Ephraim'. Simultaneously, the formulation פְּרִי בְלִי יַעֲשׂוּן ('they do not bear fruit') alludes ironically to the name 'Baal Peor' (9.10): Baal, so to speak robbed of the two *ayins* of his name, deprived of power through speech, and Ephraim, without fruit, i.e. descendants, are mirror images for each other. The question remains whether, beyond the antithetical allusion to Psalm 1, Hos. 9.16 also admits goddess symbolism.

1. Balz-Cochois, *Gomer*, and *idem*, 'Gomer oder die Macht der Astarte', *EvT* 42 (1982), pp. 37-65.

2. F. van Dijk-Hemmes, 'The Imagination of Power and the Power of Imagination', *JSOT* 44 (1989), pp. 75-88.

considered the immediate cause for the metaphor in ch. 2? She points in particular to the fact that both texts speak of זנונים ('harlotries'/signs of harlotry) and suggests that this expression may refer to a goddess in Hos. 4.12.[1] Consideration of the iconography leads to further support for this thesis. It appears evident that the woman in Hosea 2 possesses exactly those characteristics which accord with the iconography of goddess-conceptions of the eighth and seventh century: the lactating mother and the woman on the lookout for lovers, such as the 'Woman at the Window'. Furthermore, the 'whore-characteristics' in Hos. 2.4 can be elucidated iconographically: women in the service of the goddess apparently decorated their brow and their breasts, and the love goddess herself can be so presented.[2] Thus it is plausible that Hosea 2 implicates a dispute with the power of the goddess.

This dispute occurs on two levels. Fokkelien van Dijk-Hemmes focuses on the relationship between children and their mother. She makes it clear that the speaker of this monologue (Hos. 2) tries to distance the children from their mother and, according to the end of the text, declares them to be his own children (see v. 25). This can be interpreted as the prophetic struggle against the power of the goddess in Israel and for the recognition of YHWH alone. If, on a second level, the opposition of YHWH and the woman is taken into consideration, it seems to explain the relationship of the God of Israel to the goddess. First, there can be no feminine divine facing the God of Israel if only YHWH is God. In her place, Israel enters as woman. The relationship between YHWH and Israel, however, is based on an earlier action by YHWH, to whom Israel was profoundly indebted. Such a relationship could not be expressed by woman-centered imagery because that would have meant that Israel is the center,

---

1.   This reference invites deeper analysis. Within the context of a polemic against a false cult, Hos. 5.4 reads: 'a spirit of harlotry is in their midst/and they have not known YHWH'. The antithesis of that may be found in Hos. 11.9: 'a holy one (am I, El), in your midst': instead of a spirit of harlotry, YHWH himself is among them.

2.   Cf. O. Keel, 'Zeichen der Verbundenheit', in P. Casetti *et al.* (eds.), *Festschrift D. Barthélémy* (OBO, 38; Göttingen and Freiburg: Herder, 1981), pp. 159-240, 193-212.

not God. The only way to symbolize YHWH's relation to Israel is through androcentric imagery, through an androcratic marriage concept with a doubled viewpoint: the self-imposed responsibility of the husband to his wife but also his authority over her. It is within this configuration only that the erotic and sexual fascination of the goddess finds her place. Hos. 2.18-24 presents the paradisiacal honeymoon of the newly-married 'couple' YHWH and Israel and, in v. 2.22, uses the phrase, 'You will know YHWH'. Such a formulation of recognition, which can also refer to sexual intercourse, has in other passages of the Hebrew Bible a masculine subject. In our case, then, it constitutes a recognition of feminine erotic activity.[1]

3. *Implications*

A glimpse backward on the trail of the traces permits discovery of a step-by-step profile of a dispute with the power associated with a goddess in Hosea. If it appeared inadvisable to conjecturally restore the name of a goddess, consideration of wordplay leads further, and iconographic documents provide precious assistance in gaining new contours for understanding the argument implied in Hosea 4, 11, 14 and 2: texts which deal with goddess traditions.

Consideration of the textual relationships of these four

---

1. With these short remarks on Hos. 2, limited to the problematic of religious history, the text is, perceived from a feminist perspective, by no means exhausted. Aside from the article by van Dijk-Hemmes cf., for example, R.J. Weems, 'Gomer: Victim of Violence or Victim of Metaphor?', *Semeia* 47 (1989), pp. 87-104, and M.J.W. Leith, 'Verse and Reverse: The Transformation of the Woman, Israel, in Hosea 1-3', in Day (ed.), *Gender and Difference*, pp. 95-108. A biblical-theological appropriation of Hos. 2 should, in my opinion, start from the Hebrew, not the Greek version of v. 2.18. While the Greek version reads the indicative ('on that day she [the woman/Israel] will call me "my husband"'), the Hebrew text has the imperative ('call me "my husband" and not "my Baal"'): the woman's agreement to the relationship desired by YHWH is required. For greater detail concerning the possibilities of a feminist biblical theology of Hos. 2, or rather Hos. 1-3, cf. M.-T. Wacker, 'Biblische Theologie und Männerphantasie: Das Beispiel Hosea 1-3', in H. Frankemölle (ed.), *Das bekannte Buch—das fremde Buch: Die Bibel* (Paderborn, forthcoming).

chapters suggests that the goddess theme is significant in Hosea. These textual units share a striking position in the composition of the entire book, which, according to most modern commentaries, consist of the three parts 1–3, 4–11, 12–14. Hosea 1–3 is the exposition, with Hosea 2 pivotal to the presentation. Chapters 4 and 11, with their respective goddess metaphors, frame the central part, and Hosea 14 is the closing chapter of the entire book. In addition, these texts are thematically and (partially) verbally dovetailed. If Hosea 4 bewails the tree-goddess who has ensnared Israel, then Hosea 11 evokes the maternal goddess aspects of YHWH himself, and Hosea 14 closes with a cautious integration which incorporates the symbolism of the tree-goddess. In contrast, Hosea 2 is an independent unit which develops both the abhorrence of and fascination with the goddess. As Gale Yee recently demonstrated in her feminist commentary on Hosea,[1] this chapter with its paradisiacal vision of the new relationship between YHWH and Israel corresponds to the closing chapter of the book: Hos. 14.5-9 presents an equally paradisiacal picture of Israel in her fruitful land.

The obviously important position of the goddess theme is certainly due to several stages of literary production in the book of Hosea. Though this aspect could not be developed here, I wish to venture the hypothesis that this ongoing literary production (which, finally, led to the book of Hosea in its present form) is to be essentially placed in an exilic/post-exilic context.[2] The goddess topic is certainly not without support in the 'historical Hosea' but became elaborated and intensified when Hosea's message was rewritten in Judea—primarily in the Babylonian and Persian period.[3] The book of Hosea can be

1. G. Yee, 'Hosea', in C. Newsom and S. Ringe (eds.), *The Woman's Bible Commentary* (London and Louisville, KY: Westminster/John Knox Press, 1992), pp. 195-204, p. 201.

2. This appraisal results when (as noted in n. 1, p. 221) the analyses of Yee, *Tradition*, and Nissinen, *Redaktion*, constitute the basis of interpretation.

3. This literary development would correlate somehow with the transformations described by Keel and Uehlinger, *Göttinnen*, pp. 370-86. These two authors posit a development from pure tree imagery without explicit reference to a female deity (Iron II B) to a re-emergence of gynomorphic goddess imagery during the period of Iron II C in Judea (esp. the 'pillar figurines'). The argument with goddess traditions, as described by the book

regarded, therefore, as a compendium of disputes with traditions of the feminine divine in biblical Israel. This biblical text
fought as well as assimilated goddess traditions, and it is a valuable source for a religious-historical search as well as for the
feminist theological search for the 'Hebrew Goddess'.[1]

of Hosea, must especially refer to Judahites, men and women, of the declin-
ing monarchy and thereafter. On the other hand, the 'Woman at the
Window' motif, limited to the eighth century BCE, is a central argument for
an origin in the age of the 'historical Hosea', at least for Hos. 2.4-5 where
the woman/Israel is depicted like this woman at the window looking out
for lovers.

1. For detailed text analysis and fundamental arguments see my forthcoming monograph on Hosea.

Part II
ON THE PORNOPROPHETICS OF SEXUAL VIOLENCE

THE METAPHORIZATION OF WOMAN IN PROPHETIC SPEECH: AN ANALYSIS OF EZEKIEL 23*

Fokkelien van Dijk-Hemmes

The process of metaphorization of woman to a sign for something else enacts a form of disembodiment of the female subject. The imaging of woman as something else betrays habits of definition within a frame of reference that is dominated by the interests and the perceptions of the 'first' sex.[1]

The Marriage Metaphor in Hosea

From a chronological point of view, the book of Hosea is the first prophetic writing in which the relation between God and Israel is represented by the imagery of marriage.The book belongs, or at least refers, to the eighth century BCE. The marriage metaphor created in Hosea 1–3 'develops the sacred marriage of Canaanite ritual into a figure for religious apostasy'[2] and, subsequently, replaces this 'adulterous' type of marriage by an everlasting covenant in which he betrothes her to himself forever (Hos. 2.21; Eng. 2.18). According to numerous (M)[3] interpreters, the Hosean marriage metaphor should be read as a

*   From A. Brenner and F. van Dijk-Hemmes, *On Gendering Texts: Female and Male Voices in the Hebrew Bible* (Leiden: Brill, 1993), pp. 168-76. An earlier version of this essay was read at the IOSOT Congress in Leuven, August 1989. I wish to thank Professor Mieke Bal, Professor Athalya Brenner and Professor Sara Japhet for their helpful critical comments.
1.   The quotation is from the Introduction to the Utrecht Interfaculty Women's Studies Research Program, 'Women between Control and Transition'.
2.   H. Marks, 'The Twelve Prophets', in R. Alter and F. Kermode (eds.), *A Literary Guide to the Bible* (Cambridge, MA: Harvard University Press, 1987), p. 214.
3.   Male/Masculine.

parable of divine grace and forgiveness. I have argued else-where that such a prescribed reading can, and should, be challenged by an F[1] reading of the text.[2] By way of an intro-duction to the discussion of Ezekiel 23, I shall first summarize my views on Hosea 1–3.

The main part of the Hosean marriage metaphor consists of an extensive monologue spoken by the metaphorical I persona, the 'deceived husband' (ch. 2). The construction of this persona occurs in Hosea 1. In 1.2 Hosea, the prophet, is commanded to take a 'wife of harlotry' and 'children of harlotry' because the land commits 'great harlotry' by 'whoring away' from YHWH. The implication of this metaphor is that YHWH acknowledges himself as the husband of the land of Israel; and while Hosea is transformed into a metaphor of YHWH Gomer, his wife, is designated a metaphor for the land of Israel. The children (two sons and one daughter) who are born afterwards are, in their turn, immediately transformed into metaphors representing different aspects of the people's characteristics and fate.

In the first part of the monologue (Hos. 2) the I persona, YHWH/Hosea, attacks his metaphorical wife in an extremely aggressive manner. He accuses her of going after her lovers ('Baals'), and threatens several times to strip her naked. After this speech act—which exposes so much sexual violence—he then starts, from v. 16 (Eng. 14) onwards, to sing a 'love' song to her, 'Therefore, behold, I will allure her...' For the meta-phorical wife, however, this transition means that she, after having been victimized by her 'husband', now becomes his totally passive bride whose only task is to respond to his initiatives. A comparison between Hosea 2 and similar passages from the Song of Songs[3] reveals what difference it makes when

1.　Female/Feminine.
2.　F. van Dijk-Hemmes, 'The Imagination of Power and the Power of Imagination: An Intertextual Analysis of Two Biblical Love Songs: The Song of Songs and Hosea 2', *JSOT* 44 (1989), pp. 75-88; reprinted in A. Brenner (ed.), *A Feminist Companion to the Song of Songs* (The Feminist Companion to the Bible, 1; Sheffield: Sheffield Academic Press, 1993), pp. 156-70.
3.　A. van Selms, 'Hosea and Canticles', in *Studies in the Books of Hosea and Amos* (*OTSWA*, 7.8; Potchefstroom: Pro Rege, 1965), pp. 85-89. Van Selms shows that Hosea 2 contains phrases and motifs which must

the woman-in-the-text is presented not as the focalizer but, on the contrary, as the object of his focalization. A woman who, like the woman in the Song of Songs, expresses her desire for her lover is, in the Hosean context—where she is presented through his eyes and where her words are 'quoted' by him— transformed into a harlot who shamelessly goes after her lovers (in the plural!).

The Hosean marriage metaphor culminates in a call for justice. This call appears to be 'packaged' in a specifically male, misogynistic metaphorical language. The metaphor's plea, addressed to the people, to return to YHWH has a subject. It is also, and simultaneously, an example of propaganda, addressed to men, extolling an ideal patriarchal marriage in which the woman has to submit to her husband and remain faithful to him in order to prevent the birth of 'alien children' (Hos. 5.7). The effect of the metaphor's message is greatly enhanced by the prophet's alleged personal involvement in it.

Features and Functions of Pornography

I now turn to Ezekiel. In this latter prophetic book we find two examples of the marriage metaphor, in chs. 16 and 23. In the first chapter Jerusalem is metaphorized into YHWH's mis- behaving wife, while Samaria is presented merely as her sister. In the second, however, metaphorical Samaria's status too is promoted to that of YHWH's consort. The one adulterous wife is thus doubled.

The points of departure for my analysis of Ezekiel 23, to which I shall confine myself here, are two statements from Carol A. Newsom's perceptive article, 'A Maker of Metaphors: Ezekiel's Oracles against Tyre'.[1]

> It is now generally understood that far from being merely decorative, metaphors have real cognitive content. If one tries to paraphrase a metaphor, what is lost is more than just a certain

have been borrowed from love songs, the like of which were later on collected in the Song of Songs.

1. C.A. Newsom, 'A Maker of Metaphors: Ezekiel's Oracles against Tyre', in J.L. Mays and P.J. Achtemeier (eds.), *Interpreting the Prophets* (Philadelphia: Fortress Press, 1987), p. 189.

effect. What is lost is part of the meaning itself, the insight which the metaphor alone can give.

Metaphor derives much of its convincing power from the fact that it does not allow its hearers to be passive but requires them to participate in the construction of the metaphorical meanings?[1]

For the purpose of my analysis I derive the following questions from these two statements:

1. What is the specific insight which the metaphor used in Ezekiel 23 can give us? In other words, what makes it necessary to present a re-enactment of Israel's history, within this specific metaphorical language, through imagery in which Israel's behaviour is represented in terms of the conduct attributed to YHWH's two adulterous wives?
2. How does the metaphorical language used in Ezekiel 23 require or entice its target audience and modern readers to participate in the construction of its metaphorical meaning?

I want to start my analysis with the second question, which focuses attention upon the interaction between the text and the audience or reader. This question involves the issue of efficiency. How do the literary strategies deployed in the text affect the reader? How do they organize or mobilize his or her view? I refer to the audience or reader in a gendered manner not only because feminist literary theory has convincingly shown how relevant such an approach is,[2] but also because, in this case, the text itself requires us to do so. Ezekiel 23 ends with an explicit warning for women not to behave like the metaphorical harlots Oholah and Oholibah (v. 48). Thus the extended metaphor which is presented to us in this chapter speaks not

1. For an extensive treatment of the concepts behind and working of metaphors see, for instance, G. Lakoff and M. Turner, *More than Cool Reason: A Field Guide to Poetic Metaphor* (Chicago and London: University of Chicago Press, 1989).

2. Cf. J. Culler, *On Deconstruction: Theory and Criticism after Structuralism* (London: Routledge & Kegan Paul, 1983), pp. 43-64; and E. Showalter, 'Feminist Criticism in the Wilderness', in *idem* (ed.), *The New Feminist Criticism: Essays on Women, Literature and Theory* (London: Virago, 1986), pp. 243-70.

only *of* women, but also—albeit indirectly—specifically *to* women. What exactly is the message which this text conveys to women? And does it require women to participate in the construction of its metaphorical meaning in a different way from men?

As an F reader, I want to answer these questions and analyse the literary strategies deployed in the text by making use of a model which is offered by T. Drorah Setel in her article 'Prophets and Pornography: Female Sexual Imagery in Hosea'.[1] According to Setel there is a significant congruence between biblical and especially prophetic texts on the one hand, and modern pornographic depictions of female sexuality on the other hand. In both cases objectified female sexuality is used as a symbol of evil. This implies that contemporary feminist theory on the nature of female objectification can and should be applied to the examination of prophetic texts which deal with the same subject.

In summarizing the theoretical material on pornography Setel distinguishes four categories of analysis: *features, function, definition* and *causes*. Here, however, I shall confine myself to two categories only: features and function.

Setel characterizes the distinguishing *features* of pornography as follows.

1. Female sexuality is depicted as negative relative to a positive or neutral male standard.
2. Women are degraded and publicly humiliated.
3. Female sexuality is portrayed as an object of male possession and control. This includes the depiction of women as analogous to nature in general and the land in particular and, especially, in regard to imagery of conquest and domination.

The *function* of pornography can, according to Setel, be summarized as the preservation of male domination through a denial, or misnaming, of female experience. If this is accepted then I can say that the denial or misnaming of female experience should also be considered a distinguishing feature of pornography.

---

1. T.D. Setel, 'Prophets and Pornography: Female Sexual Imagery in Hosea', in L. Russell (ed.), *Feminist Interpretations of the Bible* (Philadelphia: Westminster Press, 1985), pp. 86-95.

To what extent do we find this latter feature as well as those mentioned by Setel in Ezekiel 23? The text is presented to us as a speech (*dbr*) delivered by YHWH to Ezekiel, the (male) prophet who lives in exile in Babylon and who figures as the I persona in the text: 'The word of YHWH came *to me*' (Ezek. 23.1). This means that the intended target audience is required to hear the text via Ezekiel's (fictive) ears. YHWH's speech starts like a story, and Ezekiel is addressed by him as 'Son of humanity' (*bn 'dm*).

> Son of humanity
> Two women
> daughters of one mother were there (v. 2).

The close relationship between the two sisters is emphasized by the chiastic structure of the verse: *štym nšm, bnt 'm 'ht*. No mention is made of the sisters' father. The story then continues with a description of the two sisters' conduct. The first part of this description is again constructed chiastically.

> They played the harlot in Egypt
> In their youth they played the harlot
> There their breasts were squeezed
> There the teats of their maidenhood were pressed (v. 3).

The words 'in Egypt', closely related to 'in their youth', prevent the actual or potential audience from listening to the story further as more or less interested outsiders. They are engaged, they are invited to involve themselves in it. The story about the two sisters who play the harlot, i.e. her-story, seems to present the audience's own history. In the following verse, the suspicion that the two sisters are metaphors and that, consequently, the audience itself, as part of the people of Israel, is transformed into these two metaphorical women, is confirmed.

> Their names
> Oholah the big one
> and Oholibah her sister
> They became mine
> and they bore sons and daughters
> Their names
> Samaria-Oholah
> and Jerusalem-Oholibah (v. 4).

The implicitly formulated information concerning the two sisters/cities' marriage to YHWH is enveloped by the twofold announcement of their names. Oholah, which is traditionally understood to mean '(she who has) her own tent (i.e. sanctuary)', metaphorizes the capital of Northern Israel, Samaria, while Oholibah, 'My tent (is) in her', metaphorizes Jerusalem.[1] YHWH's portrayal of himself as prepared to accept for wives two women 'who already in their youth denied their virginity'[2] must have been designed to shock the audience. After having been required to look at themselves as depraved since the very beginning of their history, they now have to shamefully acknowledge that YHWH was nevertheless willing to take the risk of a marriage-like relationship with them.

Although this might have been expected as the intended audience's response and although this in fact *is* the readerly response of most modern commentators to the beginning of our metaphorical story, one 'detail' in the text has in fact been overlooked. The activities of the two sisters—activities which are signified by *znh*, 'play the harlot'—are specified in the following part of v. 3 not as action but as receptivity. 'They' were acted upon.

> There their breasts were squeezed
> There the teats of their maidenhood were pressed.

Or, literally:

> There they [grammatically masc., see also v. 8] pressed the teats
> of their [the women's] maidenhood.

As an F reader I have some difficulties in naming such a being-acted-upon situation as 'playing the harlot', so I suggest that here we may have an example of what Setel calls 'misnaming of female experience'. It would have been more adequate to describe the events during the sisters' youth in the following manner: 'They were sexually molested in Egypt, in their youth

1. See otherwise in W. Zimmerli, *Ezechiel* (BKAT, 13.1-2; Neukirchen–Vluyn: Neukirchener Verlag, 1969), p. 542. Nevertheless, Zimmerli does not exclude the possibility that the girls' names might also contain an allusion to the meanings which have traditionally been attributed to them.

2. M.E. Andrew, *Responsibility and Restoration: The Course of the Book Ezekiel* (Dunedin, New Zealand, 1985), p. 115.

they were sexually abused'. This way, justice would have been done to the fate of these metaphorical women, and the audience would not have been seduced into viewing women or girls as responsible for and even guilty of their own violation. In short, there would have been no question of 'blaming the victim'.

Does this mean that the people whom the metaphorical women represent should actually see themselves as victims as well? This appears not to be the intention of the text. In Ezekiel 20, where we find a non-metaphorical evaluation of Israel's history, we read that Israel is accused of having been rebellious against YHWH and of worshipping idols already during its sojourn in Egypt (v. 8). This accusation, with no reference to Israel's oppression, should be viewed as YHWH's crushing response to Judah's rebellion against Babylon, undertaken in the hope of obtaining help from an Egyptian alliance during the last few years before the destruction of Jerusalem. So from ch. 20 onwards, in contrast to the foregoing chapters as well as the common prophetic view on Israel's history, Israel is indeed presented as apostate from the *very beginning* of its history. According to the illogical, arbitrary way in which Ezek. 23.3 conveys this message, Israel's sin in Egypt actually consisted of its being oppressed. Such a statement's lack of logic can apparently be made acceptable by the transformation of a people into metaphorical women. The sexual molestation inflicted upon these women serves, therefore, as a metaphor for the people's slavery in Egypt. Within an androcentric framework women can easily be seen as guilty of their own abuse. Hence, the imagery of women is indispensible for conveying a message which is a contradiction in terms: the people are guilty of their own past enslaving inasmuch as women are, by definition, guilty of their own sexual misfortunes. Referring to the first question derived from Newsom's statements, we can state that it is this specific (and illogical) M insight which the metaphor of Ezekiel 23 can give us.

Oholah's and Oholibah's Perversion

The misnaming of female experience is continued further in the metaphorical story which depicts first Oholah's and then, in much greater length and detail, Oholibah's alleged behaviour. Oholah's lusting after her Assyrian lovers by which, according to an over-zealous interpreter, she exposes her 'hankering after the flamboyance of foreign military masculinity'[1] is explained by her having enjoyed the sexual violence inflicted upon her in her youth.

> Her harlotry from (her days in) Egypt she did not abandon
> For they lay upon/raped[2] her in her youth
> And these men pressed the teats of her maidenhood
> And they pour out their harlotry upon her (v. 8).

The audience, which has already been required to perceive the metaphorical maiden's sexual abuse as harlotry, is now seduced into viewing this abuse as something Oholah had enjoyed so much that she could not do without it for the rest of her life! Her 'harlotry', however, is depicted here even more clearly as violence which is acted upon her.

The story of Oholibah too culminates in the remembrance of her youth in Egypt which is attributed to her own consciousness. Her behaviour is depicted as much more corrupt than her sister's. She not only 'lusted after' the Assyrians (v. 12), 'but she carried her harlotry further' (v. 14). After having seen 'men portrayed upon the wall, the images of the Chaldeans' (v. 14), she sends messengers for them, 'brazenly attracted by mere appearances'.[3] They, the Babylonians, 'came to her into the bed of love' (v. 17), but when she has been defiled and polluted by them, 'she turned from them in disgust' (v. 17). And despite the fact that her behaviour in its turn leads to YHWH's turning in disgust away from her 'as I had turned from her sister' (v. 18),

> She increased her harlotry
> remembering the days of her youth
> when she played the harlot in the land of Egypt
> She lusted after the paramours there
> whose organs are like the organ of asses
> and whose ejaculation is like the ejaculation of stallions (vv. 19-20).

1. Andrew, *Responsibility and Restoration*, p. 115.
2. For this meaning of *škb 't*, see also Gen. 34.1 and 2 Sam. 13.14.
3. Andrew, *Responsibility and Restoration*, p. 115.

And then, for the first time, Oholibah is directly addressed by YHWH:

> You longed for the lewdness of your youth
> when those from Egypt pressed your teats
> for your young breasts (v. 21).

The enjoyment of her own abuse, which had been attributed to Oholah, is surpassed by the perverse sexual appetite attributed to Oholibah. The latter's lusting after stallion-like males[1] is said to derive from 'the lewdness of your youth'. The depiction of Oholibah's desire in terms of the size of (animal-like) male members seems not just an example of mere misnaming of female experience, but an actual distortion of it. Instead of reflecting female desire, this depiction betrays male obsession.

In both Oholah's and Oholibah's cases, the remembrance of the sisters' youth in Egypt marks a transition from the accusation to the announcement of their punishment. The intention is probably to strengthen the audience's resolve that both metaphorical women, so perverse since their very maidenhood, indeed deserve the utterly degrading and devastating treatment to which they are to be exposed. Modern M readerly responses demonstrate how successful this literary strategy is. According to those, the sisters' torturing is appropriate and 'brings out the ironic justice of being punished by their own lovers'.[2] Thanks to the model offered by Setel, this mode of participating in the construction of the text's metaphorical meaning is no longer necessary. Setel's model enables us to recognize other distinguishing features of pornography in the description of the sisters' treatment too. Both women are degraded and publicly humiliated in order to stress that their sexuality is and ought to be an object of male possession and control.

1: In contrast to Jeremiah's marriage metaphor, where the 'woman' is metaphorized into animals (and cf. Brenner's article in this volume), the detested *male* enemies are here presented as animal-like beings.

2. Andrew, *Responsibility and Restoration*, p. 115. For similar interpretations see also Zimmerli, *Ezechiel*; W. Eichrodt, *Der Prophet Hezekiel* (ATD, 22.2; Göttingen: Vandenhoeck & Ruprecht, 1966); B. Maarsingh, *Ezechiel* (POT, 2; Nijkerk, 1988); and numerous other commentators for this chapter.

M and F Readerly Responses

Coming back to the question of whether the text speaks differently to men and to women, we can now state the following. YHWH's speech to Ezekiel transforms the people of Israel and thus the target audience, males and—at least indirectly—also females, into his metaphorical wives. Both genders are thus required to identify with the metaphorized women—especially with Oholibah, since Oholah figures chiefly as a warning signal for her 'sister'. Through Oholibah the audience is directly spoken to by YHWH several times in an utterly degrading manner. The audience is forced into seeing the shameless stupidity of their religious and political behaviour and the absolute hopelessness of their situation: Jerusalem will definitely be abandoned to destruction. The impact of that insight, which implies the utmost humiliation, apparently can only be communicated by such gender-specific metaphorical language.

The androcentric-pornographic character of this metaphorical language must indeed be experienced as extremely humiliating by an M audience forced to imagine itself as being exposed to violating enemies. Nevertheless, it is exactly this androcentric-pornographic character which at the same time offers the M audience a possibility of escape: the escape of identification with the wronged and revengeful husband; or, more modestly, identification with the righteous men who, near the end of the text, are summoned to pass judgment upon the adulterous women (v. 45). Thus, the text also functions as a specific warning to women, which is indeed contained in its penultimate verse.[1]

According to Zimmerli[2] and many other commentators, the last verses are later additions appended to ch. 23. If this is correct, the additions can be viewed as ancient M readerly responses to the metaphorical story of Oholah and Oholibah.[3]

1. There is a continuous back-and-forth movement within the text, from the metaphorization of women as cities toward the metaphorization of women per se and vice versa. Hence, any appeal to women (v. 48) should be understood as an appeal to the cities too.
2. Zimmerli, *Ezechiel*, pp. 553-55.
3. See also the M comment attached to Prov. 20.18–19—cf. Brenner in

These readerly response realize and, at the same time, testify to the possibility of escape that the text offers to its M readers.

No such possibility of escape is left to F readers. In respect to them, the metaphorization of women in Ezekiel 23 performs first and foremost a violent speech act which is even more offensive than the Hosean version: it simultaneously shapes and distorts women's (sexual) experience.

Brenner and van Dijk-Hemmes, *On Gendering Texts*, pp. 158-60.

On Prophetic Propaganda and the Politics of 'Love': The Case of Jeremiah*

Athalya Brenner

Let us agree that the Hebrew Bible is a political document. It contains ideologies of specific interest groups. It is used for achieving political ends. It exercises fundamental influence on believers, has cultural significance for non-believers. It is therefore as important to resist its unpleasant features as to celebrate its values and beauty. I want therefore to look at the flip side, at some sexist prophetic propaganda. If it were published elsewhere and today, such propaganda would have surely caused a public uproar; or, at the very least, it would be loudly challenged by feminists. I shall look at the development and utilization of one metaphor in Jeremiah: the metaphor of the divine, loving husband and his adulterous wife.

In our cultural discourse, prophetic books tend to have a privileged status that is similar to that of the Torah and the Psalms. When we discuss so-called prophetic writings we assume, explicitly, that a real person, a real 'prophet', resides in them. We say that the prophet 'hears', 'says', 'suffers'. Perhaps we need to avoid such complicity with the text. Perhaps we should remember that history, and scholarly criticism, do not necessarily support the claims those privileged texts make for themselves.

Take Jeremiah. Was the man so named real (in the sense of 'historical'), or is 'he' an imaginary, fictive figure? Did 'he' perceive himself, did 'his' audience perceive 'him', to be a prophet—which the God-in-the-text certainly did (1.5), as did

* This essay is a revised version of my Inaugural Lecture of the (rotating) Belle van Zuylen Chair, given at the Faculty of Theology, Utrecht University, in February 1993.

later compilers and editors and interpreters? Should contemporary readers regard the book attributed to 'him', a book
whose boundaries in various biblical traditions are fluid, as
prophecy? Let us remember that the referents of the Hebrew
נביא ('prophet'), נבואה ('prophecy') and their derivatives are far
from agreed upon. I therefore prefer to regard the texts
attributed to the real or literary Jeremiah, and to other
'prophets', as poetry rather than prophecy.[1] An obvious
advantage of such an approach is that it facilitates the crossing
of a barrier. Poetic authority is easier to undermine than so-
called prophetic authority.

The Jeremian passages to be discussed are ch. 2; 3.1-3; and
5.7-8. As in Hosea and Ezekiel, Israel and Judah (or Samaria
and Jerusalem) are metaphorized into a faithless wife and a
zônâ. YHWH, the metaphoric male counterpart, is the faithful
husband who is deeply affected by his wife's misbehaviour. The
descriptions of the wife's escapades and deserved punishment
are vivid and detailed. As van Dijk-Hemmes demonstrates in
her essay on Hosea,[2] metaphorized language of this sort may
pervert the language of love. And in her essay on Ezekiel[3] she
traces some pornographic properties which underlie political and
religious concerns within the presentation of the love metaphor
in Ezekiel 23. In the biblical text, Jeremiah is situated between
Hosea and Ezekiel. Let us see how the adaptation of the love
metaphor fares in this midway position.

---

1.   Cf. the dialogue in writing in *JSOT* 48 (1990). T.W. Holt ('Prophecy in
History: The Social Reality of Intermediation', pp. 2-29; and 'It is Difficult to
Read', pp. 51-54) presents a variation on the traditional approach to the
prophetic books. G.A. Auld ('Prophecy in Books: A Rejoinder', pp. 31-32)
and R.P. Carroll ('Whose Prophet? Whose History? Whose Social Reality?
Troubling the Interpetative Community Again: Notes towards a Response
to T.W. Overholt's Critique', pp. 33-49) take the opposite view. I am convinced by Auld's and Carroll's views, hence adopt their approach.

2.   F. van Dijk-Hemmes, 'The Imagination of Power and the Power of
Imagination: An Intertextual Analysis of Two Biblical Love Songs, The Song
of Songs and Hosea 2', *JSOT* 44 (1989), pp. 75-88; reprinted in A. Brenner
(ed.), *A Feminist Companion to the Song of Songs* (The Feminist Companion to
the Bible, 1; Sheffield: Sheffield Academic Press, 1993), pp. 156-70.

3.   'The Metaphorization of Women in Prophetic Speech: An Analysis of
Ezekiel 23', in this volume.

To guess author's intent is a risky business. However, one must indulge in it in order to comprehend the metaphor's function. It seems that the poet whom the text calls 'Jeremiah' wishes to tighten the bonds between his God and his target audience. It is this fair to deduce that the husband-wife metaphor is a propaganda vehicle whose employment is motivated by the following assumptions:

1. The metaphorization of human sexuality is attractive enough for securing an audience's attention and for sustaining interest.
2. In order to be effective, the metaphor should be recognized by the target audience as applicable to stock life situations or, preferably, as universally valid.
3. Female sexual behaviour is recognized by speaker and audience as potentially deviant even when unprovoked by a male partner. Therefore it is a fitting vehicle for the message intended.
4. Audience's involvement in and emotional response to the metaphor are expected.
5. The audience may thus be trapped into identification with the speaker, to the point of accepting his message.
6. The metaphor will produce guilt and shame in the audience through a rejection of the metaphorized female. The new consciousness will put an end to the illicit (from the speaker's perspective) religious and political alliances in Judah and Jerusalem.

In daily discourse many of us use love- and sex-talk for communicating religious experience, and vice versa—god-talk for sexual experience. This language practice is so common as to render the husband-wife metaphor unproblematic for both female and male readers. Furthermore, even when we agree that the metaphor's presentation in Hosea and Ezekiel contains pornographic elements, this does not absolve us from examining it afresh in the relevant Jeremian texts.

Is the husband-wife metaphor in Jeremiah pornographic, or is it 'just' sexual imagery? Five steps will be taken towards an answer: (1) the construction of a working definition of the term 'pornography'; (2) a rereading of the Jeremian (or Hosean, or

Ezekielan) metaphor; (3) an examination of other metaphors and figurations of woman in Jeremiah; (4) a comparison with another, contemporary ancient text which deals with gender roles; and finally, (5) a reading of a comparable literary intertext outside the Bible, to double-check the findings of the previous steps.

Dictionaries define pornography as the explicit description or exhibition of sexual activity in literature, films and so on. The description or exhibition is designed to stimulate erotic response rather than aesthetic pleasure. Such a definition, although widely used in popular discourse, is inadequate. It does not relate to the issue of fantasy of desire which pornography activates; we shall return to the fantasy component presently. Furthermore, such a definition does not refer to social factors, least of all gender-specific factors. In order to redress the balance, any working definition has to be supplemented by incorporating data from feminist criticism in psychology, sociology, literature and the arts.

Fantasy in pornography, as in rape, is not simply a fantasy of sex and desire. Pornographic fantasy incorporates elements of power, domination, gender relations and quite often violence. Within the fantasy desire becomes a metaphor which reflects social 'reality'. That metaphor feeds on imagination and fuels individual and collective dreams. It is both refractive and recreative. Pornographic presentations have social significance. Thus a definition must qualify the roles assigned to females (and minors; and minorities of class, colour, ideology or ethnic origin) in contradistinction to males in pornographic presentations. The definition should also relate to the degree and nature of each gender's response to the presentation. I have no quarrel with the truistic presentation of sexual desire as a primary human motive; but defining pornography 'objectively' as a stimulant to desire, without taking sociopsychological factors into account, is at best misleading.

So we turn back to Jeremiah. Let us now ask: how does the erotic metaphor work beyond securing the audience's attention? It certainly stimulates sexual fantasy. It does something else as well. The eager presentation of deviant female sexuality—and details are liberally supplied—can have one purpose only: to *shame the audience*. The more blatant the presentation, the more shocking and shameful its referent, namely the people's fickleness in forming alliances. The result of this strategy is a contrast between the metaphor and its designated purpose: pornography is expected to promote religious and political reform.

Persuasion through stigmatization, shaming as a means of bonding, and the manipulation of love are practised inside family structures and outside them—in relationship with subordinates (such as children), superiors (such as parents) and peers. The manipulation of stigmatization and shaming is a powerful tool for attaining social and political gain. The stigmatization of sexual behaviour and its abusive presentation is a trick employed by children, for instance, before they even know what the words used designate. It is commonly targetted on weak social groups, be their constituency female or male. However, because women are a much weaker social group than men, their stigmatization through pornographic presentation is much more common than that of males.[1] This holds true for the Bible as well as for other literary and visual representations, ancient and modern alike.

The Jeremian passages afford illuminating examples of this principle. Indeed, male sexuality is attacked too; however, the description of male adultery and animalistic desire in 5.7-8 is a single occurrence. All other passages which belong to the divine husband-adulterous wife metaphor are resolutely devoted to inducing shame by reference to female sexual behaviour. The practice is admitted by some commentators but, unfortunately, its gender significance is seldom acknowledged. For instance, Robert Carroll recognizes that we deal with pornography here. He writes in his OTL commentary,

> Since Hosea, religious pornography has become a standard form of abusing opponents. Once the metaphors of marriage are transferred to describing the relationship between Yahweh and Israel, then all the abuse that might be heaped on a faithless wife will become part of the arsenal of religious denunciations. This

---

1.   E. Janeway, 'Who Does What to Whom? The Psychology of the Oppressor', in A. Bach (ed.), *Ad Feminam: Union Seminary Quarterly Review* 43 (1989), pp. 133-44.

transference will explain the degree of emotion generated in such statements.[1]

I suggest that Carroll's reading is gendered by his male bias. Although he does not define what he means by 'religious pornography', Carroll claims to *understand* the metaphor—although, to be fair, he certainly does not seem to approve of it. When he goes on to warn against viewing the relevant texts as misogynistic, as some feminists do, he deconstructs himself completely. Indeed, an automatic equation of pornographic female representations and misogyny should not be adopted without due consideration. However, Carroll and other male commentators ignore some important issues. For instance: whose fantasies are enacted in the prophetic love metaphor? Whose ends do such fantasies serve? How do they do it? Upon reflection, things are not so simple. Contemporary pornographic literature by and large contains an implicit anti-female bias; if we agree on that, the same notion is applicable to the pornographic prophetic texts—hence the benefit of a comparative approach.

A female reading of the love metaphor would have a different agenda, whose origin is undeniably biased and gendered too. It would not focus on the male figurations within the story—the metaphoric husband, the messenger's voice, God. Instead, it would focus on female figurations within pornographic representations; and would append additional criteria to those of erotic stimulation and sexual fantasy.

Contemporary feminist theories define pornography by distinguishing four categories: its *features, functions, definition* and *causes*.[2] Van Dijk-Hemmes has applied the first two categories to Ezekiel 23;[3] here I shall apply all four to the Jeremian passages, then to my modern intertext, *Story of O*.[4]

---

1. R.P. Carroll, *Jeremiah: A Commentary* (OTL; London: SCM Press, 1986), p. 134.

2. T.D. Setel, 'Prophets and Pornography: Female Sexual Imagery in Hosea', in L. Russell (ed.), *Feminist Interpretation of the Bible* (Philadelphia: Westminster Press, 1985), pp. 86-87.

3. Van Dijk-Hemmes, 'The Metaphorization of Woman in Prophetic Speech'.

4. I used the English translation, although the book was originally published in French: P. Réage, *Story of O* (London: Corgi, 1972).

Features of Pornography

Female sexuality is depicted as negative in relation to a positive or neutral male sexuality. Women are publicly humiliated. Like nature and the land, they are subjected to male possession and control. They exist in order to gratify male desire—as do also minors and minorities in modern pornographic presentations.

Let us examine Jer. 2.23-25 for these features. Jerusalem, the community, is addressed by the speaker as YHWH's legitimate spouse. The words 'nation', 'community', 'city' and 'land' are grammatically female in Hebrew. However, this does not adequately account for the gendering of metaphor, or for the abuse of the metaphorical female it contains. Thus is the community addressed:

> How can you say, 'I'm not defiled, I haven't followed the Baʿals'?
> See your way in the valley, know what you've done. [You're] a
> young camel deviating from her path; [you're] a wild she-ass
> accustomed to the wilderness, sniffing the wind in her lust. Who
> can repel her desire? All who seek her needn't exhaust them-
> selves, for they shall find her in season... And you said, 'No! I
> love strangers and will follow them'.

In the metaphor, female sexuality is objectified as irregular and deviant. It is animalistic, 'natural', earthy. The metaphorized female creature is motivated neither by love nor by any other acceptable human social convention. She/it is motivated by lust. In contradistinction, male sexuality is represented by God's behaviour which, by definition, is politically, socially and morally correct. Since the 'woman' is explicitly qualified as the legal possession of her male/God (vv. 20-21), her sexual conduct violates his rights; she is therefore punishable by public exposure, a measure for measure for publicly degrading herself. The same description recurs in ch. 3: the 'woman' is in nature, her passion wild and unquenchable, her behaviour shameful.

The animalization of the metaphorized 'woman' is perhaps the most striking feature of Jeremiah 2, especially because it does not stop at the animalization stage. It is an innovation, a new development, an original contribution to prophetic por-nography. It cannot be found even in the most enthusiastic pornographic descriptions of Ezekiel 16 and 23. In Ezekiel town,

community and nation(s) are naturalized by their metaphorization into land/earth on the one hand and into women
on the other hand. As Setel and van Dijk-Hemmes show, the
two metaphors (earth and woman) are interlinked by a shared
reference: the extra-linguistic association of woman with nature
and especially the earth. This is common in pornographic as well
as other texts. The establishment of a two-way link between
woman and land facilitates an evolvement of the metaphor into
the next stage. The naturalizing of woman by animalization
constitutes a powerful new phase in the ongoing construction of
the husband-wife metaphor. This animalization cannot be
waved aside as immaterial or gender-neutral. Its intent, and the
value judgment it displays, are indicated by the animal referents
chosen: a wild she-ass, a young she-camel, neither of which is
famous for redeeming features. The metaphorization of humans
into animals is often pejorative or carries a sting: much depends
on the animal referent chosen. Furthermore, the metaphorized
'wild she-ass' is both more and less than a merely natural
animal: whoever heard of an animal who is constantly on heat,
forever lustful? Such an animal would not qualify as natural.
She/it is fabulous, mythic. Thus, the animalization of woman
argues that 'she' posits 'herself' outside the human, social order
by being (a) wild and (b) always on heat, hence (c) a mythological rather than natural creature. Let us remember: this
fantasy of womanliness must correspond to a similar fantasy of
the target audience in order for the propaganda to be effective.
Disgust and shame will not be produced unless the listeners
recognize the validity of the description for female sexual
behaviour in general. That is imperative if they are to dissociate
themselves from similar behaviour outside the sexual sphere.
The dehumanization of the metaphorical woman is the analogy
chosen to reflect the condemned, inhuman conduct of the extra-
metaphorical referent, the addressed community. An interim
stage of getting the message across is to reach out of language
by appealing to desire and emotion. A recognition that women
are (like) animals will make the metaphor work. This recognition
need not be conscious. It will be as effective, perhaps more so, if
it stimulates desire unconsciously. The hoped-for renunciation
seems like one of the reasons for using pornographic images in

the love metaphor. Is it as paradoxical as it sounds?

Does this new development express fear of the female and misogyny? If we readers feel that the textual voice disapproves of women as wild and (un)natural animals; that the target audience is drawn into sharing this disapproval; that the pornographic fantasy feeds on the view that female sexuality is uncontrollable—then, yes, misogyny underscores this dehumanized, animalized depiction. This is *not* 'just a metaphor'.

The Function of Pornography

Pornography helps to maintain male dominance through the denial or misnaming of female sexual experience. Objectification of the female is presented as universally acknowledged instead of being attributed to male predisposition against femaleness. Women are expected to identify with this perspective, through which they may be indiscriminately imaged as prostitutes, harlots and whores.[1]

In Jeremiah the woman, the community, Judah and Jerusalem and/or Israel and Samaria, is never asked to defend herself: her voice is not heard, for an adulteress deserves to be punished by divorce without further argument (3.1, 8). The message to the target audience is: if you endorse the universal truth of the metaphorized female's behaviour as it is presented; if you, males, want to preserve male social supremacy, as does the speaker; if you, females, accept the fantasy's view of your gender; if you, the community, want to forsake pornography in favour of love and loyalty; if you consider the allocation of sex roles within the metaphor valid and appropriate for the relationship between God and his community—then, well, a basic rejection of female nature informs your receptivity. You seem to support male dominance not only in the divine sphere, but also in the human domain: the metaphor's ideology cuts both ways.

The metaphorized woman is repeatedly called *zônâ*, here and in Hosea and Ezekiel. It is not clear what she is accused of: prostitution (the sale of her sexuality)? Harlotry (uncontrollable sexuality)? Whoredom (being backed by a male patron)? The distinction between the three (English) terms is blurred. To

---

1.   Setel, 'Prophets and Pornography', pp. 87-88.

complicate matters further, adultery is apparently *zenût* too, as is being a *qᵉdēšâh* (the translation 'cult prostitute' affords a splendid example of biased interpretation). The semantic confusion in the biblical text is perpetuated by biblical interpretation, as Bird has convincingly shown.[1] The biblical discourse and its metadiscourse share common premises. The indiscrimination which both discourses share amounts to a gross misnaming of female experience. Addressees and readers alike are expected to identify with and adopt God's and the poet's indignation at the supposedly stereotypical female sexual behaviour.

Feminist Definitions of Pornography

Feminist *definitions* of pornography vary. However, most feminists agree on the functionality of pornography, as presented earlier: pornography objectifies females and degrades them. It encourages female abuse and restricts female sexual choice to a state of virtual servitude. Consequently, male power is highlighted and legitimated.[2]

Reading Jeremiah 3 in this light yields unsurprising results. The figuration of one errant wife in ch. 2 has now blossomed into two errant wives. The same process is in evidence in Ezekiel: the metaphorization of one community into one wife in ch. 16 evolves into a double presentation of two communities as such wives in ch. 23. One makes two, and two lead to a generalization by drawing on male stereotypes of the female. It now becomes more evident that God/the male has been treated horridly by the wives he supposedly possesses. They (and they are actually one 'woman', in the metaphor as in life and history, for they typify 'woman') have attempted to choose their partners. They have forgotten their proper place. They are therefore guilty of social, moral and legal transgressions. The

---

1. P. Bird, 'The Harlot as Heroine: Narrative Art and Social Presupposition in Three Old Testament Texts', *Semeia* 46 (1989), pp. 397-419; and ' "To Play the Harlot": An Inquiry into an Old Testament Metaphor', in P.L. Day (ed.), *Gender and Difference in Ancient Israel* (Minneapolis: Fortress Press, 1989), pp. 75-94.

2. Setel, 'Prophets and Pornography', p. 88.

pornographic presentation asserts male domination through the control of female sexuality. Tracing the mechanism of persuasion, we notice that it moves subtly from the particular to the general, then to the ideological. Because the argumentation is analogic, its fallacy is tricky to pinpoint. Powerful gender conventions are at stake, and they are bound up with religious concerns. The enlistment of pornography as propaganda tool validates the metaphorized relationship between God and his community. This validation is accomplished by appealing to a familiar male view: women are by nature promiscuous, hence in need of containment.

Causes of Pornography

Feminists recognize that the ultimate *causes* of pornography are male insecurity and the need to affirm and reaffirm control in the face of change (Setel). Therefore, pornographic propaganda in Jeremiah (and Hosea, and Ezekiel) reflects not only the poet's political and religious concerns but also his—whoever 'he' may · have been—psychological and social concerns as a male. The love metaphor is true M literature, not just androcentric but truly phallocentric; let us note in passing the preoccupation with the male genitalia in the pornographization of males in Ezek. 23.20 and Jer. 5.8. The husband-wife metaphor is woman-suspicious: especially wife-suspicious, so much so that it is expected to be convincing when delivered by a 'Jeremiah', a fictive bachelor. However, as Freud has taught us, verbal sexual abuse—like sexual jokes—exposes fascination and desire more effectively than it masks them.[1]

Non-Pornographic Representation of Woman in Jeremiah

Far be it from me to suggest that each and every image of woman and femaleness in Jeremiah is pornographic. Indeed, there are non-pornographic representations of woman in the book: let us have a quick glance at some of them.

Jeremiah 31 has a cluster of metaphorized, type-cast women:

1. S. Freud, *Jokes and their Relation to the Unconscious* (ET; London: Pelican, 1976, 1981).

mother (v. 15), virgin (vv. 4, 21) and daughter (v. 22). The chapter contains no newly configured wife metaphor, which would have redeemed the love metaphor somewhat. The subject matter of ch. 31 is the imminent reversal of fortune for God's suffering community. Does this signify a change in role for the metaphorized females? The archmother Rachel feelingly weeps for her sons (although not for her *daughters*; perhaps she does, but the text remains mute on this point): she is totally preoccupied with her male children's fate, as a devoted mother should be. A dead mother is an asexual, safe object for veneration. Moreover, the community has miraculously become a 'virgin' again. Is this so, in the metaphor, because a virgin is by definition a more suitable spouse for a male than a tainted wife? This reversal of applied metaphor signifies fresh hopes for better male control this time, no doubt. In addition to marital male authority, paternal authority is invoked here too. When a 'daughter' figure appears toward the end of the chapter, she is too tricky for male comfort. There is no erotic imagery in this chapter, no pornography. Nevertheless, the female images conform to the pattern established earlier and complement it through the suggested reversal. They constitute an additional transference of male concern about legitimate, properly allocated gender roles to religious discourse. The quasi-female imagery in another Jeremian passage, 20.7-20, has no relevance for our topic. Although the imagery can be understood as birth imagery,[1] no gender values can be deduced from it.

Ultimately, it appears that in Jeremian pornography and outside it, even different, separate images of woman reveal analogous attitudes. The difference between the husband-wife metaphor on the one hand and the mother, virgin bride and daughter metaphors on the other hand resides neither in the particular contents nor in the underlying ideology of either, but in the vehicle chosen for presentation (the metaphors) and the message of each particular discourse.

---

1. Cf. J. Magonet, 'Jeremiah's Last Confessions: Structure, Image and Ambiguity', *HAR* 11 (1987), pp. 303-17.

An Ancient Intertext: Semonides on Women

Suspicion of women in general and wives in particular has been expressed in androcentric literature from early antiquity on. A pertinent example is the work by the ancient Greek poet Semonides, dubbed by its English translator, Lloyd-Jones, 'The first satire on women in European literature'.[1] This work can serve as a suitable intertext to Jeremiah on several counts. It advances outspokenly male perspectives about women. Chronologically, it is attributed to the seventh century BCE (which is the time slot claimed for the fictive Jeremiah too). It divides women or wives into ten categories, all metaphorized in terms of nature phenomena, eight of which are animals. The female imaged as an ass, central to the Jeremian metaphor, is present here too: 'when she comes to the act of love, she accepts any partner'.[2] This particular correspondence as well as the overall similarity between the two texts is interesting. But so are the differences. Although both poetic texts are informed by male suspicions and male needs, the Greek work refers to female sexuality in a non-pornographic manner. No stimulation of fantasy is attempted beyond the sentence quoted. This example illustrates that misogyny and pornography need not be literary bedfellows, which is what they are in the prophetic husband-wife metaphor.

A Modern Intertext: Story of O

Let us move to consider a modern piece of pornography, our so-called control text, *Story of O*. It was ostensibly authored by a woman, Pauline Réage (we shall return to the issue of authorship later). This popular French novel has been translated into several languages, filmed, and acclaimed as a breakthrough in female erotic prose by some male critics. Yet, and more widely, it is considered a pornographic novel which efficiently stimulates desire and fantasy while—like the husband-wife metaphor—betraying conventional social mores. Unlike prophetic literature,

1. H. Lloyd-Jones, *Female of the Species. Semonides on Women: The First Satire on Women in European Literature* (London: Duckworth, 1975).
2. Lloyd-Jones, *Semonides on Women*, p. 44.

Story of O is non-canonical. Nevertheless it is of undeniable literary merit, which facilitates the comparison to the Jeremiah text. A comparison between the two works may in fact begin just here. Literary merit may camouflage what should otherwise seem prominent—in the present case pornographic figurations of woman. The literary force of the Jeremian passages is beyond dispute. This, together with its canonicity and the ideology it shares with many readers, disguises the methods employed and the underlying worldview. In the prophetic metaphor features as a means for an end, while in *Story of O* it looks like an end unto itself. Nevertheless, I find the similarities between the two texts unsettling. A significant difference. And yet, in a way, prophetic pornography is more disturbing than other kinds, for it is approved of unproblematically as religious instruction. At any rate, both texts represent their own 'reality' inasmuch as they relate to sexual desire.

O is a young woman in love who remains anonymous throughout the narrative. The story-line charts a journey she agrees to undertake, a journey which is initiated by her male lover. She is gradually transformed into a naked and abused sex object whose physical or symbolic death is imminent by choice. Finally she becomes a non-person, a uterus controlled by her masters and open to all, an Orifice—but lo and behold, by her own testimony she celebrates her situation. She is aware of becoming re-educated through the intense didactic efforts of her male mentors, who have practised upon her every mental and physical violation their fantasy could invent. Now naked, with a chain through her genitals, with her skin branded and marked by beating, she is displayed as a *positive* lesson for all nubile females to emulate. But she is jubilant: she realizes that she has fulfilled her destiny, the punishment and her masters' stamp makes her belong. Initially accused of being promiscuous by nature (she is a female, is she not?), O has achieved chastity and understanding of her true female nature through sado-masochism. Now she is ready to be reborn as a male-controlled submissive female who is devoted to the ideal praxis of her gender—a conscious, self-determined bondage of love. In short, O and the narrator assure us, O has achieved 'real' feminine selfhood.

When Jessica Benjamin discusses O,[1] she points out that in the pornographic fantasy of rational(ized) violence love, control and submission are intermingled.[2] She attributes the fantasy of erotic domination to the process of differentiation between object and subject. In our culture this process entails a tension whose origin harks back to early infancy. That tension is seldom resolved successfully; instead, it is often dissolved into a gender split. Inflexible gender roles are ascribed to females and males. No mutual recognition is achieved. False nourishment is then derived by males and females from their dialectical master–slave relationship (after Hegel).

Benjamin's critique of the psychosocial factors operative in O is applicable to the Jeremian love metaphor too. A short comparison of individual details from the two texts will highlight their affinities further.

Jeremian Pornoprophetics and Story of O: Comparative Notes

In *Story of O* a reciprocal fantasy of one gender's control and the other gender's submission is expressed by the metaphor of sadomasochism. A divided mythic image is produced. Sadism represents maleness, masochism the essence of femaleness and femininity.[3] In Jeremiah, the similar fantasy—suggested also in Hosea and Ezekiel—reaches a climax. A (male) fantasy of (male) domination is acted out by equating divine authority with male power. The (male) fantasy of (female) submission becomes definitive. It is easily legitimized by a two-way application of the analogy: when God is imaged as a human male, human males can be viewed as divine. This is how metaphors work: there is interaction between sign and referent inside the metaphorical vehicle, and this has consequences. Metaphor creates its own

1. J. Benjamin, 'The Bonds of Love: Rational Violence and Erotic Domination', in H. Eisenstein and A. Jardine (eds.), *The Future of Difference* (Boston: G.K. Hall, 1980), pp. 41-70; *The Bonds of Love* (New York: Pantheon, 1988).

2. Benjamin, 'The Bonds of Love', p. 41.

3. Cf. also P.J. Caplan, *The Myth of Women's Masochism* (New York: Signet, 1987).

'reality', its own frame of reference, not to mention hierarchy. Benjamin's analysis implies that the choice of sexual metaphor is deeply rooted in male infantile fantasy. I would like to add, though, that without female desire and complicity this fantasy would not work for the female members of an audience. Neither would the implied patriarchal, androcentric, phallocentric social order be upheld.

There has been some controversy in feminist circles about the question whether it is possible that a woman wrote O, thus subscribing to male fantasy. Yes, of course; one gender's fantasy cannot survive without the cooperation of the other. But whether that reciprocation derives from one and the same source for both remains questionable. Whose (im)pure lust is it anyway?

O complies with the sadomasochistic procedures willingly; she sees herself as a subject. In her view, as narrated, she acquires a subject/partner's position by choosing to internalize her masters' value system. The consequences are the loss of her personal and sexual freedom, and the emergence of a heightened sense of shame and guilt. This is precisely what Judah, Jerusalem, Israel, the target audience, are being persuaded into doing in the Jeremian text: they are asked to acknowledge their so-called sinful ways, admit their guilt and internalize it. They are urged to feel shame, guilt and remorse as a prelude to repentance. A refusal will be punished.

O is no ordinary victim: she is co-producer of her own fate. She is convinced by her masters' verbal logic that her reeducation is necessary, that it will make her socially and morally acceptable, that it will make her desirable for male partners. Her biblical counterparts are presented as responsible for their own 'deviant' behaviour and for the dismal fate that awaits them if they do not obey the narrating voice. The literary style and voices are different in each case. Verbal violence parading as rational wisdom obtains in both.

O is requested to submit to the superior wisdom of her male mentors. The same goes for the biblical addressees in the love metaphor. They are asked to give up their independent judgment in favour of divine judgment. O is found guilty of promiscuity, hence the treatment she undergoes for her own good.

Her boundaries are violated. She is stripped naked. This is education, designed to promote her spirituality. The analogy to the biblical communities addressed as women is clear. The prophetic male voice announces that these same things will be done to them in God's name in order to remake them suitable companions for him. O views herself as a subject but she in fact becomes a dependent sex object, whereas her masters retain their independence and subjectivity. The woman Judah/Jerusalem, or Israel, is depicted as dependent on 'her' God whereas he remains her independent master. He cares, to be sure; he desires loyalty from his woman, his people. However, his subjectivity does not stem from their recognition. Like O's lovers, YHWH's domination consists of his declared omnipotence, together with a denial of his woman's separateness.

By the end of her story O has undergone a complete transmutation: from human to animal, then to an unnatural animal (a hairless owl woman). She is then possessed by her lovers in a manner reminiscent of sacrifice. The total control of the female, and her acceptance of this control, hangs upon the completion of this transmutational process. The analogy to the community's animalization in Jeremiah is obvious. The textual masters, God and his messenger, intend to subjugate this animal. They are fascinated and attracted, their attitude is ambiguous. But, naturally, they know better than an unnatural animal does. Finally, O sees her experience as a spiritual and religious journey. In the prophetic metaphor the opposite obtains. Religious alliance is metamorphosed into a kind of 'love'. The two perspectives are different enough. And yet, they look too much like the two sides of the same coin. And that makes me feel uncomfortable. Actually, acutely uncomfortable.

In Conclusion

I am a woman, white, Western, Jewish, an Israeli, middle class, heterosexual, divorced, a mother, with an academic education. I hope that, over the years, my efforts to become an F (Female/Feminine) reader have been successful. So how am I to respond to *Story of O*? I have two alternatives. The one is to identify with O, for her fantasy is—at least to a certain extent—my fantasy too, acquired by the socialization process I've undergone. The other option is to rebel against the myth of female masochism and female sexual objectification. I can refuse the recommendation—urgent demand—to achieve female selfhood at the price of independence. I can say, this is carrying things too far, this subordination of F fantasy to M (Male/ Maculine) fantasy. I do not want to be negated in order to join the symbolic male order. I am no prude; I can tolerate, sometimes enjoy, pornographic representations up to a point. But I cannot ignore the gendering effect most pornographic presentations have for persons who belong to the same anatomical sex as I do.

How am I to respond to the prophetic propaganda which depicts Judah and Jerusalem and Israel as an objectified spouse, an animalized it-woman? This propaganda cleverly constructs a stereotype: everywoman, especially everywife, is a potential deviant and should therefore be tightly controlled. By males, of course. Wife-abuse and rape should be directly linked to the worldview which makes such prophetic propaganda acceptable. Religious-political propaganda can lead to wholesale rape of women: read the news about Bosnia. So, once more, I have two alternatives. The one is to identify with the male poet's viewpoint, which is presented as God's viewpoint. The other option is to resist the kind of 'religious pornography' which is characteristic of the husband-wife metaphor. I can object to the social role it implies, no matter whether consciously or otherwise, for persons gendered as 'females'.

Toward the end of her analysis, Jessica Benjamin writes: 'The same psychological issues run through both political and erotic forms of domination, for they both embody denial of the other subject'.[1] Religious domination, be it morally just or otherwise, undoubtedly belongs to the category of political domination. And on that note, I come to my conclusion.

The religious propaganda of the prophetic love metaphor abuses female sexuality although, to be sure, it attacks male sexuality too. I do not know whether a historical person named Jeremiah (or Hosea, or Ezekiel) was responsible for the pornographic passages which bear that name in our canon. Hence, the

---

1. Benjamin, 'The Bonds of Love', p. 66.

metaphor should not be dismissed on the grounds that 'he', the prophet, was unfortunately motivated by 'his' own personal circumstances. Instead, I would like to point out that whoever composed these passages perceived men, God, women, and gender relations in a certain way. That vision, that male fantasy of desire, presupposes a complementary fantasy of female desire. The fantasy is not 'just' erotic. It is a pornographic fantasy, and so is its presentation. As an F reader, I can resist the fantasy by exposure, by criticism, by reflection. But within the present cultural system, I do so at my own peril. I was raised and educated to comply with that male fantasy and to adopt it as my very own. Like other F readers, I may deconstruct myself at times; the temptation to reciprocate this M fantasy, even to appropriate it, may still be there. Awareness helps, but the odds are against me.

DESIRE UNDER THE TEREBINTHS: ON PORNOGRAPHIC
REPRESENTATION IN THE PROPHETS—A RESPONSE

Robert P. Carroll

The women of my people you drive out from their pleasant
houses.
—Micah
Better is the wickedness of a man than a woman who does good.
—Ben Sira
Adultery is pre-text, and issues in the wrong kind of revolt; the
Revolution is post-script, and vindicates the role of process in an
adulterated world.
—Sacvan Bercovitch[1]

In memoriam Fokkelientje Geertruida van Dijk-Hemmes

Fokkelien died on 6 February 1994 and I would like this
response to her work (and Athalya Brenner's) to be read, in
some sense, as a tribute to her as a person and a scholar. She
was gentle and sensitive, a concerned person, admirable in her
scholarship and companionable in her work. Her death after a
long illness violates her scholarly performance and removes
from the guild of European biblical scholarship a much needed
and skilled voice. Those of us who knew her have lost one of
great quality, both personal and academic, and one we shall
miss for decades to come. My personal feelings about
Fokkelien's death are of deep sadness and I mourn her still as a
great loss to our profession.[2]

1. S. Bercovitch, 'The Return of Hester Prynne', in *The Rites of Assent:
Transformations in the Symbolic Construction of America* (New York and
London: Routledge, 1993), p. 238.
2. I sincerely hope that she and her work will not now suffer the fate of
being dismissed as the product of a Dead White European Female (DWEF),

It is seldom a wise move to agree to respond in print to the work of colleagues. It is never wise for a man to accept such an invitation when the colleagues are feminists. To do so is to enter a minefield of ideological contentions where all discourse is freighted with danger for the participants and all readings are open to fiercely contested struggles for signification. I am not, however, a wise man, so I have agreed to respond to the section 'Divine Love and Prophetic Pornography' in Athalya Brenner and Fokkelien van Dijk-Hemmes's very fine book for reasons other than wisdom.[1] Invited to respond to the book by Athalya, I do so because I hold the persons and work of my two colleagues in high esteem *and* also because I have written elsewhere on the topic of 'religious pornography' in the Bible, so there are some warrants for my participation here in the current discussion of an extremely interesting book.[2]

Reading Brenner and van Dijk-Hemmes

The main prophetic texts which suggest themselves for analysis under the general rubric 'religious pornography in the Bible' are Hosea 1–3, Jeremiah 2, 3 and 5 and Ezekiel 16, 20 and 23. These nine chapters contain a considerable amount of material for scrutiny and it is hardly surprising that Brenner and van Dijk-Hemmes only focus on sections of these chapters. To provide an adequate analysis of so much biblical material and of other parallel sections in the prophets, would require a further full-scale book-length treatment. It is also the case that these specific chapters represent very complex and difficult texts in the Bible.

as has happened to so many of her European male colleagues' work. This deeply racist, sexist (and liveist) attitude prevalent in some ideological circles today is indicative of a kind of fascistic atmosphere prevailing in contemporary scholarship.

1.   A. Brenner and F. van Dijk-Hemmes, *On Gendering Texts: Female and Male Voices in the Hebrew Bible* (Leiden: Brill, 1993), pp. 167-93. The two articles, by van Dijk-Hemmes and Brenner, are reproduced in this volume, pp. 244-55 and 256-74 respectively. The page numbers in this critique refer to the original publication, and the page numbers in square brackets refer to the present volume.

2.   R.P. Carroll, *Jeremiah: A Commentary* (OTL; London: SCM Press, 1986), pp. 132-80.

The interpretive issues involved in reading these narratives and poems—whatever the point of view operating in any such reading—are manifold and complicated. A very sophisticated hermeneutic is required for dealing with these texts. Any observations or criticisms which appear in this response to Brenner and van Dijk-Hemmes must be contextualized by the recognition of the complexities of the reading strategies required for adequately analysing the biblical text. The sheer amount of metaphorization going on in these complex chapters also makes interpretation of them more difficult. That is because metaphor and metonym are a complex process of representation and can easily misdirect the naive reader of texts into imagining that more or less is being said than may be the case. When the wide-ranging use of imagery, metaphors and metonyms in the Bible is taken into account, especially the tendency of the prophetic texts to cluster discrete metaphors together or to use constantly shifting metaphors (read Hosea or Isa. 40–55 as sample clusterings of metaphors and images), the modern reader of the prophets is well advised not to rush to ill-considered conclusions or to imagine that so many different and discrete metaphors necessarily add up to meaning the same thing.

Ten pages are offered by Fokkelien van Dijk-Hemmes on Ezekiel 23 in terms of the metaphorization of women in prophetic speech.[1] In point of fact women are the metaphors in the text and the thing these metaphors focus attention on are the cities of Samaria and Jerusalem (23.4). Real women may begin to make an appearance in 23.48, but the only women in the chapter are metaphors. The narrative is not about women but about cities or the communities represented by those cities. The analysis of van Dijk-Hemmes, however, is very much based on the point of view that 'the process of metaphorization of women to a sign for something else enacts a form of disembodiment of the female subject'. As a male reader my immediate response to such a claim is inevitably one of questioning. Not believing that Ezekiel 23 is about real women I am inclined not to read the metaphors as saying anything about actual women in the biblical world (of the text). I would not regard the

---

1. 'The Metaphorization of Woman in Prophetic Speech: An Analysis of Ezekiel 23', pp. 167-76 [244-55].

frequent use in the Bible of metaphorizations of men (perhaps used more often than the metaphorization of women) as representing the disembodiment of men (the male subject). Or to use the discourse of van Dijk-Hemmes, women are no more disembodied in the Bible than men are, perhaps even less so. It may be argued that all such processes of metaphorization inevitably entail disembodiment or, to express it differently, the body (male or female) is inscribed in discourse in the Bible in so many different ways that both disembodiment and embodiment take place constantly in biblical rhetoric. I cannot see any of this disembodiment of the subject taking place with exclusive reference to the female, so am not persuaded that such metaphorization is necessarily a bad thing when used of females (and not when it is used of males).

From a feminist point of view it is clearly a bad thing because the claim used by van Dijk-Hemmes as an epigraphic focalizer reads as follows:

> The process of metaphorization of woman to a sign for something else enacts a form of disembodiment of the female subject. The imaging of woman as something else betrays habits of definition within a frame of reference that is dominated by the interests and the perceptions of the 'first' sex.[1]

An exclusive focus on woman is not available to me as a man, so I find myself excluded from this kind of genderized discourse. Feminists may regard the representation of women by men (any and all such representation) as being invariably a pejorative activity and one not performed in the interests of women. That may be an arguable point of view, but it is a given of feminist readings of the Bible. From my point of view the use of metaphors of women for the community, nation, city and land in the prophets may have little to do with the representation of women as such, just as the metaphorization of men for the community and the nation in the prophets may have little bearing on the representation of men as such. But from a feminist point of view apparently the two similar uses of metaphorization

---

1. 'Metaphorization', p. 167 [244]. The citation is from the 'Introduction' to the Utrecht Interfaculty Women's Studies Research Program, 'Women between Control and Transition' (in Dutch).

processes are not symmetrical. Furthermore, I would read the text and want to emphasize the fact that the metaphorization process reflected in it represents *at best* the point of view of a few male writers or of an ideological elite directed against the community (of men and, perhaps, of women). Feminists appear to want to insist on the extension of that point of view to include all men in the society producing the biblical texts. Hence any statement read in a male-generated text will be regarded as being contaminated by the interests of all males.[1] This position I must disagree with and dissent from because I regard it to be an illegitimate generalization from a particular, and also because I do not believe it to be the case that what one, a few or some men think and say must invariably also be what *all* men everywhere think and say.

So there must inevitably be a fundamental disagreement between how I read the Bible and how the two feminists under discussion read that book. Without going into a monograph-length discussion and analysis of feminist ideology it will not be possible here to argue the case adequately, but such differences in reading strategies are fundamental to understanding this response to a very stimulating book. I think I can appreciate the objections raised by feminists to the representation of women imagined to be implicit in the metaphorization processes used by some of the biblical writers, but I really do wonder about the reading strategy entailed by this view of the matter. If the biblical writers only used negative images of women and positive images of men, then I could see the force of the objections made by feminist readers of the Bible. But that is not the case. The metaphorization processes represent negative *and* positive images both of women and men (as metaphors!) and because such representations are inevitably metaphoric their referential force is symbolic. Hosea, Jeremiah and Ezekiel use these metaphors (of women and of men) in discourse about the community, the nation, the city or the land. Only occasionally do they appear to talk about 'real' men and women—insofar as

1. In the light of the fine analysis of women's voices in the Bible given by van Dijk-Hemmes in *On Gendering Texts*, pp. 17-109, it is now rather difficult to regard the Hebrew Bible as the product of male voices *tout court*.

the rhetoric of prophecy ever talks about anything realistic.[1] I sometimes imagine that the anger expressed by feminist writers on the Bible when they deal with texts which employ the processes of metaphorization of women has to do more with a feminist commitment to outrage at any example of men daring to talk about women at all (whether real or symbolic women or even women as metaphors). As a man it is impossible for me to share such a deep sense of outrage and as an academic I cannot imagine a world of discourse where it is forbidden to talk about alterity which extends to gender. Men and women are bound to talk to and about each other and I simply do not share feminist anger that such conversational exchanges take place all the time. On the other hand, I can share a concern with any reader of the Bible who wishes to object to the ways things are expressed in the book or who wants to call into question the ideologies imagined to be operating behind the text.[2]

In her brief look at Hosea 2 and Ezekiel 23 van Dijk-Hemmes analyses the literary strategies deployed in the text using Drorah Setel's work on 'Prophets and Pornography'.[3] Setel's understanding of pornography is very much shaped by the radical feminism of Andrea Dworkin, and this means that since van Dijk-Hemmes and Brenner both follow Setel's analysis the treatment of the prophets as pornographers in their work is a Dworkinesque one. This is a highly unsatisfactory form of analysis because Dworkin is an extremist and represents an

---

1.   It would require a different article, even another book, to analyse the rhetoric of biblical prophecy in terms of referentiality. The extent to which the prophetic texts have anything to do with history is, in my opinion, still under serious discussion and debate.

2.   The role of *Ideologiekritik* in the study of the Bible is still in its infancy, but see D. Jobling and T. Pippin (eds.), *Ideological Criticism of Biblical Texts* (*Semeia* 59 [1992]). Throughout this response I use the term 'ideology' in the sense of worldview-shaping praxis, while recognizing that it can also have a deforming effect on its holders.

3.   T.D. Setel, 'Prophets and Pornography: Female Sexual Imagery in Hosea', in L.M. Russell (ed.), *Feminist Interpretations of the Bible* (Philadelphia: Westminster Press, 1986), pp. 86-95, 157-59; repr. in A. Brenner (ed.), *A Feminist Companion to the Song of Songs* (The Feminist Companion to the Bible, 1; Sheffield: Sheffield Academic Press, 1993), pp. 143-55.

extremist form of feminism. An extreme ideologue's point of view is useless for intelligent, academic analysis. Dworkin on pornography is like Hitler on the Jews—a point of view, of course, but not one that is going to contribute to a rational account of anything.[1] I stress this point here because it is necessary to give notice of the need for a strong element of *Ideologiekritik* in any approach to such ideological texts as the Bible and to such ideological writers as many feminists are.[2] Neither Brenner nor van Dijk-Hemmes actually uses Dworkin's writings in the book under discussion, but since they take up and use Setel's analysis, which is directly based on Dworkin, Dworkin's ideologically slanted work is assumed into their own analysis.[3] Since I do not accept the narrow, localized and slanted definition of pornography in Dworkin's, Setel's and van Dijk-Hemmes and Brenner's work I must register here my protest at the inadequacy of the discussion of pornography and also of the analysis of the prophets in terms of pornographic representation in the van Dijk-Hemmes and Brenner volume. The lack of a critical and reflective analysis of pornography and therefore of such representation in the prophets does, of course, allow the writers to attack the text from a feminist

1. This strong statement about Dworkin's work is based on her representation of heterosexual behaviour as concentration-camp type of activity, and reflects the difficulties I have with understanding a writer whose published work is a morass of emotive confusions (for example, the writer of the pornographic novel *Mercy* denounces men for producing pornography). I suspect double standards, and special pleading which privileges her own position here.

2. There are many different feminisms operative in the contemporary world and it is not easy to separate them into the constituent elements of a uniform ideology of feminism. For me the most helpful introductions to thinking about feminism (as a non-feminist man who is sympathetic to certain features of feminist thought) are C. Gilligan, *In a Different Voice: Psychological Theory and Women's Development* (Cambridge, MA, and London: Harvard University Press, 1982), and J.R. Richards, *The Sceptical Feminist: A Philosophical Enquiry* (London: Penguin Books, 1982).

3. What I really miss in Brenner and van Dijk-Hemmes's articles is a balanced discussion of all the differing feminist positions on pornography. In my opinion Setel ('Prophets and Pornography') uses far too narrow a base of feminist works on pornography to offer a constructive account of the matter.

perspective and I, as a non-feminist, can only object on the grounds that anybody can give any text such a treatment if a particular ideological slant is imported into the analysis. I would hope that the reading of texts must be a subtler and more sophisticated activity than just the bashing of them over the head with the blunt instrument of contemporary ideologies.

This protest by way of response is only intended to draw attention to the way in which specific ideologies can distort texts by making us read them according to the diktats of an ideology imposed on the text by the reader. Much of what passes for reader-response approaches to ancient texts is but the imposition on the text of a fixed point of view quite alien to the text. Judging by the amount of feminist readings of Hosea and Ezekiel currently available in the guild of biblical scholarship it is quite clear to me that dominant feminist ideologies enable feminist readers to read the texts in specific but very predictable ways. Yet at the same time van Dijk-Hemmes reads aspects of Hosea and Ezekiel which make the reader, any reader irrespective of gender, reflect on the text and on what may be going on in that text. Her analysis of Ezekiel 23 is one modern feminist reading of the text and it will make connections for some feminist readers between the text and their own experiences. Whereas I would prefer to deconstruct Ezekiel 23 by showing its internal incoherence at places, she seems to me to achieve a somewhat similar result by a different method. If I do not read the text as reflecting 'the denial or misnaming of female experience' (the function of pornography according to Setel and accepted by van Dijk-Hemmes), that is because I see it in metaphorization terms primarily. What is being 'described' or, better still, represented (as in any discourse) by Ezekiel is a *male* community's persistent apostasy from YHWH. He may use feminine images in the various narrative of chs. 16, 20 and 23, but not exclusively. There may well be a shift from the metaphorized community to 'real' women in 23.46-49 (depending on the force given to the phrase 'that all women may take warning' in v. 48), but that is exceptional in the narrative. I just do not follow van Dijk-Hemmes when she says that both Oholah and Oholibah 'are degraded and publicly humiliated *in order to stress* that their sexuality *is and ought to be* an object of *male possession and control*'.[1] I do not see that in the text at all. Oholah and Oholibah are metaphors of Samaria and Jerusalem, cities, not women. The images may well be drawn from male perceptions of female behaviour (whether actual or male fantasy must be left for the social historian to determine), but they are applied to the community as city and not to real women in the community. That is how metaphors work. What the Ezekiel text denounces is the behaviour of male society throughout its history. The notion that the narrative is seeking to reinforce male dominance over actual women is imposed on the text by certain forms of contemporary radical feminist ideology.

Ezekiel's rhetoric is a representation of YHWH's speech to 'himself' as he talks about Samaria (Oholah) and Jerusalem (Oholibah) *as two women*, daughters of the same mother (cf. the three sisters of Ezek. 16). These two women (cities or communities) have prostituted themselves in the past.[2] The images are developed at excessive length in order to make connections between the nation's past history in Egypt and the two nations' (Israel's and Judah's) experience of destruction by the Assyrians and the Babylonians. Chapter 23 really is an awkward mishmash of accusations, metaphors and metonyms constituting a metanarrative held together by heavy invective. It certainly invites the modern reader to deconstruct it, whether that deconstruction be of a feminist or non-feminist nature. From 23.43 the text becomes metacommentary on the over-strained metaphorization of the past (vv. 36-42 invite the speaker to judge Oholah and Oholibah). Reading this chapter again (especially under the guidance of van Dijk-Hemmes) I can see how it deconstructs itself again and again. She concludes her reading of the chapter with a very brief discussion of male and

1. 'Metaphorization of Woman', p. 175 [253].
2. I have not attempted to adjust the Hebrew *znh* to take into account current feminist distinctions between the English terms 'prostitute', 'whore' and 'harlot' (see Setel in 'Prophets and Pornography', following Dworkin). I doubt if the Hebrew *znh* will quite capture the politically correct 'sex worker', but I do recognize the point being made about how the male gaze describes (or perceives) female action. All descriptions are relativized because they reflect either the male gaze or the female gaze.

female readerly responses to the text. She feels that male readers can escape from the text whereas female readers have no escape from it. Her notion of the readers involved in reading here relates to the (original) audience of the text. I wonder about such implied audiences. Insofar as there was any such thing as an 'original audience' (implied, real or whatever) of Ezekiel's overlong diatribes (who originally read stuff such as the book of Ezekiel?), I suspect that it would not have understood such obscure prose. If it did understand anything of what was going on in such a haranguing text, then it would have comprehended the matter in terms of conventional metaphors and configurations of a traditionalist nature. Where van Dijk-Hemmes sees 'a continual back-and-forth movement within the text from the metaphorization of women as cities towards the metaphorization of women per se, and vice versa',[1] I tend to see the metaphorization of cities as women, with a slight leakage of imagery towards the end of the overlong harangue. That modern women reading Ezekiel might find its prose offensive, especially under the guidance of various feminist ideologies, is hardly surprising. Contemporary readers of ancient texts are under no obligation to tolerate the intolerable, even if in some quarters those texts are privileged as the 'Scriptures' of religious communities.

To modern readers much of the book of Ezekiel is a farrago of offensive metaphorization of human activity (both male *and* female), whether real or imaginary, for ideological purposes. Here I tend to agree with Brenner and van Dijk-Hemmes in their treatment of the various prophetic texts as propaganda. Elsewhere I have described the Hebrew Bible as 'the ideological literature of an imagined community produced in the Achaemenid or Graeco-Roman period'.[2] As such I must regard much of it as crude propaganda on behalf of the ideological elite who produced it for their own purposes. I am therefore in full sympathy with the modern reader who is a woman and who, as a womanly reader, says that these prophetic texts are offensive and unacceptable. I am, however, not as convinced as

---

1. 'Metaphorization of Woman', p. 176 n. 9 [p. 254 n. 1].
2. R.P. Carroll, 'The Hebrew Bible as Literature: A Misprision?', *ST* 47 (1993), p. 80.

van Dijk-Hemmes that male readers would necessarily find an escape from Ezekiel 23. I do not see v. 45, 'but righteous men, they shall judge them (with) a judgment of adulterous women and a judgment of women that shed blood', as an escape route for men. I read that as metaphorization drawn from the social practice of men judging adulterous women by which the speaker means that the men (and no doubt women) of Samaria and Jerusalem will be (or have been) judged by the Assyrians and the Babylonians. There may be potential for self-righteous men to misunderstand the force of the figurative language and to imagine themselves to be exempted from the judgment, but that would be a complete failure to grasp the nature of metaphoric language and a misreading of a very weak kind. While vv. 46-49 might well be read as an *applicatio* of the highly metaphorized fantasy of 23.1-45 in terms of a warning to 'real' women about the dangers of whatever *zimmâ* denotes (unchastity/lewdness/ idolatry, v. 48), I do not see how in a predominantly heterosexual society (as I imagine 'ancient' Israel to have been) such female behaviour could have been imagined to take place without male participation. Again I feel that van Dijk-Hemmes's assertion that 'the metaphorization of woman in Ezekiel 23 performs *first and foremost* a violent speech act which is even more offensive than the Hosean version: it simultaneously shapes and distorts women's (sexual) experience' (emphases added) goes too far and is driven by a modern ideological construal of the text. Without that shaping and distorting ideology the text might remain offensive, but it would not be 'first and foremost' a statement about women or their experience at all. The women in the text are metaphors, not persons.

My reading strategies make me read the text in a slightly different way from feminists, so I register here a difference of reading between me and Fokkelien van Dijk-Hemmes. Turning to Athalya Brenner's piece on Jeremiah and the poetics of (prophetic?) pornography I must register a similar intimation of a different reading strategy.[1] If my own work is the target of

1. 'On Prophetic Propaganda and the Politics of "Love"', in *On Gendering Texts*, pp. 177-93 [256-74]. Athalya and I discussed these matters when we were invited together for a *Bibelwoche* in Bendorf (Germany) in 1991.

many of her criticisms of men and the Bible I have only myself to blame because I did describe the material in Hosea and Jeremiah as 'religious pornography'.[1] It may have been a loose usage of metaphor intended to draw attention to the way many sexual metaphors in the prophets function as abuse of the community, but I did wish to signal some kind of problem in the text to readers who would delight in the Bible while abhorring pornography. I wanted to put on the agenda for discussion the fact that parts of the Bible approximate to what we would regard today as pornographic depictions of human activity. The use of the term 'pornography' was adequately justified in terms of its literal meaning 'writing of/about prostitutes' (*pornographos*) and the qualifier 'religious' signalled that the representation of such obscene language functioned in a specific way. I do not believe, of course, that there is any evidence for the existence of technical pornography among the producers of the Bible (that would be an anachronistic point of view). I was using the phrase in a metaphorical or figurative manner. Brenner and van Dijk-Hemmes however, following Setel and Dworkin, take up the notion of 'pornography' and do mean it in a modern sense. So for them there is some kind of equation between biblical texts and modern pornographic texts. This move allows them to bring to bear on the Bible the full panoply of politicized anti-pornography propaganda of sections of contemporary feminisms. Dogma and definition function here in a highly ideological manner and a monogenetic account of pornography skews the whole discussion completely.

Brenner's analysis is very dependent on that of van Dijk-Hemmes and Setel, but she focuses on Jer. 2.23-25 and Jeremiah 3. Metaphors of the community in terms of positive images of women are briefly considered and then dismissed as insignificant. There is some discussion of feminist definitions of pornography and Jeremian pornography, followed by some analysis of Pauline Réage's famous novel *Story of O*. Brenner's concluding comment on the Jeremiah material is determined by her association of the biblical text with her reactions to *Story of O* and she writes:

1.   Carroll, *Jeremiah*, p. 134.

I cannot dismiss pornographic religious propaganda which abuses metaphorized female (and, to a much lesser extent, male) sexuality on the grounds that it was unfortunately conditioned by 'his' private and social circumstances. Instead, I wish to point out that whoever composed these passages perceived women and men—not to mention God—and gender relations in a certain way. That vision, that male fantasy of desire which presupposes a corresponding and complementary mythical fantasy of female desire, is pornographic.[1]

I suspect that that is just a plain bad reading of Jeremiah, assisted by understandable reactions to a very powerful and influential postwar French novel. Jeremiah is speared in the spiking of Réage's novel and the critique of one easily passes into the critique of the other. That is closer to guilt by association that it is to responsible analysis of the biblical text. In the course of her analysis leading up to that conclusion Brenner emphasizes the animal metaphors in Jer. 2.23-24 as evidence of misogyny in the text. The 'woman-in-the-text' metaphor (there is no woman in the text, only a metaphor!) is dehumanized by being animalized and this process reflects the function of pornography as the maintenance of male domination through the denial of female experience.

Much of the charge of Brenner's analysis is carried by the feminist ideology informing it. If the readers are not feminists they will be much less impressed by the argument or captivated by any force attributed to it. As a reader, a male reader, of Jeremiah I just do *not* read the animal metaphors in 2.23-24 (there is only one animal in the Greek version of Jeremiah) as indicative of a general male view of either women or of 'woman-as-wild-animal'. I certainly do not read the metaphors as evidence of a male belief that women as wild animals must be controlled (by men). I cannot even begin to read Jeremiah 2–3 as being designed to preserve social domination of females by males.[2] The very long list of images, figures and metaphors in

1. 'Prophetic Propaganda', p. 193 [similarly, p. 274 here]. While I disagree that men are less abused by metaphorization processes in the Bible, I do agree with her that all such pornographic fantasies in the Bible ought to be resisted by modern readers. The perception of god implied by these fantasies is not one any modern reader dare entertain, let alone encourage.

2. Brenner, 'Prophetic Propaganda', pp. 184-85 [265-66].

Jeremiah 2–3 is too evenly distributed between male and female representations of the nation—never of women nor of men—for me to begin to accept this clearly modern feminist pejorative reading of the text. The voice I hear and read in Jeremiah 2–3 (and also in 5.7-8) is a voice expressing strong disapproval of the community or nation's past behaviour as wild, uncontrolled and apostate. Male *and* female metaphors are used throughout the discourses to make that point. The animal metaphors are *not* limited to female images but use male configurations also. In 5.7-8 it is male behaviour which is stigmatized using animal imagery and in Ezek. 23.20 the paramours (of Oholibah) are mocked in terms of having animal-sized penises. That is the mockery of men (foreign men perhaps) and it uses male metaphors to make the point. The target of the mockery is the male society. If using wild animal metaphors of the community as woman is to be read as misogyny, then simple logic demands that the men-as-animals metaphors must be treated as misandry. I would have to say that the prophetic texts, whether viewed as pornographic or not, are both or neither. It is special pleading of the worst kind to insist on pinning down just a favoured selection of metaphors as misogyny (a common and much favoured term of abuse in feminist discourses), while refusing to face up to the logic of that kind of discourse by acknowledging the male metaphors as misandry. The prophetic texts are certainly not exclusively misogynistic and when it is recognized that the object of all the highly rhetorical and metaphorical abuse is the community or nation (in public terms, the men) then it is arguable that they are not misogynistic in any sense. The charge of misandry can remain on the books.

The ideological voices which I hear in Ezekiel 16, 20 and 23 and Jeremiah 2, 3 and 5 are all against forms of communal behaviour connoted by sexual metaphors. They are the put-down of society by a small elite of ideologues with their own agendas coming to the fore in the space created by the denigration of all alternative accounts of society and past history. To extrapolate from such texts misogynistic messages requires an a priori and determining feminist ideology. It also requires a refusal to treat metaphor *as* metaphor when it suits a predetermined argument. No doubt metaphors can and do carry surplus meaning, but the sheer negativity of the sexual metaphors in the prophets seems to me to convey the message that the speakers or writers are against all kinds of activities, including no doubt sexual activity (if the erotic charge of the metaphors is allowed to leak back into literal descriptions), whether male or female, outside of their own social norms and values. These socio-political ideological exchanges going on in the text focus on the community or nation and not on gender, and the polemics must be seen as ongoing struggles within that society whereby different groups of ideologues sought to impose their own ideology on the representation of the past.

In disagreeing with me on Jeremiah Brenner asks some difficult questions: she writes 'Whose fantasy are they [the tex-tual images of woman]? Whom do they serve, and how do they do it?'[1] When writing my commentary on Jeremiah I found chs. 2–6 the most difficult section to comment on adequately. What I wrote, revised and rewrote yielded an unsatisfactory published version of the matter. What gave me the greatest difficulty in dealing with the text were questions quite similar to Brenner's. What is going on in these texts? Who is speaking and on whose behalf do they speak? What groups are being spoken against? What ideology or whose interests are being served by these harangues and denunciations of the community?[2] I still find it difficult to answer these questions satisfactorily. Part of the real difficulty lies in the nature of the propagandistic texts constitut-ing the section. These texts underdetermine exegetical analysis and require too much hypothetical reconstruction by the com-mentator. An *Ideologiekritik* approach to the text finds it difficult to identify the beneficiaries of such a denunciation of the com-munity and of the past. Perhaps it does serve a second temple elite or a group of ideologues in the Persian or Graeco-Roman period. On the other hand, Jeremiah 2 may be just one more ideologically slanted 'story' of the past, like Ezekiel 16, 20 and 23, designed to undermine any alternative claims to continuity with the past (Jeremiah being the constructed figure which gave the ideologues their claim on the past). My hermeneutical

---

1. Brenner, 'Prophetic Propaganda', p. 181 [261].
2. In *Jeremiah*, pp. 69-82, I treat ideology in the book of Jeremiah in terms of the interests reflected in the text.

presuppositions do not include a feminist perspective (however sympathetic I may be to some shared views of men and women), so I read these texts with much less focus on feminine metaphors as being other than metaphors. Readers such as Brenner and van Dijk-Hemmes naturally and necessarily read these texts as women and also with feminist values, so they read differently.

Pornography and Religious Abuse

It is unusual for biblical scholars to pay much attention to pornography or for them to make connections between the world in which they themselves live and the world of the texts they study. In calling the fantasy texts of the prophets 'religious pornography' I may have dug a pit for myself. On the other hand, I may not have engaged in any such digging but may have provided myself with a golden opportunity to reflect further on some of the more difficult texts in the prophets. The offending sentence reads: 'Since Hosea, religious pornography has become a standard form of abusing opponents'.[1] I think I would like to stand by that formulation of the matter, but perhaps like so much else in my commentary that sentence could have been expressed better. Taking this opportunity to rewrite the sentiment expressed there I might now say 'the use of sexual metaphors in abusing ideological opponents has been a feature of religious discourse since the Bible was written'. Such a rendering of the same thought avoids altogether the notion of 'religious pornography'. It does not, however, in any sense avoid the problem of abuse using sexual language. If I used the term 'pornography' it was as shorthand; that is, as shorthand for signalling a number of points about texts such as Jeremiah 2–3, 5; Hosea 1–3; Ezekiel 16, 20 and 23. I did also want to make connections between pornography as 'depictions of prostitutes' (whether male or female is of no consequence to me) and the rhetoric of the Bible. If it were not regarded by so many as sacred Scripture, the Bible as literature would have been banned long ago in Christian countries. It is a book full of obscene and offensive language. Like all literature produced by

1.   Carroll, *Jeremiah*, p. 134.

human cultures it has its share of bawdy material (cf. Boccaccio, Rabelais, Shakespeare, Joyce and so on).[1]

In our puritanical age such literature gives great offence, especially to ideological movements, which include various forms of contemporary feminist thought. The puritanical urge is always towards control and the domination of others. One of the most dominant forms of control is that of the censorship of literature and as various feminist ideologies are among today's ardent seekers of domination it is hardly surprising that so much feminist politics is about control and censorship. These movements desperately seek to censor and control whatever they regard as pornography, often by using the discourse of misogyny. Hence the so-called pornographic elements in the Bible have been roundly condemned by various feminists writing on biblical texts.

One way of modifying my loose usage of the term 'pornography' would be to apply to that aspect of prophetic rhetoric the term 'fantasy'. Fantasy literature is an acceptable genre in modern study.[2] It belongs with apocalypses and horror stories as a perfectly good (and politically correct) topic of study. If this fantasy aspect of the prophets also happens to contain sexual metaphors that should not pose too many problems for the modern reader because it can be contextualized within the larger sphere of fantasy literature. Everybody has sexual fantasies, so the sexual fantasies of the prophetic literature should meet with a sympathetic modern readership. Of course relativism comes into play here: one person's fantasy is another person's dangerous nightmare. What may appear to some readers as a harmless piece of speaker's utterance can to quite different readers appear as something extremely offensive or even dangerous. Politics also plays a major part here too. Offensiveness of perception all too quickly becomes political and the political inevitably moves towards mechanisms of control. Call something pornographic and it stands condemned by the politically correct and by all

1. Cf. E. Ullendorff, *The Bawdy Bible* (Oxford: The Oxford Centre for Postgraduate Hebrew Studies, 1978).

2. Cf. G. Aichele and T. Pippin (eds.), *Fantasy and the Bible* (*Semeia* 60 [1992]).

'right-minded' people. While I did wish to register a protest against and disapproval of the sexual fantasies expressed in the prophetic literature (if sexual they be), and therefore used the phrase 'religious pornography' to describe them, I only wished to indicate a site of disagreement with an ideology imagined to be inscribed in the text. I did not wish to call for censorship nor did I imagine for one moment that that imagined ideology was a male one directed (solely) against women. On the contrary, I understood, and still understand, the metaphorization processes to be symbolic and not literal. Male and female terms are used in the prophets to condemn the past, the community and also ideological opponents. There may have been women among those opponents, but it is essentially a male community (in public terms) which stands condemned by the sexual rhetoric of the prophets.[1] Feminists clearly think that the terms of abuse used in that sexual rhetoric betray more than is apparent on the surface of the language. That is a point of view with some force to it, especially in contemporary politics. If I appear to opt for a different point of view that is because I wish to resist feminist readings of the text and also to resist the logic of that position which would make the male terms of abuse indicative of misandry in the text. There is room in the world of biblical studies for many different readings of the text.

The difference in emphasis between my reading of the prophets and that taken by Brenner and van Dijk-Hemmes is simply one of focalization. When a biblical writer uses terms such as 'the man of sin/lawlessness' (deutero-Paul in Thess. 2.3) or 'anti-christ' (the Johannine letters: 1 Jn 2.18, 22), I do not for one moment entertain the suspicion (whatever the virtues of operating with the hermeneutics of suspicion might be) that one writer is anti-men, that is misandric, and the other writer is anti-Christian. That is not how language works. Equally so, when biblical writers use feminine metaphors to express disapproval of (male) behaviour I do not conclude that they are anti-women

---

1. On women as opponents see R.P. Carroll, 'Coopting the Prophets: Nehemiah and Noadiah', in E. Ulrich, J.W. Wright, R.P. Carroll and P.R. Davies (eds.), *Priests, Prophets and Scribes: Essays on the Formation and Heritage of Second Temple Judaism in Honor of Joseph Blenkinsopp* (JSOTSup, 149; Sheffield: JSOT Press, 1992), pp. 87-99.

(that is, misogynistic). I would need much further information to be able to jump to the conclusion that behind the text lies an ideology of dislike. This is the point at which Brenner and van Dijk-Hemmes bring to bear on their reading of biblical texts some modern feminist interpretations of pornography. Here also is the crux of the disagreement between our points of view. We are in another contested site of struggle for meaning. By making direct connections between some highly partisan definitions of pornography and the biblical text Brenner and van Dijk-Hemmes are able to demonstrate that the text participates in anti-women propaganda, that it is fundamentally 'sexist' in the modern jargon of feminism. There we disagree profoundly and must agree to differ. I resist the totalizing transfer of meaning from words to imagined ideologies behind the text and I also resist the partisan definitions of pornography which underwrite a political ideology of control and censorship. I am very much a resistant reader in this discussion.

By way of justification of my resistant reading strategy I should say why I resist most of the feminist readings of the Bible. I do not think that texts should be subjected entirely to a one-sided imposition of meaning by the modern reader. There should be some room in every reading for the text to resist the imposed meaning of the reader. I remain loyal to my roots in the historical-critical methodology for reading the Bible—at least to the extent that I wish to avoid the modern tendency to practise an aggravated anachronistic approach to ancient texts. I also want to resist modern ideologies which impose their own meaning on texts as if the text could only speak in a modern voice. Such impositions tend to insist on a single meaning for a text and practise a denial of the possibility of a plurality of meanings. I prefer to see texts as polysemous and therefore as being capable of resisting single-meaning readings. A specific ideological reading of a text may see in it a specific meaning, but a different reader will read it differently. What may determine the generation of meaning is a complex blend of the reader's own hermeneutical presuppositions and the text's resistance to readings generated by such approaches. The engendering of meaning is a very complex and complicated process, so I do not wish to give here any impression that reading texts (whether ancient or modern) is a simple activity. For me the aggravated anachronism of feminist readings tends to insist on finding modern values in texts or on condemning texts when they fail to yield to such inquisitorial pressure. But I would not expect to find in the Bible anything approximating to modern (or post-modern) values such as egalitarianism, liberal representative democracy or universal franchise. Nor would I expect to find in it ethics or an ethical system which I could integrate with modern life without having to alter it radically. Hence my tendency to disagree with much of contemporary readings of the Bible, whether from feminist or liberationist points of view.[1]

Some extreme or radical feminists—the definition of 'extreme' is determined by the wide spectrum of different feminisms competing for attention in the modern world—define pornography in ways which are too one-sided and partisan for me to accept as working definitions for reading the prophets (or the Bible). Much of Andrea Dworkin's work is posited on an extremely hostile misandric approach to modern life. For her, and for those feminists who think like her, heterosexual intercourse is rape *per definitionem*. Men dominate women just by being men. All consensual sexual activity is regarded as taking place between unequal genders, hence the more powerful man must inevitably rape the less powerful woman. Social betters do not seduce, they rape (see radical feminist readings of the David and Bathsheba story in 2 Sam. 12). Only gender apartheid will suffice to protect and liberate women from the power of men and the truly liberated woman is necessarily a practising lesbian. This radical position is, of course, on the extreme boundary of modern feminisms and most feminists, especially those who read the Bible, would dissent from such radicalism. Modern feminisms are a protean phenomenon of late capitalist society and very much the product of 1960s consumerist values (statistical representation is a consumerist notion). They are part of the cultural logic of late capitalism. But not all feminists situate

1.   Being a resistant reader in contemporary biblical studies is a very lonely and difficult task: so many readers wish to appropriate the Bible for their own metaphysical position, without allowing that modernist and postmodernist readers may well find that the ancient collection of books is very resistant itself to such appropriation.

themselves on the extreme boundary of feminist ideology. The kinds represented by Andrea Dworkin or Mary Daly are not the only forms of feminist thought, but Brenner and van Dijk-Hemmes draw their working definitions of pornography from the extreme end of the spectrum, so that even men who may be sympathetic to some of the central demands of feminism will find themselves alienated by a hopelessly skewed discussion. The discussion needs to be broadened much more if the term 'pornography' is to be applied to the fantasy sections of the prophets. Even then I suspect that a modern analysis of contemporary pornography will be unhelpful for understanding prophetic rhetoric.

Space does not permit an adequate discussion of pornography or even a survey of all the conflicting points on view on pornography among contemporary feminists (let alone non-feminists). Pornography is a site of fiercely contested discussion among feminists and I am not going to umpire such struggles. What I am deeply aware of in current discussions is the profound lack of consensus among feminists on the subject of pornography. Against the demands for censorship and control of (male) heterosexual pornography by some radical feminists can be heard the equally strident voices of other feminists demanding the right of access to pornography.[1] At times in these debates the issue is skewed by calling the bad thing 'pornography' and the good thing 'erotica', but this is just contemporary doublespeak for saying 'pornography' is what *you* like whereas *I* like 'erotica'. It is a self-privileging distinction without a difference. In Orwellian terms modern ideological debates too often descend into the practise of the principle 'four legs good, two legs bad'.[2] Somewhere in all this very confused and

1. See C. Whatling, 'Who's Read *Macho Sluts*?', in J. Still and M. Worton (eds.), *Textuality and Sexuality: Reading Theories and Practices* (Manchester: Manchester University Press, 1993), pp. 193-206; L. Segal and M. McIntosh (eds.), *Sex Exposed: Sexuality and the Pornography Debate* (London: Virago, 1992); and H. Geyer-Ryan, *Fables of Desire: Studies in the Ethics of Art and Gender* (Oxford: Polity Press, 1994), for a variety of differing points of view on pornography and women.

2. This famous slogan from George Orwell's allegory *Animal Farm* has the added advantage of illustrating the use of animal metaphorization similar to prophetic rhetoric. See G. Orwell, 'The Principles of Newspeak', in

confusing debate over pornography can be detected some rather old-fashioned double standards at work or even a considerable amount of *mauvaise foi*. Thus lesbian and gay factions demand the right to have free access to pornography and also the right to produce it as and when they wish (under the name 'erotica'). It is only heterosexual *pornography* which must be controlled by being banned. The matter may be expressed in a slightly different way: when society has been prevailed upon to ban pornography, lesbian and gay groups will then demand their inalienable right to pornography. It is only the control of heterosexuality which is part of the programme of women dominating men here. For me this is just politics (masquerading as scholarship and morality no doubt) producing false consciousness and I find such special pleading and double standards quite unacceptable. If pornography is what the extreme feminists say it is, then it should be banned right across the board (heterosexual, homosexual, lesbian, sadomasochism, bestiality, whatever), or if censorship is a greater political evil or danger than pornography (which I believe it to be) then pornography must be tolerated right across the board. Sauce for the goose is, I believe, sauce for the gander too!

This is where I dissent strongly from Brenner and van Dijk-Hemmes on the subject of pornography. I do not believe that the issue can be reduced to a monolithic theory of pornography, though I am quite ready to accept that the images in the Bible under discussion are pornographic. There are many ways of analysing pornography and their insistence on treating it only in terms of dominance is for me, at best, only one possible aspect of the pornographic gaze. In terms of pornography as domination matters are much more complicated than is implied by the sources used in Brenner and van Dijk-Hemmes. We might ask, 'who dominates whom in pornography?' If women produce and consume pornography, then who is dominating whom?[1] If pornography is defined as dominance, then

Nineteen Eighty-Four (London: Penguin, 1989), pp. 312-26, for the rules of Newspeak and the notion of doublespeak. Orwell's work is invaluable for any serious *Ideologiekritik* directed against modern ideological movements.

1.   On that point the work of Linda Williams is illuminating; see L. Williams, 'Pornographies On/scene, or Diff'rent Strokes for Diff'rent

presumably lesbian pornography is women dominating women and gay pornography is men dominating men. Should such pornography be banned because it is wrong for people to dominate other people or even for people to wish to be dominated? I find such analysis to be superficial in the extreme. Desire seems to me to be a better category for using with reference to pornography, a stronger and more universal category to use when analysing pornography. Who desires whom and how? That is gender-free analysis. It is symmetrical analysis which recognizes the equality of women and men. Domination may be a subset of sexual activity among consenting adults, hence its representation in pornography. But desire is a gender-free encounter between persons, whose mutuality gives expression to that desire in so many different ways. Desire, fantasy, erotic representation, domination and many other aspects of sex help to construct a very complex notion of how human beings relate to each other sexually. Pornography is only one form of the representation of sexual existence. There are many other forms of representation, but historically and socially pornography has been a contested site of struggle through the ages. Until recently pornography was banned in most countries and still is in many countries. Such censorship does not sound like men dominating women. On the contrary, it sounds much more like political power operating against men and women in the name of ideological authority. Censorship is the form true domination takes, not pornography. Censorship dominates and controls expression, representation and, above all else, liberty. It may be easy to imagine or to argue that pornography infringes somebody's freedom (the rhetoric of imagined liberty), but censorship does actually diminish real people's freedom in the name of a wide range of protective activities. Not for nothing have all the totalitarian states and puritanical ideologies absolutized the ban on pornography and all forms of sexual expression (outside marriage).

To return to the problem of the metaphorization of men, women and animals in the Bible. I would agree with Brenner and van Dijk-Hemmes that the fantasies in Hosea, Jeremiah and

Folks', in Segal and McIntosh (eds.), *Sex Exposed*, pp. 233-65, 329-32.

Ezekiel are about domination to a certain extent. But it is not domination in the pornographic sense of people dominating or being dominated, it is domination in a political or ideological sense. The so-called sexual pornography or fantasies of the prophets reflect an ideology of control and representation. The community in the past—the present status of the community keeps creeping into the text and tends to deconstruct the fantasy—is represented as male or female and these negative images vilify the community as apostate. Positive and negative images of the community under the form of men, women, animals and plants appear throughout the prophets, so the narrated images in Hosea, Jeremiah and Ezekiel must be recognized as being very conventional. The community, especially in terms of its past (Jer. 2–3; Ezek. 16, 20, 23), is metaphorized in so many different ways that it is very difficult for the modern reader to keep track of the high degree of diversity in the metaphors used. It is also too easy to lose sight of the metaphorization processes at work as representation in the text and to start imagining that the images are literal rather than metaphoric. My reading of these texts differs from those of Brenner and van Dijk-Hemmes in that it wishes to strive for a recognition of the balance of gendered images in the prophets.[1]

Feminists will ask the question 'why women?' where I would only ask 'why men and women?' Why should the community be characterized as a woman? Since the prophets use men, women, animals and plants to metaphorize the community I see no special problem in the use of feminine metaphors. But let me concede some space to the feminists by trying to respond to the question in the terms of their discourse. Why do so many of the prophetic fantasies metaphorize the community as a woman? Feminists do not like explanations which imagine the speakers to be men who have had unhappy experiences of women and wives and who speak out of the pain of such broken relationships (one explanation of Hos. 1–3). It still seems to me to be one kind of explanation. It certainly deconstructs the text. Bitter

---

1. Throughout *Jeremiah* I tried to argue for a recognition of the balanced use of gendered images in the book of Jeremiah. I still think that the abuse in Jeremiah is even-handed, even though it is also quite unpalatable for modern readers.

men speaking out of bitter experiences badmouth the community as a faithless wife or a prostitute who pursues her fantasies with other men. It is an explanation of sorts. It is not very satisfactory for many different reasons, not least being the fact that such outbursts of heartbreak or of wounded pride are among the least reliable accounts of any experience.[1] Pain and bitterness blind reason and sense. I would prefer explanations which contextualize the fantasies in their own time and social setting and which reflect possible ideological factors. After all, the fantasies are about the history of the nation and are not about the personal or sexual experiences of a man and a woman (YHWH and Israel appear under the figures of a man and a woman but are not such individuals). A penchant for troping the nation as a woman may have been culturally determined by convention or social practice. The alienation factor in Jeremiah 2–3 and Ezekiel 16, 20 and 23 may reflect a social setting where foreign women were felt to be a threat to cultural values (cf. the Ezra–Nehemiah material or Prov. 7).[2] If YHWH is married to Israel, then the community must be a woman and YHWH a man for the marriage trope to operate. Gods are usually married to goddesses, but if the ideological texts constituting the Bible are the result of a long *Kulturkampf* against goddesses, then YHWH will have to be married to a metaphor. Once upon a time YHWH had his goddess wife or wives, but in the second temple period he was married only to Israel or Jerusalem (cf. Isa. 40–66).

The marriage metaphors can be pushed further. If Israel-Jerusalem had had a long history of apostasy, as the YHWH-alone ideology insisted on reading the past, then a faithless wife or whore would have been an apt metaphor for these lengthy 'inspired historical sermons'.[3] Men and women are unreliable

1. I take it to be axiomatic for modern discussions of these gender battles that neither gender is in a position to offer objective (or 'truthful') accounts of the other gender's behaviour. *There are no neutral positions in these polemics*: we are all implicated in one side or the other.

2. On this see C.V. Camp, *Wisdom and the Feminine in the Book of Proverbs* (Bible and Literature, 11; Sheffield: Almond Press, 1985), pp. 233-54; cf. B.A. Bozak, *Life 'Anew': A Literary-Theological Study of Jer. 30–31* (AnBib, 122; Rome: Pontifical Biblical Institute, 1991), pp. 155-72.

3. See R.G. Hall, *Revealed Histories: Techniques for Ancient Jewish and Christian Historiographies* (JSPSup, 6; Sheffield: JSOT Press, 1991), pp. 48-52.

reporters on each other's activities, so men writing about the broken relationship between a man and a woman (YHWH and Israel-Jerusalem) might well produce these kinds of ranting fantasies. In waxing lyrical about YHWH's relationship to the community, city or land, but being informed by a very punitive deuteronomistic ideology of control, separation, denunciation and debunking of the past, the rhetoric of Jeremiah 2–3 and Ezekiel 16, 20 and 23 is out of control and over-metaphorized. If the mode is blame and the victim is a consort, then one of the sets of images is bound to be that of the unfaithful wife or the liberated prostitute. Modern feminism, bred in a culture of complaint with its main mode the discourse of blame, has easily recognized these poems for what they are. Many other sets of tropes are used in the Bible, but in these specific narratives the fantasy about mothers, wives, sisters and daughters has run riot. I daresay that behind the fantasies there may also be resentments of the past, dislike of the old goddesses, sexual torments or whatever, but we cannot be sure just how conventional or innovative these 'sermons' may have been. I tend to think of the Ezekiel texts as bordering on what we would now call the pathological, but I am unhappy with that anachronistic way of expressing my feelings. I do find the fantasies of Ezekiel 16, 20 and 23 bizarre and incoherent. They sound like the ravings of a drug-crazed fanatic, though they may well be the quiet, controlled, articulated and highly structured literary discourses of a sedate ideologue. I think they are incoherent and am not surprised that Brenner and van Dijk-Hemmes find them unacceptable.

Sexual images and metaphors are a constant presence in all written discourse. I cannot think of any major literature which does not use them, whether as positive or negative tropings of human behaviour or as part of general, human discourse which is inevitably metaphorized. I have used as an epigraph to this response a sentence from Sacvan Bercovitch's lengthy essay on Hester Prynne in Nathaniel Hawthorne's famous novel *The Scarlet Letter*.[1] I chose the epigraph deliberately because it uses sexual tropings to make a political point. It is easy, of course, for

---

1. Bercovitch, 'The Return of Hester Prynne', pp. 194-245.

Bercovitch to do that because he is discussing a mid-nineteenth-century novel which itself represents a historical situation by means of a sexual offence. Hester Prynne belongs to that class of nineteenth-century fictional heroines (along with Emma Bovary and Anna Karenina) whose acts of adultery are inscribed as representations of socially transgressive acts which dramatize the novelist's depiction of society. I refuse to denounce Hawthorne, Flaubert or Tolstoy as misogynists because they portray women as adulterers. Female adultery functions as a highly transgressive act in the social context of nineteenth-century European and American culture. There is an equally long literary history of fictional men as adulterers (for example, Julian Sorel), so the use of sexually transgressive acts is a dominant trope in literature. It may well reflect one of the six basic plots which determine all myths, fictions and representations in human culture. But of course Hester, Emma and Anna also expose the hypocrisy and power of men—even if they are the creations of male authors. The fantasies of Hosea, Jeremiah and Ezekiel are very different in that their 'women taken in adultery' are but metaphors and symbols, not real (fictional) people. Israel, Samaria, Jerusalem and Sodom are symbols of land, city and people, and the transgressive acts attributed to them are not seen as critical reflections on culture and conformity. On the contrary, the biblical prophets are very different kinds of critics to those who wrote the great nineteenth-century novels on female transgressive acts.[1]

There are many other ways of reading the fantasies of Jeremiah 2–3 and Ezekiel 16, 20 and 23 but space does not permit a proper analysis of such lengthy diatribes against the

1. In my opinion this is a grave defect in prophetic literature. YHWH as husband-lord as represented in the Bible is a horrendous role model for men reading the Bible (I *do* hear what feminists are saying about the Bible!). The social history of the past two millennia in the West will bear out that judgment. Sceptical literature such as Qoheleth and the laments in the Psalms speak out against the ogre of a coercive god, but ideological literature (such as the prophets) which identify the deity with Assyrian and Babylonian terror against small nations represents an entirely unacceptable image of deity for modern readers. The quotation of Ben Sira (42.14) which serves as one of the epigraphs to this response is indicative of a bad attitude towards women in the Bible.

community. The sexual tropes may disturb and bother the modern reader because they seem to be sexist in content and intent, and since in our current cultural climate feminism is part of the dominant ideology we notice these things much more acutely now. But we need to learn how to read these ancient texts without allowing our own cultural holdings to transform them into modern documents. Such sympathetic reading is not advocated here in order to hide their offensiveness from us. Our values are different from those of the text and in seeking to understand such ancient harangues it is not necessary to abandon our own ethical stances. We need to understand these texts, we do not need to adopt their values as our own. That is not a possible option for us. But the task of understanding remains. While I do disagree with Brenner and van Dijk-Hemmes on how they read these prophetic texts, I no more approve of them as rhetoric than do they. I find the pornographic style of rhetoric unpleasant and offensive. The haranguing of the community or the troping of the past in such vicious terms is most unattractive. Yet I would really like to understand these texts in order to understand what is going on in this type of discourse. One suggestion which holds promise for understanding the fantasies is to use the notion of an 'antilanguage'.[1] In the texts the writers are trying to create a different kind of society from that which prevailed in the past and such different societies generate antilanguages. Some such phenomenon is, I think, behind the lengthy harangues of Ezekiel, with traces in Jeremiah and perhaps Hosea. The attempt radically to alter everything inevitably involves violent language, overcharged rhetoric and grotesque parodies of reality. It is not difficult to recognize such features in the Ezekiel material. For a modern reader to get hung up on the surface of the words, especially on the sexual metaphors, is to misunderstand the project completely. To see Hosea, Jeremiah and Ezekiel as being merely ancient pornographers is to misread the text altogether. In my judgment feminism is here a poor reader of texts and a generator of misprisions. Feminists will think

---

1. On this concept see M.A.K. Halliday, *Language as Social Semiotic: The Social Interpretation of Language and Meaning* (London: Edward Arnold, 1978), pp. 164-82.

otherwise because their agendas of reading the Bible are different from mine. We shall just have to disagree at this point and carry on with our different reading modes.

Desire under the Terebinths

Desire rather than dominance seems to me to be the key for understanding the erotic in the Bible. But desire easily becomes dominance when it is metaphorized into forms of political and ideological propaganda. Thus the erotic becomes pornographic when it is politicized (to use a fashionable distinction in contemporary doublespeak ideological discourse). The fantasies in the prophets which contain so much 'religious pornography' or which use so many sexual images for abusing opponents move out of the sexual arena (if ever they occupied the arena of the sexual in the first place) and into politics. Here I think I may be in some agreement with Brenner and van Dijk-Hemmes in their analysis of the sexual images in the prophets. But for me this kind of political control which uses sexual imagery to abuse opponents is not an example of male control over female experience, but represents an attempt by the elite which produced these prophetic writings to control women *and* men for ideological purposes (cf. the control of men by divorce in the Ezra–Nehemiah literature).[1] Since I do not read pornography in contemporary society in terms of being 'a denial, or misnaming, of female experience' (van Dijk-Hemmes following Setel following Dworkin), because too much pornography today is produced by and for women for that definition to be true or useful, I do not read the prophetic fantasies as *mis*representations of real women's experiences. Ideology tends to misrepresent opponents by using a wide range of abusive terms, so misrepresentation in the prophetic fantasies would be misrepresentations of the community and of its past. Real people do not appear in these fantasies and the stereotypical nature of the abuse confirms this non-appearance of the real. There are no

---

1. All discussions about who is trying to control whom belong to that category of discussion which focuses on whether a glass of water or beer is half-full or half-empty; perspective is everything. The tailless fox tends to preach taillessness!

real women in Hosea 1–3, Jeremiah 2–3, 5, Ezekiel 16, 20 and 23, only metaphorized descriptions and representations of imaginary communities and imagined past histories. It is all in the imagination, in the metaphors and in the ideology.

Reading and reflecting on what Brenner and van Dijk-Hemmes have written in *On Gendering Texts* and in numerous other places, I have to admit that there is very little competent work available on 'desire in the Bible'. Apart from commentaries on and discussion of the Song of Songs, I know of no thorough-going analysis of the language of desire (*ḥmd, 'wh*, and so on), let alone an examination of how desire is inscribed in the Bible. We lack a poetics of desire for the Bible. The prophetic fantasies should be part of any such analysis, but the dynamics of metaphorization and representation should warn the reader against a foolish literalism in reading the text. The propagandistic features of the prophetic texts render prophetic language opaque. So in the most general of ways I would tend to agree with Brenner and van Dijk-Hemmes when they read against the grain of these texts and refuse to be bullied by the text into believing that the text speaks innocently of things as they were or appeared to the (imagined) speakers in the texts. Propaganda does not describe, it represents, and all such representations are constructed from many things, especially from ideology. In general feminist biblical scholars have reminded us all of a truth which is often forgotten in conventional biblical scholarship. The text is always somebody's text. It is always situated in a social context and driven by ideological concerns as well as other concerns. Readers of such texts are also situated and bring to texts their own concerns, including the ideological. Conspiring with texts readers can easily double the ideological distortion of which texts are capable. What then passes for scholarship is a mishmash of deformed readings of deforming texts and the orthodoxy generated by such deformations then becomes the distorting lens through which the Bible is read in generation after generation. Such orthodoxy has to be opposed in every generation and critical theory has to be created afresh in each generation as its way of resisting such texts.

To construct an account of desire in the Bible would run up

against two problems: the problem of representation and the problem of data. Throughout this response the aspect of representation has been to the fore. The problem of data lies in the fact that the Bible is a collection of writings from a small cultural group over a relatively short period of time, heavily edited and ideologically slanted. What we have access to in the collection of writings is a very limited account of a variety of points of view. We cannot produce a comprehensive account of desire in the second temple period from such limited texts. Even if we had further great quantities of texts they would not necessarily help us in producing a comprehensive account of desire in the province of Yehud. Reality is never entirely textual.[1] Indeed for most people reality is not textually inscribed at all. We have little or no access to how people felt and lived in ancient times, except by means of material remains and inscribed records. Such remains and texts are at best partial accounts of a variety of representations and we remain in the dark about how comprehensive they may be. The sheer lack of textual data for ancient Hebrew thought helps to circumscribe our knowledge to the point at which it is essentially ignorance. Other ancient cultures are better represented by texts and material remains. Reading accounts of desire in classical literature I am once again struck by the quantitative, as well as qualitative, difference between the Bible and Greek literature.[2] A glance at any academic library's shelves in the relevant sections will demonstrate the truth of this comparison. Just place the Hebrew Bible (and the Qumran scrolls, if you will) alongside all the ancient Greek texts and the difference between the sources for information and analysis cannot be denied. So any account of the metaphysics of desire in the Bible will inevitably be an attenuated one.

1.   While this observation is generally true, in biblical studies almost all our information is textual and Fredric Jameson's observation holds true here too, that 'history is inaccessible to us except in textual form' (F. Jameson, *The Political Unconscious: Narrative as a Socially Symbolic Act* [London: Methuen Paperback, 1983], p. 82).
2.   On this see D.M. Halperin *et al.*, *Before Sexuality: The Construction of Erotic Experience in the Ancient Greek World* (Princeton: Princeton University Press, 1990); and J.J. Winkler, *The Constraints of Desire: The Anthropology of Sex and Gender in Ancient Greece* (London: Routledge, 1990).

Space does not permit an adequate account of desire in the Bible or in the prophets. One example will have to suffice by way of conclusion. The desirable terebinths of Isa. 1.29 (cf. 57.5; 61.3 and the garden imagery of 17.10-11 and 65.3) may reflect or allude to cults of desire in the Jerusalem community, but like so much in the prophetic texts the language is highly allusive and elusive. Echoes of the gardens of Adonis may be there in the book of Isaiah, which may justify treating the garden imagery of the Bible as a subset of desire and its representations (for example, the garden in Eden is where Eve encountered the tree that was desirable in various ways; or compare the language of gardens in the Song of Songs).[1] The enterprise of elucidating desire and its constituent elements in the Bible is large enough to complicate further any account of erotic representation in the prophets, let alone the whole Bible. I mention the enterprise because I think a fully worked out account of the matter would go far towards contextualizing sexual fantasy, erotic representations and 'religious pornography' in the prophets. This would then lead to a more sophisticated treatment of the sexual imagery in the Bible than a feminist critique affords (in my opinion). It would not, however, necessarily invalidate feminist readings of the Bible because I understand them to be about modern appropriations of the text in relation to the situatedness of contemporary readers. They reflect the role of biblical texts in the *Rezeptionsgeschichte* of the Bible and in conjunction with readerly values. Feminist oppositions to the text are one more way of doing a proper *Ideologiekritik* reading of the Bible.

These then are my reflections, observations and rather lengthy response on the subject of pornographic representations in the prophets. They are an attempt to articulate my reactions to a complex set of feminist readings. I find van Dijk-Hemmes's work in section I of the Brenner and van Dijk-Hemmes book, which deals with 'traces of women's texts in the Hebrew Bible', an extremely interesting scrutiny of the text for echoes and traces of an often denied presence in the text. In accepting the general force of their arguments I am happy to recognize the

1. Cf. M. Detienne, *The Gardens of Adonis: Spices in Greek Mythology* (trans. J. Lloyd; Hassocks: Harvester Press, 1977), for Greek analogies.

womanly voices in the text. I have never doubted that women not only are represented in the text but also represent themselves in that text. For me this makes a big difference to conventional feminist claims that the Bible speaks only with the voice of patriarchy. I am not happy with the ideological constructions involved in this kind of discourse and prefer a much more nuanced account of the matter.[1] Feminists may disagree, but none of us is in a position to decide the matter because we know so very little about who wrote the Bible or under what conditions it was produced. I *differ* from Brenner and van Dijk-Hemmes in the matter of ideological commitment to feminism, but hope that we share enough common cultural values to be able to communicate with each other. The length of this response should be testimony enough to the power of their analysis and the strength of their position. I hear what they are saying and applaud the contribution they make to a more sophisticated reading hermeneutic of the Bible. A text as polysemous as the Bible permits a multiplicity of readings, so I will persist with my own reading of the difficult sexual fantasy sections in the prophets. While I do not believe that these fantasies represent real women in ancient times, I take the point that the rhetoric of such texts can be and is offensive to real women in contemporary society. All I can say to that is—mind how you read![2]

1. Which is why I prefer Gilligan (*In a Different Voice*) to Lerner (G. Lerner, *The Creation of Patriarchy* [Oxford: Oxford University Press, 1986]): it is all a matter of the different discourses used to construct the past experiences of men and women. I find all analyses of the Bible in terms of Lerner's notion of patriarchy quite unhelpful for reading that ancient text.

2. In my opinion eventually the *Ideologiekritik* approach to reading the Bible and to biblical scholarship will have to grasp the nettle of feminist interpretations of the Bible. It will be some time before there are adequate documentation and data for accomplishing such a task, but I do not doubt that one day there will begin to appear articles and books pursuing the topic 'The Empress's New Clothes or Medusa's Gaze Resisted'.

RAPE AS A MILITARY METAPHOR IN THE HEBREW BIBLE*

Pamela Gordon and Harold C. Washington

Introduction and Critical Orientation

In the Hebrew Bible cities are frequently personified as women. The context is usually military disaster and the woman is the victim. For example, the following words are addressed to Nineveh in Nah. 3.5-6:

> I am against you, says the Lord of hosts,
> and I will lift up your skirts over your face;
> and I will let nations look on your nakedness
> and kingdoms on your shame.
> I will throw filth at you
> and treat you with contempt
> and make you a spectacle.

This essay examines critically this use of sexual language and imagery in the Hebrew Bible to describe military conquest. We are especially concerned with the metaphor, so favored by the Hebrew prophets and the poet of Lamentations, of the conquered city as a raped woman. The texts we examine further problematize the failure of Deuteronomic law to categorize rape as a crime against the female victims.[1] They prompt us to ask: why does the poetry of the Hebrew Bible appear to acknowledge

*   We wish to express our thanks to: Amy Richlin, Tex Sample, Kathleen Whalen, and the participants in the 'Violence Against Women in the Biblical World' session at the 1992 annual meeting of the Society of Biblical Literature (Women in the Biblical World Section), where we presented an earlier version of this paper.

    1.   Cf. C. Pressler, 'Sexual Violence and Deuteronomic Law', in A. Brenner (ed.), *A Feminist Companion to Exodus to Deuteronomy* (The Feminist Companion to the Bible, 6; Sheffield: Sheffield Academic Press, 1994), pp. 102-12.

how devastating rape is, while the laws deny it? Our interpretation is informed by contemporary feminist critical approaches to rape and pornography, as well as recent feminist interpretation of sexual violence in ancient literatures, especially the works of the Roman poet Ovid.

Rape as a Military Metaphor

In street slang in the West today, the language of sex and the language of violence often intertwine. We frequently hear the vocabulary of intercourse used in place of the vocabulary of death and destruction. Kate Millett attributed this usage in the United States to 'our obsessive cultural habit of sexual loathing'.[1] Military language readily adopts this idiom. It appears already in military training, as an (admiring) observer of a US Marine Corps boot camp has described:

> From the moment one arrives, the drill instructors begin a torrent of misogynistic and anti-individualist abuse. The good things are manly and collective; the despicable are feminine and individual. Virtually every sentence, every description, every lesson embodies this sexual duality, and the female anatomy provides a rich field of metaphor for every degradation. When you want to create a solidary group of male killers, that is what you do, you kill the women in them. That is the lesson of the Marines. And it works.[2]

With this training, it is not surprising that combat soldiers are unselfconscious in their metaphorical reference to military operations as acts of sexual violence. Memoirs of the American Vietnam War era illustrate the soldiers' habit of describing their attacks on land, villages and people with graphic language of the violation of the female body.[3]

1. *Sexual Politics* (Garden City, NY: Doubleday, 1970), p. 292 n. 197.
2. G.F. Gilder, *Sexual Suicide* (New York: Quadrangle Books, 1973), pp. 258-59; quoted by M. Daly, *Gyn/ecology: The Metaethics of Radical Feminism: With a New Intergalactic Introduction* (Boston: Beacon Press, 1990), p. 358.
3. Daly writes: 'All male-instigated degradation of victims and enemies has as its hidden paradigm the female as Other, as victim' (*Gyn/ecology*, p. 332). As an example Daly cites the reference by American soldiers to the Vietnamese as 'gooks', for which 'the female sex is the hidden paradigm'. Compare the following names of American Army firebases in the Queson

How does this language function? We might explain it as a grotesque metonymy, taking a common aspect of warfare (i.e., rape), for the whole.[1] But clearly this is more than an incidental figure of speech; grave ideological interests are at work here. In popular discourse not only does rape metaphorically describe military assault, but the converse is true: the language of warfare is used to describe sexual 'love'.[2]

Could this be Pornography?

> I think it is sentimental to discuss the subject of war, or peace, without acknowledging that a great many people enjoy war—not only the idea of it, but the fighting itself (D. Lessing, *Prisons We Choose to Live Inside*, 1987).

> 'It is a fine day, let us go out and kill something!' cries the typical male of certain races, instinctively (O. Schreiner, *Woman and Labour*, 1911).

Currently there is great controversy over the definition and valuation of the pornographic. We use the term as it is used by those feminist critics who have focused on the contribution of

---

valley in Vietnam in 1972: 'Irene, Judy, Marge, Mary Ann, Mildred' (D. Kirk, *Tell It to the Dead: Memories of a War* [Chicago: Nelson-Hall, 1975], p. 149). Also revealing is the training jingle sung by US Marines, celebrating the frontal assault as the essence of offensive warfare: 'Hey diddle diddle, straight up the middle' (P. Caputo, *A Rumor of War* [New York: Holt, Rinehart, 1977], p. 15). The word 'diddle' has a long history in the English language as a colloquial term for sexual activity; the *Oxford English Dictionary* gives as another range of meanings for the term 'to victimize; to "do"; to do for, undo, ruin; to kill'.

1. On the ubiquity of rape in warfare, cf. S. Brownmiller, *Against Our Will: Men, Women, and Rape* (New York: Simon & Schuster, 1975), pp. 31-113. As we write in 1993 this footnote seems superfluous. Experience warns us, however, that history may not remember the women of Bosnia.

2. Cf., for example, Kate Millett's account of the protagonist in a short story by Norman Mailer, 'The Time of Her Time'. For this man, 'a female laid is a female subjugated', his penis is the 'avenger'. Enraged by a woman's assertion of intellectual autonomy, he determines to bring her home in order to 'grind it into her', 'lay waste to her little independence', leaving the woman 'caught', 'forced', and 'wounded' (*Sexual Politics*, pp. 324-25).

pornography to the power relations of patriarchal society.[1] Pornography is representation that objectifies women, exploits sexuality as means of domination, expresses hostility, and imputes defilement.[2] Recently the classicist Amy Richlin has drawn upon 'theories of representation [which], starting with the formulation of the gaze as male, trace the link between gender and violence'.[3] It is the nature of this pornographic gaze, she maintains, to take pleasure in sex *qua* violence, and in violence per se.

These features of the pornographic belong to ancient as well as contemporary literatures. Thus Richlin interprets the incidents of sexual violence in Ovid's *Metamorphoses* (she counts more than 50 tales of rape in this mythic history of the world), the *Fasti* (ten tales of rape in this poetic exposition of the Roman religious calendar), and the *Ars Amatoria* (two rapes in the witty 'Art of Loving'). It is only recently that classical scholars have become willing to designate these incidents as rape—commentators have

1.   For key contributions, see A. Dworkin, *Pornography: Men Possessing Women* (New York: Putnam, Perigee, 1981); S. Griffin, *Woman and Nature: The Roaring Inside Her* (New York: Harper & Row, 1978), and *Pornography and Silence: Culture's Revenge against Nature* (New York: Harper & Row, 1981); L. Lederer (ed.), *Take Back the Night: Women on Pornography* (New York: Bantam, 1980); A. Echols, 'The New Feminism of Yin and Yang', in A. Snitow, C. Stansell and S. Thompson (eds.), *Powers of Desire: The Politics of Sexuality* (New York: Monthly Review Press, 1983), pp. 439-59; S. Gubar, 'Representing Pornography: Feminism, Criticism, and Depictions of Female Violation', *Critical Inquiry* 13 (1987), pp. 712-41.

2.   Cf. T.D. Setel's characterization of pornographic representation: '(1) Female sexuality is depicted as negative in relation to a positive and neutral male standard; (2) women are degraded and publicly humiliated; and (3) female sexuality is portrayed as an object of male possession and control' ('Prophets and Pornography: Female Sexual Imagery in Hosea', in L. Russell [ed.], *Feminist Interpretation of the Bible* [Philadelphia: Westminster Press, 1985], p. 87).

3.   'Reading Ovid's Rapes', in A. Richlin (ed.), *Pornography and Representation in Greece and Rome* (New York and Oxford: Oxford University Press, 1992), p. 160. Richlin refers to J. Berger, *Ways of Seeing* (Harmondsworth: Penguin; London: British Broadcasting Corporation, 1972); E.A. Kaplan, 'Is the Gaze Male?', in Snitow, Stansell and Thompson (eds.), *Powers of Desire*, pp. 309-27; and T. de Lauretis, *Alice Doesn't: Feminism, Semiotics, Cinema* (Bloomington: Indiana University Press, 1984).

customarily called them 'seductions' or 'abductions'—and some who do describe these incidents as rape would argue that Ovid sympathizes affirmatively with the rape victims.[1] Richlin, however, concludes that 'the place of rape in Ovid's texts is...one where pleasure and violence intersect'. In Ovid, Richlin maintains, 'fear is beautiful'.[2] Thus she rejects the possibility that Ovid is a metapornographer, or a subversive critic of sexual aggression: 'if the *Metamorphoses* lays bare a cruel cosmos, it does so voluptuously'.[3]

Ovid also exults in the mixing of erotic and military language. Leslie Cahoon has observed that 'throughout all three books of Ovid's *Amores*, the lover's life is repeatedly described in terms either of conquering the beloved, or of being conquered, taken captive, and enslaved'.[4] Ovid adopts the motto, *militat omnis amans*, 'every lover is a soldier' (1.9), and repeatedly represents the beloved as a city to which the lover lays siege. The lover of the *Amores* resorts to rape, described in unequivocal terms. And yet, by replacing graphic sexual terms with military language the poet masks the 'lover's' offense. The language of victory drowns out the cries of the victim.

In Cahoon's view, the martial imagery for love in Ovid 'suggests that the love of the *Amores* is inherently violent and linked with the Roman *libido dominandi*'.[5] We would agree with

---

1. For a discussion of the tendency (on the part of modern translators and critics) to obscure the rapes committed by the heroes of Roman comedy by referring to acts of sexual assault as 'adventures', 'amours', and 'seductions', see Z.M. Packman, 'Call it Rape: A Motif in Roman Comedy and its Suppression in English-Speaking Publications', *Helios* 20 (1993), pp. 42-55. Commentators who rehabilitate Ovid's treatment of rape victims include: L.C. Curran, 'Rape and Rape Victims in the *Metamorphoses*', in J. Peradotto and J.P. Sullivan (eds.), *Women in the Ancient World: The Arethusa Papers* (SUNY Series in Classical Studies; Albany: State University of New York Press, 1984), pp. 263-86; and J. Hemker, 'Rape and the Founding of Rome', *Helios* 12 (1985), pp. 41-47.

2. 'Reading Ovid's Rapes', p. 165.

3. 'Reading Ovid's Rapes', p. 176.

4. L. Cahoon, 'The Bed as Battlefield: Erotic Conquest and Military Metaphor in Ovid's *Amores*', *Transactions of the American Philological Association* 118 (1988), p. 293.

5. Cahoon, 'The Bed as Battlefield', p. 294.

this assessment, adding only that the association of sexual violence, military motifs and imperial ideology is no special property of ancient Rome. This complex appears widely in ancient Near Eastern and Mediterranean cultures, wherever the urban state secures its territory and subdues others through military means. With this comparative framework in view, then, we proceed to examine rape as a military metaphor in the Hebrew Bible.

The Semantic Field of Sexual and Military Assault in Biblical Hebrew

> We have inherited a contaminated language (M. Daly,
> *Gyn/Ecology: The Metaethics of Radical Feminism*, 1978).

The technical term for rape in biblical Hebrew derives from the verbal root עָנָה II (Deut. 21.14; 22.24, 29; Gen. 34.2; Judg. 19.24; 20.4; 2 Sam. 13.12, 14, 22, 32; Lam. 5.11).[1] From a basic sense of 'to be bowed down, afflicted' in the G stem, the verb takes a meaning of 'to abuse, exploit' in the D. The verb עִנָּה occurs in contexts where a sexual sense is unlikely (for example, Sarah's treatment of Hagar, Gen. 16.6, 9), but in sexual contexts the meaning is 'to force sexual intercourse upon'.[2]

עִנָּה, however, is also used to denote military assault, or the defeat and exploitation of one nation by another. For example, the last of Balaam's oracles (notwithstanding textual difficulties), clearly envisions a punitive military expedition against Assyria, mobilized out of Cyprus:

> Ships will come from Kittim,
> and they will assault Asshur and Eber (Num. 24.24).

---

1. See *HALAT*, III, pp. 807-808.
2. Tikvah Frymer-Kensky maintains that in the contexts where עִנָּה is usually translated 'rape', only rarely does the term actually denote forcible rape. Rather it implies abusive treatment; in sexual contexts it denotes sex with someone with whom one has no right to have sex (*In the Wake of the Goddesses: Women, Culture, and the Biblical Transformation of Pagan Myth* [New York: Free Press, 1992], pp. 192, 274 n. 34). This may be arguable for contexts such as Ezek. 22.10-11, but we find incredible Frymer-Kensky's assertion that Deut. 21.10-13 'seems to imply, not only an absence of force, but a failure of sex' (p. 192). The woman is a war captive, chosen for her beauty, of whom the text stipulates 'you may go into her' (תָּבוֹא אֵלֶיהָ).

וְצִיִּים מִיַּד כִּתִּים
וְעִנּוּ אַשּׁוּר וְעִנּוּ צֵבֶר

In several contexts the action of the verb עִנָּה is attributed to the military oppressors of Israel, for example, 2 Sam. 7.10:

> And I will appoint a place for my people Israel
> …and evildoers shall abuse them no more
> וְלֹא־יֹסִיפוּ בְנֵי־עַוְלָה לְעַנּוֹתוֹ כַּאֲשֶׁר בָּרִאשׁוֹנָה
> (cf. Ps. 94.5; Isa. 60.14; Zeph. 3.19).

It would go too far to suggest that עִנָּה in these contexts should be translated 'rape', but this lexical group, including within a single semantic field the senses of 'to rape' and 'to assault, exploit militarily' certainly resembles the contemporary use of the terminology of sexual violence for military assault.

This view of the verb עִנָּה suggests that the sexual language of biblical Hebrew inscribes a pattern of domination and submission more extensively than is generally recognized. For example, the verb ענה (G) has been interpreted in erotic contexts as an instance of ענה I, and has been translated either 'to answer, respond' or 'to love'. We would argue that the term in such contexts derives from ענה II, here with the sense of 'to bend, submit'. Thus Hos. 2.16-17, for example, should be translated:

> Therefore, I will now entice her,
> and bring her into the wilderness,
> and speak to her heart…
> and there she will submit (וְעָנְתָה)
> as in the days of her youth.[1]

---

1. For עָנָה as 'to love', see A. Deem, 'The Goddess Anath and Some Biblical Hebrew Cruces', *JSS* 23 (1978), p. 27; B. Glazier-McDonald, 'Malachi 2:12: *'ēr wᵉ'ōneh*—Another Look', *JBL* 105 (1986), p. 296. The LXX, καὶ ταπεινωθήσεται, 'and she will be humbled', agrees with our rendering of וְעָנְתָה in Hos. 2.17 (compare Hos. 2.16-17 with Deut. 8.2, and cf. the comments of F.I. Andersen and D.N. Freedman, *Hosea: A New Translation with Introduction and Commentary* [AB, 24; Garden City, NY: Doubleday, 1980], p. 277).

The Besieged City as Raped Woman: Critique of a Biblical Metaphor

> Patriarchal poetry makes no mistake (G. Stein, *Bee Time Vine and Other Pieces*, 1953).

The personification of Jerusalem as 'Daughter Zion', בת ציון, occurs most often in contexts of military catastrophe.[1] In Lamentations 1–2, for example, Daughter Zion is mourned as a formerly beautiful woman, now raped and abandoned by the enemy. The description of God's punishment of Jerusalem seamlessly joins together the language of sexual and military violence. God 'strips, smashes, razes, cuts down, and lays waste'.[2] Alan Mintz comments:

> The force of this image of violation is founded on the correspondence body//Temple and genitals//Inner Sanctuary. So far have things gone that even in the secret place of intimacy to which only the single sacred partner may be admitted, the enemy has thrust himself and 'spread his hands over everything dear to her' (1.10). Violated and desolate, Fair Zion's nakedness (the Hebrew *'ervah* conveys both physical nakedness and sexual disgrace) lies exposed for the world to see.[3]

Mic. 4.11 depicts the punishment of Jerusalem as sexual humiliation:

> Now many nations are assembled against you
> saying, 'Let her be profaned,
> and let our eyes gaze upon Zion.'

---

1. See A. Fitzgerald, 'The Mythological Background for the Presentation of Jerusalem as a Queen and False Worship as Adultery in the OT', *CBQ* 34 (1972), p. 416; and *'BTWLT* and *BT* as Titles for Capital Cities', *CBQ* 37 (1975), p. 182.

2. A. Mintz, 'The Rhetoric of Lamentations and the Representation of Catastrophe', *Prooftexts* 2 (1982), p. 6.

3. Mintz, 'The Rhetoric of Lamentations', p. 4; on similar imagery in Ezek. 7.22, see J. Galambush, *Jerusalem in the Book of Ezekiel: The City as Yahweh's Wife* (SBLDS, 130; Atlanta: Scholars Press, 1992), p. 160. Note also how the language of devastation referred to Jerusalem in Lamentations corresponds to that applied to rape victims in Hebrew narrative; for example Tamar, 2 Sam. 13.20 (שממה; cf. Lam. 1.13, 16; 3.11).

Jeremiah 6 combines sexual and siege language in the depiction of an assault on Jerusalem by forces from the north: 'Prepare war against her; up, and let us attack at noon!' (6.4) cry the attackers, of whom it is said 'they will go into her'(אֵלֶיהָ יָבֹאוּ, 6.3), a phrase whose sexual connotations are undeniable. Likewise Jer. 13.20-27 describes the attack of Jerusalem as a rape. At the approach of 'those who go in' (הַבָּאִים, 13.30),[1] YHWH threatens Jerusalem with sexual abuse:

> It is for the greatness of your iniquity
> that your skirts are lifted up,
> and you are violated (13.22).
> I myself will lift up your skirts over your face
> and your shame will be seen (13.26).

Here the biblical commentators have noticed only the exposure of the woman's body, but our reading recognizes also the pornographic defacement/de-facing of the victim: as the skirt is pulled over her face the woman is dehumanized.

In Isa. 47.1-3, the city of Babylon, personified as a young woman, becomes the prey of attacking soldiers, sexually abused and humiliated:

> Come down and sit in the dust, maiden daughter Babylon!
> Sit on the ground without a throne, daughter Chaldea!
> For you shall no more be called tender and delicate.
> Take the millstones and grind[2] meal, remove your veil,
> Strip off your skirt, uncover your thigh, pass through the rivers.
> Your nakedness shall be uncovered, and your shame shall be seen.
> I will take vengeance, and I will spare no one.

To this can be compared the words addressed to Nineveh in Nah. 3.5-6 which we quoted at the beginning of this essay. These images of the besieged city as a sexually assaulted woman raise three questions: why is there a woman in this picture?; why is she beautiful?; and why is she guilty? The pornographic

---

1.   Here again the sexual connotation of the language is clear; cf. W.L. Holladay, *Jeremiah 1: A Commentary on the Book of the Prophet Jeremiah Chapters 1-25* (Hermeneia; Philadelphia: Fortress Press, 1986), p. 414.

2.   Most interpreters recognize the sexual connotations of the verb טחן in this context. Cf. *HALAT*, II, p. 358; Job 31.10; Lam. 5.13; and the commentaries.

model helps to answer these questions: the pattern here is of objectification of the female, sexual domination and abuse, and defilement. Finally we raise a fourth question, to which the pornographic model is also relevant: who is the reader?

Why is there a Woman in this Picture?

Is the prominence of this feminine figure simply a semantic accident of the feminine grammatical gender of the biblical Hebrew word for 'city', עִיר? Many interpreters seem to accept this explanation.[1] Similar feminine personifications of cities, however, occur in Mesopotamian sources where the word for city is either masculine (Akkadian ālu) or neuter (Sumerian *URU*).[2] The figure of city as woman thus cannot be explained as an incidental function of grammatical gender. Even in languages that have no grammatical gender, comparable feminine personifications inscribe patriarchal ideology.[3] In English, for example, cities, ships, nations, automobiles, and other things over which men wield power are construed as feminine (so, for example, 'the ship of State'). Likewise objects that inspire terror because they do not submit to control (for example hurricanes, until recently given women's names by American metereologists)

1. For example, J.J. Schmitt, 'The Motherhood of God and Zion as Mother', *RB* 92 (1985), p. 568; M. Biddle, 'The Figure of Lady Jerusalem: Identification, Deification and Personification of Cities in the Ancient Near East', in B. Batto, W. Hallo and L. Younger (eds.), *The Canon in Comparative Perspective* (Scripture in Context, 4; Lewiston, Queenston and Lampeter: Mellen Press, 1991), p. 175.

2. J. Lewy demonstrates that Mesopotamian cities were personified as feminine on the basis of Akkadian city names (for example, 'The city of Assur is Queen') and personal names where city names function as feminine theophoric elements ('The Old West Semitic Sun God Ḥammu', *HUCA* 18 [1944], pp. 436-54; cf. Fitzgerald, 'The Mythological Background for the Presentation of Jerusalem as a Queen', pp. 405-406; and Galambush, *Jerusalem in the Book of Ezekiel*, p. 20). Galambush likewise notes: 'In the Sumerian lamentation over the destruction of Ur (*ANET*, 455-63), the city is personified both as a queen weeping over her palace, and as the mother of the city's inhabitants' (p. 22 n. 86).

3. Cf. D. Cameron, *Feminism and Linguistic Theory* (London: Macmillan, 1985), pp. 62-71; C. Miller and K. Swift, *The Handbook of Nonsexist Writing: For Writers, Editors, and Speakers* (New York: Harper & Row, 2nd edn, 1988), pp. 75-79.

become feminine in patriarchal discourse. Control (by men) and subordination (or the lack of it, by women) are the subtexts of these feminine personifications.

Historically, the biblical figure of city as woman is thought to have originated in the common ancient Near Eastern conception of a capital city as a goddess who is the wife (thus, the subordinate possession) of the patron god of the city.[1] Thus the social base of the biblical metaphor of city as woman is the patriarchal household, with its ever present threat of violence as a sanction for the control of women (see for example Deut. 22.20-21, the law providing for the death by stoning of a young bride who is found not to be a virgin). As the husband holds mortal sway over the woman, so YHWH holds the threat of brutal retribution against the insubordinate city (or its people). The intrinsic violence of the city-as-woman metaphor is grounded in men's violent control of women in ancient Near Eastern societies.

Significantly, the biblical figure of raped woman as besieged city stands for both Jerusalem/Zion *and* foreign cities (Babylon, Ashur, and so on). Ostensibly the figure can represent both 'us' and 'them' for Israelites/Judeans, but the city as an object of violence is always a *feminine* Other, reenforcing the status of the feminine as secondary, and facilitating a pornographic objecti-fication of women by setting the female as the model victim.

Why is she Beautiful?
In Jer. 6.2 the divine voice threatens: 'the comely and delicately bred I will destroy, the daughter of Zion'. The whole of Lamentations 1–2 depicts the city as a once lovely young woman, now abused and despised. In Mic. 1.10-16, five times the inhabitants of Judean cities threatened with destruction are personified as a feminine collective 'indweller', יוֹשֶׁבֶת. The place names create a series of word-plays on the imminent destruction of the locations mentioned. The place name שָׁפִיר derives from the root שפר, 'to be beautiful', so the phrase 'go on your way, inhabitant of Shapir, in nakedness and shame' (Mic. 1.11a)

---

1.   Galumbush, *Jerusalem in the Book of Ezekiel*, pp. 20-23; Fitzgerald, 'The Mythological Background for the Presentation of Jerusalem as a Queen'.

depicts military devastation by evoking the image of the sexual humiliation of beautiful women.[1] Elsewhere Jeremiah addresses the holy city:

> And you, O desolate one,
> what do you mean dressing in scarlet
> binding on ornaments of gold,
> smearing your eyes with paint?
> In vain you beautify yourself.
> Your lovers despise you; they seek your life (Jer. 4.30-31).

How should we understand this fascination with the doomed woman's beauty? We take it as an example of the inveterate feature of patriarchal language that can be termed the '*meretrix/madonna* complex' (the whore and the virgin), a conceptual scheme that reduces woman to sexual function, constrains her role to that of the object of male control, and values the feminine figure contingent upon her accommodation to male control.[2] In the Hebrew Bible the city personified as a woman is often designated as בתולה, 'young woman' (not necessarily 'virgin', but nubile), either alone or prefixed to בת (2 Kgs. 19.21; Isa. 37.22; 47.1; Jer. 14.17; 18.13; 31.4, 21; 46.11; Lam. 1.15; 2.13; Amos 5.2).[3] As בתולה, the woman is marked as both sexually desirable and available. Before her violation, the young woman fulfills the role of virginal object of male fantasy; after she is abused, she becomes the 'harlotrous'—yet still beautiful—object of male scorn. By implying that only the beautiful are raped, these texts treat rape as though it were the 'natural' result of male desire. This serves to disguise aggression as an act of 'love'

---

1. Cf. H.W. Wolff, *Micah: A Commentary* (Minneapolis: Augsburg Fortress, 1990), p. 60: 'The play on words here is a play on meaning; what is graceful (שׁפר = 'beautiful', 'fair', BDB) will be disgraced'.

2. For the designation '*meretrix/madonna* complex', see H.C. Washington, 'The Strange Woman of Proverbs 1-9 and Post-Exilic Judean Society', in T.C. Eskenazi and K.H. Richards (eds.), *Second Temple Studies 2. Temple and Community in the Persian Period* (JSOTSup, 175; Sheffield: JSOT Press, 1994), pp. 217-42.

3. See W.F. Stinespring, 'No Daughter of Zion: A Study of the Appositional Genitive in Hebrew Grammar', *Encounter* 26 (1965), p. 139; for additional examples, Fitzgerald, '*BTWLT* and *BT* as Titles for Capital Cities', p. 168 n. 2.

and begins the process of placing the blame on the woman.

This combination of erotic pleasure and sexual violence is irredeemably disturbing. Leslie Cahoon gives a helpful assessment of similar aspects of rape incidents in Ovid. The 'lover' at *Amores* 1.7.11-18, she observes, rapes a woman, pretends to regret his violence, but then goes on to express delight in her victimization, comparing her to mythological figures such as Atalanta, Ariadne and Cassandra. 'To rate them in terms of their beauty under such circumstances', Cahoon states, 'is grotesque... As elsewhere, (e.g., *Am.* 2.5.44-46), the lover regards a woman's grief as a sexual attraction'.[1] We would argue that the biblical texts we are considering offer to the male gaze the same pornographic pleasure.[2] In the biblical context, pornography becomes an iconography of violence.

Why is She Guilty?
The manner of the *meretrix/madonna* complex is to blame the victim, regarding a woman whose sexuality is outside the control of her male master as spoiled, even if she were helplessly assaulted by another man. The woman becomes guilty by default—responsibility and victimization are collapsed into a single complex. Thus Lam. 1.8: 'Jerusalem sinned grievously, so she has become a mockery' (נִידָה). While commonly translated 'mockery', the term נִידָה inescapably alludes to the term נִדָּה, 'unclean' (cf. 1.17), hence 'menstruating' (see for example Lev. 12.2, 5; 15.19-26).[3] The text presents Daughter Zion as a

---

1.　Cahoon, 'The Bed as Battlefield', pp. 296-97.

2.　For the present we employ the concept of a 'male gaze' as a heuristic category from the theoretical discussion of pornography, leaving aside such questions as whether there is a 'female gaze': how is the possibility of women's complicity in the social function of these texts to be understood (cf. Richlin, 'Reading Ovid's Rapes', p. 160)? Distinguishing the 'male gaze' from the male reader allows us to avoid the suggestion that all men, or only men, appropriate the texts as pornographic.

3.　See Frymer-Kensky, *In the Wake of the Goddesses*, p. 269; R. Gordis, *The Song of Songs and Lamentations: A Study, Modern Translation, and Commentary* (New York: KTAV, 1974), p. 155; Hillers, *Lamentations*, pp. 9-10, 23; B. Albrektson, *Studies in the Text and Theology of the Book of Lamentations with a Critical Edition of the Peshitta Text* (Studia Theologica Lundensia; Lund: Gleerup, 1963), p. 64.

menstruating woman, thus bearing, in the masculinist view of the text, the inherent feminine stain. She is abhorrent to the male gaze: 'her uncleanness (טֻמְאָתָהּ) is upon her' (Lam. 1.9). But here we must ask whether the woman is only menstruating, or is she also bleeding from an attack? The biblical poet's use of the metaphor here has the ghastly capacity to sustain both images.

Female sexuality is viewed here as intrinsically negative, and is used as a vehicle for 'proving' the assumption that the female is inherently guilty. Establishing woman per se as guilty then legitimates masculine violence (sexual and martial) as punishment. Woman becomes the type of the failure of the people; her sexual culpability typifies the general moral guilt of the people. Both are presented as the objects of justified retribution, sexual violence against the woman, military violence against the people. The two types of violence are validated as a self-sustaining binary complex. Tikvah Frymer-Kensky offers the following commentary on the בת ציון motif:

> The Wanton Wife and Zion-as-woman express two different aspects of the imagery of God and Israel. It is a bifurcated image, almost the classic 'whore' and 'virgin'. Both represent the difficulty of being God's partner: we are angry at the 'whore' when she fails God, we are sorry for the maiden when she is punished. This image of the ruined maiden-victim enables the reader to empathize with the people, to forget the cause of the devastation and join in the sorrow.[1]

But who, we ask, is the 'we' of this commentary, and what does it mean for us uncritically to accept this bifurcation of the feminine, comporting ourselves as both 'angry at the whore' and 'sorry for the maiden'? What is the consequence of 'forgetting the cause of the devastation'? It is often asserted that the metaphorical picture of God punishing Israel in the manner of a violent husband punishing his wife does not necessarily endorse men's arbitrary and violent punishment of women. But to the assertion that this figurative complex does not identify the feminine with the guilty and does not sanction male violence against women, we would respond with the question posed by Fokkelien van Dijk-Hemmes: 'Why is Israel,

1. *In the Wake of the Goddesses*, p. 169.

first the land but then also the nation, represented in the image of a faithless wife, a harlot, and not in the image of e.g. a rapist?'[1] In other words, why is Israel (when guilty), portrayed as a sexually transgressive woman, and not as a man?

Conclusions

> Canons and cannons have more in common than the accident of sounding alike (L. Hanley, *Writing War: Fiction, Gender and Memory*, 1991).

Consequences of the Biblical Language

The results of the fusing of rape and military imagery in the Hebrew Bible are ambiguous at best. The language gives a grim and realistic reminder of the fate of women in war (Deut. 21.14; Lam. 5.11). But most problematic is the fact that the figure coopts women's experience and diminishes the first term of the comparison, the woman herself. The city, portrayed as the devastated בת ציון, may be vindicated and restored:

> You shall be a crown of beauty in the hand of YHWH,
> and a royal diadem in the hand of your God...
> For as a young man marries a young woman,
> so shall your builder marry you,
> and as the bridegroom rejoices over the bride,
> so shall your God rejoice over you (Isa. 62.3-5).

But in this conversion to a salvific motif the actual women of biblical antiquity are left behind. The renewed Holy City of post-exilic prophecy erases the reality of abused women, for whom such restoration was impossible.

Conventional commentators have often contributed to this erasure by trivializing the rape metaphor. For example, the author of the *IDBSup* article 'Zion, Daughter of', in his lengthier

---

1. Van Dijk-Hemmes is discussing Hosea here ('The Imagination of Power and the Power of Imagination: An Intertextual Analysis of Two Biblical Love Songs: The Songs of Songs and Hosea 2', *JSOT* 44 [1989], p. 85). Criticism of male lust appears elsewhere in the prophetic literature (cf. Jer 5.8), but this does not lessen the significance of the dominant pattern, where female sexuality is the principal figure for the portrayal of guilt.

1964 study of the appositional genitive, explains the rhetorical force of the metaphor by observing: 'Nothing is more touching than a ravished maiden'.[1] A basic study of the female person-ification of Jerusalem takes little account of the violence associ-ated with her apart from the gratuitous observation that 'violence done to a delicate young mother is violence indeed'.[2] An important commentator on Jeremiah decorates his discussion of ch. 6 with the supercilious remark that 'Daughter Zion...is about to become the object of unwelcome attentions'.[3] Such exegetical gallantry—often the woman is called 'girl' even if she is depicted as the mother of many children—can only deepen the dismay of some readers, who will ineluctably ask our fourth question: who is the reader? The conventional commentators assume that they, identifying with the traditional male voice, can speak for us.

Resisting the Metaphor (Why we Assert that 'Rape is Rape')
Rape as a military metaphor is masculinist language: it formulates and promotes an unchallenged masculine authority that sanctions both violent sexual acts and the mayhem of warfare. If we submit to this language uncritically, we resign ourselves to the view that 'men are like that'.[4] But resistance is imperative because no one is safe in the environment created by such rhetoric. Women are allotted the role of victim, and men are expected to pursue with equal enthusiasm both sexual domina-tion and 'war, the ultimate adventure'.[5]

If the dominant interpretive tradition has worsened the problem of rape imagery in the Hebrew Bible, how should we read the texts now? Or should we read them at all? Amy Richlin

1.   'No Daughter of Zion', p. 136; cf. W.F. Stinespring, 'Zion, Daughter Of', in *IDBSup*, p. 985.
2.   Fitzgerald, 'The Mythological Background for the Presentation of Jerusalem as a Queen', p. 416.
3.   R.P. Carroll, *Jeremiah: A Commentary* (OTL; Philadelphia: Westminster Press, 1986), p. 191.
4.   This phrase was the original working title for Virginia Woolf's pio-neering treatise on feminism as an anti-militarist movement, eventually published as *Three Guineas*; L. Hanley, *Writing War: Fiction, Gender, and Memory* (Amherst: University of Massachusetts Press, 1991), p. 62.
5.   Caputo, *A Rumor of War*, p. 6.

suggests, at the end of her study on 'Reading Ovid's Rapes', that one option is to 'blow up the canon'.[1] The classical and biblical canons, which have made such monumental contributions to the gender ideologies of 'Western civilization', can be subverted, displaced, or replaced.

We are reluctant, however, to attack one violent metaphor with another. Instead, we borrow from Richlin an answer she has borrowed from Toni Morrison. After discussing many Ovidian rapes, Richlin returns to Philomela, a victim in the *Metamorphoses* whom the rapist silences by cutting out her tongue:

> We're stuck with Philomela; she's like Beloved, the dearly beloved ghost of grief, and to be blind to her is not to exorcise her. We need to know her and keep faith with history.[2]

So we are stuck with בת ציון, the defiled and bleeding Daughter Zion. But as we acknowledge the raped women in the biblical literature, we must disengage ourselves from the company of the presumed masculine reader who sees a logic in, and takes pleasure in, the victimization of women. The literary critic Judith Fetterley, author of *The Resisting Reader* (1978), has described how patriarchal literature 'not only places women in a subordinate role but prompts the reader to identify with a point of view that is actively derogatory to women'.[3] Like Fetterley, we refuse to take that point of view.

Furthermore, we resist the metaphor; we accept neither the devastated woman as the appropriate representation of punishment, nor the conquered city as the licit object of military conquest. We reject the equation of bad women and bad cities, and we reject the idea that male violence (sexual and military) delivers just punishment. Instead we choose to take the biblical

1. 'Canons,' she continues, 'are part of social systems. We recognize the one we have as dysfunctional. It must and will change; we can surely critique the pleasure of the text without fear of breaking anything irreplaceable' ('Reading Ovid's Rapes', p. 179).

2. 'Reading Ovid's Rapes', pp. 178-79.

3. H. Montague, 'Sweet and Pleasant Passion: Female and Male Fantasy in Ancient Romance Novels', in Richlin (ed.), *Pornography and Representation* p. 246; cf. J. Fetterley, *The Resisting Reader: A Feminist Approach to American Fiction* (Bloomington and London: Indiana University Press, 1978).

figure *literally* as an emblem of the profoundest desolation, dwelling with this sense before moving facilely to a vision of redemption like that of Third Isaiah, where the raped woman is restored to the status of a cherished virginal bride. Such a transformation is possible in the theological celebration of the new Jerusalem, but it was not possible for women who suffered sexual violence in biblical antiquity, not in a culture where the only sanctioned remedy for rape, provided that the victim was young and unmarried, was for a woman to be married to her rapist. So we suggest in conclusion that it is necessary for us to renounce, for a moment, the use of the raped woman as a metaphorical figure of something else—a feminine city assaulted by an army of men. In refusing to read this biblical metaphor uncritically, we begin to unravel the linguistic network that sustains what Mary Daly has called the 'Patriarchal State of War'. Likewise, we acknowledge the incapacity of the received language to redeem the suffering of abused women through the millennia.

It has been claimed that Lam. 2.13 is one of the most important passages in biblical literature, because here the poet realizes the enormity of the destruction of the holy city by admitting the futility of his rhetoric, its incapacity to conceive the harm, much less to console.[1] We might address the biblical poet's question to the very women who provided the term of comparison for describing the broken city as a raped woman:

> What can I compare or liken to you?
> What can I match with you to console you,
> For your devastation is as vast as the sea:
> Who can heal you?

In response to this question we should observe an honest silence.

---

1. Mintz, 'The Rhetoric of Lamentations', pp. 6-7.

ANCIENT NEAR EASTERN TREATY-CURSES AND THE ULTIMATE TEXTS OF TERROR: A STUDY OF THE LANGUAGE OF DIVINE SEXUAL ABUSE IN THE PROPHETIC CORPUS*

F. Rachel Magdalene

Introduction

Phyllis Trible in her book *Texts of Terror: Literary-Feminist Readings of Biblical Narratives* analyses four tales which reflect the status of women in biblical narrative. These tales narrate stories involving the rejection, rape, dismemberment and sacrifice of women of the Hebrew Bible. Trible calls such texts 'texts of terror' and says that she 'recounts these tales of terror *in memoriam* to offer sympathetic readings of abused women...in order to recover a neglected history, to remember a past that the present eludes, and to pray that these terrors shall not come to pass again'.[1]

Trible chooses the biblical story of Jacob's wrestling at the Jabbok (Gen. 32.22-32) to ground and support her study. Her understanding of God's role in the texts of terror is revealed by the wrestling scene. She states:

> As a paradigm for encountering terror, this story offers sustenance for the present journey. To tell and hear tales of terror is

---

* A condensed version of this article was read before the Narrative Research on the Hebrew Bible Group session of the 1994 Annual Meeting of the Society of Biblical Literature. I wish to thank Judith Sanderson and Gracia Fay Ellwood for first calling my attention through their writings to the biblical metaphor 'God the rapist'. While not forgetting any of the victims of sexual violence, I also wish to dedicate this article specifically to the multitude of victims of satanic cult ritual abuse who were, and are, told over and over again: 'God is a rapist'.

1. P. Trible, *Texts of Terror: Literary-Feminist Readings of Biblical Narratives* (Philadelphia: Fortress Press, 1984), p. 3.

to wrestle demons in the night, without a compassionate God to save us. In combat we wonder about the names of the demons.[1]

Here, she expresses the view that God is either absent or present, yet acting without compassion, when we encounter these demon texts. She implies, however, that in the texts of terror themselves God is also either absent or present, yet acting without compassion: men perpetrate evil against women and God seemingly does not intervene.

This lack of intervention forces us to ponder the role of the divine in such violence against women and whether God is anywhere characterized by biblical authors as an active, rather than passive, perpetrator of gender-based violence. We find such texts within the Latter Prophets: Isa. 3.17-26; 47.1-4; Jer. 13.22-26; Ezek. 16.35-39; 23.9-10, 26-29; Hos. 2.4-5 (Eng. 2.2-3), 11-12 (Eng. 9-10); Nah. 2.7-8 (Eng. 2.6-7); 3.5, 13; and Zech. 14.2.[2]

Within these verses, God, characterized as male, is regularly threatening, in judgment, to rape, or otherwise sexually abuse, the cities of Israel, Judah and their neighbors, all characterized as female. Metaphorically then, God is seemingly quite willing to perpetrate repeated sexual assaults and abuse on women. Such texts are the ultimate in biblical texts of terror. Not only is God a passive participant in the sexual assaults on and abuse of women in the narrative portions of the Hebrew Bible by his[3] lack of intervention on behalf of the raped and abused, God is an active perpetrator of such sexual violence against women in the prophetic corpus of the Bible.

I utilize several different methodologies within this article. First, I examine, through literary analysis and feminist political theory, how the metaphor operates. Then I turn to comparative historical analysis and sociological study to reveal the origins of the metaphor and why the metaphor is used repeatedly to

1. Trible, *Texts of Terror*, p. 4.
2. While there are potentially other verses in both the poetic and narrative portions of the Bible where God is characterized as engaging in sexual abuse, I will focus my efforts upon the above named texts.
3. I use 'his' intentionally throughout this paper because, in the prophetic texts of terror, the conception of God is male. By such usage, I do not intend to suggest that this is the best understanding of God.

convey God's wrath over human disobedience. Finally, the paper addresses the feminist hermeneutical questions raised by these ultimate texts of terror.

The Metaphor

What are rape and sexual abuse? According to Brownmiller, the modern definition of rape, from a woman's point of view, is both simple and straightforward: 'If a woman chooses not to have intercourse [or, I would add, any other intimate sexual act] with a specific man and the man chooses to proceed against her will, that is a criminal act of rape'.[1] Rape is, to Brownmiller's mind, 'the real-life deployment of the penis as weapon'.[2] I define sexual abuse as 'any act with a sexual connotation or result that is used in order to objectify, dominate, hurt, or humiliate an individual'.[3] This includes such acts as rape and the public or private stripping of an individual.

Thus, the initial questions before us are: does God engage in rape or other forms of sexual abuse within the prophetic corpus, and, if so, is that how ancient Israelites understood such acts? In order to answer these questions, we must first understand that God, in the texts under study, acts in two ways. He acts directly, yet metaphorically, on the female cities of Israel, Judah and their neighbors, or he acts physically, yet indirectly through human agency, on the women of Israel and Judah.

Let us first examine the metaphorical materials. In Jer. 13.22b, God metaphorically sexually assaults Jerusalem:

> it is for the greatness of your iniquity
> that your skirts are lifted up,
> your buttocks suffer violence (my translation).[4]

1. S. Brownmiller, *Against Our Will: Men, Women and Rape* (New York: Simon & Schuster, 1975), p. 18.
2. Brownmiller, *Against Our Will*, p. 11.
3. For general discussions of sexual abuse, with definition, and its implications in a religious context see G.F. Ellwood, *Batter My Heart* (Wallingford, PA: Pendleton Hill Pamphlets, 1988); M. Fortune, *Sexual Violence: The Unmentionable Sin* (New York: Pilgrim Press, 1983); C.H. Heggen, *Sexual Abuse in Christian Homes and Churches* (Scottsdale, PA: Herald Press, 1993).
4. It should be noted that I have used the NRSV translation except

In v. 26, God continues, now de-facing and de-personalizing Jerusalem:

> I myself will lift up your skirts over your face,
> and your shame will be seen.[1]

In Nahum, God directs similar language toward Nineveh. Nah. 3.5 states:

> I am against you,
> says the LORD of hosts,
> and will lift up your skirts over your face;
> and I will let nations look on your nakedness
> and kingdoms on your shame.

where otherwise indicated. With respect to the verse under discussion, 'buttocks' is rendered as 'heels' in the euphemistic Hebrew. See also Gen. 49.19; Josh. 8.13; and BDB, p. 784. This is similar to the use of the word 'feet' in reference to male genitalia in Ruth 3.4, 7, 8, 14; Isa. 7.20; Dan. 10.6. The reader might note that the text is cleaned up in several English translations of this passage. RSV and NRSV have 'that your skirts are lifted up and you are violated'; NIV has 'that your skirts have been torn off and your body mistreated'; NEB has 'your skirts are torn off and your limbs uncovered'; JPSV has 'that your skirts are lifted up, your limbs exposed'; NJB has 'that your skirts have been pulled up and you have been manhandled' (though in their note the editors state, 'lit. "your heels have been ravished": euphemism'). One might ask: what does it mean to have one's buttocks violated in this context? Could the act of sodomy be that which is under discussion? The verb חמס appears seven times in the Hebrew Bible outside of this text (Jer. 22.3; Ezek. 22.26; Zeph. 3.4; Job 15.33, 21.27; Prov. 8.36; Lam. 2.6), having various meanings, including 'to do physical violence', 'to break laws' and 'to profane sacred ground'. While חמס does not appear to mean sexual violence in these other texts, it might well be construed to mean such here. First, the word 'skirt', שולים, and its synonym כנף, can have sexual connotations (Ezek. 16.8; Ruth 3.9; Lam. 1.9). Secondly, the lifting of the skirt is generally regarded as the precursor to the act of rape. Thirdly, any violence to the buttocks because of their location may be considered sexual violence even if there is no penetration.

1. 'Shame' is often translated in such a way to represent the female genitals. See for example R. Weems, 'Gomer: Victim of Violence or Victim of Metaphor?', *Semeia* 47 (1989), p. 92, 'private parts'; D.R. Hillers, *Treaty-Curses and the Old Testament Prophets* (BibOr, 16; Rome: Pontifical Biblical Institute, 1964), pp. 59-60, 'pudenda'; J. Sanderson, 'Nahum', in C. Newsom and S. Ringe (eds.), *The Women's Bible Commentary* (Louisville, KY: Westminster Press/John Knox, 1992), p. 218, 'genitals'.

Verse 6 reflects God's continued debasement of this woman:

> I will throw filth at you
> and treat you with contempt,
> and make you a spectacle.[1]

The stripping continues. For instance, God bares the female in Hos. 2.4-5a (Eng. 2.2-3a):

> Plead with your mother, plead—
> for she is not my wife,
> and I am not her husband—
> that she put away her harlotry from her face,
> and her adultery from between her breasts;
> lest I strip her naked
> and make her as in the day she was born... (RSV).

Hos. 2.11-12 (Eng. 2.9-10) resumes:

> Therefore I will take back
> my grain in its time,
> and my wine in its season;

1.   This case involves, at a minimum, the public exposure of the female genitalia in order to degrade the victim. Moreover, filth, which may be of any variety, including excrement, is thrown at the victim. T.D. Setel argues that in de-facing and de-personalizing the victim, such texts become pornographic because the act completely removes all vestiges of humanity from the female. The act is pornographic because it carries with it the following characteristics: '(1) female sexuality is depicted as negative in relation to a positive and neutral male standard; (2) women are degraded and publicly humiliated; and (3) female sexuality is portrayed as an object of male possession and control, which includes the depiction of women as analogous to nature in general and the land in particular, especially with regard to imagery of conquest and domination'; 'Prophets and Pornography: Female Sexual Imagery in Hosea', in L.M. Russell (ed.), *Feminist Interpretation of the Bible* (Philadelphia: Westminster Press, 1985), p. 87. See also P. Gordon and H.C. Washington, 'Rape as a Military Metaphor in the Hebrew Bible,' in this volume. Yet the text does not end there. This woman is humiliated in an even more extreme fashion through being the target of filth. For a distinct and fuller discussion of the difference between the erotic and the pornographic than is found in Setel, 'Prophets and Pornography', see A. Brenner, 'Porno-Prophetics: The Husband-Wife Metaphor Reconsidered' (unpublished paper presented at the Narrative Research on the Hebrew Bible Group session of the 1994 Annual Meeting of the Society of Biblical Literature, Chicago, IL, 21 November 1994).

and I will take away my wool and my flax,
which were to cover her nakedness.
Now I will uncover her indecency
in the sight of her lovers,
and no one shall rescue her out of my hand (my translation).[1]

God also utilizes human male agents to inflict such harm;
Jerusalem's lovers strip her in Ezek. 16.39:

And I will deliver you into their [your lovers'] hands, and they
shall throw down your platform and break down your lofty
places; they shall strip you of your clothes and take your beautiful
objects, and leave you naked and bare.

God also 'uncovers the nakedness' of cities and 'reveals their
shame'. The first Hebrew expression represents the most common language of offensive sexual intercourse in the Hebrew
Bible. For example, we often find variations on this language in
the legal materials of Leviticus.[2] Such language occurs in
Isa. 47.1-4, where God strips and deflowers Babylon as
revenge against Assyria for the evil deeds it has perpetrated
against Israel and Judah:

Come down and sit in the dust,
virgin daughter Babylon!
Sit on the ground without a throne,
daughter Chaldea!
For you shall no more be called
tender and delicate.
Take the millstones and grind meal,
remove your veil,
strip off your robe, uncover your legs,
pass through the rivers.
Your nakedness shall be uncovered,
and your shame shall be seen.
I will take vengeance,
and I will spare no one.

---

1.   The NRSV translates 'indecency' as 'shame'; the RSV as 'lewdness'.
Neither of these translations reflects the distinctiveness of the word utilized
here and only here in the Hebrew Bible.
2.   We see variations such as לגלות ערוה or תגלה ערותה. Lev. 18.6-19, 20.11,
17-21 offer us a wealth of such language. See also Gen. 9.22-23; Exod. 20.26;
Mic. 1.11.

Such rhetoric is also used at Ezek. 16.35-38. Yahweh declares against Jerusalem:

> Wherefore, O harlot, hear the word of the LORD: Thus says the Lord God, Because your shame was laid bare and your nakedness uncovered in your harlotries with your lovers... I will gather all your lovers, with whom you took pleasure, all those you loved and all those you loathed; I will gather them against you from every side, and will uncover your nakedness to them, that they may see all your nakedness. And I will judge you as women who break wedlock...are judged, and bring upon you the blood of wrath and jealousy (RSV).[1]

Ezek. 23.9-10, 26-29 are very similar; this time, however, God uses human agents. In vv. 9-10, God pronounces against Samaria:

> Therefore I delivered her into the hands of her lovers, into the hands of the Assyrians, for whom she lusted. These uncovered her nakedness...

In vv. 26-29, God proceeds against Jerusalem:

> They shall also strip you of your clothes and take away your fine jewels. So I will put an end to your lewdness and your harlotry... I will deliver you into the hands of those whom you hate, into the hands of those from whom you turned in disgust; and they shall...leave you naked and bare, and the nakedness of your harlotry shall be uncovered... (RSV).[2]

Some of the most disturbing rape language, however, can be found in Isa. 3.17, 26:

> the Lord will smite
> the heads of the daughters of Zion,
> and LORD will lay bear
> their opening...
> And her gates shall lament and mourn;
> ravaged, she shall sit upon the ground (my translation).

---

1. I selected the RSV translation over the NRSV because the language of shame is lost in the NRSV's translation of v. 36: 'Thus says the Lord God, Because your lust was poured out and your nakedness uncovered...'

2. I have used the RSV translation because the NRSV does not convey the sense of the uncovering of the nakedness in v. 29: '...and the nakedness of your whoring shall be exposed'. See Mic. 1.11 for similar language with respect to 'leaving naked and bare'.

'Opening', פּת, typically translated 'secret parts',[3] is a wordplay on the word for 'gate', פֶּתַח, or the opening of a city. Thus, the metaphor operates to equate both the city with the person of the female and the gate of the city with the vaginal opening of the female body. Nowhere in the Hebrew Bible is the military metaphor of the ravaged city as ravished female seen more clearly.[2]

So, too, do we see the gates opened for violation in Nah. 3.13:

> Behold, your troops
> are women in your midst.
> The gates of your land
> are to be opened wide to your enemies…(my translation).

Nah. 2.7-8 (Eng. 2.6-7) declares of God's action against Nineveh:

> The river gates are to be opened,
> the palace is helpless;
> It is determined that she be stripped, she be carried off,
> her maidens lamenting,
> moaning like doves,
> and beating their breasts (my translation).

Here, wet gates are opened and the captured, stripped woman is carried off for rape, while those who serve her suffer over her fate.[3]

---

1. BDB, p. 834; GKC, §§ 91c, 91f; see also the RSV and NRSV. BDB notes that some commentators emend the text to the word 'shame'. This retains the meaning, but loses the gate/vagina wordplay. Other Bibles avoid the stripping/rape imagery entirely by translating 'opening' as 'heads', 'pates', 'foreheads' or 'scalps'; see for example JPSV, NEB, NIV, NJB. This makes some sense because heads have openings and because this translation better respects the parallelism of Hebrew poetry, but it ignores the usually understood meaning of the word.

2. See generally on the issue of rape as a metaphor for war Gordon and Washington, 'Rape as a Military Metaphor'; and S. Thistlethwaite, '"You May Enjoy the Spoil of Your Enemies": Rape as a Biblical Metaphor for War', *Semeia* 61 (1993), pp. 59-75.

3. Other sexual violations of women by God may well exist within the pages of the Hebrew Bible. While Yahweh does not physically harm a female city in Mic. 4.11 and 7.10, he threatens to transgress visually the

Finally, we find a very different rape text within the prophetic corpus. In Zech. 14.2, concrete acts of rape are threatened by God against the real women of Jerusalem at the hand (or penis) of foreign male invaders. We move out of the metaphorical realm:

> For I will gather all the nations against Jerusalem to battle, and the city shall be taken and the houses looted and the women raped...

God brings the hand of war upon the land and the female inhabitants can expect to be raped as a part of the people's defeat.

Rape in the Ancient Near East

In viewing the above verses with contemporary sensibilities, God does appear to be very much capable of rape and other forms of sexual violence. One might claim, however, that the ancient Israelites did not see these acts as such. Numerous

boundaries of the female personified enemies of Israel and Judah at the time of Israel and Judah's redemption. Mic. 4.11 relates:

> Now many nations
> are assembled against you,
> saying, 'Let her be profaned,
> and let our eyes gaze upon Zion' (RSV).

Mic. 7.10 extends this:

> Then my enemy will see,
> and shame will cover her who said to me,
> 'Where is the Lord your God?'
> My eyes will gloat over her;
> now she will be trodden down
> like the mire of the streets (RSV).

Rape may not be occurring in these texts; yet another form of sexual degradation is happening to female cities through the shame-generating, piercing, gloating stare of Yahweh. The text is equally pornographic because it objectifies a woman, exploiting her sexuality as a means of domination, to express hostility, and to defile her. I am indebted to Gordon and Washington, 'Rape as a Military Metaphor' for pointing out these texts and their possible sexual meaning. See also generally Setel, 'Prophets and Pornography', and A. Dworkin, *Pornography: Men Possessing Women* (New York: Putnam, Perigee, 1981).

commentators have stated that the metaphor—city as female, deity as male—is a mere semantic accident caused by the feminine gender of the word עִיר, 'city', in biblical Hebrew.[1] Others claim that rape as we know it did not exist in the ancient world.

Pamela Gordon and Harold Washington ask, however, whether the prominence of the female metaphor is a 'semantic accident', as most interpreters seem to suggest, or whether gender ideology is at work in these texts. They argue that the latter is the case, noting that in languages that have no grammatical gender cities as well as other objects over which men wield power are typically feminine.[2] I must agree: gender-ideology is critical to the functioning of these texts.[3]

---

1. Gordon and Washington ('Rape as a Military Metaphor', p. 317) note the standard position and offer J.J. Schmitt, 'The Motherhood of God and Zion as Mother', *RB* 92 (1985), pp. 557-69, as a typical example.

2. Gordon and Washington, 'Rape as a Military Metaphor', p. 317. See also Sanderson, 'Nahum', p. 218; and *idem*, 'Micah', in Newsom and Ringe (eds.), *The Women's Bible Commentary*, pp. 215-16. Gordon and Washington ('Rape as a Military Metaphor') also note that the city is often not only a woman, but a young woman, which allows that '[b]efore her violation, the young woman fulfills the role of virginal object of male fantasy; after she is abused, she becomes the "harlotrous"...object of male scorn...' (p. 319 above). This is the case in Isa. 47.1-4 where Babylon is characterized as a virgin, yet will lose her tenderness and delicacy in the rape.

3. K.P. Darr ('Ezekiel', in Newsom and Ringe [eds.], *The Women's Bible Commentary*, p. 188) also recognizes the metaphor and says of the prophet Ezekiel: 'Ezekiel's choice of female imagery for Jerusalem and Samaria was not a poetic innovation. Cities frequently were personified as females within the Hebrew Bible and in other ancient Near Eastern texts as well. Neither was he the first to adopt marriage, with its demand for female (but not male) sexual fidelity, as a metaphor for the relationship between Yahweh and a city (the embodiment of its inhabitants). However, Ezekiel developed marital/adultery imagery more fully than had Hosea, Isaiah, or Jeremiah.' See similarly, with respect to Isaiah, S. Ackerman, 'Isaiah', in Newsom and Ringe (eds.), *The Women's Bible Commentary*, pp. 162-63. Setel ('Prophets and Pornography', p. 92) maintains that in Hosea 'the sexes of Gomer and Hosea and their respective behavior are not a random representation but a reflection and reinforcement of cultural perceptions. Hence, Hosea's metaphor has both theological and social meaning.' J. Galambush (*Jerusalem in the Book of Ezekiel: The City as Yahweh's Wife* {SBLDS, 130; Atlanta: Scholars Press, 1992], p. 23) discusses the view that the

Furthermore, there is no longer any question that rape existed in the ancient Near East. Commentators such as Trible, Gordon, Washington, Ariela Deem, Alice Keefe, Susan Thistlethwaite, Carolyn Pressler and Raymond Westbrook, among others, have long settled this point.[1] It is true, however, that the current

city as wife metaphor arose out of the context of the ancient Near East wherein a city was understood as a goddess married to a male god: 'Ezekiel's use of the marriage metaphor depends for its coherence on the culturally accepted notion that the female capital city is married to a male god. Though, as we shall see, Ezekiel is also dependent on earlier OT authors, none of the OT usage of sexual terminology to describe the relationship between the people and God can be understood apart from the status of the marriage metaphor as part of the worldview of the ancient Near East.' Galambush also notes that Ezekiel's understanding of the city's female persona colors all of his writing. Gender cannot be isolated from study of the text. While Galambush's study proceeds in a different direction from my work, it is a well-developed and provocative study of Ezekiel which I would highly recommend. On female personification in the Hebrew Bible generally see J.H. Otwell, *And Sarah Laughed: The Status of Woman in the Old Testament* (Philadelphia: Westminster Press, 1976), pp. 179-91.

1. Gordon and Washington ('Rape as a Military Metaphor', pp. 313-14), trace the use of the *piel* form of עָנָה II. In the *qal*, this verb has the general meaning 'to be bowed down or afflicted'. In the *piel*, however, the verb, within non-sexual contexts, takes on the meaning 'to humble, abuse, exploit, or debase'. Yet, in sexual contexts, the *piel* can be best translated 'to force sexual intercourse upon' or 'to rape'. See the foundational work of A. Deem, 'The Goddess Anath and Some Biblical Hebrew Cruces', *Journal of Semantic Studies* 23 (1978), pp. 25-30. Within the legal corpus, this verb is found at Deut. 21.14; 22.24; and 24.29. Non-legal sections of the Hebrew Bible also use the *piel* form of עָנָה. Within the narrative portions, it is found in the rape of Dinah (Gen. 34.2), the rape of the concubine (Judg. 19.24, 20.5), and the rape of Tamar (2 Sam. 13.12, 14, 22, 32). Based on the presence of this word, Trible (*Texts of Terror*, p. 60 n. 37) points out that '[r]ape, not incest, is Amnon's crime'. It is also found in the prophetic corpus at Ezek. 22.10, 11 to describe the sexual perversities of the men of Jerusalem who rape both unclean women and their sisters, among others. Finally, this verb is found at Lam. 5.11 to describe the raping of the women of Zion at the hands of Judah's military conquerors. This is contra, in part, T. Frymer-Kensky, 'Law and Philosophy: The Case of Sex in the Bible', *Semeia* 45 (1989), pp. 89-102; and *idem*, *In the Wake of the Goddesses: Women, Culture, and the Biblical Transformation of Pagan Myth* (New York: Free Press, 1992), p. 274 n. 34, wherein she asserts that only rarely should the *piel* of עָנָה

definition of rape is not equal to that of ancient Israel.

The concept of rape as a violation of a woman's body has taken millennia to develop. Brownmiller argues that historically rape preceded marriage:

> The earliest form of permanent, protective conjugal relationship, the accommodation called mating that we now know as marriage, appears to have been institutionalized by the male's forcible abduction and rape of the female. No quaint formality, bride capture, as it came to be known, was a very real struggle: a male took title to a female, staked a claim to her body, as it were, by an act of violence.[1]

Only later was a 'rudimentary mate-protectorate and then...[a] full-blown male solidification of power, the patriarchy',[2] established. The first piece of property in the development of 'the house of the father' was a woman. We see this repeatedly in the writing of ancient Israel.[3]

---

be translated as 'rape', and that typically the use of these particular words may imply, from a patriarchal point of view, some degree of consent: possibly an impropriety but not a rape. Yet I would maintain that the fact of consent is often a false assertion where the power differential between the two sexes is great, as it was in ancient Israel. Gordon and Washington ('Rape as a Military Metaphor', p. 313 n. 3), find her position 'incredible'. But see T. Frymer-Kensky, 'Sex and Sexuality', *ABD*, V, p. 1145, where Frymer-Kensky refers to the legal materials containing this word as 'rape laws'. A number of literary studies of rape in the Hebrew Bible now exist. See A. Keefe, 'Rapes of Women/Wars of Men', *Semeia* 61 (1993), pp. 79-97; and Trible, *Texts of Terror*, for studies of the rapes of Gen. 34, Judg. 19 and 2 Sam. 13. Thistlethwaite ('You May Enjoy the Spoil of Your Enemies'), C. Pressler ('Sexual Violence and Deuteronomic Law', in A. Brenner [ed.], *A Feminist Companion to Exodus to Deuteronomy* [Sheffield: Sheffield Academic Press, 1994], pp. 102-12), and R. Westbrook ('Punishments and Crimes', *ABD*, V, pp. 546-56) all study the legal material regarding rape.

1. Brownmiller, *Against Our Will*, p. 17.

2. Brownmiller, *Against Our Will*, p. 17.

3. It should be noted that a wife is listed among the property of a man's house in both Exod. 20.17 and Deut. 5.21. In Deuteronomy, the wife is listed as the first piece of property; in Exodus, she is listed second, after the house. Moreover, we can see the taking of brides during the assertion of military power over conquered males at work in the Hebrew Bible. For example, a virgin captive who has been raped can be made wife and divorced, but not sold into slavery, because the relationship began with a

In this environment, women had no capacity to consent to the sex act and no right to refuse it based upon her understanding of bodily integrity. Instead, according the laws of Leviticus, Numbers and Deuteronomy, and the narratives of Genesis, Judges and 2 Samuel, rape was the sexual violation of one man's property by another man.[1] It was the theft from the father of the financially valuable virginity of his daughter. It was the theft from the husband of the economically valuable and exclusive right to pleasure and reproduction lodged in his wife.[2]

Finally, rape was the means by which one group of men demonstrated their control of or authority over another group of men by forced sexual access to the human female property of

rape (Deut. 21.10-14). Thistlethwaite ('You May Enjoy the Spoil of Your Enemies', pp. 64-65) addresses this concept with respect to Deut. 20.10-17, 21.10-14; and Num. 31.9-17, 25-47. Brownmiller (*Against Our Will*, p. 33) relates concerning this right/rite: 'Fighting to secure women was on a par with fighting to secure food among ancient primitive [*sic*] tribes, an activity that still survives in certain parts of the world. The practical Hebrews, anxious to get a law on the books for all contingencies, made no bones about the status of women who were captured in war. Female captives were allowable as slaves and concubines, according to Deuteronomy, but Hebrew men were discouraged from marrying them. If a Hebrew male did marry a captive woman, unlike a Hebrew woman she could be divorced without cause or complicated rigmarole.' Moreover, we see bride capture occurring within the narrative sections of the Hebrew Bible. For example, the revenge of Dinah's brothers (Gen. 34) involves the capture of all the women and children. The civil war of Judg. 19–21 ends with the rape and carrying off of the women of Shiloh to provide wives for the surviving Benjaminites. For a discussion of these biblical episodes see Keefe, 'Rapes of Women'.

1.   Thistlethwaite ('You May Enjoy the Spoil of Your Enemies', pp. 61, 72) notes that rape is the 'theft of sexual property', and that ownership of that right has shifted over time from the father or husband to the woman. See also D.R. Mace, *Hebrew Marriage: A Sociological Study* (London: Epworth Press, 1953), p. 227, for a discussion of female sexuality as male property.

2.   For excellent discussions of the laws of rape, incest and adultery within the Hebrew Bible as violations of the property rights of men (and in the case of adultery, a violation against God), see A. Brenner, 'On Incest', in *idem* (ed.), *A Feminist Companion to Exodus to Deuteronomy*, pp. 119-42; E.A. Goodfriend, 'Adultery', *ABD*, I, pp. 82-86; J. Milgrom, 'The Betrothed Slave-Girl, Lev 19.20-22', *ZAW* 89 (1977), pp. 43-50; Pressler, *Sexual Violence*; and Westbrook, 'Punishments and Crimes', pp. 549-50, 552-54.

the weak. Brownmiller explains this latter phenomenon in the context of war as follows:

> Men of a conquered nation traditionally view the rape of 'their women' as the ultimate humiliation, a sexual *coup de grace*. Rape is considered by the people of a defeated nation to be part of the enemy's conscious effort to destroy them. In fact, by tradition, men appropriate the rape of 'their women' as part of their own male anguish of defeat. This egocentric view does have a partial validity. Apart from a genuine, human concern for wives and daughters near and dear to them, rape by a conqueror *is* compelling evidence of the conquered's status of masculine impotence. Defense of women has long been a hallmark of masculine pride, as possession of women has been a hallmark of masculine success. Rape by a conquering soldier destroys all remaining illusions of power and property for men of the defeated side. The body of a raped woman becomes a ceremonial battlefield, a parade ground for the victor's trooping of the colors. The act that is played out upon her is a message passed between men—vivid proof of victory for one and loss and defeat for the other.[1]

Thistlethwaite demonstrates Brownmiller's understanding of rape in the context of war with respect to the fate of conquered women in the wars involving ancient Israel.[2]

None of the laws or stories of the Hebrew Bible acknowledges a right residing in the female to bodily integrity or to restitution for a violation of bodily integrity. Rather, the right of protection and restitution existed in the male and the rapes of Dinah and Tamar, with the homicidal retribution on the part of their brothers, reminds us of both the seriousness of the affront to the social order of Israel which a rape constituted and the intensity of the patriarchal rage exhibited when one man or a group of men use rape to prove his or their might over another male or group of males.[3] The only appropriate response is one in

1. Emphasis supplied. Brownmiller, *Against Our Will*, p. 38.
2. Thistlethwaite, 'You May Enjoy the Spoil of Your Enemies'. See also Gordon and Washington, 'Rape as a Military Metaphor', pp. 310-12; and Sanderson, 'Nahum', p. 219. Sample biblical texts can be found at Gen. 34; Num. 31.9-17; Deut. 20.10-17, 21.10-14; Judg. 19–21; Lam. 5.11.
3. Dinah's story is found at Gen. 34. There the act of revenge implemented by her brothers is: (1) the mass murder of the male members of the tribe of her rapist; (2) the rape and enslavement of the women of that

kind, magnified many times over in degree. From the above discussion, we can see that some concept of rape, even if not a
female-oriented one, existed in ancient Israel and that patriarchal forces take seriously sexual violations which threaten the
social and economic order.

One might also argue, however, that rape is not involved in
any of these texts, but for Zech. 14.2, because they involve the
characterization of the city not as a 'good' woman but, rather,
most often as a prostitute. Prostitutes are not victimized by rape
in the ancient understanding of that word because a male property right is not violated in such sexual assaults. Sexual violence
perpetrated against such a woman would not be viewed as rape
because the woman was not under the dominion of another
male.[1] Moreover, prostitutes were righteously subject to sexual
humiliation at the hand of God because they acted outside those
roles determined as morally responsible for women.[2] Prostitutes, while critical to the functioning of patriarchal societies that
restrict the sexuality of females through male control, are nevertheless seen as wicked and, thus, as standing outside the normal
social order.[3] A prostitute could, therefore, be stripped and

tribe; and (3) the taking of the animals and wealth of the tribe. Tamar's
story is found at 2 Sam. 13 and there her brother murders her rapist.

1.   Sanderson, 'Nahum', p. 218.
2.   Sanderson, 'Nahum', p. 218.
3.   Sanderson, 'Nahum', p. 218, states: 'The role of a prostitute is an
ambivalent one in any society. The more stringently the sexuality of most
women is controlled by fathers and husbands—and thus the less available
most women are for the sexual gratification of men—the more urgently is
felt the need for women whose sexuality is not controlled by men and thus
stand outside the normal social order'. See for example Gen. 38; Josh. 2; 6;
Judg. 16.1; 1 Kgs 3.16-27; Mt. 1.5 for tolerant attitudes toward prostitution.
For a discussion of such toleration, see A. Brenner, *The Israelite Woman:
Social Role and Literary Type in Biblical Narrative* (The Biblical Seminar, 2;
Sheffield: JSOT Press, 1985), pp. 78-83. While the religious powers of ancient
Israel attempted to outlaw the practice of prostitution (see for example Lev.
19.29; 21.7, 9, 14; see also Deut. 23.18 for cult prostitution), it remained as an
institution. Sanderson, 'Nahum', p. 218, continues: 'On the other hand,
given the double standard common to patriarchal societies, the blame for
sexual activities attaches to the female only. Thus, prostitutes' activities are
deemed to be a necessary evil for the society, which means that while the
women must be tolerated, they are despised and represent fair game for

publicly humiliated or raped without consequence to the perpetrator. Any sexual assault would be viewed as legitimate retaliation for her sexual freedom and the temptation to males that she represents.[1] Thus, it cannot be said that the ancient Israelites regarded the passages under study as describing rape but, instead, a type of retribution for the perceived affront to the social order which the prostitute embodies.

Furthermore, in some of the texts before us, the cities of Israel and Judah are cast not only as prostitutes, but as wives become prostitutes. Any measure of sexual violence enacted by the husband would be tolerated in this case because the male already has exclusive right to his wife's sexuality due to the existence of the marital relationship.

In both situations, the free reign of a woman's sexuality is perceived as an offense worthy of the penalty of sexual assault. The crime is sexuality brandished; the punishment must, therefore, be both sexual and public. The woman is not violated; she is chastised through sexual savagery. To the mind of ancient peoples, these types of acts are not abusive.

Yet they are very important. Sexual violence, such as public strippings and sexual intercourse outside the normal social boundaries, against women, single, married or prostituted, is continually threatened for a legitimate social purpose. What is its significance? The answer lies in the source of the metaphor: the ancient Near Eastern treaty-curses.

The Source of the Metaphor

Much scholarly attention has been directed at the question how the ancient Near Eastern treaties and land grants impacted the formation and description of the various covenants with God set forth in the Hebrew Bible. I will not review it all here. What

vitriolic verbal attacks'. See also E.A. Goodfriend, 'Prostitution', *ABD*, V, pp. 505-10. See for example Gen. 34.31; 1 Kgs 22.38; Amos 7.17 for negative views of prostitution. P. Bird examines the fundamental ambivalence toward the prostitute in Israelite society in 'The Harlot as Heroine: Narrative Art and Social Presupposition in Three Old Testament Texts', *Semeia* 46 (1989), pp. 119-40.

1. Sanderson, 'Nahum', pp. 218-19.

is fairly clear is that there is a significant link between the ancient Near Eastern treaties and the concept of divine covenant, at least so far as the Mosaic covenant is concerned.[1] Delbert Hillers has studied this connection at length with an eye cast, in particular, toward the prophetic corpus. Building on the work of Mendenhall,[2] Hillers argues that as the treaties impacted the

---

1. See for example G.E. Mendenhall, *Law and Covenant in Israel and the Ancient Near East* (Pittsburgh: Biblical Colloquium, 1955); G.E. Mendenhall and G.A. Herion, 'Covenant', *ABD*, I, pp. 1179-1202; K. Baltzer, *Das Bundesformular* (WMANT, 4; Neukirchen–Vluyn: Neukirchener Verlag, 2nd edn, 1964); D.J. McCarthy, *Treaty and Covenant: A Study in Form in the Ancient Oriental Documents and in the Old Testament* (AnBib, 21; Rome: Biblical Institute Press, 2nd edn, 1981); *idem, OT Covenant: A Survey of Current Opinions* (Richmond, VA: John Knox, 1972); M. Weinfeld, 'The Covenant of Grant in the Old Testament and the Ancient Near East', *JAOS* 90 (1970), pp. 184-203; *idem*, 'Covenant Terminology in the Ancient Near East and its Significance in the West', *JAOS* 93 (1973), pp. 191-99; D.R. Hillers, *Covenant: History of a Biblical Idea* (Baltimore: Johns Hopkins Press, 1969); E.W. Nicholson, *God and His People: Covenant Theology in the Old Testament* (Oxford: Clarendon Press, 1986). See also M. Barré, 'Treaties in the ANE', *ABD*, VI, pp. 653-56; D. Stuart, 'Curse', *ABD*, I, pp. 1218-19; F. Fensham, 'Malediction and Benediction in Ancient Near Eastern Vassal-Treaties and the OT', *ZAW* 74 (1962), pp. 1-9; H. Tadmor, 'Treaty and Oath in the Ancient Near East: A Historian's Approach', in G.M. Tucker and D.A. Knight (eds.), *Humanizing America's Iconic Book* (Chico, CA: Scholars Press, 1982), pp. 127-52. Moreover, the discussion continues. See G.N. Knoppers, 'Ancient Near Eastern Royal Grants and the Davidic Covenant: An Examination of a Proposed Parallel' (unpublished paper presented at the Biblical Law Group session of the 1994 Annual Meeting of the Society of Biblical Literature, Chicago, IL, 20 November 1994).

2. A brief summary of Mendenhall's position follows. The ancient Near Eastern treaty is an international legal form developed to serve people across international boundaries. Moreover, it had to be a public document so that all could follow the commands of the treaty and understand the consequences for failure to follow its precepts. Treaties of the ancient Near East, often created long before Israel was established, were made between: (1) kings of relative equals, called a parity treaty; and (2) a ruling king and vassal king, called a suzerainty treaty. Both types of treaties were organized along similar lines. They had a preamble, a historical prologue, stipulations, provisions for preserving the treaty, provisions for the public reading of the treaty, a summoning of the gods so that they might act as witnesses, and a formula of curses and blessings for enforcement. This structure can also be found in, at least, the Mosaic covenant between

idea of God's covenant with the Israelites, so the treaty-curses, which were the treaties' enforcement provisions, impacted the ideas within the culture regarding the breach of that covenant.[1] Furthermore, both Israelite notions of covenant and notions regarding how the threat of the covenantal curses operated influenced the prophets in their activity.[2] Hillers, after investigating the relationship between these ancient Near Eastern treaty-curses and the prophetic corpus, suggests that many of the passages involving God's judgment on the people of Israel and Judah originated in such treaty-curses.[3]

Hillers surveyed the types of treaty-curses. They came in all varieties of maledictions and included 18 in all. The most significant for our purposes follow:

1. the city or nation will become a prostitute;
2. the city or nation will be stripped like a prostitute; and

---

Yahweh and Israel set forth in the Hebrew Bible. Mendenhall proposed that Yahweh is the superior king in a suzerainty treaty, who, after proclaiming his prior merciful and beneficent acts, offers a covenantal relationship to his people and thereby imposes upon them certain obligations. Such covenant bestows both blessings for compliance and curses for non-compliance; Mendenhall, *Law and Covenant*. He has modified this general position slightly due to the work of McCarthy and modified greatly his former position with respect to the Abrahamic and Davidic covenants due to the work of Weinfeld. See Mendenhall and Herion, 'Covenant'.

1. Hillers, *Treaty-Curses*, pp. 1-11, 80-89.
2. In support of this argument, Hillers (*Treaty-Curses*, p. 89) points out, for example, that Isa. 24.5-6 states:

> They have transgressed the laws,
> violated the statutes,
> broken the everlasting covenant.
> Therefore a curse devours the land.

Hillers makes a strong argument that all the prophets, even those of the eighth-century BCE, 'had an equal opportunity to learn [the] curses connected with a religious covenant and the same motive for using them'; Hillers, *Treaty-Curses*, pp. 83-84.

3. Hillers, *Treaty-Curses*. See also R.V. Bergren, *The Prophets and the Law* (Cincinnati: Hebrew Union College Press, 1974). Galambush (*Jerusalem*, pp. 32-35) also acknowledges the relationship between the suzerain treaties and the covenant with Yahweh in her work on the marriage metaphor in Ezekiel.

3. wives will be raped.[1]

With this knowledge, suddenly the ancient metaphor of the cities of Israel and Judah as prostitutes and wives being subject to sexual debasement at the hands of the sovereign God becomes alive for us.[2] Hillers noted the connection of the second curse to Isa. 3.17; 47.1-4; Jer. 13.22, 26; Ezek. 16.37-38; 23.10, 29; Hos. 2.4-5 (Eng. 2.2-3), 11-12 (Eng. 9-10); and Nah. 3.5.[3] According to Hillers Nah. 3.13 reflects another curse:

1. The others are:
    1. the joyful noise of the people will cease;
    2. the millstone shall stop grinding;
    3. a flood will come upon the land;
    4. the water will become contaminated;
    5. famine will come upon the land and cannibalism will ensue;
    6. the behavior of animals will change and they will dwell where the city or nation once was;
    7. ravenous wild animals shall come upon the land;
    8. weapons will be broken;
    9. warriors will become women;
    10. men will be caught like birds in a trap;
    11. incurable wounds will come upon the people;
    12. corpses will not be buried and will be instead devoured by scavengers;
    13. the scepter of the ruler will be broken;
    14. women will be unable to find men;
    15. the breasts of nursing women will dry up.

All of these find parallels in the Hebrew Bible. Moreover, the Hebrew Bible offers up two additional curses for which we do not have ancient Near Eastern parallels:

1. the nation will become like Sodom and Gomorrah; and
2. the land will be ruined and, therefore, passers-by will shudder. Hillers, *Treaty-Curses*, pp. 43-79.

2. Goodfriend ('Prostitution', p. 506), however, takes the view that God's judgment falls on Jerusalem and other cities because of the practice of prostitution within the cities. The metaphor, to her mind, operates to 'make apostasy more repulsive but also prostitution, which came to symbolize infidelity and lack of discrimination in the religious sphere as well'.

3. Hillers, *Treaty-Curses*, pp. 59-60. See also K.J. Cathcart, 'Treaty-Curses and the Book of Nahum', *CBQ* 35 (1973), pp. 179-87, who supports and extends Hillers's work with respect to the book of Nahum. Hillers

that warriors will become like women.[1]

Although several verses that we have explored are not included by Hillers, there is reason to do so. First, Hillers ignores the rhetoric of rape within these verses. He repeatedly takes the language related to 'uncovering one's nakedness' as the language of stripping rather than socially illegitimate intercourse. While the act of stripping and exposing the female's 'shame' is typically present in these verses, more is happening than the literal reading conveys. The raping of wives is more important than Hillers allows and some verses are therefore overlooked. Moreover, the wordplay on vaginal and gate openings eludes him, and, hence, the sexual abuse in these texts avoids his scrutiny.

To understand how this rhetoric is operating, let us examine Isa. 3.17-26. Verse 26 is the culmination of the castigation and stripping of the daughters of Zion in 3.16-24. This section begins with the declaration of the Lord that the daughters of Zion are haughty (v. 16) and, hence, God will inflict wounds upon their heads (v. 17a) and strip them naked (v. 17b). Then, the

---

notes that prostitution seems not to be involved in the stripping of Babylon in Isa. 47.1-4; *Treaty-Curses*, p. 60. Yet the rape of a virgin will defile her such that a life of prostitution may become her fate. Cf. Gordon and Washington, 'Rape as a Military Metaphor', p. 319, where they discuss the virgin/prostitute dichotomous thinking of the human male with respect to the sexuality of the female. Furthermore, we must remember the 'enjoyment' of the rape of a virgin as an act of war; Thistlethwaite, 'You May Enjoy the Spoil of Your Enemies'. Hillers also regards Jer. 13.22 as falling outside the prostitution metaphor; yet Jer. 13.27 recounts:

> I have seen your abominations,
> your adulteries and neighings,
> your shameless prostitutions
> on the hill of the countryside.

We should also take note of the fact that Hillers (*Treaty-Curses*, p. 58) does not make much of the curse that the city will become a prostitute. He cites only Amos 7.17 and Isa. 23.15-18 as parallels. Apparently, he is looking for very specific language such as 'your wife shall be a prostitute' (Amos 7.17) or 'she shall return to her trade, and prostitute herself with all the kingdoms of the world on the face of the earth' (Isa. 23.17). Yet I think that the extensive use of the city as prostitute metaphor finds its origins here.

1. Hillers, *Treaty-Curses*, p. 67.

stripping is described in detail (vv. 18-24). At this juncture, the subject switches from the daughters of Zion to the woman Zion. We are told that the warriors will fall in battle (v. 25) and that the gates of woman Zion will lament and mourn (v. 26a). She will be ravaged and broken, able only to sit upon the ground (v. 26b). Verse 26 depicts the opening of the 'gates' of the female and her ravishing. This is the consummation of the stripping of the vestiges of her sexual 'impropriety' that she endured in vv. 16-24. While the threatened loss of the warriors intervenes, it does not disrupt the flow of the text. Indeed, it may well signify that the protectors of the prostitute will fail and, thus, the final act of the sexual assault begun in v. 16 may take place. Consequently, Isa. 3.26 is a part of the curse wherein the prostitute is stripped (and raped) as punishment for breach of the treaty or covenant. Similar reasoning allows us to connect Ezek. 16.39 to the two prior verses which are found by Hillers to be related to the treaty-curses.

The sexual connotations of Nah. 2.7-8 (Eng. 2.6-7) and 3.13 are also ignored by Hillers. Again, this is partly the result of his failure to make the gate/vagina connection. As a result, Hillers missed the relationship between these verses and the treaty-curses. Yet v. 7 makes it clear that a female is to be stripped and this, too, Hillers apparently ignores.

Zech. 14.2 may well reflect the curse that wives will be raped, although the women of the city in the Zechariah text are not divided into those who are married and those who are unmarried. Hillers cites other biblical verses where this occurs, including 2 Sam. 16.20-22; Jer. 8.10; and Job 31.10. Then again, this verse may just reflect the realities of women in a country defeated at war.

The Religious Function of the Metaphor

Now that we have discovered that the source of the sexual assault and abuse metaphors of judgment that lie within the prophetic corpus may be found in the treaty-curses of the ancient Near East, the question we must ask is: why did these curses exist in the first instance? Again we can see patriarchal rules at work. We know that one of the ancient (and modern)[1] realities of war is that one of the victor's spoils is the rape, and possible capture for purposes of marriage or enslavement, of the women of the vanquished. Moreover, we know that the rape of other men's women is allowed in retaliation for various other types of social, economic and political violations. For example, Dinah's brothers may rape and capture the women of the tribe of Dinah's rapist in vindication of Jacob's property right which rests in Dinah's virginity. It makes sense from a patriarchal point of view that the public stripping of a nation's city/prostitutes and the rape of its city/wives are appropriate responses to the breach by that nation of its treaty with another. Such repercussions in the case of treaty-breach are a natural extension of the patriarchal dominance that produces the rape response in war.

Thus, we can now see the religious significance of the texts under study. In spite of our modern disdain for such texts, the images contained within these texts were not only acceptable to the men of ancient Israel, they meaningfully conveyed the message to return to the fold of the Israelite covenantal relationship with God. The public stripping or rape of the female cities of Israel and Judah is a perfect medium to convey the message that Israel has breached its covenant with God and that the natural consequences, well known to all because treaties were publicly announced documents, will flow therefrom. In a patriarchal system where God is the chief patriarch, he has total access to the females of his underlings, including its cities. Given the nature of ancient Near Eastern treaties and their curses, the public sexual humiliation or rape of the underlings' cities/women is an appropriate response to any perceived or actual violations of existing agreements between God and his people. God's threat of sexual violence will seem quite real in the ancient

---

1. For example, the rape of the women of Bosnia. See Thistlethwaite, 'You May Enjoy the Spoil of Your Enemies'; and C.A. MacKinnon, 'Turning Rape into Pornography: Postmodern Genocide', *Ms.* 4.1 (1993), pp. 24-30. Moreover, rape is so accepted as an integral part of war that a contemporary book on war crimes might not even mention the problem. See for example R.A. Falk, G. Kolko and R.J. Lifton (eds.), *Crimes of War* (New York: Random House, 1971).

setting and will evoke compliance with the covenant.

Furthermore, in those cases where the prophet announced God's salvation or renewal of the people, God's revenge against those who subjugated Israel and Judah also must have fallen within patriarchal structures. Raping the women of one's conquered enemy was the only 'just' response in light of the rights of war. Less would have called God's power as chief patriarch into question.[1]

Finally, the religious metaphor, God the rapist, was effective because the language is highly provocative and thus draws our attention. Renita Weems acknowledges this when she asserts with respect to Hosea:

> For what was the case in ancient Israel remains the case in modern times: talk about sex and sexuality tends to provoke, rouse, humiliate, and captivate people. Such language certainly arrests the imagination.[2]

The prophets well utilized the language of sexual violence to call Israel and Judah back to obedience in their relationship with God and to judge their enemies.

---

1.   It is critical to remember God's role in war in ancient Israel. Wars were religious events. G. von Rad (*Der heilige Krieg in alten Israel* [Göttingen: Vandenhoeck & Ruprecht, 1969]) coined the term 'Holy War' to describe Israel's relationship to war. Others hold related but not identical views of war in ancient Israel. See for example R. Smend, *Yahweh War and Tribal Confederation* (Nashville: Abingdon Press, 1970). As Thistlethwaite ('You May Enjoy the Spoil of Your Enemies', p. 68), states, '[t]he theological purposes read into the conduct of biblical war are to serve Yahweh and the ends of Yahweh'. Yet Yahweh leads these wars as well. He is chief warrior as well as chief patriarch and the chief warrior must rape if he is to partake fully in the bounty of war. But see Gen. 14 where the warrior Abram offers up the full bounty to the kings of Shalem and Sodom, which characterizes Abram as especially noble. Cf. R. Magdalene, 'The Legend of Abraham the Warrior in First Century Judaism with an Emphasis on the Writings of Josephus' (unpublished paper for the University of Denver/Iliff School of Theology, August 1993).

2.   Weems, 'Gomer: Victim of Violence?', p. 89.

The Hermeneutical Question

Regardless of the usefulness of this metaphor in ancient Israel, we must acknowledge that times have changed and women now possess their own 'sexual property'. This metaphor must be addressed from the perspective of modern readers. Traditional commentators have often handled the problem by trivializing it.[1] This is an inadequate solution. A wide range of feminist literature has discussed alternative biblical hermeneutics in similar cases.[2] The question is whether the texts before us can be redeemed in any way or whether we must abandon them, having simply pointed out their patriarchal bent and historical context. For many authors, redemption of the texts is impossible. Judith Sanderson decries the continued use of such metaphor because it is 'a destructive view of women's bodied self'.[3] As previously discussed, Setel calls the use of the metaphor 'pornographic'.[4] Gordon and Washington call us to 'resist the metaphor'.[5] In solidarity with all victims of sexual abuse, both in the text and beyond it, both in the ancient world and in the modern one, I must agree with them and stand against the continued use of this metaphor.[6]

---

1. See the brief but important discussion of this point in Gordon and Washington, 'Rape as a Military Metaphor', pp. 322-23.

2. Several good summaries of these methods are found in: C. Osiek, 'The Feminist and the Bible: Hermeneutical Alternatives', in A.Y. Collins (ed.), *Feminist Perspectives on Biblical Scholarship* (Chico, CA: Scholars Press, 1985), pp. 93-105; S.H. Ringe, 'When Women Interpret the Bible', in Newsom and Ringe (eds.), *The Women's Bible Commentary*, pp. 1-9; K.D. Sakenfeld, 'Feminist Uses of Biblical Materials', in Russell (ed.), *Feminist Interpretation of the Bible*, pp. 55-136; *idem*, 'Feminist Perspectives on Bible and Theology: An Introduction to Selected Issues and Literature', *Int* 42 (1988), pp. 5-44; E. Schüssler Fiorenza, 'Remembering the Past in Creating the Future: Historical-Critical Scholarship and Feminist Biblical Interpretation', in Collins (ed.), *Feminist Perspectives on Biblical Scholarship*, pp. 43-64; and T.D. Setel, 'Feminist Insights and the Question of Method', in Collins (ed.), *Feminist Perspectives on Biblical Scholarship*, pp. 93-106.

3. Sanderson, 'Nahum', p. 220.

4. Setel, 'Prophets and Pornography'.

5. Gordon and Washington, 'Rape as a Military Metaphor', pp. 323-25.

6. Some commentators try to deal with the problem by calling us to

Today we celebrate women's claim to full humanity. Women are beings with the right to accept or reject sexual advances. Rape is no longer a property violation lodged in the male but, instead, a physical violation of a woman. Where God metaphorically sexually assaults a woman or leads human males to rape human females, he is a rapist. This understanding of God, while once admittedly religiously informative, is now highly violative of those potentially subject to rape—both women and children. It undermines their trust in and reliance upon God.[1] Women and children have for too long been forced to be dependent on

take the metaphor less literally. Weems ('Gomer: Victim of Violence?', p. 100 [discussing the work of S. McFague, *Metaphorical Theology* (Philadelphia: Fortress Press, 1982)]), for example, points out that the metaphor becomes particularly problematical when it 'succeeds': 'The problem arises when the metaphor "succeeds", meaning that the reader becomes so engrossed in the pathos and the details of the metaphor that the *dissimilarities* between the two are disregarded. When that happens, McFague points out that God is no longer *like* a husband, God *is* a husband; namely that the thing specified *becomes* the signification itself. In this case, a risky metaphor gives rise to a risky deduction: here, to the extent that God's covenant with Israel is like a marriage between a man and a woman, then a husband's physical punishment against his wife is as warranted as the punishment of Israel. It is the risk of oversimplification and rigid correspondence'. Emphasis supplied. J.J. Schmitt also warns us about hanging on rigidly to such metaphors for God: '[T]he Bible reader of today must realize the danger of taking literally these descriptions of the indescribable. The prophets used whatever images they thought appropriate for their society. Their statements remain part of the theology of 8th- and 7th-century Israel' ('Prophecy [Preexilic Hebrew]', *ABD*, V, pp. 485). I do not find this tack particularly helpful.

1. Sanderson ('Nahum', p. 218) states concerning this issue: 'In the face of massive violence against women in modern western societies, it is very difficult for women to read biblical stories of men's violence against women and even worse to read biblical imagery of God's violence against women... Even though one realizes that all language about God is metaphorical and that God can be imaged only through human analogies, it is nevertheless painful to read God's activity of judgment portrayed as sexual violence.' See also pp. 220-21. G.F. Ellwood (*Batter My Heart*) and D.R. Blumenthal (*Facing the Abusing God: A Theology of Protest* [Louisville, KY: Westminster Press/John Knox, 1993] pp. 240-46) discuss the theological, hermeneutical and psychological issues involved with such abusive texts.

those who abuse them physically, sexually and emotionally. We must not continue to perpetrate such dependence in the religious realm.[1]

Conclusion

The prophets and their redactors, from the eighth century BCE to the early fourth, depicted the cities of Israel and Judah as women whose sexuality is outside of the control of men. God, the covenantal marriage partner, or male authority figure, thus has the right to chastise any behavior flowing from such freedom through acts of sexual violence. Moreover, such women are subject to this violence because their men, the nations, have breached their treaty with their suzerain, Yahweh. The language, formed in reliance upon the treaty-curses of the ancient Near East, strongly evokes the notion of covenant with its attendant responsibilities in the mind of the ancient Israelite listener. Through the metaphor, one would be reminded of the covenant, one's obligations thereunder, and the breadth of the potential consequences for any breach thereof. Thirdly, the ancient Near Eastern patriarchal understanding of justice required the use of such a metaphor. The cities of the enemies of Israel and Judah are subject to sexual violence because they are victims of the divine warrior who implements exacting execution of his patriarchal wrath and authority. At this point, we understand much about these metaphors and how they came into existence. There is some comfort in understanding the how and why of the imagery of sexual assault in the Hebrew Bible. Yet to women of old and to those of us in the present, these texts are indeed the ultimate texts of terror: God not only does not intervene to prevent sexual assault, the Deity is fully prepared to be among the perpetrators of such. Because victims of sexual abuse are conditioned in the process of their abuse to continue to focus on the perpetrator by struggling with the how

1. For several excellent discussions of the damage many biblical and Christian doctrines cause those subject to sexual violence, see Heggen, *Sexual Abuse*; J.C. Brown and C.R. Bohn (eds.), *Christianity, Patriarchy, and Abuse: A Feminist Critique* (Cleveland: Pilgrim Press, 1989); and A. Imbens and I. Jonker, *Christianity and Incest* (Minneapolis: Fortress Press, 1992).

and the why of the abuse, at the expense of respecting their experience and of their healing,[1] it is insufficient for us to understand how the texts are operating, it is insufficient for us to understand why the texts exist, that is, their historical context. We must stand against the use of such texts as religious metaphor. Toward that end, as Trible has done in her work, we must grieve for the victims of the metaphor who have suffered under patriarchal views of God. Then we must join Trible in her memorial to the victims in and of biblical texts. Finally, we must say and pray in chorus with Trible, 'Never again!'

1.   See generally E. Bass and L. Davis, *The Courage to Heal: A Guide for Women Incest Survivors of Child Sexual Abuse* (San Francisco: Harper Collins, 2nd edn, 1992); M. Beattie, *Codependent No More: How to Stop Controlling Others and Start Caring for Yourself* (San Francisco: Harper & Row, 1987); J. Bradshaw, *Homecoming: Reclaiming and Championing Your Inner Child* (New York: Bantam Books, 1990); *idem, Bradshaw On: Healing the Shame that Binds You* (Deerfield Beach, FL: Health Communications, 1988); *idem, Bradshaw On: The Family. A Revolutionary Way of Self Discovery* (Deerfield Beach, FL: Health Communications, 1988); Fortune, *Sexual Violence*; A. Miller, *For Your Own Good: Hidden Cruelty in Child-Rearing and the Roots of Violence* (trans. Hildegarde Hannum and Hunter Hannum; New York: Farrar, Straus, Giroux, 1984); *idem, Thou Shalt Not Be Aware: Society's Betrayal of the Child* (trans. Hildegarde Hannum and Hunter Hannum; New York: Farrar, Straus, Giroux, 1983); *idem, The Drama of the Gifted Child* (trans. R. Ward; New York: Basic Books, 1981; originally published as *Prisoners of Childhood*); C. Olksana, *Safe Passage to Healing: A Guide for Survivors of Ritual Abuse* (San Francisco: HarperCollins, 1994); and A.W. Schaef, *Co-Dependence: Misunderstood* (San Francisco: Harper & Row, 1986).

Part III
SHOULD WE TRUST THE GOD OF THE PROPHETS?

Nancy R. Bowen

Elisabeth Schüssler Fiorenza, in her book *Bread Not Stone*, states that 'the basic insight of liberation theologies and their methodological starting point is that all theology knowingly or not is by definition always engaged for or against the oppressed'.[1] Rosemary Radford Ruether has argued that what is holy, the true nature of things, is that which promotes the full humanity of women.[2] These two statements point to a critical issue for feminist biblical interpretation. The issue is how a text functions within communities of faith. Does the interpretation of a text function in the community to which it is addressed to liberate those who are oppressed? One of the tasks of feminist biblical interpretation is to seek interpretations that function to promote such liberation. Then we can call the Bible truly holy.

In the task of seeking liberating interpretations feminist biblical interpreters have raised the question of how biblical images of God are appropriated. In modern history feminist biblical interpreters and theologians have focused on traditionally male or patriarchal images of the deity (such as king, father) versus female or goddess images of the deity (such as nurturer, Mother, Wisdom). A primary concern of these studies has been to critique the ways in which the male images of the deity have historically been used to devalue women and to limit their roles in society. The complementary concern has been to recover and claim as positive and liberative for women the female images of

1. E. Schüssler Fiorenza, *Bread Not Stone* (Boston: Beacon Press, 1984), p. 45.
2. R.R. Ruether, 'Feminist Interpretation: A Method of Correlation', in L.M. Russell (ed.), *Feminist Interpretation of the Bible* (Philadelphia: Westminster Press, 1985), p. 115.

the deity. In this article I want to look at an image of God that as far as I can tell has historically not been used either for or against women. This image however is seen as problematic and unredeemable in other ways. The image of God that I am going to explore is the image of YHWH as deceiver. What I wish to explore is whether this troublesome image of the deity can be interpreted in such a way that it functions for the oppressed and the promotion of the full humanity of women.

The text that is at the center of this investigation is Ezek. 14.1-11. In this passage some elders come to Ezekiel apparently to inquire of the prophet for a word from YHWH.[1] Rather than answering them as would be expected, Ezekiel instead uses this as an occasion to utter an oracle of judgment against these elders. Why is it a problem for the elders to come to the prophet? The answer may lie in the elders' understanding of the covenant relationship with YHWH. We can only speculate as to the situation the elders were hoping YHWH would address. Since this text can most likely be situated in the period between the first deportation of exiles from Judah in 597 BCE and the fall of Jerusalem in 587 BCE[2] there are numerous possibilities in light of that national crisis. Perhaps they were questioning how this disaster could have come upon Judah or perhaps they were wondering when the chastisement would end. Whatever the question may have been, the elders would have understood that as members of the covenant community experiencing a situation of distress, an inquiry of YHWH should result, if possible, in relief from their distress. To go to a prophet assumes that mediation is possible. It assumes continuity in the covenant relationship.

1.   In Ezek. 8.1 and 14.1 the text does not explicitly state the purpose of the visit by these elders. Ezek. 20.1 and 33.31 specifically state that they have come to seek a word from YHWH. By inference, this would be assumed to be the case also in 8.1 and 14.1.

2.   Chapters 1–24 form a primary unit within the book. In its final form both the dated sections (1.1–3.15; 8.1–11.25; 20.1-44; 24.1-14) which are in chronological order and the theme (primarily oracles of judgment) set these chapters within this ten-year period. See M. Greenberg, *Ezekiel 1–20* (AB, 22; Garden City, NY: Doubleday, 1983), pp. 3-6, and W. Zimmerli, *Ezekiel I* (trans. R. Clements; Hermeneia; Philadelphia: Fortress Press, 1979), pp. 68-74.

However, the expectation of these elders is problematic for two reasons. First, the theology of the book of Ezekiel is clear that YHWH has already severed the covenant relationship that would have been the basis for that expectation.[1] Secondly, the oracle against the elders indicates that in keeping 'idols in their hearts' they have committed an offense that would require punishment, not a favorable hearing.[2] The announcement of judgment toward these elders thus resoundingly negates their assumption that the covenant relationship is still in effect. Therefore, the decision by the elders to go to another prophet is again the occasion for another announcement of judgment. Indeed, when the elders seek another prophet the text says that if this other prophet speaks a word to them, then that word is a result of YHWH's having deceived that prophet (v. 9). The result of this action is that both the elders and the prophet will then be eliminated from the midst of the people.

Why is it a problem for this other prophet to respond to the elders? In the context of this passage it might be fair to say that it is because the prophet should have known better. In 3.26 God tells Ezekiel that he shall be 'speechless'. This does not mean that Ezekiel never speaks. Rather, Ezekiel is forbidden to intercede for the people since the basis for that intercession, the covenant relationship, has been broken.[3] On that basis, *no* prophet would be able to intercede and offer a word to one who inquired. The fact that this other prophet does so is attributed to YHWH's activity. YHWH deceives the prophets, in a sense 'tricking' the prophet into giving the elders a word. Reading between the lines, the deception is that in giving a word to the prophet to speak YHWH indicates to the other prophet that mediation was still possible when, in fact, it was not. The nature of the deception is to cause the prophet to accept as true or valid what is actually false or invalid.

What is problematic about this text is that YHWH engages in the activity of deception. This passage and others similar to it

1. T. Raitt, *A Theology of Exile: Judgment/Deliverance in Jeremiah and Ezekiel* (Philadelphia: Fortress Press, 1977), pp. 67-74, 77-78.
2. Zimmerli, *Ezekiel I*, pp. 146, 306-307.
3. R.R. Wilson, 'An Interpretation of Ezekiel's "Dumbness"', *VT* 22 (1972), pp. 95-96.

(1 Kgs 22.19-23; Jer. 20.7-13) have obviously been troubling for theologians. It is troubling because it stands in stark contrast to passages that are very clear that such activity should be considered to be against God's very nature.[1] It is beyond the limits of this article to deal with the question of whether this contrast can be resolved. Rather, I would like to raise the question of whether it can be liberating to hold out the possibility that God is not always trustworthy. When I asked one of my students this question she responded with a resounding 'no'. She was very clear that her view of God would not tolerate God acting in such a way. For her, a liberating God was one who was compassionate, who healed and did not hurt. To view God as a deceiver seemed abusive to her. It is true that at first glance it does not seem possible that divine deception could possibly be liberating. But I would like to suggest that there is a way to find liberation in this understanding of God.

There are two other places in the Hebrew Bible where God's activity with regard to prophets is understood as deception, 1 Kgs 22.19-23 and Jer. 20.7-13. These three passages all share a common vocabulary word for the act of deception (Heb. *pth*). In addition, these three passages have in common that they all occur in contexts of transition from an old situation to a new

---

1. J.J.M. Roberts, 'Does God Lie? Divine Deceit as a Theological Problem in Israelite Prophetic Literature', in J.A. Emerton *et al.* (eds.), *Congress Volume Jerusalem 1986* (VTSup, 40; Leiden: Brill, 1988), p. 211. 'The OT characterizes YHWH as a god of truth (Ps. 31.6) or faithfulness (Deut. 32.4) who is just and right (Deut. 32.4; Ps. 92.16, 119.137; 145.17) and without iniquity (Deut. 332.4; Ps. 92.16). His word and judgements are straight (Ps. 33.4) and true (Ps. 19.10, 119.137, 151-60) and altogether righteous (Ps. 19.10). He does not lie, because he is not a man that he should lie or change his mind (Num. 23.10; 1 Sam. 15.29); what he says he will do, and what he promises he will bring to pass (Num. 23.19).'

Also, note that some who recognize the tension still argue that YHWH does not deceive. See E.F. Siegman, *The False Prophets of the Old Testament* (Washington, DC: Catholic University of America, 1939) and I.O.A. Ude, 'False Prophets in the Old Testament' (PhD dissertation, Fuller Theological Seminary, 1979). These two authors use an 'evolutionary approach'. YHWH as the cause of false prophecy is viewed as the 'naive conception of primitive times' (Siegman) or 'evidence of immature theology and an unethical conception of prophecy' (Ude).

situation. In 1 Kings it is the transition from the rule of Ahab and the end of the Omride dynasty to that of a new king, Jehu, and a new dynasty.[1] In Jeremiah and Ezekiel it is the transition from the time of the monarchy to the time of exile. In each instance YHWH's act of deception is directed toward the *old* situation. The deception is mediated through a prophet or prophets. And the nature of the deception is to maintain the antagonist within the old situation, but in doing so it brings about the demise of that old situation.

In 1 Kings 22 the deception is directed against the king of Israel, Ahab. Prior to 1 Kings 22 the end of Ahab's rule has already been predicted (1 Kgs 21.21, 27-29). When the kings of Israel and Judah are deciding to go to battle, 400 prophets of the king of Israel are deceived by God. They favorably predict Ahab's victory in battle. The result of this deception encourages Ahab to continue in his role as king. However, through this favorable oracle (deception) Ahab is lured into a battle in which he is killed.

In Jer. 20.7-13 the situation is a little more complicated. Here the deception is directed against Jeremiah. Even though he thinks that YHWH may have possibly deceived him the book as a whole vindicates YHWH. The accusation however arises because of YHWH's apparent failure to bring about the destruction of Judah and Jerusalem that Jeremiah has been announcing as the word of YHWH (4.19-21, 29; 5.16-17; 6.22-26; 8.14, 16; 10.19-20; 12.10-13). In the face of Babylonian aggression, this word stands in contradiction to the prophets who say that the word of YHWH is that Judah and Jerusalem will *not* fall (5.12-13; 6.13-14; 7.1-15; 8.10-12; 14.13-14). If, however, YHWH *has* deceived Jeremiah, the nature of the deception is to encourage

---

1. This interpretation is based upon reading the text in its final form. There are those that question whether this incident originally involved Ahab. See A. Campbell, *Of Prophets and Kings: A Late Ninth-Century Document* (Washington, DC: Catholic Biblical Association of America, 1986), pp. 1, 98; S. De Vries, *Prophet Against Prophet* (Grand Rapids: Eerdmans, 1978), pp. 93-111, 124; J. Gray, *I and II Kings* (OTL; Philadelphia: Westminster Press, 2nd edn, 1970), pp. 414-18; J. Miller and J. Hayes, *A History of Ancient Israel and Judah* (Philadelphia: Westminster Press, 1986), pp. 298-301.

Jeremiah to continue in his role as a prophet announcing the coming destruction. The conclusion we are invited to reach is that the word of judgment was then not the true word of YHWH, and it could be claimed that Jeremiah's opponents were the true prophets! However, the result of continuing in that role will be to make Jeremiah a false prophet and to lead to his destruction by his enemies (20.10).

And as we have seen in Ezekiel, the deception is directed toward the elders. The word that the prophet gives the elders as a result of YHWH's deception encourages them to continue in their belief that the covenant relationship with YHWH remains intact. The result, however, is that YHWH will eliminate them from the midst of the people. In a symbolic way their destruction represents the end of any who would still hold to the belief that the covenant relationship with YHWH was still intact even though it had ended.

In summary, it appears that YHWH acts as a deceiver in times of transition, that this is mediated through a prophet and that the deception serves to maintain the old situation but only in such a way as to bring about its demise. This being the case, how can we explain this divine activity?

One possible answer to this lies in the 'monotheizing tendency' of the Hebrew Bible. In comparative studies of Israelite religion with the religions of the ancient Near East it is clear that there are numerous adaptations of ancient Near Eastern myth contained within the Hebrew Bible.[1] The monotheizing tendency refers to that process by which Israel transfers attributes or aspects of ancient Near Eastern deities to YHWH because Israel affirms that there is but *one* god and not many.[2] The

1. Some who have highlighted these connections between the Hebrew Bible views of YHWH and the broader ancient Near Eastern context include F.M. Cross, *Canaanite Myth and Hebrew Epic* (Cambridge, MA: Harvard University Press, 1973); B. Lang, *Monotheism and the Prophetic Minority* (Sheffield: Almond Press, 1983), pp. 13-59; C.L. Seow, *Myth, Drama, and the Politics of David's Dance* (HSM, 46; Atlanta: Scholars Press, 1989).

2. On this process see J. Sanders, *Canon and Community* (Philadelphia: Fortress Press, 1984), pp. 51-52, 56-57. Sanders (p. 56) speaks of a fourfold process by which Israel adapted the traditions of its neighbors. Israel depolytheized what it learned, monotheized it, Yahwized it, and then Israelitized it.

result of this process is that YHWH frequently acts like the gods
Baal and El,[1] and occasionally like one of the goddesses such as
Anat (or Hathor, Exod. 4.24-26; or various Hittite goddesses
and the Egyptian goddess Isis who assist at births, Ps. 22.9-10).[2]
I would like to suggest that one motif transferred to YHWH
from other gods is that of trickster, and that this motif will give
new insights into the image of YHWH the deceiver and will lead
to seeing how this divine activity can function in a liberating
manner. I will demonstrate this by comparing YHWH's activity in
the texts under discussion to that of the goddess Inanna in the
story of 'The Transfer of the Arts of Civilization from Eridu to
Erech (Uruk)'.

In this story the goddess Inanna turns the tables on her
grandfather, the god Enki. Briefly sketched, the action of the
story is as follows. Inanna travels to Eridu, the city where Enki
resides. At the palace, Enki and Inanna get into a drinking
match. Already drunk, Enki begins toasting the goddess. After
each toast he offers her groups of the *me*, or divine ordinances
that govern everything from the high priesthood and godship
to judgment-giving and decision-making. This happens fourteen
times, until Enki has given Inanna all the *me*. Enki commands
that Inanna be allowed to reach the city of Uruk safely, so
Inanna loads all of the *me* onto her boat and departs for her
city.

When he sobers up Enki discovers that all the *me* are gone.
Upon inquiry he discovers he has given them to Inanna, where-
upon he attempts to recover them. But Inanna successfully
thwarts his attempts and safely reaches Uruk where, when the
boat is unloaded, more *me* than were originally presented to
Inanna are discovered. Enki concedes defeat and the *me* are
allowed to remain at Uruk as the two cities become allies.[3]

One possible way to analyze this story is from the perspective
of contemporary theories regarding trickster figures. Carole
Fontaine has argued that in this myth Inanna is portrayed as a

1.   See especially Cross, *Canaanite Myth*, and Seow, *Myth*.
2.   C. Fontaine, 'The Deceptive Goddess in Ancient Near Eastern Myth:
Inanna and Inaras', *Semeia* 42 (1988), p. 86.
3.   This is summarized from Fontaine, 'The Deceptive Goddess', pp. 88-
89.

'trickster'.[1] A primary characteristic of these figures is that they are consummate and continuous trick-players and deceivers.[2] Susan Niditch points out that in trickster tales 'success [by the trickster] is achieved in a irregular, roundabout way, by deception, a trick'.[3] Thus, Inanna successfully acquires all the *me* in the roundabout way of taking advantage of her drunk grandfather.

Inanna's story is not the only instance in ancient Near Eastern mythology where one of the members of the pantheon or heavenly council engages in such trickery and deception. For example, in the Babylonian pantheon the deity that is most frequently associated with such activity is Enki. In the story of Atra-Hasis Enki successfully thwarts the desire of the god Enlil to destroy humankind by a flood. Having been previously outmaneuvered by Enki, Enlil binds the gods by an oath not to let humankind know that the flood would happen. However, Enki manages to get around this by warning the human Atra-Hasis by pretending to speak, not to him, but to the wall of his hut.[4]

Another aspect of the story about Inanna and Enki is that the story mythologically represents the historical reality of the rise of Uruk over Eridu as the city with the political power of the day. That is, this story is about a transition of power. How that transition came about is explained as the successful tricking by Inanna (the patron deity of Uruk) of Enki (the patron deity of Eridu).

This aspect of the story, that it provides an explanation for a transition from one situation to another, can also be illuminated by trickster theories. Tricksters often appear at the points of growth and change in a society.[5] By their trickery they disrupt

1. Fontaine, 'The Deceptive Goddess', p. 87.
2. W. Hynes, 'Mapping the Characteristics of Mythic Tricksters: A Heuristic Guide', in W.J. Hynes and W.G. Doty (eds.), *Mythical Trickster Figures: Contours, Contexts and Criticisms* (Tuscaloosa: University of Alabama Press, 1993), pp. 35-36.
3. S. Niditch, *Underdogs and Tricksters* (San Francisco: Harper & Row, 1987), p. 49.
4. W.G. Lambert and A.R. Millard, *Atra-Hasis: The Babylonian Story of the Flood* (Oxford: Clarendon Press, 1969).
5. W.J. Hynes and W.G. Doty, 'Introducing the Fascinating and Perplexing Trickster Figure', in *Mythical Trickster Figures*, pp. 4, 8.

the present order. But when order is restored, it may not be restored to what it was before. The trickster, through his or her tricks, may prepare the way for adaptation, change, or even total replacement of the world that is disrupted.[1] Thus, after Inanna's trick on Enki, Uruk rises to a prominence and fame that it had not previously known.

That a trickster is able to break open the possibility of such change is a function of a trickster's standing outside of normal categories. As one who stands outside of these categories the trickster can act to bridge them.[2] In this way tricksters become associated with creativity. Not being bound by conventional categories, they are able to create or imagine new alternatives. In addition, their creative solutions often function to perform socially valuable deeds.[3] Thus, Inanna through her creative drinking match is able to bring the *me*, which represent all of the arts of civilization, to Uruk. In a similar way, Enki faces the problem of how to get around the oath he made to Enlil. His creative solution is to talk to the wall of Atra-Hasis's hut, thereby performing a socially valuable deed, saving humanity · from the coming destructive flood.

I would like to suggest that in the biblical texts in which YHWH is portrayed as a deceiver we have a memory of the 'trickster' deity who is a member of the heavenly council. In adapting this ancient Near Eastern myth Israel transfers to YHWH this trickster role. We know that because of the process of monotheizing Israel could not have a separate deity who plays this role. So we find that it is YHWH who acts with some trickster-like characteristics.[4]

What YHWH faces is how to make the transition from an old situation to a new situation. YHWH's 'success' in solving the

1. W. Hynes, 'Inconclusive Conclusions: Tricksters—Metaplayers and Revealers', in *Mythical Trickster Figures*, p. 212.

2. K.M. Ashley, 'Interrogating Biblical Deception and Trickster Theories: Narrative of Patriarchy or Possibility?', *Semeia* 42 (1988), pp. 105-106; Hynes, 'Mapping', pp. 34-35.

3. Hynes, 'Inconclusive Conclusions', pp. 211-14.

4. 1 Kgs 22 comes closest to preserving the ancient Near Eastern pantheon. There it is a 'spirit' in the heavenly council who deceives the prophets.

problem is achieved in an irregular, roundabout way through deception. In each story YHWH's 'creative solution' to the problem lies in the deception of prophets. I think that the reason all these stories occur in connection with prophets is because prophecy is a suitable medium for deception. And in the disruption of the current order through such trickery YHWH is able to break open the possibility for a new order not yet imagined.

Now, how might this understanding of YHWH's activity as deceiver function in a liberative way? The way I have located such a possibility is in seeing the situation we are in today as dynamically equivalent to the situations found in the above texts.[1] That is, it is my belief that we find ourselves today in a situation of transition. I believe this transition to be one from principles of religion and society that marginalize one group of persons as less than fully human, to principles that seek the full participation of all persons within society.

If we seek to understand how YHWH is at work in this transition, perhaps we could say that she has a few tricks up her sleeves. It is one of the characteristics of tricksters to disrupt present orders, which creates the possibility of an alternative reality. One of the characteristics of YHWH's deception in the biblical stories is that the deception leads those in the old situation to believe that they can continue on their present course: Ahab as king, Jeremiah as prophet of doom, the elders as believing in the continuity of the covenant. In such seeming maintenance of the status quo YHWH, in the end, disrupts that status quo by bringing about its demise. And so, when I see resistance to this transition, such as the continued limited role of women in some religious traditions and the virtual exclusion of gays and lesbians from all aspects of religious life, perhaps we can see YHWH at work 'deceiving' those who stand within the status quo into believing that they can continue on their present course. Even though the resistance is painful, this also gives hope—for we know the eventual result of the deception will be the destruction of the old situation.

In many ways such an understanding of YHWH's activity is analogous to other stories in the Hebrew Bible. In particular it

---

1. J.A. Sanders, 'Hermeneutics', *IDBSup*, p. 406.

calls to mind the activity of YHWH in hardening Pharaoh's heart (Exod. 4.21; 9.12; 10.1, 20, 27; 11.10; 14.4, 8, 17). This activity of YHWH prevents Pharaoh from allowing the Hebrews to leave while at the same time providing the opportunity for the display of YHWH's glory in the resulting exodus. It also calls to mind the message Isaiah is directed to give to the people (Isa 6.9-10, NRSV):

> Keep listening, but do not comprehend;
> Keep looking, but do not understand.
> Make the mind of this people dull,
>   and shut their eyes,
> so that they may not look with their eyes,
>   and listen with their ears,
> and comprehend with their minds,
>   and turn and be healed.

When the prophet inquires, 'How long, O Lord?', the answer is, 'Until cities lie waste/ without inhabitant, and houses without people/ and the land is utterly desolate' (v. 11). Then again, perhaps YHWH has in mind some 'creative solutions' that we have not yet conceived.

There are several issues that this interpretation raises that need to be addressed. The first has to do with whether one stands within the old or the new situation. For example, if we consider the transition to be essentially about a shift in power, a reversal in the locus of power from the present powerful to the powerless (as in 1 Sam. 2.1-10 and Lk. 2.46-55), then I know at times that I must consider the possibility that I stand also within the old situation and that I might therefore stand on the receiving end of YHWH's deceptive activity.

The second issue has to do with the moral character of deception. It is not morally or ethically very comfortable to consider the possibility that YHWH does, in fact, on occasion lie. However, according to trickster theories this is another aspect of the trickster. The trickster stands as morally neutral, as somehow outside the language of moral norms (of good and evil).

> Of tricksters and gods of myth, Lévi-Strauss argues that they are halfway between two polar terms and must therefore retain something of the duality, be contradictory—good and bad at the

same time. Not surprisingly, they give rise to ambivalent responses.[1]

Tricksters cannot be defined or captured by any category or classification. The trickster is often 'out of bounds'. 'No borders are sacrosanct, be they religious, cultural, linguistic, epistemological, or metaphysical.'[2] In typical tricksterish fashion this may function to disrupt our conceptions of YHWH.

The final issue is the question of whether the biblical situation and the contemporary situation are in fact dynamically equivalent. In the biblical texts that were examined, the transitions involved were not necessarily from situations of oppression to situations of liberation. If the biblical transitions, however, are viewed as shifts of power from one group to another, the analogy becomes more precise.

Even with the need to confront these issues, I hope that a feminist reading of this troubling activity of YHWH will open the door to future feminist readings of other troubling aspects of YHWH's activities.

1. Ashley, 'Interrogating Biblical Deception', p. 106. Ashley cites C. Lévi-Strauss, 'The Structural Study of Myth', in *Structural Anthropology* (trans. C. Jacobson and B. Schoepf; New York: Basic Books, 1963), pp. 226-27.

2. Hynes, 'Mapping', p. 34.

BIBLIOGRAPHY

Ackerman, S., '"And the Women Knead Dough": The Worship of the Queen of Heaven in Sixth-Century Judah', in P.L. Day (ed.), *Gender and Difference in Ancient Israel* (Philadelphia: Fortress Press, 1989), pp. 109-22.

—'Isaiah', in Newsom and Ringe (eds.), *The Women's Bible Commentary*, pp. 162-63.

Adler, E.J., 'The Background for the Metaphor of Covenant as Marriage in the Hebrew Bible' (PhD dissertation; Berkeley: University of California, 1990).

Ahlström, G.W., *Royal Administration and National Religion in Ancient Palestine* (Studies in the History of the Ancient Near East, 1; Leiden: Brill, 1982).

Aichele, G., and T. Pippin (eds.), *Fantasy and the Bible* (*Semeia* 60 [1992]).

Albrektson, B., *Studies in the Text and Theology of the Book of Lamentations with a Critical Edition of the Peshitta Text* (Studia Theologica Lundensia; Lund: Gleerup, 1963).

Albright, W.F., *Archaeology and the Religion of Israel* (Baltimore: Johns Hopkins University Press, 2nd edn, 1946).

Andersen, F.I., and D.N. Freedman, *Hosea: A New Translation with Introduction and Commentary* (AB, 24; Garden City, NY: Doubleday, 1980).

Anderson, B.W. (ed.), *The Books of the Bible* (New York: Charles Scribner's Sons, 1989).

Anderson, G.A., *Sacrifices and Offerings in Ancient Israel: Studies in their Social and Political Importance* (Atlanta: Scholars Press, 1987).

Andrew, M.E., *Responsibility and Restoration: The Course of the Book Ezekiel* (Dunedin, New Zealand, 1985).

Ashley, K.M., 'Interrogating Biblical Deception and Trickster Theories: Narrative of Patriarchy or Possibility?', *Semeia* 42 (1988), pp. 105-106.

Auld, G.A., 'Prophecy in Books: A Rejoinder', *JSOT* 48 (1990), pp. 31-32.

Baltzer, K., *Das Bundesformular* (WMANT, 4; Neukirchen–Vluyn: Neukirchener Verlag, 2nd edn, 1964).

Balz-Cochois, H., 'Gomer oder die Macht der Astarte: Versuch einer feministischen Interpretation von Hos 1–4', *EvT* 42 (1982), pp. 37-65.

—*Gomer: Der Hohenkult-Israels im Selbstverständnis der Volksfrommigkeit* (Europäische Hochschulschriften, 23.191; Frankfurt: Peter Lang, 1982).

Barré, M., 'Treaties in the ANE', *ABD*, VI, pp. 653-56.

Barton, J., 'History and Rhetoric in the Prophets', in M. Warner (ed.), *The Bible as Rhetoric* (London and New York: Routledge, 1990), pp. 53-55.

Bass, E., and L. Davis, *The Courage to Heal: A Guide for Women Incest Survivors of Child Sexual Abuse* (San Francisco: Harper Collins, 2nd edn, 1992).

Batten, L.W., 'Hosea's Message and Marriage', *JBL* 48 (1929), p. 257.

Batto, B., *Studies on Women at Mari* (Baltimore: Johns Hopkins University Press, 1974).

Baumgartner, W., 'Miszellen', *ZAW* 33 (1913), p. 78.

Beattie, M., *Codependent No More: How to Stop Controlling Others and Start Caring for Yourself* (San Francisco: Harper & Row, 1987).

Benjamin, J., 'The Bonds of Love: Rational Violence and Erotic Domination', in H. Eisenstein and A. Jardine (eds.), *The Future of Difference* (Boston: G.K. Hall, 1980), pp. 41-70.

—*The Bonds of Love* (New York: Pantheon, 1988).

Bercovitch, S., 'The Return of Hester Prynne', in *The Rites of Assent: Transformations in the Symbolic Construction of America* (New York and London: Routledge, 1993), p. 238.

Berger, J., *Ways of Seeing* (Harmondsworth: Penguin; London: British Broadcasting Corporation, 1972).

Bergren, R.V., *The Prophets and the Law* (Cincinnati: Hebrew Union College Press, 1974).

Berlin, A., *Poetics and Interpretation of Biblical Narrative* (Sheffield: Almond Press, 1983).

Biddle, M., 'The Figure of Lady Jerusalem: Identification, Deification and Personification of Cities in the Ancient Near East', in B. Batto, W. Hallo and L. Younger (eds.), *The Canon in Comparative Perspective* (Scripture in Context, 4; Lewiston, Queenston and Lampeter: Mellen Press, 1991), p. 175.

Bird, P., ' "To Play the Harlot" ': An Inquiry into an Old Testament Metaphor', in Day (ed.), *Gender and Difference in Ancient Israel*, pp. 75-94.

—'The Place of Women in Ancient Israelite Cultus', in P.D. Miller, Jr, P.D. Hanson and S.D. McBride (eds.), *Ancient Israelite Religion: Essays in Honor of Frank Moore Cross* (Philadelphia: Fortress Press, 1987), pp. 397-419.

—'The Harlot as Heroine: Narrative Art and Social Presupposition in Three Old Testament Texts', *Semeia* 46 (1989), pp. 119-40.

Birkeland, H., *Zum Hebräischen Traditionswesen: Die Komposition der Prophetischen Bücher des Altes Testament* (Oslo: Jacob Dybwad, 1938).

Blau DuPlessis, R., 'Psyche, or Wholeness', *Massachusetts Review* (Spring 1979), pp. 77-96.

Bloch-Smith, E., *Judahite Burial Practices and Beliefs about the Dead* (JSOTSup, 123; Sheffield: JSOT Press, 1992).

Blumenthal, D.R., *Facing the Abusing God: A Theology of Protest* (Louisville, KY: Westminster Press/John Knox, 1993).

Bouyer, L., *La Bible et l'évangile* (Paris: 1951).

Bozak, B.A., *Life 'Anew': A Literary-Theological Study of Jer. 30–31* (AnBib, 122; Rome: Pontifical Biblical Institute, 1991).

Bradley, A.C., *Shakespearean Tragedy* (New York: Macmillan, 1949).

Bradshaw, J., *Bradshaw On: The Family: A Revolutionary Way of Self Discovery* (Deerfield Beach, FL: Health Communications, 1988).

—*Bradshaw On: Healing the Shame that Binds You* (Deerfield Beach, FL: Health Communications, 1988).

—*Homecoming: Reclaiming and Championing Your Inner Child* (New York: Bantam Books, 1990).

Bratsiotis, N.P., '*îš*', *TDOT*, I, pp. 222-35.

Braulik, G., 'Die Ablehnung der Göttin Aschera in Israel', in M.-T. Wacker and
E. Zenger (eds.), *Der eine Gott und die Göttin* (QD, 135; Freiburg: Herder,
1992), pp. 106-36.

Brenner, A., 'Porno-Prophetics: The Husband-Wife Metaphor Reconsidered'
(unpublished paper presented at the Narrative Research on the Hebrew Bible
Group session of the 1994 Annual Meeting of the Society of Biblical
Literature, Chicago, IL, 21 November 1994).

—*The Israelite Woman: Social Role and Literary Type in Biblical Narrative* (The Biblical
Seminar, 2; Sheffield: JSOT Press, 1985).

Brenner, A. (ed.), *A Feminist Companion to Exodus to Deuteronomy* (The Feminist
Companion to the Bible, 6; Sheffield: Sheffield Academic Press, 1994).

Brenner, A., and F. van Dijk-Hemmes, *On Gendering Texts: Female and Male Voices
in the Hebrew Bible* (Leiden: Brill, 1993).

Brichto, H.C., 'Kin, Cult, Land and the Afterlife—A Biblical Complex', *HUCA* 64
(1973), pp. 1-54.

—'The Case of the Soṭah and a Reconsideration of Biblical "Law"', *HUCA* 46
(1975), pp. 55-70.

Brown, E.M., *Patterns of Infidelity and their Treatment* (Frontiers in Couples and
Family Therapy, 3; New York: Bronner/Mazel, 1991).

Brown, J.C., and C.R. Bohn (eds.), *Christianity, Patriarchy, and Abuse: A Feminist
Critique* (Cleveland: Pilgrim Press, 1989).

Brown, S.L., *The Book of Hosea with Introduction and Notes* (London: Methuen,
1932).

Brownmiller, S., *Against Our Will: Men, Women and Rape* (New York: Simon &
Schuster, 1975).

Buber, M., *Der Glaube der Propheten* (Darmstadt, 2nd edn, 1984).

Buber, M., and F. Rosenzweig, *Die Schrift and ihre Verdeutschung* (Berlin: Schocken
Books, 1936).

Bucher, C., 'The Origin and Meaning of ZNH Terminology in the Book of Hosea'
(PhD Dissertation, Claremont Graduate School, 1988).

Budde, K., 'Zu Text und Auslegung des Buches Hosea', *JBL* 45 (1926), p. 285.

Burns, R.J., *Has the Lord Indeed Spoken Only through Moses? A Study of the Biblical
Portrait of Miriam* (SBLDS, 84; Atlanta: Scholars Press, 1987).

Burroughs, J., *An Exposition of the Prophecy of Hosea* (Edinburgh: James Nichol,
1643).

Buss, M.J., *The Prophetic Word of Hosea: A Morphological Study* (BZAW, 111; Berlin:
Töpelmann, 1969), p. 11.

Byng-Hall, J., 'Resolving Distance Conflicts', in A.S. Gurman (ed.), *Casebook of
Marital Therapy* (New York and London: Guilford, 1985).

Cahoon, L., 'The Bed as Battlefield: Erotic Conquest and Military Metaphor in
Ovid's *Amores*', *Transactions of the American Philological Association* 118
(1988), p. 293.

Calvin, J., *Commentaries on the Twelve Minor Prophets. I. Hosea* (trans. J. Owen;
Edinburgh: Edinburgh Printing Company, 1846).

Cameron, D., *Feminism and Linguistic Theory* (London: Macmillan, 1985).

Camp, C.V., *Wisdom and the Feminine in the Book of Proverbs* (Bible and Literature
Series, 11; Sheffield: Almond Press, 1985).

Camp, C.V., and C.R. Fontaine (eds.), *Women, War and Metaphor* (*Semeia* 61 [1993]).

Campbell, A., *Of Prophets and Kings: A Late Ninth-Century Document* (Washington, DC: Catholic Biblical Association of America, 1986).

Caplan, P.J., *The Myth of Women's Masochism* (New York: Signet, 1987).

Caputo, P., *A Rumor of War* (New York: Holt, Rinehart, 1977).

Carasik, M., 'Who Were the "Men of Hezekiah" (Proverbs xxv 1)?', *VT* 44 (1994), pp. 289-300.

Carroll, R.P., 'Rebellion and Dissent in Ancient Israelite Society', *ZAW* 89 (1977), p. 190.

—*Jeremiah: A Commentary* (OTL; London: SCM Press, 1986).

—'Whose Prophet? Whose History? Whose Social Reality? Troubling the Interpetative Community Again: Notes towards a Response to T.W. Overholt's Critique', *JSOT* 48 (1990), pp. 33-49.

—'Coopting the Prophets: Nehemiah and Noadiah', in E. Ulrich, J.W. Wright, R.P. Carroll and P.R. Davies (eds.), *Priests, Prophets and Scribes: Essays on the Formation and Heritage of Second Temple Judaism in Honor of Joseph Blenkinsopp* (JSOTSup, 149; Sheffield: JSOT Press, 1992), pp. 87-99.

—'The Hebrew Bible as Literature: A Misprision?', *ST* 47 (1993), p. 80.

Cathcart, K.J., 'Treaty-Curses and the Book of Nahum', *CBQ* 35 (1973), pp. 179-87.

Cathcart, K.J., and R.P. Gordon, *The Aramaic Bible. XIV. The Targum of the Minor Prophets* (Edinburgh: T. & T. Clark, 1989).

Chaney, M., 'Bitter Bounty: The Dynamics of Political Economy Critiqued by Eighth-Century Prophets', in R.L. Stivers (ed.), *Reformed Faith and Economics* (Lanham, MD: University Press of America, 1989), pp. 15-30.

Cheyne, T.K., *Hosea, with Notes and Introduction* (Cambridge: Cambridge University Press, 1887).

Clements, R.E., 'Understanding the Book of Hosea', *RevExp* 72 (1975), pp. 405-23.

Clines, D.J.A., 'Hosea 2: Structure and Interpretation', in E.A. Livingstone (ed.), *Studia Biblica 1978, I: Papers on Old Testament and Related Themes* (JSOTSup, 11; Sheffield: JSOT Press, 1979), p. 99.

Coats, G.W., *Rebellion in the Wilderness: The Murmuring Motif in the Wilderness Traditions of the Old Testament* (Nashville: Abingdon Press, 1968).

Cody, A., *A History of Old Testament Priesthood* (AnBib, 35; Rome: Pontifical Biblical Institute, 1969).

Cogan, M., *Imperialism and Religion: Assyria, Judah, and Israel in the Eighth and Seventh Centuries BCE* (Missoula, MT: Scholars Press, 1974).

Cohen, G., 'The Song of Songs and the Jewish Religious Mentality', in *Studies in the Variety of Rabbinic Cultures* (Philadelphia: Jewish Publication Society, 1991), p. 6.

Coogan, M., 'Canaanite Origins and Lineage: Reflections on the Religion of Ancient Israel', in P.D. Miller *et al.* (eds.), *Ancient Israelite Religion* (Philadelphia: Fortress Press, 1987), pp. 115-16.

Cooper, G.A., 'God's Gamble: Hosea 11.1-9', *Third Way* 15.8 (1993), p. 20.

Coote, R.B., and M.P. Coote, *Power, Politics, and the Making of the Bible: An Introduction* (Minneapolis: Fortress Press, 1990).

Coote, R.B., and K. Whitelam, *The Emergence of Early Israel in Historical Perspective* (The Social World of Biblical Antiquity, 5; Sheffield: Almond Press, 1987).

Coppens, J., 'L'histoire matrimoniale d'Osée', *BBB* 1 (1950), pp. 39-40.

Crane, W.E., 'The Prophecy of Hosea', *BSac* 89 (1932), p. 481.

Cross, F.M., *Canaanite Myth and Hebrew Epic* (Cambridge, MA: Harvard University Press, 1973).

Crowfoot, J.W. *et al.*, *Samaria-Sebaste*. II. *The Ivories* (London, 1938); III. *The Objects* (London, 1957).

Culler, J., *On Deconstruction: Theory and Criticism after Structuralism* (London: Routledge & Kegan Paul, 1983).

Curran, L.C., 'Rape and Rape Victims in the *Metamorphoses*', in J. Peradotto and J.P. Sullivan (eds.), *Women in the Ancient World: The Arethusa Papers* (SUNY Series in Classical Studies; Albany: State University of New York Press, 1984), pp. 263-86.

Daly, M., *Gyn/ecology: The Metaethics of Radical Feminism: With a New Intergalactic Introduction* (Boston: Beacon Press, 1990).

Damian, P., 'Letter 59', in T.P. Halton (ed.), *The Fathers of the Church: Medieval Continuation*. II. *Peter Damian, Letters 31-60* (trans. O.J. Blum; Washington: Catholic University of America Press, 1990), pp. 394-403.

Darr, K.P., 'Ezekiel', in Newsom and Ringe (eds.), *The Women's Bible Commentary*, p. 188.

Dash, L., *When Children Want Children* (New York: William Morrow, 1989).

Davidson, A.B., 'Hosea', in J. Hastings (ed.), *A Dictionary of the Bible* (Edinburgh: T. & T. Clark, 1904), p. 421.

Davies, G.I., *Hosea* (NCB; London: Marshall, Morgan & Scott; Grand Rapids: Eerdmans, 1992).

Davies, G.I., *Hosea* (OTG; Sheffield: JSOT Press, 1992).

Davies, S., 'The Canaanite-Hebrew Goddess', in C. Olson (ed.), *The Book of the Goddess: Past and Present* (New York: Crossroad, 1985), pp. 68-79.

Day, J., 'A Case of Inner Scriptural Interpretation', *JTS* 31 (1980), pp. 314-15.

—'Asherah in the Hebrew Bible and Northwest Semitic Literature', *JBL* 105 (1986), pp. 385-408.

Day, P.L., 'Why is Anat a Warrior and a Hunter', in D. Jobling, P.L. Day and G.T. Sheppard (eds.), *The Bible and the Politics of Exegesis* (Cleveland: Pilgrim Press, 1991), pp. 141-46.

Day, P.L. (ed.), *Gender and Difference in Ancient Israel* (Minneapolis: Augsburg Fortress, 1989).

De Vries, S., *Prophet Against Prophet* (Grand Rapids: Eerdmans, 1978).

Dearman, J.A., *Property Rights in Eighth-Century Prophets: The Conflict and its Background* (Atlanta: Scholars Press, 1988).

Deem, A., 'The Goddess Anath and some Biblical Hebrew Cruces', *JSS* 23 (1978), pp. 25-30.

Deissler, A., *Hosea* (Die Neue Echter Bibel, 4.8; 1981).

DeRoche, M., 'Structure, Rhetoric, and Meaning in Hosea 4:4-10', *VT* 33 (1983).

Detienne, M., *The Gardens of Adonis: Spices in Greek Mythology* (trans. J. Lloyd; Hassocks: Harvester Press, 1977).

Dever, W., 'Ashera, Consort of Yahweh? New Evidence from Kuntillet 'Ajrud', *BASOR* 255 (1984), pp. 21-38.

—'Some Drawings and Inscriptions on Two Pithoi from Kuntillet 'Ajrud', *VT* 37 (1987), pp. 180-211.

Dietrich, M., and O. Loretz, *Jahwe und seine Aschera* (Ugarit.-Bibl. Literatur, 9; Münster, 1992).

Dijk-Hemmes, F. van, 'The Imagination of Power and the Power of Imagination: An Intertextual Analysis of Two Biblical Love Songs, The Song of Songs and Hosea 2', *JSOT* 44 (1989), pp. 75-88; reprinted in A. Brenner (ed.), *A Feminist Companion to the Song of Songs* (The Feminist Companion to the Bible, 1; Sheffield: Sheffield Academic Press, 1993), pp. 156-70.

Douglas, M., *In the Wilderness: The Doctrine of Defilement in the Book of Numbers* (JSOTSup, 158; Sheffield: JSOT Press, 1993).

Dresner, S.H., 'The Return of Paganism', *Midstream* June/July 1988, p. 32.

Duhm, B., *Die Zwölf Propheten: In den Versmassen der Urschrift* (Tübingen: Mohr, 1910).

—*Anmerkungen zu den Zwölf Propheten* (Giessen, 1911).

Dworkin, A., *Pornography: Men Possessing Women* (New York: Putnam, Perigee, 1981).

Echols, A., 'The New Feminism of Yin and Yang', in A. Snitow, C. Stansell and S. Thompson (eds.), *Powers of Desire: The Politics of Sexuality* (New York: Monthly Review Press, 1983), pp. 439-59.

Edelman, D., 'Huldah the Prophet—of Yahweh or Asherah?', in A. Brenner (ed.), *A Feminist Companion to Samuel and Kings* (The Feminist Companion to the Bible, 5; Sheffield: Sheffield Academic Press, 1994), pp. 231-50.

Edwards, M., and E. Hoover, *The Challenge of Being Single* (New York: New American Library, 1975).

Eichrodt, W., *Der Prophet Hezekiel* (ATD, 22.2; Göttingen: Vandenhoeck & Ruprecht, 1966).

Ellwood, G.F., *Batter My Heart* (Wallingford, PA: Pendleton Hill Pamphlets, 1988).

Emmerson, G., 'A Fertility Goddess in Hosea IV 17-19?', *VT* 24 (1974), pp. 492-97.

—*Hosea: An Israelite Prophet in Judean Perspective* (JSOTSup, 28; Sheffield: JSOT Press, 1984).

Ewald, G.W., *Commentary on the Prophets of the Old Testament. I. Joel, Amos, Hosea and Zechariah* (trans. J.F. Smith; London: Williams & Norgate, 1875).

Ewald, H., *Die Propheten des Alten Bundes. I. Hosea* (Stuttgart, 2nd edn, 1867).

Exum, J.C., *Fragmented Women: Feminist (Sub)Versions of Biblical Narrative* (JSOTSup, 163; Sheffield: JSOT Press, 1993).

Eybers, I.H., 'The Matrimonial Life of Hosea', *OTWSA* 7.8 (1964-65).

Falk, R.A., G. Kolko and R.J. Lifton (eds.), *Crimes of War* (New York: Random House, 1971).

Farr, G., 'The Concept of Grace in the Book of Hosea', *ZAW* 70 (1958), p. 103.

Fensham, F., 'Malediction and Benediction in Ancient Near Eastern Vassal-Treaties and the OT', *ZAW* 74 (1962), pp. 1-9.

Fetterley, J., *The Resisting Reader: A Feminist Approach to American Fiction* (Bloomington and London: Indiana University Press, 1978).

Fisch, H., 'Hosea: A Poetics of Violence', in *Poetry with a Purpose: Biblical Poetics and Interpretation* (Bloomington and Indianapolis: Indiana University Press, 1988), p. 141.

Fisher, E.J., 'Cultic Prostitution in the Ancient Near East? A Reassessment', *BTB* 6 (1976), pp. 225-36.

Fitzgerald, A., '*BTWLT* and *BT* as Titles for Capital Cities', *CBQ* 37 (1975), p. 182.

—'The Mythological Background for the Presentation of Jerusalem as a Queen and False Worship as Adultery in the OT', *CBQ* 34 (1972), p. 416.

Fohrer, G., *Die Propheten des 8. Jahrhunderts* (Gütersloh, 1974).

Fontaine, C., 'Queenly Proverb Performance: The Prayer of Puduhepa (KUB XXI, 27)', in K.G. Hogland, E.F. Huwiler, J.T. Glass and R.W. Lee (eds.), *The Listening Heart: Essays in Wisdom and the Psalms in honor of Roland E. Murphy, O. Carm.* (JSOTSup, 58; Sheffield: JSOT Press, 1987), pp. 95-126.

—'The Deceptive Goddess in Ancient Near Eastern Myth: Inanna and Inaras', *Semeia* 42 (1988), p. 86.

Fortune, M., *Sexual Violence: The Unmentionable Sin* (New York: Pilgrim Press, 1983).

Freedman, H., and M. Simon (eds.), *Midrash Rabbah* (London: Soncino Press, 1983).

Frei, H., *The Eclipse of Biblical Narrative* (London: Yale University Press, 1980).

Freud, S., *Jokes and their Relation to the Unconscious* (ET; London: Pelican, 1976, 1981).

Frymer-Kensky, T., 'Law and Philosophy: The Case of Sex in the Bible', *Semeia* 45 (1989), pp. 89-102.

—*In the Wake of the Goddesses: Women, Culture, and the Biblical Transformation of Pagan Myth* (New York: The Free Press, 1992).

—'Sex and Sexuality', *ABD*, V, p. 1145.

Fuchs, E., 'The Literary Characterization of Mothers and Sexual Politics in the Hebrew Bible', *Semeia* 46 (1989), pp. 151-66.

—'Contemporary Biblical Literary Criticism: The Objective Phallacy', in V.L. Tollers and J. Maier (eds.), *Mappings of the Biblical Terrain: The Bible as Text* (Bucknell Review; London and Toronto: Bucknell University Press, 1990), pp. 134-42.

Galambush, J., *Jerusalem in the Book of Ezekiel: The City as Yahweh's Wife* (SBLDS, 130; Atlanta: Scholars Press, 1992).

Geyer-Ryan, H., *Fables of Desire: Studies in the Ethics of Art and Gender* (Oxford: Polity Press, 1994).

Gilder, G.F., *Sexual Suicide* (New York: Quadrangle Books, 1973).

Gilligan, C., *In a Different Voice: Psychological Theory and Women's Development* (Cambridge, MA, and London: Harvard University Press, 1982).

Ginsberg, H.L., 'Hosea, Book of', *EncJud*, VIII, pp. 1010-25.

—'Studies in Hosea 1–3', in M. Haran (ed.), *Yehezkel Kaufmann Jubilee Volume* (Jerusalem: Magnes Press, 1960), pp. 50-69 of the English Section.

—'Lexicographical Notes', in *Hebräische Wortforschung* (VTSup, 16; Leiden: Brill, 1967), pp. 73-75.

—*Tanakh: A New Translation of the Holy Scriptures* (Philadelphia: Jewish Publication Society, 1985).

Ginzberg, L., *The Legends of the Jews* (Philadelphia: Jewish Publication Society, 1968).

Glazier-McDonald, B., 'Malachi 2:12: *'ēr w^e'ōneh*—Another Look', *JBL* 105 (1986), p. 296.

Goodfriend, E.A., 'Adultery', *ABD*, I, pp. 82-86.

—'Prostitution', *ABD*, V, pp. 505-10.

Gordis, R., 'Hosea's Marriage and Message', in *idem* (ed.), *Poets, Prophets, and Sages: Essays in Biblical Interpretation* (Bloomington: Indiana University Press, 1971), pp. 230-54.

—*The Song of Songs and Lamentations: A Study, Modern Translation, and Commentary* (New York: KTAV, 1974).

Gottwald, N., *The Tribes of Yahweh: A Sociology of the Religion of Liberated Israel, 1250-1050 BCE* (Maryknoll, NY: Orbis Books, 1979).

—*The Hebrew Bible: A Socio-Literary Introduction* (Philadelphia: Westminster Press, 1985).

Graetz, N., 'The Haftorah Tradition and the Metaphoric Battering of Hosea's Wife', *Conservative Judaism* 45 (1992).

Gray, J., *I and II Kings* (OTL; Philadelphia: Westminster Press, 2nd edn, 1970).

Greenberg, M., *Ezekiel 1–20* (AB, 22; Garden City, NY: Doubleday, 1983).

Griffin, S., *Woman and Nature: The Roaring Inside Her* (New York: Harper & Row, 1978).

—*Pornography and Silence: Culture's Revenge against Nature* (New York: Harper & Row, 1981).

Gruber, M.I., 'The *qādēš* in the Book of Kings and in Other Sources', *Tarbiz* 52 (1983), pp. 167-76 (in Hebrew).

—'The *qᵉdēšāh*—What was her Function?', *Beersheva* 3 (1988), pp. 45-51 (in Hebrew).

—'The Hebrew *qᵉdēšāh* and her Canaanite and Akkadian Cognates', *UF* 18 (1986), pp. 133-48 (repr. in *idem*, *The Motherhood of God and Other Studies* [South Florida Studies in the History of Judaism, 57; Atlanta: Scholars Press, 1992], pp. 17-47).

—'The Motherhood of God in Second Isaiah', *RB* 3 (1983), pp. 251-59 (repr. in *idem*, *The Motherhood of God and Other Studies* [South Florida Studies in the History of Judaism, 57; Atlanta, GA: Scholars Press, 1992], pp. 3-15).

Gubar, S., 'Representing Pornography: Feminism, Criticism, and Depictions of Female Violation', *Critical Inquiry* 13 (1987), pp. 712-41.

Haag, E. (ed.), *Gott der einzige: Zur Entstehung des Monotheismus in Israel* (QD, 104; Freiburg: Herder, 1985).

Hackett, J.A., 'Can a Sexist Model Liberate Us? Ancient Near Eastern Fertility Goddesses', *JFSR* 5 (1989), p. 69.

Hadley, J., 'The Khirbet el-Qom Inscription', *VT* 37 (1987), pp. 50-62.

Hall, R.G., *Revealed Histories: Techniques for Ancient Jewish and Christian Historiographies* (JSPSup, 6; Sheffield: JSOT Press, 1991).

Halliday, M.A.K., *Language as Social Semiotic: The Social Interpretation of Language and Meaning* (London: Edward Arnold, 1978).

Halperin, D.M., *et al.*, *Before Sexuality: The Construction of Erotic Experience in the Ancient Greek World* (Princeton: Princeton University Press, 1990).

Halpern, B., '"Brisker Pipes than Poetry": The Development of Israelite Monotheism', in J. Neusner *et al.* (eds.), *Judaic Perspectives on Ancient Israel* (Philadelphia: Fortress Press, 1987), pp. 93-94.

Hampson, D., 'Christianity Will Always Be a Male Religion', *The Independent*, 15 November 1992.

Hanley, L., *Writing War: Fiction, Gender, and Memory* (Amherst: University of Massachusetts Press, 1991).

Harper, W.R., *A Critical and Exegetical Commentary on Amos and Hosea* (Edinburgh: T. & T. Clark, 1905).

Harris, R., 'Biographical Notes on the Naditu Women of Sippar', *JCS* 16 (1962), pp. 1-12.

—'Independent Women in Ancient Mesopotamia', in B.S. Lesko (ed.), *Women's Earliest Records: From Ancient Egypt and Mesopotamia* (BJS, 166; Atlanta: Scholars Press, 1989), pp. 145-56.

—'Inanna-Ishtar as Paradox and a Coincidence of Opposites', *History of Religions* 30 (1991), pp. 261-78.

Hayes, J.H., 'Hosea's Baals and Lovers: Religion or Politics?', paper delivered at the AAR/SBL Annual Meeting in New Orleans, 1990.

Heggen, C.H., *Sexual Abuse in Christian Homes and Churches* (Scottsdale, PA: Herald Press, 1993).

Heilbrun, C.G., 'The Character of Hamlet's Mother', in *Hamlet's Mother and Other Women: Feminist Essays on Literature* (London: The Women's Press, 1991), pp. 9-17.

Hemker, J., 'Rape and the Founding of Rome', *Helios* 12 (1985), pp. 41-47.

Herbert, A.S., *The Book of the Prophet Isaiah: Chapters 1–39* (Cambridge: Cambridge University Press, 1973).

Herman, J., *Trauma and Recovery: The Aftermath of Violence from Domestic Abuse to Political Terror* (New York: Basic Books, 1992).

Heschel, A.J., *The Prophets* (New York: Harper & Row, Schocken Books; Philadelphia: Jewish Publication Society, 1962).

Hestrin, R., 'The Cult Stand from Ta'anach and its Religious Background', in E. Lipinski (ed.), *Phoenicia and the East Mediterranean in the First Millennium BC* (Studia Phoenicia, 5; Leuven: Peeters, 1987), pp. 61-77.

—'The Lachish Ewer and the Ashera', *IEJ* 37.4 (1987), pp. 212-23.

—'Understanding Asherah', *BARev* 17.5 (1991), pp. 50-59.

Hillers, D., *Treaty-Curses and the Old Testament Prophets* (BibOr, 16; Rome: Pontifical Biblical Institute, 1964).

—*Covenant: History of a Biblical Idea* (Baltimore: Johns Hopkins Press, 1969).

—*Lamentations: Introduction, Translation, and Notes* (AB; Garden City, NY: Doubleday, 1972).

—'Analyzing the Abominable: Our Understanding of Canaanite Religion', *JQR* 75.3 (1985), pp. 253-69.

Holladay, J., 'Religion in Israel and Judah under the Monarchy: An Explicitly Archaeological Approach', in P.D. Miller *et al.* (eds.), *Ancient Israelite Religion* (Philadelphia: Fortress Press, 1987), p. 278.

Holladay, W.L., *Jeremiah 1: A Commentary on the Book of the Prophet Jeremiah Chapters 1-25* (Hermeneia; Philadelphia: Fortress Press, 1986).

Holt, T.W., 'It is Difficult to Read', *JSOT* 48 (1990), pp. 51-54.

—'Prophecy in History: The Social Reality of Intermediation', *JSOT* 48 (1990), pp. 2-29.

Hooks, S., 'Sacred Prostitution in Israel and the Ancient Near East' (PhD dissertation; Hebrew Union College, 1985).

Hopkins, D., 'The Dynamics of Agriculture in Monarchical Israel', in

K.H. Richards (ed.), *Society of Biblical Literature Seminar Papers 1983* (Chico, CA: Scholars Press, 1983), p. 196.

Hugenberger, G.P., *Marriage as a Covenant* (VTSup, 52; Leiden: Brill, 1994).

Hynes, W., 'Mapping the Characteristics of Mythic Tricksters: A Heuristic Guide', in W.J. Hynes and W.G. Doty (eds.), *Mythical Trickster Figures: Contours, Contexts and Criticisms* (Tuscaloosa: University of Alabama Press, 1993), pp. 35-36.

—'Inconclusive Conclusions: Tricksters—Metaplayers and Revealers', in *Mythical Trickster Figures*, p. 212.

Hynes, W.J., and W.G. Doty, 'Introducing the Fascinating and Perplexing Trickster Figure', in *Mythical Trickster Figures*, pp. 4, 8.

Imbens, A., and I. Jonker, *Christianity and Incest* (Minneapolis: Fortress Press, 1992).

Jacobs, J., 'Triennial Cycle', *JewEnc*, XII, pp. 254-57.

Jameson, F., *The Political Unconscious: Narrative as a Socially Symbolic Act* (London: Methuen Paperback, 1983).

Janeway, E., 'Who Does What to Whom? The Psychology of the Oppressor', in A. Bach (ed.), *Ad Feminam: Union Seminary Quarterly Review* 43 (1989), pp. 133-44.

Janzen, J.G., 'Metaphor and Reality in Hosea 11', *Semeia* 24 (1982).

—'Song of Moses, Song of Miriam: Who is Seconding Whom?', *CBQ* 54.2 (1992), pp. 215-16; reprinted in A. Brenner (ed.), *A Feminist Companion to Exodus to Deuteronomy* (A Feminist Companion to the Bible, 6; Sheffield: Sheffield Academic Press, 1994), pp. 187-99.

Jaroš, K., 'Die Motive der Heiligen Bäume und der Schlange in Gen 2-3', *ZAW* 92 (1980), pp. 204-15.

Jeremias, J., *Der Prophet Hosea übersetzt und erklärt* (ATD, 24.1; Göttingen: Vandenhoeck & Ruprecht, rev. edn, 1983).

Jobling, D., and T. Pippin (eds.), *Ideological Criticism of Biblical Texts* (*Semeia* 59 [1992]).

Johnson, B., 'Interview', in I. Salusinszky (ed.), *Criticism and Society* (London and New York: Methuen, 1987), pp. 169-70.

Johnston, J., *Lesbian Nation: The Feminist Solution* (New York: Simon & Schuster, 1973).

Junker, H., 'Textkritische, formkritische und traditionsgeschichtliche Untersuchung zu Os 4,1-10', *BZ* 4 (1960), p. 170.

Kaplan, E.A., 'Is the Gaze Male?', in A. Snitow, C. Stansell and S. Thompson (eds.), *Powers of Desire: The Politics of Sexuality* (New York: Monthly Review Press, 1983), pp. 309-27.

Keefe, A., 'Rapes of Women/Wars of Men', *Semeia* 61 (1993), pp. 79-97.

Keel, O., 'Zeichen der Verbundenheit', in P. Casetti *et al.* (eds.), *FS D. Barthélémy* (OBO, 38; Göttingen and Freiburg: Vandenhoeck & Ruprecht, 1981), pp. 159-240.

—'JHWH in der Rolle der Muttergottheit', *Orientierung* 53 (1989), pp. 123-32.

—*Das Recht der Bilder gesehen zu werden* (OBO, 122; Freiburg and Göttingen, 1992), pp. 203-208.

Keel, O. (ed.), *Monotheismus im Alten Israel und seiner Umwelt* (BibB, 14; Freiburg: Universitätsverlag, 1980).

Keel, O., and C. Uehlinger, *Göttinnen, Götter und Gottessymbole* (QD, 134; Freiburg: Herder, 1992).

Keel-Leu, H., *Vorderasiatische Stempelsiegel* (OBO, 110; Freiburg and Göttingen, 1991).

Kinet, D., *Ba'al und Jahwe: Ein Beitrag zur Theologie des Hoseabuches* (Frankfurt, 1977).

Kirk, D., *Tell it to the Dead: Memories of a War* (Chicago: Nelson-Hall, 1975).

Knight, G.A.F., *Hosea: Introduction and Commentary* (London: SCM Press, 1960).

Knoppers, G.N., 'Ancient Near Eastern Royal Grants and the Davidic Covenant: An Examination of a Proposed Parallel' (unpublished paper presented at the Biblical Law Group session of the 1994 Annual Meeting of the Society of Biblical Literature, Chicago, IL, 20 November 1994).

Koch, K., *The Prophets*. I. *The Assyrian Period* (trans. M. Kohl; Philadelphia: Fortress Press, 1983).

—'Aschera als Himmelskönigin in Jerusalem', *UF* 20 (1988), pp. 97-120.

Köhler, L., *Theologie des Alten Testaments* (Tübingen, 4th edn, 1966).

Kreuzer, S., 'Gott als Mutter?', *TQ* 169 (1989), pp. 123-32.

Kühlewein, J., ''*īš*', *THAT*, II, p. 135.

Lakoff, G., and M. Turner, *More than Cool Reason: A Field Guide to Poetic Metaphor* (Chicago: University of Chicago Press, 1989).

Lambert, W.G., and A.R. Millard, *Atra-Hasis: The Babylonian Story of the Flood* (Oxford: Clarendon Press, 1969).

Landy, F., *Hosea* (Readings; Sheffield: Sheffield Academic Press, forthcoming).

Lang, B., 'The Social Organization of Peasant Poverty in Biblical Israel', *JSOT* 24 (1982), pp. 47-63.

Lang, B., *Monotheism and the Prophetic Minority* (Sheffield: Almond Press, 1983).

Lang, B. (ed.), *Der einzige Gott: Die Geburt des Biblischen Monotheismus* (Munich, 1981).

Lauretis, T. de, *Alice Doesn't: Feminism, Semiotics, Cinema* (Bloomington: Indiana University Press, 1984).

Lederer, L. (ed.), *Take Back the Night: Women on Pornography* (New York: Bantam, 1980).

Leith, M.J.W., 'Verse and Reverse: The Transformation of the Woman, Israel in Hos. 1-3', in P.L. Day (ed.) *Gender and Difference in Ancient Israel* (Minneapolis: Fortress Press, 1989), pp. 95-108.

Lemaire, A., 'Les inscriptions de Khirbet el-Qôm et l'Ashérah de Jhwh', *RB* 84 (1977), pp. 595-60.

Lemche, N.P., *Early Israel: Anthropological and Historical Studies on Israelite Society before the Monarchy* (Leiden: Brill, 1985).

—*Ancient Israel: A New History of Israelite Society* (Biblical Seminar, 5; Sheffield: JSOT Press, 1988).

Lenski, G., *Human Societies: A Macrolevel Introduction to Sociology* (New York: McGraw-Hill, 1970).

Lerner, G., 'The Origin of Prostitution in Ancient Mesopotamia', *Signs* 11 (1986), pp. 236-54.

—*The Creation of Patriarchy* (Oxford: Oxford University Press, 1986).

Lévi-Strauss, C., 'The Structural Study of Myth', in *Structural Anthropology* (trans. C. Jacobson and B. Schoepf; New York: Basic Books, 1963), pp. 226-27.

Lewy, J., 'The Old West Semitic Sun God Hammu', *HUCA* 18 (1944), pp. 436-54.

Lipshitz, A., *The Commentary of Rabbi Abraham Ibn Ezra on Hosea* (New York: Sepher-Hermon Press, 1988).

Lloyd-Jones, H., *Female of the Species. Semonides on Women: The First Satire on Women in European Literature* (London: Duckworth, 1975).

Lohfink, N., 'Zu Text und Form von Os 4,4-6', *Bib* 42 (1961), pp. 301-31.

Long, C.H., *Significations: Signs, Symbols, and Images in the Interpretation of Religion* (Philadelphia: Fortress Press, 1986).

Loretz, O., "Anat-Aschera (Hos. 14,9) und die Inschriften von Kuntillet 'Ajrud', *SEL* 6 (1989), pp. 57-65.

Lundbom, J.R., 'Poetic Structure and Prophetic Rhetoric in Hosea', *VT* 29 (1979), pp. 300-308.

—'Contentious Priests and Contentious People', *VT* 36 (1986), p. 57.

Maarsingh, B., *Ezechiel* (POT, 2; Nijkerk, 1988).

Mace, D.R., *Hebrew Marriage: A Sociological Study* (London: Epworth Press, 1953).

Macintosh, A.A., *The Independent*, 16 November 1992.

MacKinnon, C.A., 'Turning Rape into Pornography: Postmodern Genocide', *Ms.* 4.1 (1993), pp. 24-30.

Magdalene, R., 'The Legend of Abraham the Warrior in First Century Judaism with an Emphasis on the Writings of Josephus' (unpublished paper for the University of Denver/Iliff School of Theology, August 1993).

Magonet, J., 'Jeremiah's Last Confessions: Structure, Image and Ambiguity', *HAR* 11 (1987), pp. 303-17.

Malamat, A., '*Ummatum* in Old Babylonian Texts and its Ugaritic and Biblical Counterparts', *UF* 11 (1979), pp. 534-35.

Marks, H., 'The Twelve Prophets', in R. Alter and F. Kermode (eds.), *A Literary Guide to the Bible* (Cambridge, MA: Harvard University Press, 1987), p. 214.

Martin, J.D., 'Israel as a Tribal Society', in R.E. Clements (ed.), *The World of Ancient Israel: Sociological, Anthropological and Political Perspectives* (Cambridge: Cambridge University Press, 1989), pp. 95-118.

Mayes, J.L., *Hosea: A Commentary* (OTL; Philadelphia: Westminster Press, 1969).

Mayr, F.K., 'Patriarchalisches Gottesverständnis? Historische Erwägungen zur Trinitätslehre', *TQ* 152 (1972), pp. 224-55.

Mays, J.L., *Hosea: A Commentary* (OTL; Philadelphia: Westminster Press, 1969).

McCarter, P.K., 'Aspects of the Religion of the Israelite Monarchy: Biblical and Epigraphic Data', in P.D. Miller *et al.* (eds.), *Ancient Israelite Religion* (Philadelphia: Fortress Press, 1987), pp. 146-49.

McCarthy, D.J., *OT Covenant: A Survey of Current Opinions* (Richmond, VA: John Knox, 1972).

—*Treaty and Covenant: A Study in Form in the Ancient Oriental Documents and in the Old Testament* (AnBib, 21; Rome: Biblical Institute Press, 2nd edn, 1981).

McFague, S., *Metaphorical Theology* (Philadelphia: Fortress Press, 1982).

Mendenhall, G.E., *Law and Covenant in Israel and the Ancient Near East* (Pittsburgh: Biblical Colloquium, 1955).

—'The Hebrew Conquest of Palestine', *BA* (1962), pp. 66-87.

Mendenhall, G.E., and G.A. Herion, 'Covenant', *ABD*, I, pp. 1179-1202.

Meschel, Z., 'Did Yahweh have a Consort? The New Religious Inscriptions from the Sinai', *BARev* 5 (1979), pp. 24-35.

Meyers, C., 'Of Drums and Damsels', *BA* 45.1 (1991), pp. 16-27.

Milgrom, J., 'The Betrothed Slave-Girl, Lev 19.20-22', *ZAW* 89 (1977), pp. 43-50.

Miller, A., *The Drama of the Gifted Child* (trans. R. Ward; New York: Basic Books, 1981; originally published as *Prisoners of Childhood*).

—*Thou Shalt Not Be Aware: Society's Betrayal of the Child* (trans. Hildegarde Hannum and Hunter Hannum; New York: Farrar, Straus, Giroux, 1983).

—*For Your Own Good: Hidden Cruelty in Child-Rearing and the Roots of Violence* (trans. Hildegarde Hannum and Hunter Hannum; New York: Farrar, Straus, Giroux, 1984).

Miller, C., and K. Swift, *The Handbook of Nonsexist Writing: For Writers, Editors, and Speakers* (New York: Harper & Row, 2nd edn, 1988).

Miller, J., *Seductions: Studies in Reading and Culture* (London: Virago, 1990).

Miller, J., and J. Hayes, *A History of Ancient Israel and Judah* (Philadelphia: Westminster Press, 1986).

Millett, K., *Sexual Politics* (Garden City, NY: Doubleday, 1970).

Mintz, A., 'The Rhetoric of Lamentations and the Representation of Catastrophe', *Prooftexts* 2 (1982), p. 6.

Montague, H., 'Sweet and Pleasant Passion: Female and Male Fantasy in Ancient Romance Novels', in A. Richlin (ed.), *Pornography and Representation in Greece and Rome* (New York and Oxford: Oxford University Press, 1992), p. 246.

Mosis, R., 'Die Wiederherstellung Israels', in *idem* and R. Lothar (eds.), *Der Weg zum Menschen* (FS A. Deissler; Freiburg: Herder, 1989), pp. 110-33.

Mullen, E.T., *Narrative History and Ethnic Boundaries: The Deuteronomistic Historian and the Creation of Israelite National Identity* (Atlanta: Scholars Press, 1993).

Munich, A., 'Notorious Signs, Feminist Criticism and Literary Tradition', in G. Greene and C. Kahn (eds.), *Making a Difference: Feminist Literary Criticism* (London: Methuen, 1985), pp. 238-59.

Murray, R., *The Cosmic Covenant: Biblical Themes of Justice, Peace and the Integrity of Creation* (London: Sheed & Ward, 1992).

Nestle, E., 'Miszellen', *ZAW* 29 (1909), pp. 233-41.

Newman, M.L., Jr, *The People of the Covenant: A Study of Israel from Moses to the Monarchy* (New York: Abingdon Press, 1962).

Newsom, C.A., 'A Maker of Metaphors: Ezekiel's Oracles against Tyre', in J.L. Mays and P.J. Achtemeier (eds.), *Interpreting the Prophets* (Philadelphia: Fortress Press, 1987), p. 189.

Newsom, C., and S. Ringe (eds.), *The Women's Bible Commentary* (Louisville, KY: Westminster Press/John Knox, 1992).

Nicholson, E.W., 'Israelite Religion in the Pre-Exilic Period: A Debate Renewed', in J.D. Martin and P.R. Davies (eds.), *A Word in Season* (JSOTSup 42; Sheffield: JSOT Press, 1986).

Nicholson, E.W., *God and His People: Covenant Theology in the Old Testament* (Oxford: Clarendon Press, 1986).

Niditch, S., *Underdogs and Tricksters* (San Francisco: Harper & Row, 1987).

Nissinen, M., *Prophetie, Redaktion und Fortschreibung im Hoseabuch* (AOAT, 231; Neukirchen–Vluyn: Kevelaer, 1991).

Noth, M., *Numbers: A Commentary* (OTL; Philadelphia: Westminster Press, 1968).

Nyberg, H.S., *Studien zum Hoseabuche* (Uppsala, 1935).

O'Connor, M.P., 'The Pseudo-Sorites in Hebrew Verse', in E.W. Conrad and

E.G. Newing (eds.), *A Ready Scribe: Perspectives on Language and Text. Essays in Honor of Francis I. Anderson's Sixtieth Birthday* (Winona Lake, IN: Eisenbrauns, 1987), p. 243.

Oden, R., *The Bible Without Theology: The Theological Tradition and Alternatives to It* (San Francisco: Harper & Row, 1987).

Olksana, C., *Safe Passage to Healing: A Guide for Survivors of Ritual Abuse* (San Francisco: HarperCollins, 1994).

Olyan, S.M., *Asherah and the Cult of Yahweh in Israel* (SBLMS, 34; Atlanta: Scholars Press, 1988).

Orwell, G., 'The Principles of Newspeak', in *Nineteen Eighty-Four* (London: Penguin, 1989).

Osiek, C., 'The Feminist and the Bible: Hermeneutical Alternatives', in A.Y. Collins (ed.), *Feminist Perspectives on Biblical Scholarship* (Chico, CA: Scholars Press, 1985), pp. 93-105.

Oswald, H.C., *Luther's Works. XVIII. Lectures on the Minor Prophets* (St Louis, MO: Concordia, 1975).

Otwell, J.H., *And Sarah Laughed: The Status of Woman in the Old Testament* (Philadelphia: Westminster Press, 1976).

Packman, Z.M., 'Call it Rape: A Motif in Roman Comedy and its Suppression in English-Speaking Publications', *Helios* 20 (1993), pp. 42-55.

Pardes, I., *Countertraditions in the Bible* (Cambridge, MA: Harvard University Press, 1992).

Paterson, J., 'Hosea', in F.C. Grant and H.H. Rowley (eds.), *A Dictionary of the Bible* (Edinburgh: T. & T. Clark, 2nd edn, 1963), p. 397.

Plaskow, J., *Standing Again at Sinai: Judaism from a Feminist Perspective* (San Francisco: Harper & Row, 1990).

—'Anti-Judaism in Feminist Christian Interpretation', in E. Schüssler-Fiorenza (ed.), *Searching the Scriptures. I. A Feminist Introduction* (New York: Crossroad, 1993), pp. 117-29.

Premnath, D.N., 'Latifundialization and Isaiah 5.8-10', *JSOT* 40 (1988), pp. 49-60.

Pressler, C., 'Sexual Violence and Deuteronomic Law', in A. Brenner (ed.), *A Feminist Companion to Exodus to Deuteronomy* (The Feminist Companion to the Bible, 6; Sheffield: Sheffield Academic Press, 1994), pp. 102-12.

Pritchard, J.B., *Palestinian Figurines in Relation to Certain Goddesses Known through Literature* (New Haven: American Oriental Society, 1943).

Rabinowitz, L.I., 'Haftarah', *EncJud*, XI, pp. 1342-45.

Rad, G. von, *Theologie des Alten Testaments* (Munich, 4th edn, 1965).

—*Old Testament Theology. II. The Theology of Israel's Prophetic Traditions* (trans. D.M.G. Stalker; Edinburgh: Oliver & Boyd, 1965).

—*Der heilige Krieg in alten Israel* (Göttingen: Vandenhoeck & Ruprecht, 1969).

Raitt, T., *A Theology of Exile: Judgment/Deliverance in Jeremiah and Ezekiel* (Philadelphia: Fortress Press, 1977).

Réage, P., *Story of O* (London: Corgi, 1972).

Reisner, G.A., *et al.*, *Harvard Excavations at Samaria* (Cambridge, MA: Harvard University Press, 1924).

Richards, J.R., *The Sceptical Feminist: A Philosophical Enquiry* (London: Penguin Books, 1982).

Richlin, A., 'Reading Ovid's Rapes', in *idem* (ed.), *Pornography and Representation in Greece and Rome* (New York and Oxford: Oxford University Press, 1992), p. 160.

Ringe, S.H., 'When Women Interpret the Bible', in Newsom and Ringe (eds.), *The Women's Bible Commentary*, pp. 1-9.

Ringgren, H., *"ab'*, *TDOT*, I, pp. 1-19.

—'*qādēš'*, in H.-J. Fabry and H. Ringgren (eds.), *Theologisches Worterbuch zum alten Testament* (Stuttgart: Kohlhammer, 1989), IV, pp. 1200-1201.

Roberts, J.J.M., 'Myth versus History: Relaying the Comparative Foundations', *CBQ* 38 (1976), pp. 1-13.

—'Does God Lie? Divine Deceit as a Theological Problem in Israelite Prophetic Literature', in J.A. Emerton *et al.* (eds.), *Congress Volume Jerusalem 1986* (VTSup, 40; Leiden: Brill, 1988), p. 211.

Robertson Smith, W., *The Religion of the Semites* (New York: Meridian Books, 2nd edn, 1956).

Robinson, T.H., 'Hosea bis Micha', in *idem* and F. Horst (eds.), *Die Zwölf Kleinen Propheten* (Tübingen: Mohr, 1938), p. 20.

—*Hosea* (HAT, 1.14; Tübingen: Mohr, 2nd edn, 1954).

Rowley, H.H., 'The Marriage of Hosea', *BJRL* 39 (1956), p. 222.

—'The Marriage of Hosea', in *Men of God: Studies in Old Testament History and Prophecy* (London: Nelson, 1963).

Rudolph, W., *Hosea* (KAT, 13.1; Gütersloh: Gerd Mohn, 1966).

Ruether, R.R., *Sexism and God-Talk: Toward a Feminist Theology* (Boston: Beacon Press, 1983).

—'Feminist Interpretation: A Method of Correlation', in L.M. Russell (ed.), *Feminist Interpretation of the Bible* (Philadelphia: Westminster Press, 1985), p. 115.

Ruppert, L., 'Erwagungen zur Komposition and Redaktionsgeschichte von Hosea 1-3', *BZ* 26 (1982), pp. 208-23.

Saggs, H.F.W., *The Encounter with the Divine in Mesopotamia and Israel* (London: Athlone Press, 1978).

Saiving Goldstein, V., 'The Human Situation: A Feminine View', *JR* 40 (1960), pp. 100-12; reprinted in C.P. Christ and J. Plaskow (eds.), *Womanspirit Rising* (San Francisco: Harper, 1979), pp. 25-42.

Sakenfeld, K.D., 'Feminist Uses of Biblical Materials', in L.M. Russell (ed.), *Feminist Interpretation of the Bible* (Philadelphia: Westminster Press, 1985), pp. 55-136.

—'Feminist Perspectives on Bible and Theology: An Introduction to Selected Issues and Literature', *Int* 42 (1988), pp. 5-44.

Sanders, J., *Canon and Community* (Philadelphia: Fortress Press, 1984).

—'Hermeneutics', *IDBSup*, p. 406.

Sanderson, J., 'Micah', in Newsom and Ringe (eds.), *The Women's Bible Commentary*, pp. 215-16.

—'Nahum', in Newsom and Ringe (eds.), *The Women's Bible Commentary*, p. 218.

Sawyer, J.F.A., 'Daughter of Zion and the Servant of the Lord in Isaiah: A Comparison', *JSOT* 44 (1989), pp. 89-107.

Schaef, A.W., *Co-Dependence: Misunderstood* (San Francisco: Harper & Row, 1986).

Schmitt, J.J., 'Prophecy (Preexilic Hebrew)', *ABD*, V, pp. 485.

—'The Gender of Ancient Israel', *JSOT* 26 (1983), pp. 115-25.

—'The Motherhood of God and Zion as Mother', *RB* 92 (1985), pp. 557-69.

—'The Wife of God in Hosea 2', *BR* 34 (1989), pp. 5-18.

Schroer, S., 'Die Zweiggöttin in Israel/Palästina', in M. Küchler and C. Uehlinger (eds.), *Jerusalem* (FS O. Keel and H. Keel-Leu; NTOA, 6; Freiburg, 1987), pp. 201-25.

—*In Israel gab es Bilder* (OBO, 74; Freiburg and Göttingen, 1987), pp. 21-45.

Schüngel-Straumann, H., 'Überlegungen zum Jahwe-Namen in den Gottesgeboten des Dekalogs', *TZ* 38 (1982), pp. 496-506.

—'Mutter Zion im Alten Testament', in T. Schneider and H. Schüngel-Straumann (eds.), *Theologie zwischen Zeiten und Kontinenten: Für Elizabeth Gossmann* (Freiburg: Herder, 1993), pp. 19-43.

Schüssler Fiorenza, E., *Bread Not Stone* (Boston: Beacon Press, 1984).

—'Remembering the Past in Creating the Future: Historical-Critical Scholarship and Feminist Biblical Interpretation', in A.Y. Collins (ed.), *Feminist Perspectives on Biblical Scholarship* (Chico, CA: Scholars Press, 1985), pp. 43-64.

Schüssler Fiorenza, E. (ed.), *Searching the Scriptures. I. A Feminist Introduction* (New York: Crossroad, 1993; London: SCM Press, 1994).

Schwartz, R., 'Adultery in the House of David: The Metanarrative of Biblical Scholarship and the Narratives of the Bible', *Semeia* 54 (1991), pp. 35-56.

Scolnic, B., 'Bible Battering', *Conservative Judaism* 45 (1992), p. 43.

Scott, M., *The Message of Hosea* (New York: Macmillan, 1921).

Segal, L., and M. McIntosh (eds.), *Sex Exposed: Sexuality and the Pornography Debate* (London: Virago, 1992).

Sellers, O.R., 'Hosea's Motives', *AJSL* 41 (1924–25), p. 244.

Sellin, E., *Das Zwölfprophetenbuch* (Leipzig/Erlangen, 1922).

Selms, A. van, 'Hosea and Canticles', in *Studies in the Books of Hosea and Amos* (OTSWA, 7.8; Potchefstroom: Pro Rege, 1965), pp. 85-89.

Seow, C.L., *Myth, Drama, and the Politics of David's Dance* (HSM, 46; Atlanta: Scholars Press, 1989).

Setel, T.D., 'Feminist Insights and the Question of Method', in A.Y. Collins (ed.), *Feminist Perspectives on Biblical Scholarship* (Chico, CA: Scholars Press, 1985), pp. 93-106.

—'Prophets and Pornography: Female Sexual Imagery in Hosea', in L.M. Russell (ed.), *Feminist Interpretations of the Bible* (Oxford: Basil Blackwell, 1985), pp. 86-95.

Showalter, E., 'Feminist Criticism in the Wilderness', in *idem* (ed.), *The New Feminist Criticism: Essays on Women, Literature and Theory* (London: Virago, 1986), pp. 243-70.

Siegman, E.F., *The False Prophets of the Old Testament* (Washington, DC: Catholic University of America, 1939).

Silver, M., *Prophets and Markets: The Political Economy of Ancient Israel* (Boston and The Hague: Kluwer-Nijhoff, 1983).

Smend, R., *Yahweh War and Tribal Confederation* (Nashville: Abingdon Press, 1970).

Smith, M., 'God Male and Female in the Old Testament: Yahweh and His "Asherah"', *TS* 48.2 (1987), pp. 333-40.

Smith, M.S., *The Early History of God* (New York: Harper & Row, 1990).

Snaith, N.H., *Amos, Hosea, and Micah* (London: Epworth Press, 1959).

Stager, L., 'The Archaeology of the Family in Ancient Israel', *BASOR* 260 (1985), p. 22.

Sternberg, M., *The Poetics of Biblical Narrative: Ideological Literature and the Drama of Reading* (Bloomington: Indiana University Press, 1985).

Stinespring, W.F., 'Zion, Daughter Of', in *IDBSup*, p. 985.

—'No Daughter of Zion: A Study of the Appositional Genitive in Hebrew Grammar', *Encounter* 26 (1965), p. 139.

Stoebe, H.J., 'rḥm', *THAT*, II, pp. 761ff.

—*Hosea* (*THAT*, II).

Stuart, D., 'Curse', *ABD*, I, pp. 1218-19.

—*Hosea–Jonah* (WBC; Waco, TX: Word Books, 1987).

Tadmor, H., 'Treaty and Oath in the Ancient Near East: A Historian's Approach', in G.M. Tucker and D.A. Knight (eds.), *Humanizing America's Iconic Book* (Chico, CA: Scholars Press, 1982), pp. 127-52.

Tadmor, M., 'Female Cult Figurines in Late Canaan and Early Israel: Archaeological Evidence', in T. Ishida (ed.), *Studies in the Period of David and Solomon and Other Essays* (Winona Lake, IN: Eisenbrauns, 1982), pp. 170-71.

Thistlethwaite, S., '"You May Enjoy the Spoil of Your Enemies": Rape as a Biblical Metaphor for War', *Semeia* 61 (1993), pp. 59-75.

Tigay, J.F., *You Shall Have No Other Gods: Israelite Religion in Light of Hebrew Inscriptions* (Atlanta: Scholars Press, 1986).

Todd, A.S., *Old Testament Theology* (Philadelphia: Westminster Press, 1957).

Tolbert, M.A., 'Protestant Feminists and the Bible: On the Horns of a Dilemma', in A. Bach (ed.), *The Pleasure of Her Text: Feminist Readings of Biblical and Historical Texts* (Philadelphia: Trinity Press International, 1990), p. 5.

Torczyner, H., 'Dunkle Bibelstellen', in *FS K. Marti* (BZAW, 41; Berlin, 1925), pp. 274-80.

Tötterman, K.A.R., *Die Weissagungen Hoseas bis zur ersten assyrischen Deportation (I - VI,3): Nebst einem Commentar des Karäers Jephet ben Ali zu Hos. Cap. I - II,3* (Helsingfors, 1879).

Toy, C.H., 'Note on Hos. 1–3', *JBL* 32 (1913), p. 77.

Trible, P., 'Bringing Miriam out of the Shadows', *BR* 5 (1989), pp. 14-25, 34; reprinted in A. Brenner (ed.), *A Feminist Companion to Exodus to Deuteronomy* (The Feminist Companion to the Bible, 6; Sheffield: Sheffield Academic Press), pp. 166-86.

—'Depatriarchalizing in Biblical Interpretation', in E. Koltun (ed.), *The Jewish Woman: New Perspectives* (New York: Schocken Books, 1976), pp. 217-40.

—*God and the Rhetoric of Sexuality* (Philadelphia: Westminster Press, 1978).

—*Texts of Terror: Literary-Feminist Readings of Biblical Narratives* (Philadelphia: Fortress Press, 1984).

Ude, I.O.A., 'False Prophets in the Old Testament' (PhD dissertation, Fuller Theological Seminary, 1979).

Ullendorff, E., *The Bawdy Bible* (Oxford: The Oxford Centre for Postgraduate Hebrew Studies, 1978).

Vaux, R. de, 'Les fouilles de Tell el-Far'ah, près Naplouse', *RB* 53 (1951), pp. 541-89.

Vogels, W., 'Osée-Gomer car et comme Yahweh Israël, Os 1-3', *NRT* 103 (1981), pp. 722-23.

Wacker, M.-T., 'Frau-Sexus-Macht: Eine feministische Relecture des Hoseabuches', in *Der Gott der Manner und Frauen: Theol. z. Zeit* 2 (Düsseldorf: Patmos, 1987), pp. 101-25.

—'Gefährliche Erinnerungen', in *idem* (ed.), *Theologie-feministisch* (Düsseldorf, 1988).

—'Matriarchale Bibelkritik—ein antijudaistisches Konzept?', in L. Siegele-Wenschkewitz (ed.), *Verdrängte Vergangenheit, die uns bedrängt* (Munich, 1988), pp. 181-242.

—'Gott als Mutter?', *Concilium* 25 (1989), pp. 523-28.

—'Feminist Theology and Anti-Judaism: The Status of the Discussion and the Context of the Problem in the FRG', *JFSR* 7.2 (1991), pp. 109-16.

—'Aschera oder die Ambivalenz des Weiblichen', in *idem* and E. Zenger (eds.), *Der eine Gott und die Göttin* (QD, 135; Freiburg: Herder, 1992), pp. 137-50.

—'Kosmisches Sakrament oder Verpfändung des Körpers?', in R. Jost *et al.* (eds.), *Auf Israel Hören* (Freiburg und Luzern, 1992), pp. 47-84.

—'Biblische Theologie und Männerphantasie: Das Beispiel Hosea 1–3', in H. Frankemölle (ed.), *Das bekannte Buch—das fremde Buch: Die Bibel* (Paderborn, forthcoming).

Wallis, G., '*ăhab*', *TDOT*, I, pp. 99-118.

Washington, H.C., 'The Strange Woman of Proverbs 1-9 and Post-Exilic Judean Society', in T.C. Eskenazi and K.H. Richards (eds.), *Second Temple Studies 2. Temple and Community in the Persian Period* (JSOTSup, 175; Sheffield: JSOT Press, 1994), pp. 217-42.

Waterman, L., 'The Marriage of Hosea', *JBL* 37 (1918), p. 201.

Weems, R., 'Gomer: Victim of Violence or Victim of Metaphor', *Semeia* 47 (1989), pp. 87-104.

Weinfeld, M., 'The Covenant of Grant in the Old Testament and the Ancient Near East', *JAOS* 90 (1970), pp. 184-203.

—'Covenant Terminology in the Ancient Near East and its Significance in the West', *JAOS* 93 (1973), pp. 191-99.

—'Kuntillet 'Ajrud Inscriptions and their Significance', *SEL* 1 (1984), pp. 121-30.

Weiser, A., *Das Buch der zwölf kleinen Propheten* (ATD, 24; Göttingen: Vandenhoeck & Ruprecht, 5th edn, 1967).

Wellhausen, J., *Die Kleinen Propheten übersetzt und erklärt* (Skizzen und Vorarbeiten, 5; repr.; Berlin, 4th edn, 1963).

Westbrook, R., 'Punishments and Crimes', *ABD*, V, pp. 546-56.

Westenholtz, J.G., 'Tamar, *Qedesa, Qadistu*, and Sacred Prostitution in Mesopotamia', *HTR* 82.3 (1989), pp. 245-65.

Whatling, C., 'Who's Read *Macho Sluts*?', in J. Still and M. Worton (eds.), *Textuality and Sexuality: Reading Theories and Practices* (Manchester: Manchester University Press, 1993), pp. 193-206.

Whitt, W.D., 'The Divorce of Yahweh and Asherah in Hos. 2.4-7, 12ff.', *SJOT* 6 (1992), pp. 31-67.

Williams, J.G., *Women Recounted: Narrative Thinking and the God of Israel* (Sheffield: Almond Press, 1982).

Williams, L., 'Pornographies On/scene, or Diff'rent Strokes for Diff'rent Folks', in

L. Segal and M. McIntosh (eds.), *Sex Exposed: Sexuality and the Pornography Debate* (London: Virago, 1992), pp. 233-65.

Wilson, R.R., 'An Interpretation of Ezekiel's "Dumbness"', *VT* 22 (1972), pp. 95-96.

—*Prophecy and Society in Ancient Israel* (Philadelphia: Fortress Press, 1980).

Winkler, J.J., *The Constraints of Desire: The Anthropology of Sex and Gender in Ancient Greece* (London: Routledge, 1990).

Winnicott, D., *Playing and Reality* (London: Routledge & Kegan Paul, 1991).

Winter, U., *Frau und Göttin: Exegetische und ikonographische Studien zum weiblichen Gottesbild im Alten Israel und in dessen Umwelt* (OBO, 53; Göttingen: Vandenhoeck & Ruprecht, 1983).

Wolff, H.W., 'Hoseas Geistige Heimat', in *Gesammelte Studien zum alten Testament* (Munich: Chr. Kaiser Verlag, 1964), pp. 241-43.

—*Hosea: A Commentary on the Book of the Prophet Hosea* (trans. G. Stansell; Hermeneia; Philadelphia: Westminster Press, 1974).

—*Dodekapropheton I. Hosea* (BKAT, 14.1; Neukirchen–Vluyn: Neukirchener Verlag, 3rd edn, 1976).

—*Micah: A Commentary* (Minneapolis: Augsburg Fortress, 1990).

Wright, C., *God's People in God's Land: Family, Land, and Property in the Old Testament* (Grand Rapids, MI: Eerdmans, 1990).

Wünsche, A., *Der Prophet Hosea übersetzt und erklärt* (Leipzig, 1868).

Yee, G., 'Hosea', in Newsom and Ringe (eds.), *The Women's Bible Commentary*, pp. 195-204.

—*Composition and Tradition in the Book of Hosea: A Redaction-Critical Investigation* (SBLDS, 102; Atlanta: Scholars Press, 1987).

Zayadine, F., 'Une tombe du fer à Samarie-Sébaste', *RB* 75 (1968), pp. 562-85.

Zenger, E., ' "Durch Menschen zog ich sie..." (Hos. 11.4): Beobachtungen zum Verständnis des prophetischen Amtes im Hoseabuch', in L. Ruppert, P. Weimar and E. Zenger (eds.), *Künder des Wortes: Beiträge zur Theologie der Propheten* (Würzburg, 1982), pp. 183-201.

Zimmerli, W., *Ezechiel* (BKAT, 13.1-2; Neukirchen–Vluyn: Neukirchener Verlag, 1969).

—*Ezekiel I* (trans. R. Clements; Hermeneia; Philadelphia: Fortress Press, 1979).